THE AGE OF ARISTOCRACY
1688–1830

A HISTORY OF ENGLAND

General Editor: Lacey Baldwin Smith

THE MAKING OF ENGLAND: TO 1399

C. Warren Hollister
Robert C. Stacey
University of Washington, Seattle
Robin Chapman Stacey
University of Washington, Seattle

THIS REALM OF ENGLAND: 1399–1688

Lacey Baldwin Smith
Northwestern University

THE AGE OF ARISTOCRACY: 1688–1830

William B. Willcox
Walter L. Arnstein
University of Illinois, Urbana-Champaign

BRITAIN YESTERDAY AND TODAY: 1830 TO THE PRESENT

Walter L. Arnstein
University of Illinois, Urbana-Champaign

THE AGE OF ARISTOCRACY
1688–1830

Eighth Edition

William B. Willcox

Walter L. Arnstein
University of Illinois, Urbana-Champaign

HOUGHTON MIFFLIN COMPANY   BOSTON   NEW YORK

Editor-in-Chief: Jean Woy
Associate Editor: Leah Strauss
Associate Production/Design Coordinator: Lisa Jelly
Senior Cover Design Coordinator: Deborah Azerrad Savona
Manufacturing Manager: Florence Cadran
Senior Marketing Manager: Sandra McGuire

Cover design: Walter Kopec
Cover art: Colman, Samuel (1780–1845), *St. James's Fair, Bristol*. City of Bristol
  Museum and Art Gallery.

Printed in the U.S.A.

Library of Congress Catalog Card Number: 00-133908

ISBN: 0-618-00103-4

23456789-QF-05 04 03 02 01

To Charlotte

Contents

Illustrations

Maps

Charts and Graphs

Foreword

Carl Becker once complained that everybody knows the job of the historian is "to discover and set forth the 'facts' of history." The facts, it is often said, speak for themselves. The businessperson talks about hard facts; the statistician refers to cold facts; the lawyer is eloquent about the facts of the case; and the historian, who deals with the incontrovertible facts of life and death, is called a very lucky fellow. Those who speak so confidently about the historian's craft are generally not historians themselves; they are readers of textbooks that more often than not are mere recordings of vital information and listings to dull generalizations. It is not surprising, then, that historians' reputations have suffered; they have become known as peddlers of facts and chroniclers who say, "This is what happened." The shorter the historical survey, the more textbook writers are likely to assume godlike detachment, spurning the minor tragedies and daily comedies of humanity and immortalizing the rise and fall of civilizations, the clash of economic and social forces, and the deeds of titans. Anglo-Saxon warriors were sick with fear when Viking "swift sea-kings" swept down on England to plunder, rape, and kill, but historians dispassionately note that the Norse invasions were a good thing; they allowed the kingdom of Wessex to unite and "liberate" the island in the name of Saxon and Christian defense against heathen marauders. The chronicler moves nimbly from the indisputable fact that Henry VIII annulled his marriage with Catherine of Aragon and wedded Anne Boleyn to the confident assertion that this helped produce the Reformation in England. The result is sublime but emasculated history. Her subjects wept when Good Queen Bess died, but historians merely comment that she had lived her allotted three score years and ten. British soldiers rotted by the thousands in the trenches of the First World War, but the terror and agony of that holocaust are lost in the dehumanized statistic that 765,399 British troops died in the four years of war.

In a brief history of even one "tight little island," the chronology of events must of necessity predominate, but if these four volumes are in any way fresh and up-to-date, it is because their authors have tried by artistry to step beyond the usual confines of a textbook and to conjure up something of the drama of politics, the humdrum of every day life, and the pettiness, as well as the greatness, of human motivation. The price paid will be obvious to anyone seeking total coverage. There is relatively little in these pages on literature, the fine arts, or philosophy, except as they throw light on the uniqueness of English history. On the other hand, the complexities, uncertainties, endless variations, and above all the accidents that bedevil the design of human events — these are the very stuff of which history is made and the "truths" that this series seeks to narrate and preserve. Moreover, the flavor of each volume varies according to the tastes of its author. Sometimes the emphasis is political, sometimes economic or social, but the presentation is always impressionistic — shading, underscoring, or highlighting to achieve an image that will be more than a bare outline and will recapture something of the smell and temper of the past.

Even though each book was conceived and executed as an entity capable of standing by itself, the four volumes were designed as a unit. They tell the story of how a small and insignificant outpost of the Roman Empire hesitantly, and not always heroically, evolved into the nation that has probably produced and disseminated more ideas and institutions, both good and bad, than any state since Athens. Our hope is that these volumes will appeal both individually, to those interested in a balanced portrait of particular segments of English history, and collectively, to those who seek the majestic sweep of the story of a people whose activities have been wonderfully rich, exciting, and varied. In this spirit this series was originally written and has now been revised for a seventh time, not only to keep pace with new scholarship but, equally important, to keep it fresh and thought-provoking to a world becoming both more nostalgic and more impatient of its past.

Time has not left this series untouched since its inception in 1966. As the four volumes have changed over seven revisions, so also have their authors. William B. Willcox of the University of Michigan and Yale University, a decade before his death in 1985, turned responsibility for revising volume III, *The Age of Aristocracy,* over to Walter L. Arnstein of the University of Illinois, and now, five revisions later, this volume belongs to him although Willcox's name still appears on the title page. In September of 1997 C. Warren Hollister, the author of volume I, *The Making of England,* died, and the series has been fortunate in persuading Robin and Robert Stacey of the University of Washington to take on the revision of the volume. A new generation is emerging to keep our four volumes abreast of the changing needs and interests of educators and students.

The writing of history is always a collective enterprise, and so the authors of this series would like to thank the following reviewers who made valuable suggestions for the eighth edition: Lorraine Atreed, Holy Cross College; Joel D. Benson, Northwest Missouri State University; Katherine French, SUNY–New Paltz; Amy M. Froide, University of Tennessee–Chattonooga; Helen Hundley, Wichita State University; Susan K. Kent, University of Colorado; Newton Key, Eastern Illinois University; Fred M. Leventhal, Boston University; Muriel C. McClendon, University of California–Los Angeles; and Joseph P. Ward, University of Mississippi.

Lacey Baldwin Smith

Preface

Professor William Bradford Willcox, the original author of this volume, was born in Ithaca, New York, on October 29, 1907, and died in New Haven, Connecticut, on September 15, 1985. He was educated at Cornell University and at Yale; the latter institution conferred the Ph.D. degree in 1936. In the course of his forty-year-long academic career, he taught at Williams College (1936–1941), the University of Michigan (1941–1970), and Yale University (1970–1976). He was the author of three other books on British history (one of them the winner of the Bancroft Prize) and the editor of a fourth in addition to *The Age of Aristocracy*. Professor Willcox moved to Yale University in 1970 to become the general editor of *The Papers of Benjamin Franklin*, and he continued that task even after retirement; Volumes 15 through 25 of that monumental series were published under his editorship.

When I was asked some years ago to assist in the preparation of a third and then a fourth edition of *The Age of Aristocracy*, I did not see it as my task to tamper in any significant way with the widely acknowledged strengths of the book as first written: the accounts and analyses of warfare, of the fundamentals of politics, and of the attitudes and the way of life of the aristocracy. I did somewhat expand, however, those sections of the book that deal with economic and demographic history, the social history of the lower classes, popular culture, the history of ideas, and Ireland. In the process I reorganized the original nine chapters into four chronological parts subdivided into a total of thirteen chapters. I am also responsible for all of the tables, a majority of the maps, most of the illustrations, and the much revised bibliography.

Of necessity, I have found myself solely responsible for the fifth, the sixth, the seventh, and now the eighth edition of the book. Although some sections dealing with politics and the history of warfare have been condensed, much that Professor Willcox wrote remains as he composed it. In each edition, however, I have brought the bibliography up to date as well as the historiographical footnotes that may be found in each chapter. In the more recent editions, I have also added illustrations and included an appendix detailing the reigns of monarchs, the duration of ministries, and estimates of population between 1688 and 1830. I have enlarged as well several sections of the books, including those on Anglo-Scottish and Anglo-Irish relations. For the sixth edition, I rearranged Part II topically so that Chapter 3 deals with the structure of society, Chapter 4 with the structure of politics and the age of Walpole, Chapter 5 with international relations and war, and Chapter 6 with the world of ideas as reflected in philosophy, literature, education, and in the lives of Lord

Chesterfield and Samuel Johnson. A new section, "The Roles of Women," was incorporated into Chapter 3. Additional passages involving gender relations, education, Ireland, the history of medicine, and the cost of living in the eighteenth-century have been amplified in the eighth edition.

Over the years a number of noted historians have read all or large portions of the text and have provided helpful suggestions. They include Professor Daniel Baugh of Cornell University, Professor Lois Schwoerer of George Washington University, Professor James McCord of the College of William and Mary, Professor Marjorie Morgan of Southern Illinois University, Professor Perez Zagorin of the University of Rochester, and reviewers chosen by Houghton Mifflin Company. A number of graduate students at the University of Illinois have also assisted me in a manner both menial and substantive, in preparing successive editions for publication. Dr. John Beeler (now of the University of Alabama), helped with the sixth edition; Dr. Christopher Prom (now of the University of Illinois Archives) helped with the seventh edition; and Mr. David Kamper did so with the eighth edition.

When I completed the preparation of the fourth edition eighteen years ago, Professor Willcox suggested that I indicate in the Preface that he had "provided his cordial assistance in and endorsement of" that continuing process of amendment and revision necessary for any historical survey that remains in print for more than three decades. I should like to think that, had he been in a position to do so, Professor Willcox would have placed a comparable seal of approval on this eighth edition of a book that should keep his name in print well into the twenty-first century.

W. L. A.

About the Authors

William B. Willcox (1907–1985) earned a Ph.D. from Yale University and taught at the University of Michigan and then at Yale, where he edited eleven volumes of *The Letters and Papers of Benjamin Franklin*. His other publications included *Star of Empire: A Study of Britain as a World Power, 1485–1945* (1950), and *Portrait of a General: Sir Henry Clinton in the War of Independence* (1964).

Walter L. Arnstein holds a Ph.D. from Northwestern University. He is Professor Emeritus at the University of Illinois at Urbana-Champaign, where from 1968 to 1998 he taught British History; in 1989 the university also named him Jubilee Professor of the Liberal Arts and Sciences. He has held fellowships at Clare Hall of Cambridge University and at the Institute for Advanced Studies in the Humanities of the University of Edinburgh. He has served as President of the Midwest Victorian Studies Association, the Midwest Conference on British Studies, and the North American Conference on British Studies. He has also served on the editorial boards of the *American Historical Review, The Historian*, and *Albion*. His other publications include *The Bradlaugh Case* (1965; new ed., 1984), *Protestant Versus Catholic in Mid-Victorian England* (1982), *Britain Yesterday and Today: 1830 to the Present* (8th ed., 2001); as editor and contributor, *Recent Historians of Great Britain* (1990); as editor and compiler, *The Past Speaks: Sources and Problems in British History Since 1688* (1981; second ed., 1993); and, as author, eight articles about Queen Victoria.

THE AGE OF ARISTOCRACY
1688–1830

PART ONE

THE FRUITS OF REVOLUTION

1688 to 1714

THE BATTLE OF BLENHEIM (1704)
(Bettmann/Corbis)

The Glorious Revolution

The seventeenth century in Britain was one of revolution. In 1642 a series of political and religious disputes in England — complicated by rebellions in Charles I's other kingdoms, Scotland and Ireland — led to civil war. The partisans of king and Parliament — the Cavaliers and the Roundheads — transferred their debate from the council chamber to the battlefield, and by the time the decade ended, King Charles I had been tried and executed, the monarchy abolished, and the Church of England disestablished by the victors of that struggle. The 1640s secured the authority of Parliament, but the 1650s dramatized the fact that it was easier to overthrow a system of government than to find an acceptable substitute. After the death of Charles I in 1649, the land was governed by Oliver Cromwell, a country gentleman who had risen from obscurity through the ranks of the parliamentary army and who held from 1653 until his own death in 1658 the title of Lord Protector. Cromwell proved an able general and a sincere religious reformer, but his rule as Lord Protector rested ultimately on military power. One political experiment followed another, and not until two years after Cromwell's death was a stable government restored in the person of King Charles II, the son of Charles I.

King and Parliament

The nation seemed to require both king and Parliament, and after 1660 it had both. Yet the Restoration failed to resolve some important questions: Could the monarch set aside laws passed by Parliament, and would he appoint ministers acceptable to that body? Would Parliament supply the funds to enable the monarch and his ministers to defend the interests of the kingdom in peace and war? Would the Church of England once again serve as the sole legal religious organization, or were Protestant dissenters and Roman Catholics to gain formal toleration? This last question proved particularly troublesome in the later 1670s, when it became clear that Charles II's successor would be his brother James, a Roman Catholic convert, and when Lord Shaftesbury and his followers sought to pass an Exclusion Bill denying him the throne. They were known as Whigs, their opponents as Tories. Charles ultimately defeated the controversial bill by not summoning Parliament at all during the last four years of his reign. His brother succeeded peacefully in 1685, but within three years, he provoked another revolution, an event caused in part by the constitutional uncertainties that still enveloped the relationship between king and Parliament. Equally important, however, were questions of religion and of foreign policy. Would England become an ally, a neutral, or an enemy of Roman Catholic France? A final determinant of that revolution was the personalities of two men, King James II and his nephew and son-in-law William of Orange.[1]

The Reign of James II (1685–1688)

James II came to the throne under auspicious circumstances. After the Exclusion Crisis of 1679–1681, the unsuccessful attempt to exclude him from the right of succession because of his earlier conversion to Roman Catholicism, a reaction had set in in favor of the crown. James's newly elected Parliament of 1685 was as cooperative as he could possibly have hoped for. It granted him the money he sought and, for the moment, overlooked his Catholicism. A methodical and conscientious monarch, sincere in his religious profession, James was also an obstinate and unimaginative man — or perhaps he was too imaginative. His dream of returning Britain[2] to Roman Catholicism had withered with the death of his great-grandmother, Mary Queen of Scots, and its ghost had apparently been laid to rest at the time of the Popish Plot of 1678–1679. Yet from the moment of his accession, James worked stalwartly and stupidly to realize this dream. What he attempted to do — to turn back the historical clock — is usually described as reactionary. In the European context

---

[1]The "Glorious Revolution" is discussed in detail in numerous works, including Stuart E. Prall, *The Bloodless Revolution: England, 1688* (1972), and J. R. Jones, *The Revolution of 1688 in England* (1972). Two helpful collections of essays inspired by the tricentenary of the occasion are Lois G. Schwoerer, *The Revolution of 1688: Changing Perspectives* (1992), and J. R. Jones, *Liberty Secured? Britain Before and After 1688* (1992). The events of 1688–1689 have been set in a broader context by Geoffrey Holmes, *The Making of a Great Power: Late Stuart and Early Georgian Britain, 1660–1722* (1993); by J. R. Jones in *Country and Court: England 1658–1714* (1978); and by Thomas Babington Macaulay in that classic early-Victorian example of history writing as a fine art, *A History of England from the Accession of James II*, ed. Sir Charles Firth, 6 vols. (1913–1915). Stephen B. Baxter, *William III and the Defense of European Liberty, 1660–1702* (1966), and John Miller, *James II: A Study in Kingship* (1977), are two highly relevant biographies. Although some historians have judged the Revolution Settlement of 1688 and after as constituting no more than a change of monarchs, most agree that — even if it scarcely altered the social structure of the kingdom — it significantly transformed its political institutions.

[2]*Britain* at this time had no precise political meaning, because until 1707 the island of Great Britain remained divided into two kingdoms with a common sovereign, England (including Wales) and Scotland. However, the two were deeply involved with each other, and the inclusive words *Britain* and *British* are convenient in referring to the island as a whole. The phrase "British Isles" is often used when referring to the archipelago of Great Britain, Ireland, and numerous small nearby islands (such as the Isle of Man and the Hebrides).

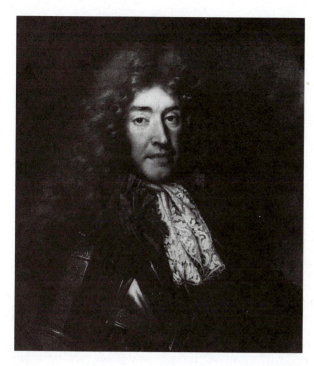

King James II (1685–1688) Within three years of his accession he had aroused a whirlwind of hostility because of his apparent desire to reimpose Roman Catholicism. *(National Maritime Museum, London)*

of the 1680s, however, James might well be described as a modernizer. Indeed, in the era of Louis XIV of France, both religious unity (under Roman Catholic auspices) and an efficient royal absolutism seemed to be the wave of the future. A national parliament dominated by landed aristocrats, each powerful in his own locality, might be dismissed as a vestige of the Middle Ages that would in due course fade away, just as France's Estates-General had done.

Within just three years, James succeeded in alienating almost every powerful group in English society. He infuriated the Anglican Church not merely by practicing his Catholic faith in public but also by insisting on complete equality for Catholics, in defiance of the law as it then stood. He made his Jesuit chaplain a member of the Privy Council, and he appointed Catholics to govern Scotland (where he reigned as King James VII), to command the English navy, and to lead the English army stationed in Ireland. He antagonized the universities by insisting that Oxford colleges name Roman Catholics as their heads and by dismissing *en masse* the fellows of Magdalen College when they refused to do so. He offended a majority of country squires by keeping a large standing army and by supplanting numerous county lords-lieutenant and hundreds of justices of the peace with men who lacked wealth and prestige but who were regarded as especially loyal to the king. He angered Parliament by failing to summon it after 1685 and by challenging its laws. He either dispensed with, in individual cases, the legal restrictions that Parliament had imposed on Roman Catholics, Quakers, and Presbyterians, or he suspended such laws altogether. Finally, he revoked the charters of numerous corporate boroughs and the City of London, intending to change the franchise rules so as to "pack" the next Parliament.

Englishmen who felt increasingly unhappy about these actions could take comfort in the fact that James II, at fifty-five, was no longer a young man and that eventually his Protestant daughter Mary would succeed him. In June 1688, however, James had the audacity to become a father once more, this time of a son by his second wife, the Catholic Mary of Modena. To the dismay of many of James's subjects, the new heir would be brought up as a Catholic and take legal precedence over his Protestant elder half-sisters, Mary and Anne. Although many Protestants denounced the baby as an imposter smuggled secretly into the queen's bedchamber, most Catholics hailed him as a miracle. James, never noted for his tact, immediately announced that the pope had agreed to be the boy's godfather. Ten days after the birth, seven English political leaders sent an "invitation" to William of Orange indicating that the kingdom was ready for a change. "The . . . people are so generally dissatisfied with the present conduct," they reported, "in relation to their religion, liberties and properties (all which have been greatly invaded) and they are in such expectation of their prospects being daily worse, that your Highness may be assured there are nineteen parts of twenty of the people throughout the kingdom who are desirous of a change; and who, we believe, would willingly contribute to it, if they had such a protection to countenance their rising, as would secure them from being destroyed. . . ."[3]

The Role of William

In any explanation of the Revolution of 1688–1689, the role of William is as important as that of James. William had been connected with the Stuart dynasty since birth. His mother was the sister of Charles II and James II; he thus stood in the line of succession to the English and Scottish thrones even before 1677, when he married the most immediate heir, James's daughter Mary. Although critics of Charles II and James II had at times appealed to William for aid, he had steered a studiously neutral course. He had no desire to usurp or to gain by conquest what he and his wife would someday inherit by law. Only when the Church of England, to which his wife was devoted, seemed in danger of being displaced, when her inheritance was about to be taken from her, and when James jeopardized the very survival of the English monarchy, did William agree to act. If there were to be a rebellion, he was willing to guide it. He would come not as William the Conqueror but as William the Deliverer.

William served the Dutch Republic as stadholder; in everything but name he was a constitutional monarch. Small in size and population but

[3]Cited in E. N. Williams, *The Eighteenth-Century Constitution: Documents and Commentary* (1960), p. 8

for two generations the leading commercial nation of northern Europe, the Netherlands had experienced a cultural renaissance, had founded colonies in the Americas, Africa, and the East Indies, and had served as the bulwark of a tolerant Protestantism. Since 1672 William had strived to make his land the keystone of a military coalition prepared to withstand the expansionist ambitions of the colossus of the age, the France of Louis XIV. William's foreign policy hinged on persuading England to cease being a secret ally of France or even a neutral and to join his coalition instead.

William quietly assembled an army of Dutch, English, and German troops as well as refugee Huguenots (French Protestants). He received the secret assent of the Dutch Estates-General for his venture while giving Louis XIV cause to think that the assembled troops would move up the Rhine (where French influence was increasing) rather than across the Channel. Early in November 1688, William's flotilla of 250 ships was swept by a "Protestant wind" past the becalmed English fleet, and on November 5 it landed 15,000 men at Torbay in southwestern England.

James reacted to the prospect of invasion with a sudden reversal of policy. He now promised to maintain the privileges of the Church of England. He replaced the Catholic admiral of the fleet with a Protestant. He reinstated the fellows of Magdalen College, Oxford. He restored the charter of the City of London. Such steps seemed so obviously the result of fear rather than of change of heart that they were credited more to William than to James. The former, in a declaration issued before he sailed, called on the people of England to aid him in his "Design" so that the nation might be freed from "arbitrary government and slavery" and so that the evils that had beset the English Constitution might be "fully redressed, in a free and legal Parliament. . . ." One by one, the leading men of England deserted James's court and declared their allegiance to William. James's younger daughter Anne did so, as did his leading general, John Churchill, and scores of lesser men in both the army and the county militia.

As William's troops advanced toward London, James lost all courage. He decided not to fight at all but to flee to France, where he had sent his wife and baby son. He disguised himself, hired a fishing boat, and dropped the Great Seal — the symbol of royal power — into the Thames. A group of Kentish fishermen accidentally recognized the king and brought him back to London, where William, eager to avoid a direct confrontation, wisely allowed him to escape a second time. By that time, William had taken command of the English army, which James at the last moment had sought to disband. New parliamentary elections were held in both England and Scotland, but because these Parliaments were summoned without royal writ, they are known as Conventions. The English Convention met in late January 1689 in an atmosphere of enormous tension, while tracts and pamphlets offering conflicting advice poured from the presses.

Whigs and Tories

The crisis had for the moment brought Whig and Tory together, but the parties threatened to turn on each other again. Many issues separated them. The Tories were the champions of the crown and of the Church of England, the Whigs the champions of Parliament and of the dissenting Protestants outside the established Anglican Church. Although both Tories and Whigs disliked Roman Catholics, until the Revolution the Tories, professing their duty to obey the king, muted their hostility in order to remain obedient. The two parties also differed significantly on foreign policy: The Whigs, partly because of their ties with the Dutch and partly because of their stalwart Protestantism, adopted a belligerent stance toward France, which was replacing the Dutch Republic as England's chief commercial rival and ranked as the major Catholic power of Europe. The Tories, who drew strong support from the rural gentry, had little desire to be pulled into a continental war, from which the merchants might profit but for which the gentry would be taxed. So divisive were these issues that nothing short of a political miracle could have induced the two parties to collaborate.

James had worked that miracle by forcing the Tories to choose between their loyalty to the crown and their devotion to Anglicanism, for the two were now in conflict. Most Tories responded, however reluctantly, by momentarily discarding their theory that an anointed king could not lawfully be resisted and by allying with the Whigs to safeguard the familiar institutions of the country. The alliance was precarious, but the alternative appeared to be civil war. With the lesson of the Cavaliers and Roundheads fresh in memory, the leaders of 1688 were so determined to keep their own revolution from getting out of hand that they were willing to forget past quarrels. Yet they had their awkward moments. In the autumn of 1688, only James's decision to flee the kingdom saved them from bloodshed. In the Convention, they argued long and bitterly before agreeing to settle the crown jointly on William and Mary and to draw up a statement of grievances and rights.

Once they reached their decision, the revolution in England was virtually complete. It still had a stormy course to run in Scotland, however, and an even stormier one in Ireland, as we shall see. By the spring of 1689, however, there was no longer any danger that the attack on James would, like the attack on his father Charles I, unloose the flood of radicalism.

Adroitly managed, the Revolution remained orderly for another reason as well: It was widely accepted by the general public and, even more significantly, by the oligarchs who dominated the political world of the day. Although these men might disagree violently on specific issues, they agreed on the fundamental point that their legal position must be safeguarded from arbitrary royal encroachment. Some churchmen refused to take the authorized oath of allegiance to William and Mary and consequently lost their posts; they were known as "nonjurors." Those

Tories for whom old principles proved more important than their position as oligarchs remained loyal to their exiled king. For them, as for Shakespeare,

> The breath of worldly men cannot depose
> The deputy elected by the Lord.

These nostalgic royalists were known as Jacobites, from Jacobus, the Latin form of James, and they and their descendants continued intermittently to protest and agitate for more than half a century. The majority of the country's ruling families felt satisfied, however, with the Revolution Settlement.

The Revolution Settlement in England

The men who engineered the accession of William and Mary were less abstract political theorists than workaday politicians who concentrated on the needs of the moment.[4] On the one hand, they branded as unconstitutional certain past actions of King James II, whom they accused of abdicating the crown and leaving the throne vacant. They then settled the crown jointly on William and Mary, with full regal power to be exercised by William in the name of both. On the other hand, accepting the fiction that James's son was a fraud, they insisted that they were not making the crown elective, because the succession was to go to William and Mary's children and, if they had none, to Mary's younger sister Anne and her children. They also addressed the status of Protestant dissenters in England, and they found ways to ensure that Parliament would meet annually and, by means of the Triennial Act of 1694, that members of the House of Commons should be elected every three years. These constituted substantial achievements, but they were also incomplete. The position of the House of Commons made up only one part of a larger question, the relationship between Parliament and the executive branch of the government. This relationship was to remain in a state of intermittent tension for generations to come. Statutes to the contrary notwithstanding, the future of the crown would also remain uncertain until after the accession of the house of Hanover in 1714, as would the position of English dissenters. Anglo-Scottish relations were in flux until the Act of Union of 1707. All that the Revolution settled, in short, could have easily been unsettled during the years that followed.

Those years were filled with difficulties.[5] The fiscal system of Charles II and James II had proved inadequate, and new ways of financing the state had to be found. Influencing all the developments of the period, furthermore, was a great foreign war that ground on, except for a five-year

---

[4]W. A. Speck, *Reluctant Revolutionaries: Englishmen and the Revolution of 1688* (1989).

[5]Most of these problems are discussed, in clear and concise topical essays, in Geoffrey Holmes, ed., *Britain After the Glorious Revolution* (1969).

Parliament offers the crown to William and Mary (February 16, 1689) The engraving is based on a romanticized painting of the scene a hundred years later by James Northcote (1746–1831). *(Bettmann/Corbis)*

intermission, from 1689 to 1713. In the heat generated by armies fighting abroad and parties quarreling at home, the Revolution Settlement remained fluid. It did not cohere into a stable system of government until after the war ended and the Hanoverians had replaced the Stuarts on the throne of England.

The Whigs and Tories of the 1690s were no more democrats than Charles I had been. They would have shared his view that the common people had no claim to a role in government but only a right to a government that safeguarded their lives and goods. The oligarchs were ready enough to speak in the name of the people, however, and in the Bill of Rights of 1689 they agreed that *all* freeborn English possess "their undoubted rights and liberties." These included the right to petition, the right to jury trial, and freedom from "excessive bail," "excessive fines," and "cruel and unusual punishment."[6] However, the right to direct participation in government still eluded altogether people such as farm laborers, domestic servants, and common sailors. Like the right to bear arms, that privilege went only to Protestant property-owners. If the state itself existed for the preservation of property, as John Locke argued, then only men of substance should have a voice in determining, primarily through the legislature, the actions of the state.

Although the Revolution of 1688–1689 had demonstrated the ultimate importance of Parliament, the executive authority of the monarch had not been subordinated to the authority of that institution. The ministers of the crown, although they normally sat in the House of Lords or

---

[6]Lois G. Schwoerer, *The Declaration of Rights, 1689* (1981), provides the fullest account of the evolution and implications of the document that became the Bill of Rights.

the House of Commons, were not servants of Parliament but of the king. A major part of their service to him, it is true, consisted of marshaling enough votes in the two houses — the first hereditary, the second elected — to ensure passage of legislation acceptable to him. Their position therefore depended on their parliamentary influence, and when they lost influence, they usually lost office; but the king alone determined their tenure. He could, if he chose, keep for a time the most unpopular ministers to carry out the most unpopular policy. Parliament might eventually force him to negotiate, but it had no means of securing from him the men and measures of its choice. It might bankrupt a government by withholding funds or overturn a minister by the cumbersome process of impeachment. What Parliament could not do was to implement its will through the day-to-day operation of the ministry. Its power remained in essence negative.

The Tories of 1689 were still keenly conscious of the fact that the monarch remained the kingdom's chief executive and that a monarch whose title was in dispute was likely to be challenged by other claimants to the throne. In order to stabilize the Revolution Settlement by capping it with a legally and religiously valid crown, they made every effort to invest William and Mary with a reasonable facsimile of James II's legitimate sovereignty. The Whigs cared less about such legalism. A few of them had even played with the idea of supplanting a hereditary monarchy with a republic. After 1689, the labels of Whig and Tory, in the words of a modern historian, "distinguished those who welcomed the Revolution as a notable constitutional advance from those who grudgingly accepted it as a sinful and infinitely regrettable necessity."[7] In order to control the sovereign, the Whigs were even willing to tamper with the law of heredity. Although they admitted a role for the royal prerogative, they intended to keep it subordinate to the will of the oligarchy as expressed through Parliament, that citadel of oligarchic power. Precious little divinity, in consequence, hedged their king.

The Whig position was writ large in the statutes of William's reign. The Bill of Rights guaranteed the House of Commons control of its own procedure and ended the royal claim to suspend or dispense at will with acts of Parliament. The Act of Settlement (1701) provided judges with security of tenure, subject only to impeachment and removal by Parliament. Thus they gained that independence from the crown for which they had struggled since the days of James I. In 1689, the first in a series of Mutiny Acts established parliamentary control over the army by legalizing martial law — the basis of all military discipline — for only a stipulated period. The acts have been renewed continuously from that day to this, usually for a year at a time, and have achieved two purposes

---

[7]J. P. Kenyon, *The Stuarts: A Study in English Kingship* (1959), p. 189. This short, well-written, and vivid account is focused, as the title indicates, on the personalities of the sovereigns. J. P. Kenyon also wrote *Revolution Principles: The Politics of Party, 1689–1720* (1977).

at once — to subject the army to periodic parliamentary examination and to ensure that Parliament was in session at least once a year. Last, but far from least, the course of the Revolution underlined the Whig principle, emphasized by Locke, that the state rests on a contract between government and governed. In the Bill of Rights, the people of England, represented by the Lords and Commons in Parliament, "claim, demand, and insist upon" specific liberties and *then* declare that William and Mary are joint sovereigns. Although leaders of the Convention did not in fact bargain with Prince William, the point that the settlement conveyed is unmistakable: Sovereignty is not an indefeasible right but rather the result of an agreement in which subjects offer their allegiance on the condition that the crown maintain their liberties. If the condition is violated, the contract is void.

The enthronement of William and Mary was the beginning, not the end, of the problem of the succession. Late in 1694, Mary died unexpectedly of smallpox. Only thirty-two, she had borne no children. William remained king for his lifetime. At his death, according to the Bill of Rights, the throne would pass to his sister-in-law, James's younger daughter Anne, and then to her offspring by her husband, a dull Danish prince. Anne became pregnant eighteen times; the result was twelve miscarriages, one stillbirth, and four children who died in infancy. In 1700, the death of her fifth child, the eleven-year-old duke of Gloucester, dashed the hope of carrying on even the semilegitimate line of James's Protestant daughters. That line would end at Anne's death, and the question of who would succeed her had to be settled all over again.

There were two possibilities. One was to bring back James or his son by his second marriage, both Roman Catholics. The other was to turn to the nearest Protestant branch of the Stuarts. This remote branch was represented by James I's granddaughter Sophia, the widowed electress of Hanover, and her son, the elector George.[8] Bringing in the Hanoverians, petty German princes with their wholly German outlook, not only might extinguish the glamor of royalty but also might embroil Great Britain in the politics of central Europe. Restoring the Catholic Stuarts would have even worse consequences: Their faith and their heritage almost committed them to undoing the Revolution. Even the Tories could not stomach that prospect. In 1701, the year after the death of Anne's last child and the year before King William died, a Parliament dominated by Tories passed the Act of Settlement, which stipulated that after Anne's tenure, the throne should pass to the Hanoverian line. Thus the Tories, for the moment, confessed the untenability of their doctrine of legitimacy, for they passed into law their opponents' principle that the crown was at the disposition of Parliament — but only for the moment. The Tories' creed

---

[8]The family tree on page 13 shows how the problem arose. Sovereigns are in Roman capitals, and the claimants after 1700 are in italics.

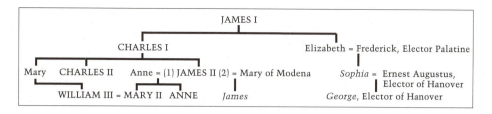

of legitimacy died hard, and within a decade the Jacobites among them schemed to bring the son of James II back to his father's throne.

If Whigs and Tories could be brought together in a crisis by their hatred of Roman Catholicism, they stood poles apart in their attitude toward Protestant dissenters. The Tories, traditional champions of the Anglican Church, wished to maintain the restrictive policy against such dissenters that the Clarendon Code of the 1660s had imposed. The Whigs had long ago realized that the code had failed in its purpose: to make life so unpleasant for its victims that they would return to the fold of the established church. Instead, legal harassment had merely kept the Presbyterians, Congregationalists, Baptists, and other sects a discontented minority. That minority had proved so loyal to the parliamentary cause, however, despite all the blandishments of Charles II and James II, that the Whigs considered dissenters humble champions of Whiggism who deserved their reward. By 1689, even the Tories agreed to make some grudging concessions to them. The question was how far to go, and here the two parties locked horns.

The conflict led to a compromise that did no more than open the door to comprehensive religious liberty. The Toleration Act of 1689 did not cover Roman Catholics, Jews, or that small body of Protestants who denied the doctrine of the Trinity (the later Unitarians); it did not apply to Ireland; it did not give English dissenters political rights, for they remained excluded from local and national government. It did, however, relieve all other English Protestants, including the Quakers, from the restraints on their civil liberty and freedom of worship that the Clarendon Code had imposed, and it made them, for the first time, full-scale participants in all aspects of national life except that of holding public office. There the entrée remained the one set up by the Test Act of 1673 — taking communion in the established Church of England. A particular form of the Eucharist remained the hallmark of the ruling class.

Whatever its limitations, the Toleration Act had significant implications for about half a million of the five-and-a-half million people who lived in England and Wales. The act made it possible for dissenters to worship in public meetinghouses rather than in private homes. More than 2,500 such houses were licensed during the twenty years after 1689, and in London they soon outnumbered Anglican parish churches by a ratio of two to one. Whereas the act did not go far enough for the dissenters and their parliamentary champions (who had to be at least nominal Anglicans to hold office), it stretched much too far for most Tories. The latter objected particularly to the manner in which some dissenters wormed their way into office by the practice known as occasional conformity, or taking Anglican communion once a year to satisfy the letter of the law. Tories also resented the way in which the expiration of the Licensing Act in 1694 had liberated heretical and anticlerical pamphleteers from government censorship. Critics of the government were also freed from press censorship, but they still had to abide by a strict libel law. Most of all, Tories disliked the way in which the legal authority of the Church of England had been undermined, first by James II and now by William III and his Parliament. In the past, church courts had vigorously addressed cases ranging from blasphemy and failure to attend church to marriage, adultery, and illegitimate births. Now they found it difficult to exert such legal discipline. The spiritual revival of the 1690s took the form not of a legally strengthened state church but of voluntary organizations. The Society for the Promotion of Christian Knowledge and the Society for the Propagation of the Gospel, for example, set up charity schools and parish libraries and sent missionaries to the American colonies; in colonial Virginia the College of William and Mary was chartered in 1693 in order to train such missionaries. In the meantime, members of the Society for the Reformation of Manners used the civil law courts to initiate prosecutions for immorality against their neighbors. The proper role of the Church of England remained very much in dispute after 1689, for on the issue of dissent, more than on most other issues, the Tories took a reactionary stand and tried to undo the measure of toleration that had been instituted. The religious struggle, like the uncertainty over the succession, helped to keep the whole settlement in suspense until the day of Queen Anne's death.

The Turnabout in Foreign Policy

Behind these domestic conflicts, and often overshadowing them, loomed another and far greater conflict. The upheaval that ousted King James II was a revolution not only in internal affairs but also in foreign policy, for it launched the English into European involvements that they had scarcely known before. Since the 1660s, when Louis XIV had begun to reach for the hegemony of western Europe, the English government had done nothing to stop him. In fact, twice it had helped him by fighting the Dutch Republic, the power that barred his way to the lower Rhine. The rest of the time, England's kings had preserved a largely benevolent neutrality. As long as Britain's chief executive was Charles II or James II, both of them first cousins of Louis, thoroughgoing war against France was out of the question. Neutrality ended, however, when William became king.

By the 1680s, the Dutch Republic lay squarely in the path of French aggression, and its stadholder was forging a European coalition against Louis. William was a mediocre soldier but a skilled diplomat, and it was largely in the cause of his diplomacy that he made his bid for the British throne. When he succeeded, he brought his subjects into their first continental coalition with the Grand Alliance of 1689 — Sweden, Spain, Savoy, the Holy Roman Empire, Bavaria, Saxony, the Palatinate, and the Dutch Republic. Britain thus unknowingly began that series of struggles against France that is often called the second Hundred Years' War, a duel of giants that occupied almost half of the next 125 years and that profoundly influenced the history of the world.

Britain's rulers did not go to war merely because they took William as their king; they had reasons of their own. English merchants had increasingly grown alarmed at the rise of French commerce and naval power; diplomats had realized that Louis, if he secured for France the "natural" frontiers of the Pyrenees, Alps, and Rhine, would upset the balance of power in Europe; parliamentarians had fretted over his efforts to bribe ministers of the crown; Protestants had come to see in him a new Philip of Spain, scheming to bring the British Isles back into the arms of Rome. Louis's revocation in 1685 of the Edict of Nantes, which had granted religious toleration to French Huguenots, had induced as many as 50,000 of them to flee to England as refugees. They established themselves in London and in smaller English cities as textile manufacturers, goldsmiths, glassmakers, and wine merchants. The Huguenots did not merely provide the English with additional reasons to oppose France, but thousands of them and their descendants also fought in England's armies.[9] The causes of war antedated the Revolution, and the coming of William made war almost impossible to avoid.

Tories and Whigs agreed on opening the struggle but not on how far to carry it. France was too strong to bring down quickly, and the Tories had no taste for long years of fighting. Their party had firmer ties with landed gentlemen than with overseas merchants, and the gentry neither knew nor cared much about distant dangers in Europe. Their background and tradition made them isolationists; and, even when they themselves sat on the benches of Parliament and confronted the affairs of the world, they tended to restrict their vision to the rural limits of squire, vicar, and justice of the peace. They disliked the French more as foreigners than as a threat to the balance of power; they detested papists but did not see in Louis the malevolent champion of Rome. Willing as they were to embark on war, they thus had no overpowering incentive to prolong a conflict that impressed them more as the Dutch stadholder's than as their own.

They had one compelling reason *not* to fight — the taxes that a long war entailed. The system of taxation rested in part on excise duties on alcoholic beverages as well as on salt and leather. A third of all national tax revenue was based on a tax on land, the form of property easiest to identify and to assess; and by 1689 the land tax stood at 20 percent of assessed

---

[9]Robin D. Gwynn, *Huguenot Heritage* (1985). Within two generations, the French refugees were almost completely to intermarry with the English population. They disappeared, therefore, as a distinct ethnic minority.

value. Landowners, who formed the backbone of the Tory party, paid what many of them considered, with some reason, a disproportionate share of the nation's bills. As the campaigns in Europe dragged on from year to year and the cost mounted, so did discontent in Tory circles. Long before the second of the two big wars of the era had ended in 1713, the Tories had become the party of peace.

The wars that began in 1689 were to bring not only costs but also benefits: financial innovations; long-term changes in the relations of England to both Ireland and Scotland; a significant enhancement of the status of Great Britain as a power in Europe and the wider world. The dramatic nature of such changes was not evident, however, during the first phase of the conflict, which lasted from 1689 to 1697. It was known as the War of the League of Augsburg, or simply as King William's War. It comprised a number of naval battles and annual campaigns on land, but it provided a clear-cut victory for neither France nor its enemies. The nature of the Grand Alliance created a problem that would recur several times in the future — how to hold the alliance together. The states that composed it, because they surrounded France, were exposed to attack and destruction piecemeal; the French stood at the center of a circle and could strike at the circumference wherever they pleased. The allied war effort depended on effective communications among Spain, northern Italy, central Europe, the Dutch Republic, Scandinavia, and the British Isles. The distances involved were enormous, but the British had an advantage, if they could develop it, that would more than compensate for the French advantage of position. Moving supplies and armies was slower and more cumbersome by land than by sea, and naval control of the waters around Europe would give the allies the upper hand. A successful war of coalition, in short, depended on the strategic exertion of sea power.

As an instrument of such power, the Royal Navy of 1689 seemed a weak reed. It had not seen action since the third Dutch war, fifteen years before, and its performance then had been lamentable. Now it had been overtaken by the French navy in both numbers of ships and tactical skill. Yet in some ways the navy had grown more effective than in the days of its past glory, first under Elizabeth I and then under the Roundheads. The warship had become differentiated from the commercial carrier; no longer could merchant ships usefully be converted into line-of-battle ships, as they had been against the Armada. Naval careers had become differentiated from military ones; gone were the amphibious heroes of Cromwell's time, like Robert Blake and George Monck and Prince Rupert, who had transformed themselves from generals into admirals. The "senior service" was emerging as a specialized profession. The kingdom had also made a start on establishing a marine corps, on training young men systematically for a career at sea, and on maintaining naval reserve officers in peacetime. The challenges that remained centered on building and manning more ships and learning how to use them.

The Revolution Settlement in Ireland

King William's War opened with a crisis in which sea power played a paramount part. In March 1689, King James landed in Ireland, which he intended to use as a base for reconquering the British throne. Two years earlier, he had appointed a faithful Roman Catholic, the earl of Tyrconnel, as his Irish lord-lieutenant, and the latter had placed all the major political, judicial, and military offices in Roman Catholic hands. In 1689, the Irish took advantage of James's presence to induce him to summon a Parliament that immediately set to work for Irish independence by condemning to death some two thousand leaders of the Protestant Ascendancy in Ireland and confiscating their estates. Most Protestant leaders fled to the northern province of Ulster, where they proclaimed William and Mary king and queen and organized an army of their own with which they defended Londonderry and Enniskillen against James's besieging force. Because the French had the upper hand at sea, it seemed only a matter of time, however, before the entire island fell under James's control. William could not come to the rescue unless the navy could clear a way for him, but the navy had no idea how to do that. Fortunately for him, in this instance the French admirals proved equally inept.

The result was what looks by hindsight like a comedy of errors, although it was in fact more a comedy of ignorance. In the summer of 1690, the French concentrated their efforts against the Anglo-Dutch fleet in the English Channel and defeated it. Then, instead of capitalizing on their victory by blockading Ireland, they did nothing. Meanwhile, King William sailed (with a convoy of only six warships) to Carrickfergus in Ulster, where he began the march south toward Dublin, James's capital. William's army of English, Irish Protestant, Dutch, Danish, and French-Huguenot troops met James's army of French and Irish Catholics at the Battle of the River Boyne. Although William's deputy commander was killed and an Irish cannonball grazed the king's shoulder, his frontal assault succeeded. James, his troops in retreat, sought refuge on a French warship and fled back to France. The remnants of his army held out until October 1691, still with little support from the sea, and then in the Treaty of Limerick surrendered on reasonable terms. The French had lost the best chance in their history of turning Ireland into a satellite. By the time they tried again a century later, the British had learned how to handle a navy.

William's victory served to save the Revolution at the cost of the Irish.[10] If James had triumphed or even had maintained his grip on part of the island, he might have regained his hold on parts of England, but such prospects dimmed as soon as he scuttled back under Louis's wing and became a pensioner of France. The exiled king never again landed in

---

[10]The process is described in detail in S. J. Connolly, *Religion, Law, and Power: The Making of Protestant Ireland, 1660–1760* (1992). See also J. C. Beckett, *The Making of Modern Ireland, 1603-1923* (2nd ed., 1981) and Francis G. James, *Ireland in the Empire, 1688–1770* (1973).

The Battle of the Boyne   The American-born painter Benjamin West (1738–1820) provides a romanticized depiction of King William III at the battle scene. *(Mary Evans Picture Library)*

the British Isles, and the Jacobites who waited for him there grew more and more discouraged. They had to nourish their faith on a secret ritual; when one of them toasted "the king," with his wineglass held over a goblet of water, he meant that he was toasting the king-over-the-water. Such antics revealed a fidelity that they prudently concealed from neighbors loyal to the new regime. From the Battle of the Boyne to the end of the wars, the Jacobite cause, whether in Ireland or Scotland or England, was the cause of France as well as of James. It was therefore tinged with treason.

English and, in the short run, Scottish Jacobites paid chiefly in heartache for their failure, but Ireland paid a heavier price. English kings had laid claim to all or part of neighboring Ireland ever since the 1170s, when the island was divided among numerous clans and tribal kingdoms. During the late Middle Ages, direct English influence was confined to "the English pale," the east-coast area surrounding Dublin; but during the Tudor era, English influence grew once more. Poynings' Law (1494) subordinated the separate Irish Parliament to the authority of the English crown, and in 1541 that Parliament and most Irish chieftains acknowledged Henry VIII as "King of Ireland." Ireland was then subdivided in the English manner into thirty-two counties, and during the later sixteenth century, English church leaders sought to bring Protestantism (in the form of Anglican theology and liturgy and the English language) to Ireland as well. During the reign of Elizabeth I (1558–1603), many Irish, seeking to protect their Gaelic language and culture, came to identify their cause with the reinvigorated Roman Catholicism of the era of Europe's "wars of religion." From that time on, religion served as a major stumbling block to Anglo-Irish amity. English fears that Ireland might become an enemy base intensified when Irish rebels against English overlordship sought — and sometimes received — the aid of Spain or France. The lands of defeated Irish rebels were therefore usually confiscated and granted to noblemen friendly to the English crown. The most successful confiscation brought thousands of Scottish and English settlers to "plantations" in Ulster during the reign of King James I (1603–1625).

The events of 1689–1691 thus constituted the third time in a century that many Irish had turned on their rulers and had met defeat. The unsuccessful rebellion against Elizabeth I and James I had been followed by another in the 1640s against the Long Parliament. Oliver Cromwell had avenged the latter uprising in a savage military campaign that was followed by additional confiscations. Only one-fourth of all Irish land remained thereafter in the hands of Roman Catholic property owners. During the 1690s, the Anglo-Irish rulers of the emerald isle exacted a vengeance more civilized than that of the Cromwellians but at least as effective. They repudiated the policy of religious toleration that King William III had at first supported, and used the Irish Parliament to strengthen the penal laws against Roman Catholics. The latter were neither to buy land nor to inherit it from Protestants. When a Catholic landowner died, the law compelled him to divide his lands equally among all his surviving sons. Catholic tenant farmers for the most part lost the protection of custom and were transformed into "tenants at will" whose rents could be raised and who could be turned out at their landlord's whim. Under the circumstances, thousands of Catholic landholders found it prudent to convert to Protestantism. Catholics who did not were also barred from several trades and professions and were forbidden to serve in either the Irish Parliament or as local government officials. They could neither vote nor sit on juries; nor could they serve as teachers, constables, sailors, or soldiers. As a consequence, 14,000 Irish soldiers chose to serve with King Louis XIV of France. Even some Protestants of Ulster, who had held a beachhead for William, were decreed second-class subjects. Most of them were Presbyterians of Scottish descent, and an act passed in 1704 excluded them also from the right to hold public office in Ireland. Membership in the Dublin Parliament was limited, from then on, to the minority who belonged to the Irish branch of the Church of England.

This largely Anglo-Irish elite thus used the Dublin Parliament to impose its rule and a high degree of public order on an Ireland long embittered by violence and sectarian tensions. The Westminster Parliament added repressive legislation of its own in the form of trade restrictions.

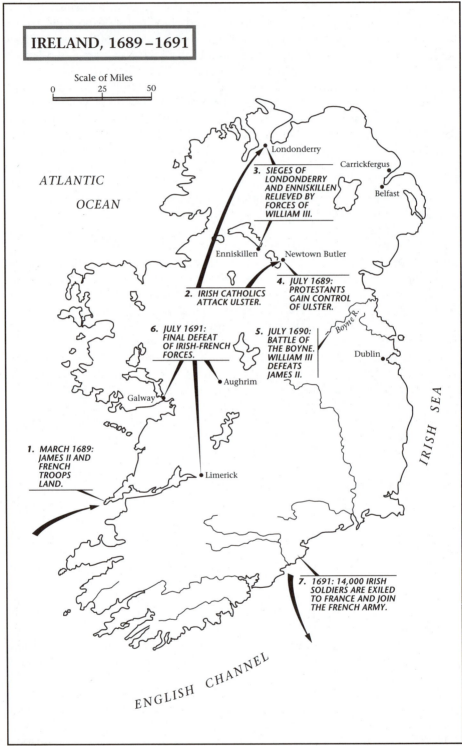

IRELAND, 1689–1691

Scale of Miles

0   25   50

ATLANTIC

OCEAN

Londonderry

Carrickfergus

Belfast

3. SIEGES OF LONDONDERRY AND ENNISKILLEN RELIEVED BY FORCES OF WILLIAM III.

Enniskillen

Newtown Butler

2. IRISH CATHOLICS ATTACK ULSTER.

4. JULY 1689: PROTESTANTS GAIN CONTROL OF ULSTER.

Boyne R.

6. JULY 1691: FINAL DEFEAT OF IRISH-FRENCH FORCES.

5. JULY 1690: BATTLE OF THE BOYNE. WILLIAM III DEFEATS JAMES II.

Dublin

Aughrim

Galway

1. MARCH 1689: JAMES II AND FRENCH TROOPS LAND.

Limerick

IRISH SEA

7. 1691: 14,000 IRISH SOLDIERS ARE EXILED TO FRANCE AND JOIN THE FRENCH ARMY.

ENGLISH CHANNEL

Although it encouraged Ireland's linen industry, it forbade the Irish to export woolen goods either to foreign lands or to Britain's colonies. Indeed, it treated Ireland as a colony. During the eighteenth century, Ireland remained predominantly a land of Gaelic-speaking peasants engaged in subsistence farming, although pockets of industry, commerce, and cultural life existed, such as Dublin, the second-largest city in the British Isles. Nor were all the penal laws and economic restrictions consistently enforced: In spite of numerous hardships, some 1,000 Roman Catholic priests and 4,000 monks and nuns carried on their work. The penal laws may have stemmed from fear on the part of the Anglo-Irish Ascendancy and the English, but it remains fair to conclude, as Edmund Burke did later in the century, that in British history they constituted an "unparalleled code of repression" motivated by "national hatred and scorn towards a conquered people." During no other era did the majority of the Irish population suffer from such obvious subjugation as during the first three-quarters of the eighteenth century.

In Scotland, unlike Ireland, William and Mary gained the crown by an affirmative vote of the Scottish Convention summoned by William. Although defeated at the Convention, the Jacobites remained popular in the country at large, and many of them prepared to fight. Only the death of their ablest military leader, Viscount Dundee, at the Battle of Killiecrankie in July 1689 allowed William to extend his rule over the Scots. During William's reign, however, the nature of the long-term relationship between the still-separate kingdoms of England and Scotland remained uncertain.

Financial Innovations

The Revolution Settlement had yet another facet: the reordering of public finance.[11] By 1689, the archaic fiscal system that the Stuarts had inherited from the Tudors, although improved at the Restoration, was far from the system of a modern state. England had ample money, but much of it lay idle; the wealthy had grown accustomed to keeping coins and gold bars locked up in safes or buried in their gardens. Until such treasure could be readily channeled into investment, whether in private enterprise or government securities, commercial growth languished, and financing a prolonged war was impossible. The nation needed mechanisms for tapping its wealth, and these were found. Although complex and undramatic, they were as much responsible as the navy for Britain's emergence as a great power.

---

[11]The most authoritative modern account is P. G. M. Dickson, *The Financial Revolution in England: A Study in the Development of Public Credit, 1688–1756* (1967). John Brewer places the subject in broader context in *Sinews of Power: War, Money, and the English State, 1688–1783* (1988). J. H. Clapham provided the classic account of the most significant financial innovation in *The Bank of England*, 2 vols. (1944).

The public debt provides one example. By the early 1690s, the government clearly could not continue to finance the war by increasing taxation or by engaging in short-term borrowing. The solution was to create a system of permanent borrowing — to issue annuities, not repayable but bearing interest for specified terms of years; investors could thus buy a guaranteed income from the state. By 1696, the system had fully developed, and what had once been a short-term loan to the government became a government security. So began the national debt. The method did not solve the financial problems of the state with one stroke; debt rarely does. It did, however, permit the government to utilize private capital more freely than before, and, in this case, to channel it into war-making.

Almost from the start, the evolution of the public debt had intimate links with the rise of the Bank of England. Here many factors came into play, two of which proved especially significant. The first was the government's need for an agency to administer the complicated machinery of the debt; the second was the rising demand for a reliable form of paper currency. Private banking, largely in the hands of London goldsmiths, had flourished since the Restoration and had already developed the two techniques that chiefly concern citizens of today — the personal check and the bank note (or, as it is known in the United States, "the bill") that constitutes paper currency. The check is in essence an order to the banker to pay from money deposited, the note a promise by him to pay from his own resources. By the 1690s, bank notes had become a kind of informal currency that supplemented gold and silver coins. Their value depended, however, on the financial reputation of the particular bank that issued them and might vary enormously from firm to firm and year to year. What was needed was a bank of issue that was as far above suspicion as Caesar's wife.

In 1694, a group of Whig financiers struck a bargain with the government. They lent it £1,200,000 at a lower interest rate than that on the debt and in return were chartered as a bank with certain unique privileges, which grew as the years passed. Soon the new corporation, the Bank of England, had the entire management of the debt and a monopoly of joint-stock banking,[12] and it was the largest institution licensed to issue bank notes. Its volume of business grew so great, and its connection with the government so close, that it commanded the confidence of the business community. In the course of the eighteenth century, its notes became what they remain to this day: the dominant paper currency of Great Britain. From the beginning, the Bank thus held a unique position as both a private corporation and an arm of the state.

Many Tories vehemently fought the Bank on the grounds that it was a Whig device for tying the financial world to the power of the Whig party. If that party was synonymous with the cause of the Revolution,

---

[12]The Bank of England was the only bank owned not by an individual or by a small number of partners but by a large number of (long-term or short-term) investors who thereby created a corporation that became, in effect, an institutional entity with a life of its own.

The Customs House   One of the buildings that helped make London the kingdom's financial center in the 1690s and after. *(The British Museum, Grace Collection)*

the Tories' point was well taken. Political changes tend to endure when money is invested in them; Henry VIII, for example, reinforced the breach with Rome by transferring the monastic lands to new owners, who soon saw in Catholicism a threat to their pocketbooks as well as their souls. An analogous process unfolded in the 1690s: The Revolution became a gigantic vested interest; the more money poured into government securities and the more powerful the Bank of England grew, the more the new financial structure of the nation fused with its political structure. A Jacobite restoration would threaten not only those who governed under William and later under Anne but also those who invested in government, and security-holders were far more numerous and formidable than officeholders. By the 1710s, some 40,000 such security-holders existed, including a few aristocrats and country gentlemen, some foreigners, a significant minority of women (unmarried heiresses and widows), and a majority of London-based merchants and financiers.

The Bank also strengthened the sinews of sea power, which protected the Revolution from external threats. The climax of the naval war came in 1692, when Louis attempted an invasion, only to see his fleet destroyed under the eyes of his army off the Normandy coast in the Bay of La Hogue. After that the needs of the land war increasingly drained his resources away from the navy, while the British pushed a ship-building program that soon won them predominance at sea. Ships were so expensive, however, that only the creation of the Bank permitted the Royal Navy to function. Half of the initial loan of 1694, with which the Whig bankers bought their charter, went at once to the treasurer of the navy. Throughout the war, and the War of the Spanish Succession that followed, English squadrons plowed through distant seas because suitable arrangements had been made in the London money market. Almost a third of the cost of King William's War was met by borrowed money, while the remainder was paid by excise taxes, customs duties, and the land tax. The medieval theory that the king could, except in time of war, "live of his own" (that is, pay for all the expenses of government with the income from his personal lands and with taxes voted to him for life) evaporated. Instead, Parliament grew accustomed to meeting annually in order to levy taxes and authorize their expenditure. A series of short-run expedients was being transformed into a financial system.

The thirteen years of William's reign thus encompassed far-reaching change: The constitution was altered; religious dissent was legally tolerated; Ireland was pacified effectively, if harshly; Scotland was secured; and England fought its first great postmedieval European war and achieved the financial means for waging it. In 1697, peace returned to Europe as eight years of war ended with the Treaty of Ryswick. The tide of Louis's aggression ebbed, and he was forced to restore most of his recent conquests and to permit the Dutch to garrison defensive fortresses in the Spanish Netherlands, which separated the Dutch Republic from France. In the peace treaty, Louis also recognized William, instead of James, as king of England and Anne as William's successor.

For these solid achievements, the Dutch king might have expected some thanks from his new subjects, but he received few. Even the men who had invited him in 1688 had harbored doubts about him, and he lacked both the virtues and vices by which his uncle, Charles II, had endeared himself to much of the public. During his first years as king, William benefited from the popularity of his graceful queen consort, Mary II. Although not well educated for the role, from 1690 on, for five successive years, she served as loyal and capable regent for as long as half a year at a time while William waged war in Ireland or on the continent. Many of his new subjects continued to view William as a foreigner, however — as a cold, withdrawn man who reserved his scant affections for the Dutch Republic. He possessed Charles's political acumen without his laziness, and a deeper insight into European diplomacy than any sovereign since Elizabeth, but these qualities did not truly impress England's political leaders, who were far more interested in managing their king than in learning from him. While the war lasted, they were forced to cooperate with him after a fashion, but the moment peace was signed, they made his life miserable. Parliament forced the sale of Irish lands that the king had granted his favorites, slashed his standing army, and packed home his beloved Dutch guards. After a decade on the throne, he was on such bad terms with the political leaders who had called him to it that he talked of quitting the country.

Yet he could not act on these words for the same reason that he had been unable to resist the call in 1688. The storm clouds of a new and greater crisis were looming over Europe, and he dared not lose such control as he had over British policy. The four years of peace after 1697 stretched his gift for diplomacy to the limit, first as he warded off the coming storm and then as he prepared for it. Parliament was asleep, and he could only hope that it would wake in time to meet the danger. The "Glorious Revolution" was now history, but the Revolution Settlement remained in great danger of being unsettled.

CHAPTER 2

The Reign of Queen Anne

Prolonged and expensive as King William's War had been, it proved to be no more than the first act in England's dramatic conflict with the France of Louis XIV. During the last months of William's life, the kingdom immersed itself in a worldwide conflict, the War of the Spanish Succession, that would grind on for eleven years, a time that coincided almost precisely with the reign of Queen Anne (1702–1714). That war also had important implications for party politics, government finance, and Anglo-Scottish relations.[1]

The War of the Spanish Succession (1702–1713)

The question that confronted Europe at the opening of the eighteenth century was what to do with a state too weak to determine its own future. The state, or rather the collection of states, was the empire of the Spanish Habsburgs. With Spain as its focus, the empire included the Spanish Netherlands, possessions in Italy, and most of Central and South America. The crown of these vast dominions rested on the head of a weak and sickly king, Charles II, who had no direct heirs. What would happen when he died?

The answer would affect the whole power structure of the continent. By 1700 two principal contenders vied for the inheritance, both claiming it by right of descent: Archduke Charles of Habsburg, a younger son of the Austrian branch of the family headed by the Holy Roman Emperor; and

---

[1]The early eighteenth century is discussed in the works by Brewer, Holmes, and J. R. Jones cited in Chapter I as well as in two classic works of the 1930s, G. M. Trevelyan's *England Under Queen Anne*, 3 vols. (1930–1934), and Sir Winston Churchill's account of his distant ancestor, *Marlborough, His Life and Times*, 6 vols. (1933–1939). Institutional changes are taken up in J. H. Plumb, *The Origins of Political Stability in England, 1675–1725* (1967), and parliamentary activities in Geoffrey Holmes, *British Politics in the Age of Anne*, rev. ed. (1987). In his recent overview, *Politics Under the Later Stuarts: Party Conflict in a Divided Society, 1660–1715* (1993), Tim Harris agrees that a genuine two-party political rivalry took shape during those decades. Relevant biographies include Corelli Barnett, *Marlborough* (1974); Roy A. Sundstrum, *Sidney Godolphin: Servant of the State* (1992); Edward Gregg, *Queen Anne* (1979); and Frances Harris, *A Passion for Government: The Life of Sarah, Duchess of Marlborough* (1992).

Philip of Bourbon, the grandson of Louis XIV.[2] Neither could succeed to the entire Spanish empire without threatening the balance of power, in one case by reestablishing the old Habsburg predominance of the early sixteenth century, in the other by creating an even more menacing Bourbon predominance. The only way to maintain the balance was to split the prize and give part to each claimant. Even Louis XIV approved of this idea as an alternative to a European war, and he and King William agreed to a partition treaty. The Austrian Habsburgs refused to cooperate, however, and the king of Spain was not so weak or so lacking in Spanish patriotism as to see his empire carved up. He willed it in its entirety to Philip with the proviso that, if the Bourbon refused, the entire empire should go to Archduke Charles. Then, in 1700, King Charles II of Spain died.

Louis faced a difficult choice. He might respect the partition treaty, which could well mean fighting Austria for his grandson's share, or accept for him the entire empire and fight all who objected. He chose the second alternative and thereby ensured war against Austria. Britain was far from ready to fight, but during 1701 Louis acted as if he were trying to force its hand: He moved his troops into the Spanish Netherlands, announced that France would henceforth enjoy special trading privileges with Spanish America, and in September, when James II died, he formally recognized his cousin's son as James III, king of England and Ireland, and as James VIII of Scotland. Almost simultaneously, Louis banned British imports into France and urged his grandson, Philip, to do the same in Spain. These actions gave Britain major war aims — to preserve the Dutch Republic from French dominance, to redress the balance of power, to safeguard the Protestant succession in England against a Stuart pretender who was the protégé of France, and to protect British trade in Europe and overseas. When King William returned from the continent after organizing another coalition, he found that Parliament at last stood solidly behind him. The War of the Spanish Succession had begun.

William did not live to manage the conflict. He had never been robust, and this latest crisis drained his stamina. In February 1702, he fell from his horse and broke his collarbone; two weeks later he was dead. Fortunately for both his countries, however, he left behind a military leader much more talented than he was — John Churchill, then earl and later duke of Marlborough, the most brilliant soldier-diplomat of modern history.

Marlborough, like William, possessed a cool intelligence and almost infinite patience; unlike William, he was endowed with tact, good looks, and the charm to melt stone. Under this winning surface, he proved greedy and unscrupulous, like most of the men about him. In a peaceful era, he might have left no more of a mark than they did; but in wartime his genius, aided by the luck that brought him to power, carried his name across Europe. He had launched his career as a trusted servant of James II (who had taken Marlborough's sister as a mistress), had deserted

---

[2]The family tree on page 28 shows how the claims arose. Claimants after 1700 are in italics.

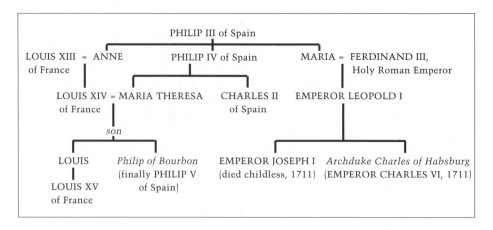

James at the critical moment of the Revolution and been rewarded with an earldom by the new sovereigns, and had then begun to intrigue with James again. William never liked nor, for good reason, trusted the earl but was compelled as time passed to bring him into prominence. Although the king did not know what talent lay hidden in his slippery servant, he did know that Marlborough's wife Sarah was the close friend and confidante of Princess Anne and that the couple would play a crucial part in the new reign.

So they did. Anne seemed born to be dominated by someone, and Sarah possessed the personality to dominate. The new queen's life had been dogged by both embarrassment and misfortune. Her mother, a commoner whose marriage to the future James II had first been kept secret, had died early. Her father had long been estranged from her by differences of religion and politics. Her husband, Prince George of Denmark, was a stupid man who drank too much. He remained faithful to the queen, but politically he proved a lightweight, and in 1708 he died. (According to tradition, the prince never learned more than a single English sentence: "Is it possible?" — admittedly a phrase suitable for a great variety of occasions.) All of Anne's children had died in childbirth or in childhood, and by the time she ascended the throne, she appeared prematurely aged; she was sickly, corpulent, dull-witted, narrowly pious, and suspicious of all except her few friends. Yet friends she had to have, and those whom she trusted she trusted completely — for the time being. Her strong sense of duty prevailed over her ill health sufficiently to permit her regularly to attend debates in the House of Lords; she was the last monarch to do so. She also conferred with her ministers, presided at cabinet meetings, and made known her often strongly held opinions. If Queen Anne did not succeed in making her court the center of cultural splendor in London, it was not for want of trying.[3]

---

[3]See Robert O. Bucholz, *The Augustan Court: Queen Anne and the Decline of Court Culture* (1993).

The Duchess of Marlborough The brilliant wife of Britain's premier general was, for a time, the queen's best friend. *(National Portrait Gallery, London)*

Anne's deep devotion to Sarah, though spiced with a touch of fear, lasted for years and extended to Sarah's husband. The queen was scarcely on the throne before Marlborough became the power behind it; he was made commander-in-chief, a duke, and a Knight of the Garter. His duchess bullied Anne in his interest and provided the strange liaison that tied the direction of the war to the source of executive power in St. James's Palace.

For a link with Parliament, Marlborough trusted primarily the manipulations of Queen Anne's leading civilian minister, Lord (Sidney) Godolphin, a moderate Tory. His chief responsibility was to hold together in Parliament a working majority that would support the war. Success in this task depended in great measure on military victories, which hinged, in turn, on how well the allies could coordinate their efforts. They were again scattered across the map of Europe: Britain, the Dutch Republic, Austria, some of the German states, and later Savoy and Portugal. The second coalition had the same weakness that had undermined King William — dispersion — whereas France enjoyed new advantages. Its armies already occupied Spain and the Spanish Netherlands and commanded the lower Rhine; and France had won the alliance of Bavaria in southern Germany, a wedge thrust between Anglo-Dutch and Austrian power. France consequently embarked on the War of the Spanish

Queen Anne (1702–1714)
The last of the Stuarts
was a doggedly dutiful
monarch. *(The Granger
Collection)*

Succession in a vastly stronger position than it had possessed in King William's War in 1689.

Politics and geography created three main theaters of operations, to which a fourth was soon added. The three were the Low Countries, the Danube valley, and northern Italy; the fourth was Spain. Each of the continental allies had its own interests. The Austrians determined to defend themselves on the Danube while they acquired the Spanish possessions in Italy, and they wanted to see Archduke Charles made king of Spain only if they did not have to do the fighting there. Neither the British nor the Dutch, at the start, dreamed of doing it for them. The Dutch focused on the Low Countries and, like the French in the First World War, opposed any distant operations that weakened the defense of their own soil. Only the British, secured at home by sea power, were in a position to see both the struggle as a whole and the need to coordinate its many parts. They were not inclined to do so, however, and Marlborough's chief task was to imbue them with his own broad vision.

Many of Britain's leaders were impervious to his vision, but no one could resist his charm. Lord Chesterfield,[4] who knew Marlborough well, has left a sketch of him that deserves quoting:

---

[4]Philip Stanhope, the fourth earl of Chesterfield, was a noted eighteenth-century political figure, diplomat, and letter writer, whose "world" will be discussed further in Chapter 6.

He was eminently illiterate, wrote bad English and spelled it worse. . . . His figure was beautiful, but his manner was irresistible by either man or woman. It was by this engaging, graceful manner that he was enabled, during all his war to connect the various and jarring powers of the grand alliance and to carry them on to the main object of the war, notwithstanding their private and separate views, jealousies, and wrong-headednesses. Whatever court he went to (and he was often obliged to go himself to some testy and refractory ones), he as constantly prevailed and brought them into his measures.

During the first two years of the struggle, Marlborough did not notably prevail with either Parliament or Britain's allies. Although he showed his skill by parrying the French threat to the Netherlands, the danger to Austria steadily intensified; by the spring of 1704, the French and Bavarians were poised for a blow at Vienna that might well knock the Habsburgs out of the war. Neither the Tories nor the Dutch could see the danger. Marlborough did, and he rose to it. In the deepest secrecy, having taken only the queen and Godolphin into his confidence, he ordered the British, Dutch, and German army in the Low Countries to set off on a lightning march to the Danube. There at Blenheim, in August, he won the first great victory to come to a British general in Europe since the Middle Ages. King Louis's army was shattered, his marshal a captive in Marlborough's coach; and Versailles received its first word of the disaster in letters from prisoners of war. After Blenheim, France, although still far from defeated, was forced progressively onto the defensive. The gilded panoply of the French regime, which had fascinated and terrified Europe for half a century, was shown at last to be vulnerable.

The Duke of Marlborough
England's great general led a European coalition against France. The duke is depicted by Sir Godfrey Kneller (1646–1723), England's premier portrait painter during the late seventeenth and early eighteenth centuries.
(Bettmann/Corbis)

Meanwhile, British sea power made itself felt in the Mediterranean. In the autumn of 1703, the Royal Navy helped to induce the duke of Savoy, Louis's ally in northwestern Italy, to change sides and bring into the coalition an army of 16,000 men. Almost simultaneously, Portugal likewise deserted France for Britain, thereby changing the whole face of the war. The allies now had a base for the conquest of Spain and began to take seriously the idea of installing the archduke in Madrid. This war aim aroused the enthusiasm of the powerful merchants, Dutch and British, who were eager to enlarge their trade; Spain and its overseas empire under Habsburg rule would be their happy hunting ground.

Philip V, backed by French land power, reigned in Madrid, however. Ousting him would require a naval attack and therefore command of the sea. For that purpose, the Portuguese harbor of Lisbon was inadequate, because a fleet based there could not control the Mediterranean coast of Spain or contain the French fleet based at Toulon. What the allies needed was a base in the Mediterranean that had a good harbor and that was immune to land attack — in other words, an island. The obvious place was Port Mahon on Minorca, in the Balearic Islands. Here the British established themselves in 1708 and remained for seventy-five years.

Meanwhile they had picked up another prize. In 1704, a British admiral, frustrated by a cruise in which he had accomplished nothing, had attacked and captured the Rock of Gibraltar. Although its harbor was too small to serve as a base, Gibraltar was invaluable as a point from which to observe any hostile fleet that entered or left the Mediterranean. Gibraltar and Minorca, lying off the coast of Spain near Barcelona, together would provide the keys to naval operations off southern Europe: Large ships based on Port Mahon could blockade enemy squadrons in the harbors of the mainland; if a squadron ran the blockade and made for the open Atlantic, frigates based on Gibraltar could follow it and call up a battle fleet from Minorca or Britain. This became the strategy of the future, but it took many years to develop. Britain, retaining its two conquests at the end of the war, had no inkling that for generations to come, they would be worth far more than Marlborough's many victories.

Those victories continued after Blenheim, for the duke never lost a major battle. Yet his triumphs proved inconclusive, and their principal effect was to breed violent controversy at home about the conduct of the war. As one campaign dragged on to the next, the Tories became more and more restive, the Whigs more and more ambitious. Marlborough's strategy now had as its political aim the expulsion of King Philip from Spain, and as its military aim the invasion of France by way of the Spanish Netherlands and Flanders. The Tories believed (rightly) that these aims were unattainable and urged instead what came to be called a "bluewater" policy: concentrating on the war at sea while supporting Britain's continental allies by subsidies, which cost less than the interminable land war. In contrast, the Whigs fixed their eyes on the Spanish prize, and Marlborough's victories made them overconfident. They dreamed of a France conquered by invasion from the Low Countries, of Louis brought

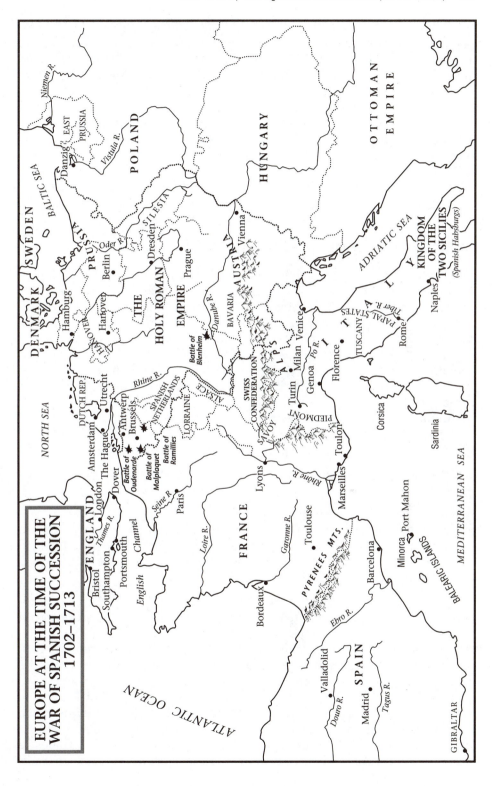

EUROPE AT THE TIME OF THE
WAR OF SPANISH SUCCESSION
1702–1713

to his knees and his grandson exiled from Madrid, and of Spain and Spanish America opened to British trade. Year after year, however, Louis refused to kneel, and the Spaniards held to their Bourbon king. The Whig formula, "No peace without Spain," seemed a recipe for war without end.

In order to carry on the conflict, Marlborough and Godolphin turned more and more during those years from the Tories to the Whigs, and by 1708 the Whigs dominated the queen's ministry. The duchess of Marlborough persuaded a doubtful Queen Anne to go along with this process for a time, but by 1710 a royal and popular reaction in favor of the Tories was well under way. By then the years of war had fundamentally altered both the constitution and the institutions of England and Scotland.

England and Scotland: Uneasy Union

During the War of the Spanish Succession, the troubled relationship between the separate kingdoms of England and Scotland was permanently altered by the Act of Union of 1707. Since 1603 the two kingdoms had known the same monarch, but in a century as unstable as the seventeenth, a union of crowns had led neither to a union of cultures nor to a sense of security. It remained readily conceivable that eventually the two kingdoms might once more go their separate and perhaps hostile ways. Not that the situation in Scotland was identical to that in Ireland. For a majority of the Irish, the civil war of the 1640s and the accession of William III in 1689 had brought disaster. For many Scots, the clouds of war and revolution included silver linings. In their dealings with the English, the Scots enjoyed three great advantages over the Irish:

- a separate parliament whose decisions London could not automatically overrule;
- an implacably Protestant church; and
- a fighting force that commanded respect. Seventeenth-century Scotland was not strong enough to avoid temporary defeat and partial domination by England, but it was too powerful to be exploited as Ireland had been.

Most Scots had resented the "sword government" of Oliver Cromwell's Ironsides during the 1650s, but they deemed the Restoration of 1660 at best a partial improvement. They still looked on the Stuart dynasty as in one sense their own, and they found Charles II personally congenial. Ardent Presbyterians deplored, however, the manner in which the restored monarch eradicated all Scottish legislation since 1633 and reimplanted bishops on top of their Presbyterian structure of kirk session, presbytery, and synod. Scottish merchants fumed at the manner in which the English Parliament curtailed their trade with both England and its overseas colonies. The Scots dealt with the first of these grievances in 1689, when militant Presbyterians gained a majority of seats in Scotland's own Convention. That convention, after drafting a lengthy Claim of Right, offered the Scottish throne to William and Mary on the condition that the Presbyterian Church be recognized as the national church of Scotland. The condition was promptly met, and the northern kingdom finally shook off the rule of the hated bishops, against whom many Scots had struggled for a hundred years.

William soon learned that the Convention had not spoken for all Scots. While he consolidated his position in England and launched a military expedition to Ireland, Scottish Highlanders found occasion to quarrel with Lowlanders, and old clan rivalries reemerged in the wild hills and glens of the north. The Highlands were still a land of chieftains and followers rather than of landowners and tenant farmers, and many clan chieftains had grown accustomed to a high degree of local independence. Most Highlanders spoke Gaelic, a Celtic language unrelated to English, rather than Lowland Scots, a tongue closely related to English. Nor did the Presbyterian kirk have a strong influence among them. Not surprisingly, many Highlanders became Jacobites, supporters of the exiled King James, whom they looked on not as ruler of a modern state but as head of Clan Stuart. In 1689, as noted earlier, some of them rose and were suppressed by force, the first of numerous Jacobite rebellions that broke out over half a century. In 1692 the Macdonalds of Glencoe, who had dragged their feet in making peace with King William, were butchered by soldiers drawn from a rival clan, the Campbells. This massacre, for which William had not had direct responsibility but which he condoned, further undermined his popularity in Scotland.

These troubles coincided with a weakening of the king's political control over Scotland. Since the Restoration of 1660, the Scottish Parliament had been dominated by the executive; privy councillors responsible to the monarch had picked a committee of members of Parliament that arranged most of its business. After the Revolution of 1688–1689, this committee disappeared, and Parliament changed its character: No longer a tool of royal authority, it spoke to a distant sovereign with an increasingly independent voice. That sovereign had to work with two legislatures, English and Scottish, each meeting regularly and jealous of its own prerogatives. Any friction that arose between them would place the crown in a most uncomfortable position.

Friction did arise, largely from economic causes. The Scots were turning to trade and commercial ventures overseas with the zeal that they had shown for the theological niceties of John Calvin. English financial and mercantile interests, entrenched in the Westminster Parliament and determined to keep the resources of the empire for themselves, feared Scottish competition even more than Irish. In the 1690s, a Company of Scotland formed to trade with the Indies, Africa, and Spanish America. The directors attempted, indeed, to establish a colony at the Isthmus of Panama, which one promoter looked on as "the door of the seas, and the key to the universe." After London financiers had refused English investment in the company, the Scots took it over as a national enterprise, undeterred by William's failure to support them. William's ambassador then found himself in the extraordinary position of trying to explain to the Spanish court that, although a group of William's subjects had invaded Spanish territory, Spain should bear William no ill will, because those subjects were defying their king. The Company of Scotland collapsed less because of Spanish resistance than because of the inexperience of their directors: They sent too few supplies; they did not know how to cope with the tropical diseases that felled the colonists; they underestimated the difficulty of building a road across the isthmus; and when they withdrew in 1699, three of their four ships sank in a storm. The Scots blamed the English for the entire debacle.

Early in Anne's reign, the Scottish Parliament found occasion to assert national autonomy in political terms. The climax came with the passage of the Scottish Act of Security of 1704, which provided that the dynastic union of the two countries, unless it were amended in a way to satisfy the Scots, should end at Anne's death. The Scottish crown would then go to a Protestant Stuart, but not necessarily to the same one who wore the crown of England. When the queen refused to sign the act, the Edinburgh Parliament followed the old English parliamentary tactic of putting pressure on the crown by refusing to appropriate the taxes needed to pay for day-to-day government. Anne signed, the measure became law, and the crisis came to a boil. The English Parliament took up the challenge by passing an Alien Act that, within a few months, would have proclaimed all Scots in England foreigners and therefore forbidden to inherit property there. It would also have halted altogether the importation of Scottish cattle and linen.

Waiting for time to heal the quarrel in the middle of a world war seemed highly dangerous, for at any moment Anne's death might open the northern kingdom to the French. If the existing constitutional relationship was unworkable, the only alternative to complete separation was a closer union. Members of a committee drawn from the English and Scottish Parliaments overcame their mutual suspicions sufficiently to begin negotiations that in due course achieved a compromise, the Act of Union of 1707.[5] By the decision of their respective Parliaments, the two nations were amalgamated in the Kingdom of Great Britain, with the Union Jack as its flag. Scotland retained its own traditions of local government, its own courts, and its own system of laws, which had been codified back in 1681 by James Dalrymple, Viscount Stair, in his *Institution of the Laws of Scotland*. Dalrymple had woven Scottish statutes and

---

[5] Brian P. Levack skillfully sets the scene in *The Formation of the British State: England, Scotland, and the Union, 1603–1707* (1987). In *Scotland and the Union* (1977), David Daiches has supplied a concise and readable account. P. W. J. Riley's *The Union of England and Scotland* (1979) concentrates on the short-term political ambitions of leading negotiators. This era of Scottish history is set in context by Rosalind Mitchison in *A History of Scotland* (2nd ed., 1982) and by the same author in *Lordship to Patronage: Scotland, 1603–1745* (1983), Vol. 5 of *The New History of Scotland*.

The Act of Union (1707)   The 2nd Duke of Queensberry, Royal Commissioner in Scotland, formally presents the document to Queen Anne. *(Granger Collection)*

judicial decisions into a pattern guided more by the Roman than by the English Common Law tradition. Scotland would also continue to have the Presbyterian kirk as its own official religion, although subsequent laws extended toleration to other Christian denominations as well. Scotland received 45 of the 558 seats in the House of Commons of the new combined Parliament, and Scottish peers were to elect 16 of their number to sit in the combined House of Lords. Edinburgh remained the legal capital, but the political capital for Scots was now Westminster, and a Scottish Parliament was not to meet in Edinburgh again until 1999.

Such junior-partner status represented a harsh reality. Scotland, with a third of the island's area, had less than a sixth of its population and, according to a contemporary estimate, only a thirty-ninth of its wealth. Union gave the Scots a most important economic concession, however: free trade with England and throughout the empire. The island of Great Britain thereby became the largest free-trade area in Europe. The Scots, who, during the decade before 1707, had staggered under a series of unusually poor harvests in addition to the Panama disaster, could at last export their cattle, their linens, and their raw wool duty free. The union was an act of necessity on both sides, not of choice, and it remained extremely unpopular with numerous Scots and Englishmen for years to come. It was the result, however, of forces that had been drawing the two countries together for two centuries.

When Henry VII's daughter Margaret Tudor had gone as a bride to Edinburgh in 1503, her father had said that in this marriage alliance between the two kingdoms, the larger kingdom would pull the smaller one into its orbit. Time proved him right. The first pull came at the beginning of Elizabeth's reign, when the Scots threw off Catholicism, broke away from France, and called on England for aid; the next came when the House of Stuart moved its court from Edinburgh to London; the third came during the Puritan Revolution, which brought the two countries into more intimate contact than ever before — sometimes in collaboration, sometimes in war — and culminated in a brief political union forced on the Scots by the Cromwellian Protectorate. The two kingdoms independently preferred William III to James II, and in the midst of the outburst of economic and military activity that swept the whole island at the turn of the century, the idea of a voluntary and enduring union periodically raised its head. Moderates in both lands ultimately succeeded in mitigating ancient hatreds and jealousies in the interest of promoting economic prosperity, military safety, and dynastic security. In the process they may not have fashioned a British nation, but they did create a British state.[6]

Administration and Politics in Wartime

It is customary to look on the Glorious Revolution as weakening the executive and strengthening the legislative and judicial branches of the British government. The appraisal is accurate in that, from 1689 on, not a year went by without a meeting of Parliament; and, by the practice of William and the dictate of the Act of Settlement, judges were now appointed for life and in no sense subject to dismissal at the monarch's pleasure. These limitations on the crown gave rise to the eighteenth-century theory of the English Constitution, that Britain possessed a "mixed government," a happy balance of executive, legislative, and judicial power. The Constitution was considered balanced in yet another way: the forms of government first defined by the ancient Greeks — the monarchical, the aristocratic, and the popular — were exemplified respectively by the sovereign, the House of Lords, and the House of Commons.

In the age of William and Anne, Britons still regarded their monarch as personally in charge of the executive branch of government. William served quite literally as the commander-in-chief of the kingdom's armies; Anne presided over all the formal meetings of her leading ministers, called "cabinet councils," which took place almost every Sunday and lasted for several hours. Her officers of state generally belonged to one of the houses of Parliament, but Anne considered them her ministers. As she once explained: "All I desire is my liberty in encouraging and employing all those that concur faithfully in my service, whether they are called Whigs or Tories, not to be tied to one or the other. . . ."[7]

---

[6]In her revisionist survey, *Britons: Forging the Nation, 1707–1837* (1992), Linda Colley contends that eighteenth-century English people and Scottish people did, to an increasing degree, define themselves as Britons.

[7]Cited in G. M. Trevelyan, *England Under Queen Anne* (1930), 1:175

Shipwreck   The French fleet was not the only hazard to Britain's navy. In 1707 a storm swept several vessels into the rocks of the Scilly Isles (off England's southwest coast). *(Mary Evans Picture Library)*

A period of war might necessitate yearly meetings of Parliament to vote taxes and authorize army discipline, but in the eighteenth century, as in the twentieth, war was likely to strengthen the executive branch of government. At the very least, it vastly increased the number of people employed by the crown. The royal court was no longer expanding, but various departments of state were growing rapidly, especially the Admiralty, the War Office, and the Treasury. During the war years, the British navy doubled in size, until it maintained more than 300 ships and some 50,000 sailors and ranked as the largest in Europe; it employed more people than any other industry in the country. The army grew even more quickly, and though far from the largest in Europe, it employed 70,000 men by 1711. Both services, furthermore, required a far more complex bureaucratic structure than ever. The navy, for example, built dockyards that employed more than 2,000 workers each and that constituted the largest industrial units in the land. A navy victualing office in London that extended over five acres bought and distributed each year millions of pounds of beef, pork, butter, and cheese, as well as millions of gallons of beer.

The biggest nonmilitary branch of the national government was the Treasury, whose growth too stemmed from war and the taxation and the government borrowing that war necessitated. The Customs, the Excise, the Mint, and the Tax Office all came under the jurisdiction of the Treasury, and new tax collectors were employed as new taxes were imposed — taxes on land, on salt, on servants, on paper, on glass, and even on hackney cabs. The employees of the enlarged Treasury were not all noted for honesty or efficiency; patronage, as well as merit, determined their appointment. Yet they compared favorably with their continental counterparts, and the increasing number of career government servants demonstrated sufficient ability to raise the necessary funds and pay the expenses of war.

Although the growing executive branch of the government was a potential force for political stability, parliamentary strife was not — and never in English history had party rivalry been so lively as in the reign of Queen Anne. The Triennial Act of 1694 guaranteed a general election every three years, although not all seats were contested each time. The total English electorate grew for a time to over 250,000, one adult male in four or five; electioneering proved rowdy, and bribery was prevalent. Party rivalry between Whigs and Tories centered not only on a struggle for office but also on genuine differences of both principle and emphasis. By the middle years of Anne's reign, the Whigs had become the war party, the party of parliamentary management and government finance, and the party of the aristocratic magnates, cosmopolitan in outlook and sympathetic to religious dissenters and overseas traders. The Tories had the backing of some of London's most successful brewers, builders, and clothiers. Predominantly, however, they were the party of the country squires, fearful of the influence of the burgeoning bureaucracy, eager to reduce taxes and electoral corruption, suspicious of foreigners abroad and of religious dissenters at home. By 1710 they had also become the peace party. Interparty strife, although sometimes confused by factional division and moderated by members of Parliament who consistently supported the queen's ministers, was the order of the day. Yet the contestants did not yet acknowledge either the legitimacy or the utility of such party rivalry, and winners were still tempted to impeach or to exile losers. Political opposition to the queen's ministers looked suspiciously like potential treason, and as the final years of Anne's reign demonstrated, a change of party dominance might even alter the succession to the throne.

The Twilight of the Stuart Era (1710–1714)

Every year seemed to bring another victory by Marlborough's forces over the French: the Battle of Ramillies (1706), the Battle of Oudenarde (1708), the Battle of Malplaquet (1709). Yet somehow peace seemed further away than ever, because thus far the anti-French alliance had failed to budge the grandson of Louis XIV off the Spanish throne. On all other points in dispute, the French seemed eager to make peace, but the Whigs refused to negotiate. Tory landowners wondered whether a conspiracy was at work on the part of the new "moneyed interest" to impoverish both them and the Anglican clergy, a quarter of whose income went in taxes to help pay the

Thanksgiving Service in St. Paul's Cathedral Queen Anne and members of both houses of Parliament give thanks for Marlborough's victory at Ramillies (1706) in Christopher Wren's newly completed structure. *(The British Museum, photo by Weidenfeld and Nicolson)*

costs of war. Queen Anne grew increasingly disenchanted with the bullying from the duchess of Marlborough and transferred her affections to Abigail Masham, a relative of the moderate Tory leader Robert Harley. She distrusted advisers who appeared to mock princes and churchmen alike.

The rising tide of discontent came to a head with the impeachment and trial of Dr. Henry Sacheverell. A handsome young High Church clergyman, Sacheverell utilized Guy Fawkes Day, 1709, to preach an explosive sermon in London against religious dissenters, occasional conformists, unlicensed schools, "moderate" bishops, and all who questioned the pre-1689 doctrines of loyalty and obedience to monarch and church. The Whig government decided to prosecute Sacheverell for the sermon and thereby brand all such Tory ideas as Jacobitical and treasonous. The House of Commons duly impeached the preacher for "high crimes and misdemeanors," but the tactic backfired. In the House of Lords, Sacheverell's advocates shrewdly defended him as the victim of misrepresentation by enemies of the Church of England. One hundred thousand copies of his sermon were sold, and London's streets were filled by a turbulent pro-Sacheverell mob, "a symbol of populist resentment of the Bank, of wealthy city dissenters, and of a Whig war policy that seemed to be undermining the domestic economy."[8] Dissenter meeting-houses were wrecked and the Bank of England attacked. Although the House of Lords, by a vote of 69–52, declared him guilty, Sacheverell escaped with a minimal sentence: a three-year suspension from public preaching. He became the hero of the hour as church bells were rung, toasts were drunk, and celebrations were held in his honor.

In the summer of 1710, the queen dismissed Godolphin as her chief minister and replaced him with Harley. The Tories also triumphed in the parliamentary elections that followed in November. They committed themselves to making peace, and for domestic reasons, they had to make it quickly. At the queen's death, which might come at any moment, they dreamed of a Stuart restoration. The Tories had never liked the prospect of a Hanoverian king, even though they themselves had passed the Act of Settlement; and since 1701, they had grown increasingly intrigued by a Stuart youngster, growing up in France, whom the Jacobites called James III and others called the Pretender. If he could be persuaded to change his religion, he might make a Tory king — *provided* that the war had ended by the time the question arose. Even the most fervent Tory did not expect the British public to welcome in time of war a monarch who was a pensioner of France.

Two factors helped the government in its hurried efforts to make peace and force the treaty through Parliament:

Archduke Charles succeeded to the Habsburg dominions in 1711 as the emperor Charles VI. His accession undermined the Whig argument for conquering Spain, because success there would unite the Austrian and Spanish empires under a single crown and thereby upset the balance of power.

The queen gave her ministers the support they needed to force the treaty through the House of Lords. The upper house, unlike the lower, was still dominated by Whigs, for it was immune to the electorate. Without royal intervention, the Lords could not be coerced. Anne could pack the house, however, and she did so at the end of 1711 by creating twelve new Tory peers. Her action carried more weight than she or her ministers realized. Two greater crises of the future, in 1832 and 1911, would be resolved by monarchs (at the behest of their leading ministers) threatening to take the same course, and the fact that Anne had set a precedent would ultimately suffice to bring the Lords to heel.

Thus in 1713 Britain and France finally ended their war with the Treaty of Utrecht. Britain's reluctant allies followed suit the next year, and the Utrecht Settlement proved a landmark in both European and British history. France accepted the Hanoverian succession to the British throne and banished the Pretender; in return, the allies recognized Philip V as the rightful king of Spain and of the Spanish overseas empire, on the

---

[8]Gary Stuart De Krey, *A Fractured Society: The Politics of London in the First Age of Party, 1688–1715* (1986). See also Geoffrey Holmes, *The Trial of Dr. Sacheverell* (1973).

condition that he never inherit the French throne. The Austrian Habsburgs received the former Spanish possessions in Italy; and the Spanish Netherlands (modern Belgium) became the Austrian Netherlands, their border with France garrisoned by Dutch troops to protect the road to Amsterdam. Spain ceded Gibraltar and Minorca to Britain, and by an agreement known as the *asiento* accorded to British merchants a monopoly on importing slaves into Spanish America and granted limited trading rights there.[9] In North America, France ceded Hudson's Bay, Nova Scotia, and Newfoundland to Britain. These were the dry details.

The settlement respected the principle of the balance of power by giving something to every strong belligerent. The Dutch gained security for their frontiers. The Austrian Habsburgs gained the whole of the European Spanish empire, except Spain itself, and so increased their weight in the scales of power to balance the Bourbon acquisitions. France gained a dynastic, and therefore a political and economic, link with Spain and South America but lost part of the inheritance for which Louis had originally gone to war. Only Britain, among the major contestants, seemed to make minor gains: a rock by the Straits of Gibraltar, a Mediterranean island, and some North American wilderness. But appearances were deceptive.

The settlement furthered the long-standing British interest in keeping a strong power out of the Low Countries; the Austrian Netherlands were henceforth protected by the Dutch and governed by the distant Habsburgs. British merchants gained concessions that strengthened their long-standing claims to a share of the trade with Latin America. The Royal Navy, faced with the possibility that the Franco-Spanish fleets might unite against it in overwhelming strength, received in Gibraltar and Minorca the bases it needed to keep Bourbon forces in the Atlantic separated from those in the Mediterranean. In short, Britain came out of the struggle with little to show on the surface for eleven years of fighting but with solid foundations for its power.

The end of the war marked the beginning of a final, bitter domestic crisis. Its crux was the succession, but it also involved the status of landowners, taxation, and religion. In 1711 the Tory Parliament passed a law making only substantial landowners eligible for election to the House of Commons. Wealth in the form of bank deposits or stock holdings did not count. Two years later, Parliament substantially reduced the burden of the tax on land. On the subject of religious dissent, the Tories were as intolerant as ever. In 1711 they banned the practice of occasional conformity to evade the Test Act and three years later gave the Church of England a monopoly on secondary education; dissenters now could neither hold office nor keep their children from Anglican indoctrination. With even their precarious position of 1689 in jeopardy, the dissenters looked for deliverance to the Whigs and Hanover. The Tories, in turn, could rely on a large segment of the country squires and on a body of Anglican

---

[9]See Chapter 5.

clergy that appeared to be strengthening anew its claims to be England's sole established religion.

Persecuting a minority might win votes for the Tories, but it did not solve their basic dilemma over the succession of the crown. Time was running out; Anne, who had fallen dangerously ill in December 1713, was unlikely to live many months longer, and some preparation had to be made for a legitimate candidate to succeed her — but who? If Hanover was unpopular with the Tory government, the Tories were even more unpopular with Hanover. The elector George became sole heir to the throne when his mother Sophia died early in 1714, and George believed that the great Tory achievement, the Treaty of Utrecht, had flagrantly betrayed the interests of the German states in general and Hanover in particular. Unless the angry elector could be shorn of power before he set foot in England, the Tory ministers would be finished, politically if not physically. Yet as the nearest Protestant in the royal succession, George — in accordance with the Act of Settlement of 1701 — remained Anne's legal heir. The Tories' sole alternative to George was the Pretender, who, far from giving them help, dashed their hopes in the spring of 1714 by announcing that he would not abandon his Catholic faith for the sake of a throne.

As spring gave way to summer, the unity of the Tory ministry began to disintegrate in a quarrel between its two leading members. Robert Harley, earl of Oxford, was an enigmatic and skillful politician who wanted to wait on events in the hope of profiting from whatever came. Henry St. John, viscount Bolingbroke, sought to gather into his hands the full power of the state by putting his agents into every position of influence. How he intended to use the power is not clear to this day, because he never got the chance to demonstrate it: Lord Oxford stood in his way. The two men, who by now detested each other on a number of grounds, fought for the upper hand. On July 27, Bolingbroke won; Oxford was dismissed. But the victor had only three days in which to try to exploit his victory. By July 30, with the queen obviously dying, few men wanted to risk their necks for Bolingbroke's schemes. The moderates gained control, and a stream of orders went out to prepare the way for the coming of the Hanoverian. On the morning of August 1, the last of the Stuarts died. Edema and a bad heart in a woman prematurely old ended Bolingbroke's career and destroyed his party, and he of all men had reason to remember his *Macbeth:*

> She should have died hereafter;
> There would have been a time for such a word.

The years 1713–1714 constitute a watershed in British history. They marked the end of a quarter-century of wars, from which Britain emerged as the major sea power of Europe and during which the changes set in motion in 1688 were completed and secured. *If* defeat of the Royal Navy had ever opened the way to invasion and a Stuart restoration, *if* Scotland had broken the dynastic union and resumed its independence, *if* the Bank of England had failed, *if* the Pretender had turned Protestant, and *if* Anne had lived a few months longer, Britain's subsequent history would have differed greatly, but such historical speculation is of limited value. All that can be said is that the Revolution Settlement was never really safe until George I was proclaimed king and was not in serious jeopardy thereafter. The settlement, like the people who made it, combined political wisdom and expediency, as well as principles and grasping self-interest. It arose from the dust of battling parties in Westminster and battling armies in Europe. When the dust finally cleared, it was revealed as the structure of Britain's Augustan Age.

PART TWO

THE WHIG OLIGARCHY
1714 to 1763

SPEAKER ARTHUR ONSLOW POINTS TO SIR ROBERT WALPOLE IN THE HOUSE OF
COMMONS, 1730 *(The National Trust)*

CHAPTER 3

The Structure of Society

Asociety, past or present, can be described only in generalizations, which by their nature must remain partial at best. Observers of a contemporary society can at least live in it, but historians must view it through the eyes of men and women long dead, who may have experienced their times on the basis of expectations and preconceptions far different from our own. The generalizations that historians apply to past centuries must also rest on evidence that is often contradictory and incomplete.[1]

This is no modern discovery. It was clear to a sophisticated observer in the reign of George II and underlay his skeptical view of the data that make history. "Do we ever hear the most recent fact related exactly in the same way," the earl of Chesterfield asked, "by the several people who were at the same time eyewitnesses of it? No. One mistakes, another misrepresents, and others warp it a little to their own turn of mind or private views. A man who has been concerned in a transaction will not write it fairly; and a man who has not, cannot." Chesterfield went on to caution his son, in his study of the past, to remember the complexities and inconsistencies of human nature with which history grapples — the fluctuations of passion and will, the accidents of bodily health, the elements of pettiness and evil in the best of people, of greatness in the worst.

In this passage, nevertheless, the earl was urging upon his son the value of studying history. That study was becoming, as never before, the recognized prerequisite for understanding the present, which is the reason that the eighteenth century saw the beginning of history-writing in the modern sense. And, although generalization remains hazardous, we know a great deal about the aristocrats and squires and their dependents among

---

[1]Although at times unduly cynical, at other times unduly sunny, the best single introduction to the subject of this chapter remains Roy Porter, *English Society in the Eighteenth Century* (2nd ed., 1990). In *Progress and Poverty: An Economic and Social History of England, 1700–1850* (1996), Martin J. Daunton has provided a reliable recent overview. Other relevant works that remain of value are complementary books by John Rule, *Albion's People: English Society, 1714–1815* (1992), and *The Vital Century: England's Developing Economy, 1714–1815* (1992), as well as Charles Wilson, *England's Apprenticeship, 1603–1763* (1965); and T. S. Ashton, *An Economic History of England: The Eighteenth Century* (1955).

whom Lord Chesterfield moved, from their politics and architecture to the management of their estates and their views of life. (Some of these subjects are explored further in Chapters 4 and 6.)

"Such is the constitution of civil society," wrote the eighteenth-century English historian Edward Gibbon (1737–1794), "that, whilst a few persons are distinguished by riches, by honours, and by knowledge, the body of the people is condemned to obscurity, ignorance, and poverty." Generalization therefore becomes even more hazardous when we try to examine the lives of the vast majority of British men and women who were not at or near the top of the social hierarchy. In the course of the past two generations, however, numerous historians have reminded us of how much circumstantial evidence is available about their lives: in judicial records, in obscure pamphlets and newspapers, in surviving diaries, in travelers' accounts, in pictures, in buildings, and even on tombstones.

The England of Gregory King

The eighteenth century was not so absorbed with statistics as the nineteenth and twentieth centuries would be, but it was more so than the sixteenth or early seventeenth centuries. The kingdom increasingly resorted to large-scale government borrowing and nationally organized tax collections. Some merchants at Edward Lloyd's coffeehouse in London were developing the principles and practices of insurance — for ships, fire protection, and human lives. In 1699 Isaac Newton, the most esteemed scientist of the day, was appointed to the Treasury office of Master of the Mint, and its standards of accuracy proceeded to improve. Surviving business and household accounts reveal the conscientiousness with which many men and women recorded every penny and shilling that they spent — and sometimes saved.

There was no national census in Britain until 1801, however, so demographers seeking to calculate the population of the preindustrial world and its growth or decline have had to make do with indirect evidence drawn from parish registers and tax records. They have also used the estimates made by contemporaries. By general consent, the most reliable guide to the population and social structure of early-eighteenth-century England was provided in 1696 by Gregory King, the secretary to the Commissioners of the Public Accounts. He justified his "Natural and Political Observations and Conclusions upon the State and Condition of England" on the basis that, in the midst of a long and expensive war, knowledge of "the true state and Condition" of its people and their wealth "must be of the Highest Concern. . . ." Because historians generally agree that the population grew slowly during the first half of the eighteenth century, King's figures provide an approximate guide for that entire period.

Gregory King's assumptions are as revealing as his conclusions. He assumed, for one thing, that the fundamental unit of society was not the individual but the family. Furthermore, he took for granted what social historians have recently confirmed — that the nuclear family (made up of father, mother, and children) had become the fundamental social unit in the British Isles and northern Europe long before the Industrial Revolution.

Admittedly, a nuclear family might last for only a few years, because young men were not encouraged to marry until they could afford to set up a household with wife and children. Both farmers and journeymen tended to marry in their late twenties, with their wives a year or two younger. In the first half of the century, the death rate was high. The average person lived about thirty-five years (in contrast to seventy-five or more in our day), and only one parent in two could expect to survive long enough to see a child grow to adulthood. Because many marriages were cut short by death, most families included no more than four children. Historians continue to dispute whether English men and women of the time consciously sought to limit the size of their families, but surviving evidence of magic spells and special herbs suggests that many of them tried. Most people also knew that a nursing mother was less likely to become pregnant again right away. Miscarriages and stillbirths were common, and abortion did not become illegal in England until 1803.[2] Strong social pressure existed against illegitimate children, but society had considerable toleration for unmarried women who became pregnant, provided that they married before the child was born. The lot of illegitimate children was unenviable. Whether they ended up in a foundling hospital or, when somewhat older, were found apprenticeships by the local parish overseers of the poor, only a minority reached adulthood. In most families, by the time a boy had entered his teens, he would have left home as apprentice to a shopkeeper or a craftsman or even a chimney sweep; most girls would have become farm or household servants.

In the higher social strata, the family included a number of unmarried live-in household servants. Modern scholars conclude, indeed, that King underestimated both the size of the average household and the annual income of the top families in the land. Many families of farmers, merchants, tradesmen, and artisans also included live-in servants and apprentices. A widowed parent, a spinster aunt, or a bachelor uncle might be found at all social levels, but the nuclear family was the norm.

If King's estimates are correct, it is equally clear that early eighteenth-century England was a highly inegalitarian society. About one-fourth of the total national income went to 3.5 percent of all families, whereas three-fifths of the population shared a sixth of that income. King's own comments took such a state of affairs for granted. Indeed, he praised the families of nobles, merchants, professionals, shopkeepers, and artisans for "increasing the wealth of the kingdom," while criticizing vagrants, paupers, and even common laborers, cottagers, seamen, and soldiers for decreasing its bounty. His criterion was whether income ex-

---

[2]Angus McLaren, *Reproductive Rituals: The Perception of Fertility from the Sixteenth to the Nineteenth Century* (1984).

POPULATION AND SOCIAL STRUCTURE OF ENGLAND IN 1688, ACCORDING TO GREGORY KING, 1696

Number of families	Rank, degrees, titles, and qualifications	Heads per family	Number of persons	Yearly income per family £
160	Temporal lords	40	6,400	2,800
26	Spiritual lords	20	520	1,300
800	Baronets	16	12,800	880
600	Knights	13	7,800	650
3,000	Esquires	10	30,000	450
12,000	Gentlemen	8	96,000	280
5,000	Persons in greater offices	8	40,000	240
5,000	Persons in lesser offices	6	30,000	120
2,000	Merchants and traders by sea	8	16,000	400
8,000	Merchants and traders by land	6	48,000	200
10,000	Persons in the law	7	70,000	140
2,000	Eminent clergymen	6	12,000	60
8,000	Lesser clergymen	5	40,000	45
40,000	Freeholders of the better sort	7	280,000	84
140,000	Freeholders of the lesser sort	5	700,000	50
150,000	Farmers	5	750,000	44
16,000	Persons in sciences and liberal arts	5	80,000	60
40,000	Shopkeepers and tradesmen	4½	180,000	45
60,000	Artisans and handicrafts	4	240,000	40
5,000	Naval officers	4	20,000	80
4,000	Military officers	4	16,000	60
50,000	Common seamen	3	150,000	20
364,000	Laboring people and out-servants	3½	1,275,000	15
400,000	Cottagers and paupers	3½	1,300,000	6½
35,000	Common soldiers	2	70,000	14
—	Vagrants	—	30,000	—
1,360,586			5,500,520	—

ceeded or fell short of expenditure. Those whose income surpassed expenditure won praise for investing in the commerce and industry of the kingdom. Those in the lower half of society were thought all too liable to resort to the charity of others or to the parish overseer of the poor.

The society that Gregory King analyzed evidently recognized a wide array of gradations of social status that in practice roughly paralleled annual income. Yet King ranks government officials above merchants, and clergymen above freeholders, even though merchants and freeholders were materially better off. The society that King describes was in no sense castebound; some individuals found it possible, both legally and practically, to climb the social ladder or to topple from it. Nor is it appropriate to describe the society as based on class. True, a small group of

A Village Pillory   In the countryside, as in London, the pillory was used both to punish criminals and to entertain the public. *(Mary Evans Picture Library)*

legally defined aristocrats sat atop the social ladder, whom one was well advised to address as "Your Lordship," or "Your Worship," or "Sir." But which of the groups that King classified ought to be defined as "middle-class" and which as "lower-class" is sometimes far from apparent: Such phrases are either too simple to represent human reality or too "fuzzy around the edges." What is clear is that relatively few members of eighteenth-century English society were "class-conscious" in the manner that some of their nineteenth- and twentieth-century descendants came to be. Most people were far more conscious of their precise relationship to those immediately above them and below them on the societal ladder than they were aware of those on their own level elsewhere in the land. Their loyalty thus went less to a class than to a community. The people with whom a landed aristocrat or a country squire concerned himself in the course of a day or a year were in no sense limited to his own rank in society. They included the immediate members of his family, a bevy of household and estate servants, his tenant farmers, and, only slightly further removed, the village parson, the local tradesmen, and the neighborhood artisans. True, they deferred to him, and should he have been appointed justice of the peace, then he and his fellow justices meeting four times a year in "quarter sessions" possessed the legal authority to supervise their behavior; but in times of distress they expected his assistance. Many of them might owe their position or that of their children to his patronage, and they might extend comparable patronage at a lower level to servants, day laborers, and apprentices. When the landed squire entered Parliament, he readily pictured himself as responsible for and representative of his particular portion of the country. Members of different social ranks thus tended to be tied to one another by complex relationships of patronage and dependence.

In Chapter 13 of the novel *Joseph Andrews* (1742), Henry Fielding compares the pattern of patronage and dependence to "a kind of ladder."

> Early in the morning arises the postillion, or some other boy, which no great families, no more than great ships, are without, and falls to brushing the clothes and cleaning the shoes of John the footman; who being dressed himself, applies his hands to the same labours for Mr. Second-hand, the squire's gentleman; the gentleman in the like manner, a little later in the day, attends the squire; the squire is no sooner equipped than he attends the levee of my lord; which is no sooner over, than my lord himself is seen at the levee of the favourite, who, after the hour of homage is at an end, appears himself to pay homage to the levee of his sovereign. Nor is there, perhaps, in this whole ladder of dependence, any one step at a greater distance from the other than the first from the second, so that to a philosopher the question might only seem whether you would choose to be a great man at six in the morning or at two in the afternoon. And yet there are scarce two of these who do not think the least familiarity with the persons below them a condescension, and, if they were to go one step farther, a degradation.

The Aristocracy and the Gentry

As Gregory King's chart suggests, the top rung of England's social ladder during the eighteenth century was occupied by aristocrats and country squires and their families. Aristocrats had the right to sit in the House of Lords. Members of the squirearchy or gentry, although they did not bear the title of duke, marquess, earl, viscount, or baron, nevertheless were likely to play a significant role in government (at least at the local level). Their wealth, like that of the nobles, derived primarily from the ownership of a large landed estate. Whatever ties landed gentlemen might also have to commerce and banking, their prestige derived for the most part from their estates and from the imposing country houses in which many of them lived.

The average J.P. (Justice of the Peace), like the average M.P. (Member of Parliament), was an amateur who lacked formal training in the law and who expected to devote no more than a few weeks or, at most, a few months each year to his governmental responsibilities. Gentlemen had careers and might spend considerable time at them, but they rarely entered their professions prepared by formal education. If they joined either of the armed services, they did not attend a university — let alone a military or naval academy — but were trained in the regiment or at sea: one admiral remarked that for forty years his ship "has been the only university he has been permitted to study at." If they elected a political career, they were likely to start with an education at a "public school" (a fee-paying boarding school such as Eton or Harrow or Westminster) and either the university of Oxford or Cambridge. A few might also gain exposure to the law at one of the Inns of Court in London; but then, when they secured local office or a seat in Parliament or membership in the cabinet, they learned "on the job," relying on their wits and, with luck, an experienced secretary.

This is not to say that gentlemen were uneducated. Almost all of them were versed in the classics and had some command of French, while many were well grounded in history and informed by foreign travel and wide reading. What they lacked was education in the principles and theory of what they were doing: they were improvisers rather than specialists and would have scorned being anything else. Their self-assurance, even when they were ignorant, was that of men who know that they are to the manor born; their amateur status was synonymous with their being gentlemen.

George Frederick Handel (1685–1759)   In 1711 Handel moved to London where he became the favorite composer and conductor of both courtiers and ordinary citizens. *(National Portrait Gallery, London)*

Their rule often proved inefficient. They could waste both time and money. They sometimes made decisions based on inadequate information and unexamined premises; they ignored much that cried out to be done. Yet they also achieved surprising results in the hundred-odd years that their regime lasted. They conquered an empire overseas, fought France to a standstill and eventually to defeat in Europe, presided at home over an economic revolution in agriculture and industry, and brought the art of living among the favored few to a high peak. They had faults aplenty, but they also possessed the energy to make their system work.

Early Georgian society, for all its self-assurance, was less sophisticated than it became later in the century. The court did much to set its tone, and the sovereign to set the tone of the court. Anne had been no patron of the arts, and even by comparison with her, the first two Hanoverians were boors — witness the bluff comment of George II, in his Germanic English, "Damn the Bainters, and the Boets Too!" Only for music did the first two Georges make an exception: Both became loyal patrons of George Frederick Handel (1685–1759), German by birth, Italian by musical training, and English by residence and naturalization. Handel dedicated his *Royal Water Music* to George I, and many of Handel's thirty-six Italian operas were performed before the king. In his later career, the composer specialized in oratorios, unstaged operas performed in concert halls to English texts, the best-remembered of which, *The Messiah*, was first performed in Dublin in 1742. Handel helped to implant choral singing in the English musical tradition, and he helped make mid- and late-eighteenth-century London a mecca for numerous other continental musicians.

Many powerful magnates did provide patronage to painters and poets, musicians and architects, but their taste was far from impeccable; they often mistook ostentation for elegance. An example in point is Blenheim Palace, completed at the beginning of the period. When Parliament voted the duke of Marlborough a great country house, a fashionable architect, Sir John Vanbrugh, was commissioned to design it. The duke himself had much to do with the plans, and after his death his termagant duchess brought the work to completion. The palace bears the impress of Marlborough's personality. "As the Pharaohs built their Pyramids, so he sought a physical monument which would certainly stand, if only as a ruin, for thousands of years. About his achievements he preserved a complete silence, offering neither explanations nor excuses for any of his deeds. His answer was to be this great house."[3]

Although the "house" — three acres of it — answers no questions explicitly, it does tell something about what the duke and his age deemed monumental. The palace is not only huge but as ponderous as the Great

[3]Churchill, *Marlborough*, Vol. 6 (1939), p. 319. For an illustration of Blenheim and additional comments about eighteenth-century architecture, see Chapter 10. In *The Aristocracy in England, 1660–1914* (1986), J. V. Beckett provides a sympathetic overview. In *Aristocratic Century: The Peerage of Eighteenth-Century England* (1984), John Cannon focuses on the fewer than two hundred families at the top of the social hierarchy.

Pyramid. Its heaviness is accentuated by the fact that it broods over one of the most serene and spacious parks in England. The mass of the building is enough in itself to explain the epitaph on the gravestone of Vanbrugh, its architect: "Lie heavy on him, Earth, for he laid many a heavy load on thee." Massiveness, though, is not the only characteristic; another is multiplicity. Despite the symmetrical plan, the sense of unity dissolves in a maze of pavilions, wings, colonnades, and indentations; the eye struggles to race from window to cornice to statuary to pilaster without ever coming to rest. The interior is of a piece with the facade: monumental staircases, vast rooms hung with tapestry or gleaming with marble (some of it real, some painted on the walls), and never a quiet moment. This is the architecture of show, a collection of impressive parts jostling each other for preeminence, like politicians jostling for office. The restless energy within the structure creates an imposing chaos.

The same restlessness ran through much of society, although it did not always appear on the surface. Many members of the eighteenth-century nobility and gentry added to their country houses or built new ones, securing, if they were fortunate, the services of Lancelot "Capability" Brown (1716–1783), the prime landscape architect of the age. This onetime kitchen gardener had acquired his nickname from his habit of concluding a prospective client's estate survey with the comment that he saw "great capability of improvement here." Brown would dam rivers to create artificial lakes, shear away old hillsides and build new ones, cut away underbrush and plant whole groves of trees — all in order to provide a series of varied but serene parkland views to be admired from the

Blenheim Palace   The structure built in honor of the duke of Marlborough — the most monumental private home ever built in Britain. *(Blenheim Palace, Oxfordshire/Bridgeman Art Library, London)*

manor house and from the winding gravel walks with which Brown would surround the structure.

The inhabitants of such country houses seemed to have an almost inexhaustible appetite for social life. They loved to hunt wild game — such as hares, deer, partridges, and pheasants — and in order to safeguard the pleasure for themselves, they enacted harsh antipoaching laws to exclude most members of the lower orders from such sport. Many of the wealthy gambled large sums at horse races; and, according to one foreign observer, racehorses received "all the care and tender treatment that favorite children can expect from a parent." They loved to eat and to drink as well, and large country houses all boasted their own breweries. They also took pleasure in dancing and in attending what they called an assembly—defined in 1751 as "a stated and general meeting of the polite persons of both sexes, for the sake of conversation, gallantry, news and play." The invention of carriages with springs made it possible for country squires and their wives to travel to London in relative comfort and also to take the waters at Bath or at one of the other fashionable spas; there they sought to socialize as well as to recover from the "nervous disorders" with which many of the well-to-do felt afflicted. The great lords usually owned permanent town houses in London (in which they lived for six months or more each year), but aristocrats and gentry alike retained their country roots.[4] If only because their architectural and social ambitions tended to exceed their income, many of them were perpetually in debt, but only a handful lost their estates altogether.

Unlike most continental landlords, the English gentry were not themselves farmers with large numbers of peasants working for them directly. Although each estate might boast a small home farm to supply the household with produce and fresh dairy products, most of the estate was leased, often in large tracts, to rent-paying tenants, known in England as farmers. A nobleman's or a squire's status as primarily a rent-collector enabled him to serve as a local official or Member of Parliament and still have time for the vigorous life of a country gentleman. He was wise, however, not to take the economic foundations of that life for granted. In all likelihood, his estate was formally "entailed." That meant that he had only a life interest in it and was pledged to keep it intact, so that it might be inherited at his death by his eldest son. If the estate was not entailed, dividing it among several sons would fatally lower their positions in the world. How, then, could he keep the estate together and also provide for his children? Not by sitting still, but only by exploring every possible way to increase the family fortunes.

One way was matrimonial. If a father could find rich wives for his boys and rich husbands for his girls, his troubles would be over. Even if he could do nothing more than find an heiress for his eldest son, he might then

---

[4]Mark Girouard is concerned with both the architectural setting and the inhabitants' social customs in *Life in the English Country House* (1978). In *English Landed Society in the Eighteenth Century* (1963), G. E. Mingay deals with estates, large and small, and the way they were managed.

stretch the estate so that it would provide a good income not only for his prospective widow, but substantial dowries for his daughters and allowances for his younger sons during their entire lifetime. The conscientious father, however, would rarely try to make a marriage alliance with a monster or a moron, no matter how well endowed with earthly goods. Indeed, the mid-eighteenth-century aristocratic family in England was likely to show both greater affection and a more pronounced sense of equality between husband and wife, more direct involvement in the bringing up of children, and a wider degree of detachment from the ever-present household servants than had comparable families during the Tudor and Stuart eras.[5] Admittedly, a father seeking spouses for his children concerned himself as much with social status and financial stability as with love. Achieving his goal required luck in finding wealth, diplomatic and business acumen in bargaining with the other set of parents, and shrewd lawyers in drawing up the contract. Such contracts, though they could not guarantee happy marriages, often ensured the survival of families.

Fathers found the largest market for rich husbands and wives among those who had more money than lineage. The *nouveaux riches* of the day, who had made their fortunes in banking, commerce, or the wool trade, or abroad in the service of the East India Company or one of its lesser competitors, were eager to rise above their origins into the gentry or even the aristocracy. To do so, they first had to settle on the land, then to contract judicious marriages. No one could begin the climb toward gentility until he had severed all active connection with trade and bought a country estate; then he could inaugurate the long series of moves by which his children might gain admission to country society. A daughter with a large dowry might catch the eye of an impoverished peer or squire. A son would go to an acceptable school such as Eton, then to Oxford or Cambridge, then perhaps to Europe for a year or two of polishing on what was called the Grand Tour. If his father had enough wealth, on his return he would be eligible to marry, perhaps even the daughter of an impoverished earl: such a marriage would in all likelihood make him socially acceptable by right of his wife. Their son, two generations removed from money grubbing, would rank as a gentleman above reproach. In this and similar ways, the oligarchy continually took in new blood. "Trade in England," said Daniel Defoe, ". . . has peopled this nation with gentlemen. . . . The tradesmen's children, or at least their grandchildren, come to be as good gentlemen, statesmen, parliament-men, privy councilors, judges, bishops, and noblemen as those of the highest birth and the most ancient families."[6]

---

[5]The entire subject is explored in Lawrence Stone, *The Family, Sex, and Marriage in England, 1500–1800* (1977), and in Randolph Trumbach, *The Rise of the Egalitarian Family: Aristocratic Kinship and Domestic Relations in Eighteenth-Century England* (1978). After studying surviving legal records in detail, Stone has conceded in a more recent work, *Uncertain Unions: Marriage in England, 1660–1753* (1992), that a significant number of well-to-do as well as propertyless Britons permitted themselves a high degree of sexual freedom at a time when the state of marriage law was confused.

If upward mobility affected at least some eighteenth-century landed families, then so did downward mobility. Although a careful father would use all his connections, relatives, and influential friends to find openings for his sons in the world in which they were reared, he might not necessarily succeed. Take the case of an imaginary country squire, Sir Roger Broadacres, Bart., the father of six sons. Broadacres's estate would be entailed on young Roger, the eldest, who would expect to inherit it along with the baronetcy. No problem there. The second son would be marked out for a commission in the army, and Lady Broadacres's cousin at the War Office would be expected to watch out for his advancement. The third son, if a studious lad, might be educated for a post in the Church of England, in which an uncle was a bishop. If a fourth son found the sea attractive, his godfather (a captain in the Royal Navy) might advance a career there. The prospects for the fifth and sixth sons would be slim, however. Sir Roger might apprentice one with the family attorney to be trained in the law and the other with the wool merchants who had long marketed the produce of the family sheep. At least two of the six sons (and their families) would therefore "descend" from the world of the gentry.

A man in Sir Roger's position had to do more than provide for his children by arranging marriages and pulling strings; he also had to look sharply to his income. The status, perhaps the survival, of his family depended on how well he used his land, and during the eighteenth century, many of his ilk became leaders as well as beneficiaries of agricultural improvement. Charles Townshend, a secretary of state in the 1720s, retired from politics in order to pioneer the utilization of root crops and to win historical renown as "Turnips Townshend." Such men had an economic incentive, of course, but money was not their only motivation. Like Antaeus, they drew their strength from the earth, and familiarity with it was in their blood. The discovery that it had greater potential than they had dreamed of challenged their adventurousness, and they responded by improving agriculture with the same energy that they brought to politics and empire building.

The Farmers

In early eighteenth-century England, industrialization still lay in the future, but in no sense was the country a wholly self-sufficient agricultural society. Many more people worked at farming than at any other economic activity, but there existed a sizable population of artisans, merchants, and other town and city folk who bought their food in the shop or the market-

---

[6]In the most thorough study thus far of English upward social mobility through the centuries, *An Open Elite? England, 1540–1880* (1984), Lawrence and Jeanne Stone argue that the degree of such upward mobility has been exaggerated. Yet the statistics collected by the authors suggest that, in each generation, one landed family in five had "risen" from commerce and the professions. See the review by Harold Perkin in the *Journal of British Studies* (October 1985).

place rather than growing it themselves. Even family farmers specialized in particular crops from which they derived their cash income.

Independent family farms, whose owners were known as yeomen, continued to be found, but large estates were becoming more common. These estates constituted units of ownership rather than of production, for most of the land that they encompassed was rented out, on long lease or short, to tenants who, with members of their family and hired hands, cultivated the soil. By the end of the century, some three-quarters of the agricultural land was worked by such tenant farmers. Many of them had once been small freeholders who had sold out to the great landowners in return for capital to invest in cattle, seed, fertilizer, and plows.

In the first half of the eighteenth century, farmers remained very much dependent on the success or failure of each year's harvest. Hay-making and harvesting would not only absorb all available local labor but also attract thousands of young workers from Ireland and Wales, who then returned home for the winter. A run of bad harvests in the early decades of the century gave way to a series of plentiful ones in the 1730s and 1740s. Farm production not only kept up with but surpassed a slowly growing population, so that food prices fell and Britain became an exporter of wheat, malt, and barley to continental Europe. Although a blessing for Londoners, the decline in food prices caused many tenants to fall behind in their rents. Landlords, compelled to concede rent reductions, received a new incentive to increase agricultural efficiency.

One revolutionary discovery in agriculture was that land need not lie fallow in order to regain its fertility. This simple fact undermined the system of cultivation that had prevailed in the more fertile areas of England from time immemorial: The arable land of a manor was divided into two or three great fields, each subdivided into the lord's and tenants' strips. In the two-field system, one of the two fields lay fallow each year; in the three-field system, one of the three. In any given year, therefore, at least a third of the fertile land of the country bore nothing but weeds. Consequently, the land produced insufficient fodder to keep all the cattle through the winter, and many had to be slaughtered every fall. These limitations on the supply of grain and meat seemed to be imposed by the nature of the soil; century after century, no one thought to question whether they might be imposed by human ignorance.

The acceleration in scientific activity that began with the Restoration entailed learning to question, and as one of its earliest inquiries, the Royal Society investigated methods of farming and breeding. At the same time, pioneers introduced the practice, long a commonplace in Flanders, of judiciously rotating crops to keep all fields producing every year. Wheat one summer, turnips the next, then oats or barley, then clover, then wheat again — this was the cycle that significantly altered the pattern of British agriculture. The primary rationale behind crop rotation was that the new crops, turnips or clover, both replenished the soil and provided winter fodder for cattle. Bigger and better-fed herds gave the farmer more meat to sell and more manure for fertilizing, which made for more and better crops and hence still larger herds. Simultaneously came the first experiments with the scientific breeding of sheep and cattle for meat. Over the century, the typical British pig, small and hairy, was thus transformed into a large, fat, and essentially hairless animal. Slowly but cumulatively, rural life was changing.

The rotation of crops and the new emphasis on stock breeding forced a change in the face of the countryside. Now that the old system, two or three open fields divided into strips, was no longer necessary, landholders gradually came to realize how wasteful it was. To rotate crops most efficiently meant consolidating scattered strips into a single holding. Analogously, the only way to improve farm stock was to prevent the animals' habitual grazing together over the fallow ground, a practice that ensured "the haphazard union of nobody's son with everybody's daughter," and to segregate them for breeding purposes. Improving crops and meat, in other words, required enclosed land. The requirement was met by the enclosure movement, which meant the conversion of strips and pasture rights in the open field, under communal supervision, into individual fields and pastures, walled or fenced, in which each owner or tenant could do as he pleased. Additional enclosures in the English midlands by act of Parliament would excite intense controversy later in the century (see Chapter 9), but recent historical research has shown that two-thirds of the land had already been enclosed when the century began.[7]

In a society still largely rural, such changes had momentous ramifications. The predominance of the landed interest, unchallenged until after the Napoleonic Wars, did not rest solely on turnips and clover, mutton and beef; for wealth accrued from many other sources. The wealth most accessible to the landowner was that which lay in his fields. The more profit his farmers made, the fatter his rent rolls grew. As harvests improved over the decades, the income of the progressive squire with a few acres and of the magnate with scattered estates advanced accordingly.

Eighteenth-century laws protected grain growers from foreign competition and even granted a bounty to those who exported grain abroad. Such exports would decline later in the century when a growing population caught up with and threatened to overtake the available food supply. Upper-class menus could be very elaborate, but for most farm and town laborers, bread (made of wheat or rye), cheese, and beer (made of barley and hops) served as food staples. By midcentury, imported tea and sugar had become part of that diet as well. Those who could afford it ate beef several times a week, while the rest made do with occasional mutton or bacon, and, in coastal areas, fish. In Scotland and northern England, oat porridge and oat bread were customary, whereas in Lancashire, as in Ire-

---

[7]See J. R. Wordie, "The Chronology of English Enclosure, 1500–1914," *Economic History Review* (November 1983). Also relevant are E. L. Jones, *Agriculture and the Industrial Revolution* (1974), and Volume V (1640–1750) of *The Agrarian History of England and Wales* (1984) edited by Joan Thirsk.

land, potatoes increasingly became a standard food. Cabbage and other leafy vegetables were available but often spurned.

Not only did some tenant-farm families seek to supplement their income with hand-loom spinning and weaving, but many other economic activities also depended on agriculture. Even a small village could support a blacksmith, a shoemaker, a tailor, a glazier (to fix and repair windows), and a thatcher (to construct cottage roofs). Wheat made its way from the farms to millers, bakers, distillers, and starchmakers. Cattle provided hides for tanners and ultimately for dealers in leather goods. Soap-boilers and candlemakers used the fat derived from cattle and sheep, and the wool shorn from the latter provided the textile industry with its raw material.

Merchants and Artisans

Eighteenth-century industry was thus largely sustained by a variety of individual rural craftsmen. In London and in several other regions, however, relatively large-scale, specialized forms of manufacture had developed. Textiles predominated, and in the eighteenth century woolen cloth continued to serve, as it had for four hundred years, as England's most important nonagricultural product. As late as 1740, woolen cloth reportedly constituted one-third of all English manufactured goods. No wonder that Parliament had long been eager to make sure that domestic raw wool was reserved for English producers, not smuggled abroad, and that Parliament protected these same textile manufacturers from foreign competition. Wool was manufactured in a variety of grades and forms, and, although total production is estimated to have risen by 50 percent between 1700 and 1760, the industry underwent no technological revolution during this period. In Devon the industry indeed declined just as it reached its heyday in Norfolk; in Norwich and vicinity, 12,000 hand looms kept some 72,000 weavers busy. The industry flourished most in Yorkshire, where labor was cheaper and the merchant-capitalist organizers more enterprising. Like most other industries, woolen cloth manufacture was concentrated not in factories but in small workshops. Much of the work took place in the very cottages in which the workers lived, and the major task of the merchant-clothier was to superintend the multifaceted process by which the wool was spun in one place, woven in a second, fulled (or thickened) in a third, dyed in a fourth, and sold in yet another.

Other textiles were produced as well. The Lombe silk factory that operated in Derby during the 1720s foreshadowed the pattern of manufacture of the early nineteenth century. The complex machinery, which had been copied from an Italian model and which supposedly involved "97,746 wheels, movements, and parts," drew its power from a waterwheel and employed more than 300 women and children working day and night on successive twelve-hour shifts. Silk manufacture eventually declined; linen manufacture, in contrast, advanced in both northern Ireland and Scotland. In Lancashire a group of English entrepreneurs took advantage of an act

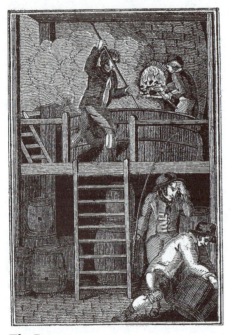

The Brewer

The Cooper (or Barrel-maker)

The Tallow Chandler (or Candle-maker)

The Letterpress Printer

Four Eighteenth-Century Artisans at Work   *(Mansell/Time)*

that levied high tariffs on cloth from India in order to launch a cotton industry that later in the century would become an economic giant.

Before the 1760s, there took place no revolutionary transformation in
the manufacture of metals any more than in the production of textiles.
But forges, anvils, smithies, and glassworks utilized an increasing
amount of coal: The amount mined more than doubled during the first
sixty years of the century. Some 10,000 nailmakers transformed perhaps
half of the iron output of the English Midlands into nails. Techniques
continually improved. A workshop industry such as watchmaking entailed considerable division of labor, as some workers made dials, others
cases, and yet others wheels and springs. By midcentury, some 120,000
clocks and watches were produced each year in London; of these, 70,000
were exported abroad. During the eighteenth century, a watch became
less a luxury than a necessity for British gentlemen, craftsmen, and
tradesmen (if not yet for their wives); and before giving way to the Swiss
in the nineteenth century, British watchmakers produced about half the
world's output. In specific skills, Dutch, French, and German artisans
were on a par with, or superior to, the English; but by 1757 one Englishman could boast that "few countries are equal, perhaps none excel, the
English in the number of contrivances or their Machines to abridge
labour." Although in many regions the pace of change remained slow, observers discerned bustle and vitality. Daniel Defoe adopted a Chamber-
of-Commerce tone when, in his *Tour of the Whole Island of Great
Britain* (1724–1726), he boasted of

> the new Buildings erected, the Old Buildings taken down; New Discoveries
> in Metals, Mines, Minerals; new Undertakings in Trade; Inventions, En-
> gines, Manufactures, in a Nation pushing and improving as we are: These
> Things open new Scenes every Day, and make England especially show a
> new and different Face in many Places, on every occasion of surveying it.

Yet the work of artisans could prove dangerous, and a late eighteenth-
century pamphleteer reminded his readers that

> scarcely are we fed, lodged, clothed, warmed, without sending multi-
> tudes to their grave. The collier [coal-handler], the clothier, the painter,
> the gilder, the miner, the makers of glass, the workers in iron, tin, lead,
> copper, while they administer to our necessities, or please our taste and
> fancies, are impairing their health and shortening their days.[8]

Life in London

In the England and Wales of 1700, more than four out of five people lived
in villages housing fewer than 2,500 inhabitants. However, the number
who resided in provincial towns was growing; a century later, three
persons in ten were urban rather than rural.[9] Increasingly, families in the

---

[8]Cited in Rule, *Albion's People*, p. 25.

middle ranks of society — merchants, bankers, lawyers, well-to-do shop-keepers — strove to emulate the aristocracy's pattern of life to the extent that their income allowed. In the process they were changing the complexion of their cities and towns. The lath-and-plaster dwellings of Tudor times were giving way to brick houses built in classical style, with big windows and spacious rooms. The finer houses had water supplied by wooden pipes to the ground floor. The ambitious fitted out their rooms with carpets, mirrors, and mahogany furniture. Streets were often paved and widened and sometimes lit by oil lamps, and many towns boasted not only elegant churches but also assembly rooms, music rooms, theaters, bookshops, and circulating libraries.

One urban area stood out from all the rest, however, as indeed it still does: London constituted a unique phenomenon. In 1700, when Bristol and Norwich claimed perhaps 30,000 people each and Edinburgh was just a little more populous than that, the number of inhabitants of London approached a staggering 600,000. It was in the process of overtaking Paris as the largest city in Europe. Fewer than one-third of London's people now lived within the old city walls. The metropolis that one Englishman in nine called home had not merely spread westward along the Thames and linked up with Westminster, where Parliament met and judges sat, but also had swallowed up a score of small villages to the east and the north. Until 1747 the London Bridge of nursery rhyme fame sufficed as the sole land link with Southwark and the suburbs to the south, but two more bridges were added at midcentury. For the enthusiastic Defoe, London was made

> *glorious* by the Splendor of its Shores, gilded with noble Palaces, strong Fortifications, large Hospitals and publick Buildings; with the greatest Bridge, and the greatest City in the World, made famous by the Opulence of its Merchants, the Encrease and Extensiveness of its Commerce; by its invincible Navies and by the innumerable Fleets of Ships sailing upon it, to and from all Parts of the World.

Other eighteenth-century observers were troubled by the implications of the growth. The novelist Tobias Smollett saw midcentury London as "an over-grown monster; which, like a despotical head, will in time leave the body and extremities without nourishment and support." Visitors commented more prosaically on "the smoke, which being mixed with a constant fog, covers London." Coal had replaced wood as the prime fuel for cooking and for heating homes and workshops; as a consequence, one

---

[9]See P. J. Corfield, *The Impact of English Towns, 1700–1800* (1982), and Peter Borsay, *The English Urban Renaissance: Culture and Society in the Provincial Town, 1600–1770* (1989), as well as Chapter 3, "The Progress of Politeness," in Paul Langford's contribution to the *New Oxford History of England* series, *A Polite and Commercial People: England, 1727–1783* (1989). M. Dorothy George, *London Life in the Eighteenth Century* (1925) remains a classic guide to life in the kingdom's sole metropolis. It may be supplemented with George Rudé, *Hanoverian London, 1714–1808* (1971), and Peter Earle, *The Making of the English Middle Class: Business, Society, and Family Life in London, 1660–1730* (1989).

Farming in the 18th Century   The *Universal* Magazine (1748) displays the latest horse-drawn plows. *(Bettmann/Corbis)*

pessimist feared that "the inhabitants must at last bid adieu to all hopes of ever seeing the sun."

Some 40 percent of London's work force labored in industrial enterprises like shipyards, breweries, and textile workshops. Commerce played a yet more important role, first because London served as the kingdom's largest port, where as many as 1,400 sailing vessels might at any given time compete for the opportunity to load or unload their wares. Second, it was a community of markets and exchanges, such as Billingsgate for fish, Covent Garden for fruits and vegetables, and Smithfield for meat. "Every county," wrote Defoe, "furnishes something for the supply of London." There was cider from Devon, cheese from Cheshire, and cattle from the Scottish Highlands. From East Anglia, drovers urged on thousands of geese and turkeys that waddled to the capital on their own feet if not on their own volition.

Many of the kingdom's 60,000 professionals were employed in, or were attracted to, London: civil servants, lawyers, clergymen, and physicians, though the last-named found themselves competing both with surgeons and with the apothecaries (pharmacists) who set themselves up as unofficial medical "general practitioners." Although the Scottish-born John Hunter (1728–1793) pioneered important advances in surgery, doctors had few remedies for diseases such as gout, a painful swelling in the feet that was most likely to afflict well-to-do gentlemen who ate too much rich food and drank too much alcohol. Blood-letting became so commonly prescribed (if altogether illusory) a remedy for every malady that London's physicians named their professional journal for their preferred blood-letting instrument, *The Lancet*.[10]

Numerous bankers, stockbrokers, publishers, musicians, and architects could also be found in London. Such professionals and their families constituted part of the "consumer revolution" that was turning London into the kingdom's shopping mecca. Open-air market stalls remained the most common sites for selling food-stuffs and other wares, but in London they were supplemented by permanent retail establishments. The bright, glass-fronted, and bow-windowed shops that lined mile after mile of London's streets fascinated foreign visitors:

> Behind the great glass windows absolutely everything one can think of is neatly, attractively displayed, in such abundance of choice as almost to make one greedy. Now large slipper and shoe shops for anything from adults down to dolls, can be seen; now fashion-articles or silver or brass shops, books, guns, glasses, the confectioner's goodies, the pewterer's wares, fans etc.

This German observer went on to praise the silks, chintzes, and muslins (for women's dresses), the china and glass and lamp shops, as well as the fruiterers who sold apples and grapes and such exotic wares from afar as figs, oranges, and pineapples.[11] Most shops in London and in the provincial towns were much smaller establishments that concentrated on groceries, fabrics, cutlery, and dishes. By the 1770s, so many of these had sprung up that the economist Adam Smith became the first person to describe the kingdom as "a nation of shopkeepers."

For well-to-do country families who built town houses around elegant new squares — each with its private park in the center — London was not merely the political, legal, and commercial capital of the realm but also its social center, the site of "balls and assemblies," of theaters, and of pleasure gardens such as Vauxhall and Ranelagh. Having paid their shilling admission, visitors could wander along Vauxhall's winding wooded paths, illuminated at night by hundreds of decorated oil lamps. They could listen either to nightingales or to outdoor singers and fiddlers, and stop at pavilions to dance or to purchase wine, cider, or beer and slices of beef or ham — so thin, according to a contemporary critic, that you could read a newspaper through them. Indeed, London's first daily newspaper began publication in 1702; by 1760 there were four. Young men often escorted young women down garden paths that turned so confusingly that, according to one observer, "the most experienced mothers have often lost themselves in looking for their daughters." The gardens at Ranelagh, reputedly more sedate, centered on a huge rotunda, inside which visitors could promenade and listen to music. The rotunda

---

[10]See, e.g., Roy Porter and G.S. Rousseau, *Gout: The Patrician Malady* (1998), and Douglas Starr, *Blood: An Epic History of Medicine and Commerce* (1999).

[11]Sophie von La Roche (1786) is cited in Neil McKendrick, John Brewer, and J. H. Plumb, *The Birth of a Consumer Society* (1982), p. 79. See also Hoh-Cheung and Lorna H. Mui, *Shops and Shopkeeping in Eighteenth-Century England* (1989), and Carole Shammas, *The Pre-Industrial Consumer in England and America* (1990).

balcony was divided into fifty-two open alcoves where groups of seven or
eight could eat, observe, listen, and wait for the outdoor fireworks that
climaxed the evening.

Only a fourth of the people who lived in eighteenth-century London
had been born there. In addition to drawing large numbers of professionals, merchants, and gentry, the city also attracted tens of thousands of
the destitute from the countryside, along with immigrants from Ireland,
Scotland, continental Europe, and even several thousand erstwhile black
slaves from sub-Saharan Africa. Many of the Africans were fitted out in
exotic livery and feathered turbans to serve as pages in wealthy London
households. All these immigrants helped produce the variety celebrated
by Ned Ward, the early eighteenth-century rhymester:

> Young Drunkards reeling, Bayliffs dogging,
> Old Strumpets plying, Mumpers progging [beggars scrounging],
> Fat Dray-men squabling, Chair-men ambling,
> Oyster-Whores fighting, School-Boys scrambling,
> Street-Porters running, Rascals batt'ling,
> Pick-pockets crowding, Coaches rattling,
> News bawling, Ballad-wenches singing,
> Guns roaring, and the Church-Bells ringing.

London was a dangerous and often brutal metropolis in which favorite public amusements included cockfights, bullbaiting, and wrestling
matches between half-nude women. Some people found diversion in the
Tower of London, where the crown jewels, medieval weapons and suits of
armor, and the royal menagerie were on display, while others peered rev-
erently at the lavish tombs in Westminster Abbey. Still others sought out
curio collections. The most elaborate and well-organized of these, Sir
Hans Sloane's, was bought for the nation in the 1750s with funds raised
by a government-sponsored lottery and transformed into the British
Museum. Londoners could also visit wax museums, peep shows featur-
ing mechanical figures operated by clockwork, and freak shows advertising giants and dwarfs, three-breasted women and two-headed men, and
what a later generation came to call Siamese twins.[12] On Sundays sight-
seers paid their pennies for the right to gape at the lunatics behind the
bars of Bethlehem Hospital, whose name was contracted into "Bedlam."
Others stared at — or even stoned — convicted criminals bound to the
pillory or watched the floggings at Bridewell (the "House of Correction")
and the hangings at Tyburn. Henry Fielding, the novelist and magistrate,
was moved to complain that "we sacrifice the lives of men not for the reformation but for the diversion of the populace." Whatever the punishment, crime continued to flourish, and in 1718 London's city marshal
lamented that it was "the general complaint of the taverns, the coffee-

---

[12]In *The Shows of London* (1978), Richard D. Altick writes informatively about numerous
largely forgotten chapters in the history of popular culture. In *Hogarth: A Life and a
World* (1997), Jenny Uglow tells us about the uniquely successful pictorial chronicler and
humane satirist of eighteenth-century London life.

English Money in the Eighteenth Century

4 farthings = 1 penny (1 d.)
6 pennies = 1 sixpence
12 pennies (or pence) = 1 shilling (1 s.)
2½ shillings = 1 half crown
5 shillings = 1 crown
20 shillings = 1 pound (£1)
21 shillings = 1 guinea

It is all but impossible to readily translate the prices and wages of 1700 into those of 2000. We know that a unskilled or semiskilled laborer might earn £15 to £25 a year and that a live-in domestic servant might earn no more than £3 a year (in addition to room and board). According to Boswell's *Life of Johnson*, a man might survive at bare respectability in early eighteenth-century London for £30 a year (of which £4 would pay for a rented room). Such a person might breakfast on bread and milk for a penny, dine for six-pence, and spend threepence in a coffee house.

In the course of three centuries, both wages and the costs of clothing, food, and shelter have altered at significantly different rates, but in order to translate the approximate values of 1700 into those of 2000, one might multiply the figures of 1700 by 300 to obtain an approximation in British pounds and by 500 to obtain an approximation in American dollars.

houses, the shop-keepers, and others, that their customers are afraid when it is dark to come to their houses and shops for fear that their hats and wigs should be snitched from their heads or their swords taken from their sides, or that they may be blinded, knocked down, cut or stabbed."

London was a magnet for all elements of society, including the poor. To them it offered variety, excitement, and the chance to make a dishonest penny, but it extended neither security nor comfort. During the first half of the eighteenth century, the urban death rate was significantly higher than the rural, and, according to one estimate, of every four children born in London during those decades, only one survived to the age of five. The mass of the urban poor lived on the edge of subsistence in conditions that would have made a modern slum seem like paradise. Home meant one

BRITISH OUTPUT OF SPIRITS, 1700–1770
(in millions of gallons)

YEAR

Adapted from T. S. Ashton, *An Economic History of England: The Eighteenth Century* (1972), p. 243.

room per family — often in a garret or a cellar — and as many as eight adults and children in the family bed. The houses lacked both piped-in water and plumbing, and the gutters outside the door served as sewers. Overcrowding eliminated privacy and almost assured sexual promiscuity.

Those who could afford to do so escaped in the evening to the tavern or alehouse. Never did so large a number of English men and women find it so easy to drown their sorrows as during the 1720s, 1730s, and 1740s — the so-called "gin age." That potent beverage had become easy to distill from domestic grain, and thousands of gin-shops opened in London during the early years of the century. Although farmers, distillers, and retailers all profited, the disastrous consequences had become apparent by 1736, when the preamble to an act of Parliament observed that "the drinking of spirituous liquors or strong waters is become very common, especially among the people of lower and inferior rank, the constant and excessive use whereof tends greatly to the destruction of their healths, rendering them unfit for useful labours and business, debauching their morals, and inciting them to perpetuate all manner of vices. . . ." It required several additional acts of Parliament, a widespread change of attitude, and a rise in grain prices before high license fees and strict enforcement of the law brought the "gin mania" to an end in the early 1750s.

Taverns served not only as social centers but also as unofficial employment agencies and as places where workers collected their pay. Except for apprentices and household servants, most of whose income came

Gin Lane, by William Hogarth (1697–1764)   *(North Wind Picture Archives)*
A caption at the bottom of the print reads:

> Gin, cursed Fiend with Fury fraught,
> Makes human Race a prey;
> It enters by a deadly Draught,
> And steals our Life away.
>
> Virtue and Truth, driv'n to Despair,
> It's Rage compells to fly,
> But cherishes, with hellish Care,
> Theft, murder, perjury.
>
> Damn'd Cup! That on the vitals preys,
> That liquid fire contains
> Which Madness to the Heart conveys,
> And rolls it thro' the veins.

Beer Street, by William Hogarth (1697–1764)   *(North Wind Picture Archives)*
A caption at the bottom of the print reads:

> Beer, happy produce of our Isle
> Can sinewy Strength impart,
> And wearied with fatigue and Toil
> Can cheer each manly Heart.
>
> Labour and Art upheld by Thee
> Successfully advance,
> We quaff Thy balmy Juice with Glee
> And water leave to France.
>
> Genius of Health, thy Grateful Taste
> Rivals the Cup of Jove,
> And warms each English generous Breast
> With Liberty and Love.

in the form of room and board, London laborers were very much part of a money economy. Skilled craftsmen might join trade guilds, which involved initiation rites and oaths, mutual support in times of dearth, and occasional strikes. Artisans who earned pay on a piecework basis were not generally noted for thrift and forethought, however. As one observer complained in 1772: "If a person can get sufficient in four days, to support himself for seven days, he will keep holiday the other three, that is he will live in riot and debauchery."[13] After a rowdy weekend, many workmen would take off Monday ("St. Monday") as well. London wages tended to be high when work was available, but preindustrial London, like most of the Third World in our time, was plagued with chronic underemployment. In trades that suffered one or more slack seasons a year, laborers all too often found themselves imprisoned for debt or seeking relief from the parish overseers of the poor.

The Roles of Women

In eighteenth-century England, a majority of women were legally subordinate to men — in youth to their fathers; later, to their husbands. Wives in turn could not be punished for crimes such as theft and burglary because the law assumed that they acted under the authority of their husbands. As William Blackstone noted in his *Commentaries on the Laws of England* (1765–1769), that assumption had guided English law for a thousand years. Such an exemption from punishment did not apply, however, to convictions for murder, treason, or operating a brothel. Inasmuch as each divorce required an individual act of Parliament, which only the rich could afford to procure, most marriages ended only through death. In the lower ranks of society, some marital unions were broken by the husband's desertion, and women mistreated by their husbands could obtain a judicial "surety of the peace."

Two groups of women — unmarried heiresses and widows — possessed a good deal of legal power and sometimes significant economic influence (as business proprietors). They even had some political influence as voters by proxy. The life of the duchess of Marlborough reminds us that aristocratic married women might also exercise much sway behind the scenes at court. It was generally agreed, however, that men and women differed profoundly in their natures and in their abilities. A sexual double standard also enjoyed wide acceptance. As the midcentury sage Dr. Samuel Johnson observed, "The chastity of women is of all importance, as all property depends on it." By contrast, "wise married women don't trouble themselves about infidelity in their husbands. . . . The man imposes no bastards upon his wife."

As has already been suggested, the day-to-day lives led by women depended most of all on their rank in society. In aristocratic and gentry

---

[13]Cited in Porter, *English Society in the Eighteenth Century*, p. 6.

families, wives were expected to superintend l... duce heirs, and to play a crucial role in the edu... and in the all-important preparation of their daug... market." While their husbands hunted foxes, shot... bled at the racecourse, wives found time to pay so... parties, attend dances, play cards, embroider line... They might take comfort in books such as *Pamela*, by Samuel Richardson (1698–1761). Its moral was a n... were by nature more rational and women by natu... then it was equally true that good women served ...arge by teaching higher standards of morality than did selfish and predatory men.

Some unmarried women and widows in the middle ranks of society conducted businesses of their own, even as married women were involved with cooking, gardening, and marketing as well as with assisting their husbands in their business or profession. Those who sought to ape their betters grew increasingly reluctant, however, to dirty their hands. According to one late-eighteenth-century critic, the well-off farmer's wife now saw herself as a lady who "would faint at the idea of attending a market, like her mother or grandmother, with a basket of butter, pork, roasting pigs or poultry, on her arm."[14] Female midwives, common earlier in the century, increasingly gave way to male doctors attending at childbirth, and an exceptional female surgeon of the 1780s survived only because she sent no bill unless she had cured the patient.

Feminist trailblazers were few in the eighteenth century, but there were some. Writer Mary Astell (1668–1731) pleaded with her fellow gentlewomen to raise themselves from the world of fashion, cards, and tea-table gossip: "How can you be content to be in the World like Tulips in a Garden, to make a fine *show* and be good for nothing?" Mary Wortley Montagu (1689–1762) distinguished herself as a poet and letter writer. A sojourn in Constantinople, where her husband served as British minister to Turkey, led her to introduce into Britain the practice of inoculation against smallpox, one of the dreaded diseases of the age; the faces of those who survived were often permanently disfigured. Inoculated patients were deliberately infected with a mild form of smallpox in order to ward off the hazards of a more serious attack later. The practice remained controversial, but the fact that it was adopted by the royal family caused it to become widespread. Catherine Macaulay (1731–1791) wrote a much-acclaimed eight-volume *History of England* that surveyed the seventeenth century.

In the lower ranks of society, most women worked both inside the home (as cooks, cleaners, launderers, and child-raisers) and outside. A handful of women also disguised themselves as men and went to sea as common

---

[14]Cited in Ivy Pinchbeck, *Women Workers and the Industrial Revolution 1750–1850*, new ed. (1969), p. 34. The wider subject may be explored further in the volumes by Porter and Langford cited earlier, in Amanda Vickery, *The Gentleman's Daughter: Women's Lives in Georgian England* (1998), and in Vivien Jones, ed., *Women in the Eighteenth Century* (1990), a collection of excerpts drawn from pamphlets, sermons, novels, and guides to conduct.

all shopkeepers expected their wives to help mind the store, and
farmers expected them to share some of the work, but a midcentury
or from Sweden learned to his surprise that in England unlike at home,
it belongs to the men to tend the cattle, milk the cows, and to perform all
the work in the arable fields and meadows. . . ." A survey of surviving London court records[15] reveals that in the metropolis, three married women in
five and more than four unmarried women in five were accustomed to paid
employment. Of these a quarter worked in domestic service and a fifth
were employed in the making or mending of clothes. Smaller numbers
served as nurses, barmaids, and streetsellers. Like their male counterparts,
women in the lower ranks of society found it necessary from time to time
to rely on assistance from the parish overseers of the Poor Law.

The Poor Law

The Elizabethan Poor Law of 1601 had placed an enormous responsibility
on the parish, the smallest unit of civil as well as ecclesiastical government. Each year, the parish had to choose two overseers of the poor to
levy a tax called the "poor rate" on local property-holders, to be used for
relief of those too young, too old, or too sick to help themselves. The
overseers also sought to find employment for the parish's able-bodied
but jobless. Although the Elizabethan Poor Law was amended in detail
from time to time, it provided the basic framework of social welfare in
England for well over 200 years. Such a system was unique to England
and Wales: In Europe's Roman Catholic lands, the church was expected
to aid the poor; in eastern Europe, the extended family was expected to
help. Ireland had no Poor Law, and under Scottish law, parishes were permitted, but not required, to levy a "poor rate."

Each person was entitled to assistance in his or her parish of settlement: the parish where a husband lived in the case of a wife, where a father lived in the case of a child, where born in the case of an illegitimate
child. What the law did not do was to set up a national or even a county
administrative system to supervise the work of the overseers: they were
unpaid nonprofessionals whose efficiency and whose sympathy for their
charges varied from parish to parish.

Studies of surviving parish records suggest that, although many overseers felt a greater sense of responsibility to the parish rate payers than to
the "undeserving poor," they did not leave paupers and aging widows to
starve. These unfortunates received a small weekly allowance and at
times bedding, cooking utensils, and shoes. When they fell ill, the parish
paid the local doctor to prescribe quinine for fevers and "Godfrey's cordial" or "Daffy's elixir" for other ailments. When they died, the parish
paid for the funeral and the burial. Orphaned children were supported un-

---

[15]Peter Earle, "The Female Labour Market in London in the late 17th and early 18th Centuries," *Economic History Review* (August 1989).

til they were old enough to be apprenticed. Unmarried pregnant women might be bribed to move to the next parish so that their offspring would not become a parish liability, but when that ploy failed, the parish paid for a midwife and searched for the father. Although fewer than 10 percent of the people of the average parish were seen as incorrigibly poor, as many as 50 percent might seek parish aid at least once in their lifetime because of a personal or national crisis.

The Elizabethan Poor Law required overseers to put the able-bodied to work, but this task proved difficult. Some parishes bought supplies of wool to set women to spin or used jobless men to repair roads and wells, but the cost of supervision generally exceeded the monetary gain. During the early eighteenth century, parishes received permission to solve the problem by joining forces to set up workhouses in which the poor were to be brought together, given food and shelter of a sort, and put to work. Enthusiasts hoped that these workhouses would give pauper children enough elementary training so that they, "instead of being bred up in irreligion and vice to an idle vagabond life, will have the fear of God before their eyes, get habits of virtue, be inured to labour, and thus become useful to their country." Reality often defied such hopes. The rules of one London workhouse insisted that inmates attend church on Sunday or forfeit supper; those who missed church twice were to be confined inside the workhouse for six months. Separate dormitories housed men and women and boys and girls — with three children or two adults per bed — and inmates had to be in bed by nine in the summer and by eight in the winter. Such a regime deterred all but the truly needy from seeking parish aid. Many a workhouse became a dumping ground where the aged as well as the young, the ill as well as the healthy, were jammed together in filthy buildings that bred disease and despair.

The people of eighteenth-century Britain lived in a paradoxical society in which elegance in architecture, furniture, and sometimes in manners went hand in hand with widespread callousness and cruelty, a clamorous and abusive press, and intermittent riots. Election-time tumults in numerous communities in 1715 led to the passage of the Riot Act later that year. The statute permitted local magistrates to "read the Riot Act" to an assembly of twelve or more. Those who failed to disperse within the hour could be found guilty and punished. The rapidity with which capital offenses were added to the statute book in the early eighteenth century testifies to the sense of concern of such magistrates. They lacked any police force more formidable than the parish constable; only on rare occasions did they summon the regular army to halt a riot. The threat of hanging aimed to keep the populace in awe, but the great majority of those convicted of capital offenses were ultimately spared the noose. Thus in a typical year (1740), seventeen men and one woman were hanged in England. Those convicted of theft and burglary were far more likely to be sentenced to "transportation," a term of servitude and then eventual release in one of the North American colonies, most often Virginia, Maryland, or Pennsylvania.

Both rich and poor appealed to the common law, and when dissatisfied, Britons of the day appeared ever ready to fight for their rights as they saw them. When a new turnpike road or an enclosure of common land undermined ancient custom, or when a bad harvest created a bread shortage, or when a change of fashion led to a depression in a particular trade, laborers and their wives often resorted to vocal and violent protests. In similar fashion, even the unenfranchised often took a keen interest in parliamentary election contests in which they had no right to vote. Carl Philip Moritz, a German visitor, expressed amazement at the manner in which "a crowd of people mainly of the lowest class" gathered in a London square and listened to orators who

> bowed low to this rabble and always addressed them as "gentlemen" . . . when one sees here how the lowliest carter shows an interest in public affairs; how the smallest children enter into the spirit of the nation; how everyone feels himself to be a man and an Englishman — as good as his king and his king's minister — it brings to mind thoughts very different from those we know when we watch the soldiers drilling in Berlin.[16]

Food riots were a recurring small-town phenomenon, and at least once a decade, a particular cause would rouse "the London mob" to a flurry of destruction. Even the king's ministers at times had their windows smashed and had to arm themselves against assault.[17] Yet the first half of the century witnessed neither a political overturn, nor an explosion in population, nor a revolution in industry. The mood of the age favored individual achievement and self-assertion in war, trade, and politics rather than popular subordination to some national master plan.

---

[16] *Journeys of a German in England in 1782*, translated and edited by Reginald Nettel (1965), pp. 55–56.

[17] In an influential article, "The Moral Economy of the English Crowd in the Eighteenth Century" (1971), reprinted in *Customs in Common* (1991), E. P. Thompson argued that such outbursts were neither random nor spontaneous but a rational and ritualized expression of an older set of values, in which the necessity of providing food at a fair price took precedence over private profit and in which the activities of grain dealers and bakers were minutely regulated and bread prices fixed by law. In "The 'Moral Economy' of the English Crowd: Myth and Reality," John Stevenson casts doubt on both the extent and consistency of such assumptions. (Anthony Fletcher and John Stevenson, eds., *Order and Disorder in Early Modern England* [1985]). Stevenson is also the author of *Popular Disturbances in England, 1700–1870* (1979). Thompson and his associates in D. Hay et al., *Albion's Fatal Tree: Crime and Society in Eighteenth-Century England* (1975), and Peter Linebaugh in *The London Hanged: Crime and Civil Society in the Eighteenth Century* (1992) look on the criminal law as predominantly an instrument of class oppression. A recent survey by Douglas Hay and Nicholas Rogers, *Eighteenth-Century English Society* (1997) similarly sees the era as dominated by social conflict between a tiny upper class and a gigantic lower class. In contrast, John Brewer and John Styles, eds., in *An Ungovernable People: The English and Their Law in the Seventeenth and Eighteenth Centuries* (1980), emphasize that eighteenth-century society involved more than two classes and that the rich, the poor, and those in between all appealed to the law, a law that gave legitimacy to the authority of the upper ranks and at the same time limited that authority. The most detailed study of the way the criminal law was applied is J. M. Beattie, *Crime and the Courts in England, 1660–1800* (1986)

CHAPTER 4

Politics in the Age of Walpole

Life in eighteenth-century London was often turbulent, but the king-dom's underlying social structure remained remarkably stable. Society was organized in a hierarchical manner, with a small group of landowning families at the top furnishing political, social, cultural, and — to a lesser degree — economic leadership. This chapter first examines the manner in which the government came to operate under such aristocratic influence during the decades after 1714. Then it traces the rise and eventual decline of the leader who dominated Britain's political world during the 1720s and 1730s, Sir Robert Walpole.

The Defeat of Toryism

The political role of the oligarchy changed after 1714 because the Tories, who had played so prominent a role during the reign of Queen Anne, were prevented, for the indefinite future, from holding national office. Out of the deep cleavage that had resulted in civil war in 1642 had come the Whigs and Tories of the Restoration — one the intellectual heirs of the Roundheads, the other of the Cavaliers; and from the 1670s until the death of Anne, the party struggles had swirled above an undercurrent of violence. Great issues had been at stake in religion and in domestic and foreign policy, and they had all been tied to the disposition of the crown. Although not political parties in a twentieth-century British sense, for a time the Tories and the Whigs had shown significant elements of parliamentary cohesion and discipline and even of national organization. Whig and Tory ministries had alternated in power. With the arrival of the Georges came the supremacy of the Whigs and a less tempestuous political atmosphere.

The Glorious Revolution had shaken the twin pillars of Tory principle: the Anglican Church as the sole church of the kingdom and the royal prerogative as divinely ordained. Toleration of Protestants outside the church had been legalized, and God's laws of hereditary monarchy had been in part subordinated to man's law made in Parliament. Until 1714, the Tories continued to champion the ideal of a Church of England that

79

kept in legal check both Roman Catholics and non-Anglican Protestants and to hope for a restoration of the divine-right Stuart monarchy in the person of the son of the exiled King James II. After 1714 their twin principles lay shattered and, at least at the national level, their party was relegated to minority status.

The Whigs extended the practice of toleration in a typically pragmatic fashion. Parliament repealed the legislation of Anne's reign against dissenters. Although it left the Test Act and the Clarendon Code, as modified in 1689, on the statute book, it passed annual "indemnity acts" to prevent the legal prosecution of dissenters who held local government office. In England, politically ambitious dissenters tended to move into the Anglican fold, and the total number of non-Anglican Protestants declined during the first half of the eighteenth century. The status of those who remained excited far less controversy than before. Their acute grievances had eased, and their religious zeal flagged. Many of them settled down, alongside the Anglicans, to what the historian Edward Gibbon was to call, somewhat cynically, "the fat slumbers of the church."

If religious dissent ebbed as a major political issue after 1714, so too did the veneration of monarchy. George I was sufficiently colorless to dissipate the last wisps of Tory romanticism, and his court proved as dull as he. In his early years, he had divorced and imprisoned his charming young wife for a love affair and had probably had her lover murdered; but by the time he came to England, in his midfifties, he had lost the glamor of scandal without having acquired that of royalty. He lacked a regal aura. He never learned to speak English, and he appalled his courtiers when, on his arrival, he was unable to distinguish the different ranks of the peerage.[1] Except when it seemed absolutely necessary politically, he shunned the pomp that his office demanded. Although he impressed his German associates as a reasonable, kind-hearted man, highly knowledgeable about European diplomacy, he failed to win the affection of his new subjects. Lord Chesterfield found the king gross even in his pleasures. "No woman came amiss to him," he reported, "if they were very willing and very fat. . . . The standards of his Majesty's taste made all those ladies who aspired to his favor, and who were near the suitable size, strain and swell themselves like the frogs in the fable to rival the bulk and dignity of the ox. Some succeeded, and others burst."

The Tories could not worship a crown that rested on such a head, but George would not have welcomed them even if they had. He recognized that he owed his throne to the Whigs and accordingly gave them the plums of office: Tories became locked in permanent and apparently hopeless opposition. A few of the erstwhile Tories turned Jacobite, scheming for the day that never arrived when a Stuart would again rule. Others

---

[1] J. H. Plumb provides caustic pen portraits of George I and his immediate successors in *The First Four Georges* (1956). Ragnhild Hatton's assessment in *George I: Elector and King* (1978) is far more favorable. John M. Beattie presents a detailed account of the royal household in *The English Court in the Reign of George I* (1967).

came to terms with the new regime, called themselves Whigs, and joined the scramble for office. The rest became disgruntled onlookers, perennial opponents of Whig ministries that they criticized as expensive and corrupt. As late as 1741, however, 135 of 489 members of Parliament still called themselves Tories.

As a result of the demotion of Toryism to apparently permanent minority status, Britain, for more than half a century after 1714, did not have two parties in any meaningful sense at the national level.[2] A significant minority of Tories continued to serve in local government as Justices of the Peace, as deputy lieutenants of a county, and as members of land-tax commissions. Everyone who aspired to national office was by definition, however, a Whig, and the important political conflicts of the period took place among cliques within this party. As the balance of power shifted between the cliques, ministries came and went. There was always an opposition, and its leaders thundered against corruption in government, but they were usually trying to increase their nuisance value in order to force their way into office, and they quickly changed their tune when they got there. Although politics remained tumultuous, the tumult differed from that under the later Stuarts: The struggle centered more on place and less on principle. Only the Jacobites, with their antiquated adherence to principle, could on occasion revive the earlier threat of civil war. The rest of the time, the politics of Whiggism produced only factional skirmishing.

The Cabinet and Parliament

Great causes and principles do not necessarily give rise to important developments, which often unfold during undramatic times. So it was with the first half-century of the Hanoverians, when the very dullness of the new monarchy contributed to the rise of cabinet government. George I and his son, who succeeded him in 1727 as George II, had some prestige because they were kings, and more because advancement depended on their favor; but, except in some matters of foreign policy, they lacked the will for leadership that their predecessors had demonstrated. Consequently, a subtle shift of executive power set in, from the sovereign to his ministers. The ministers became less agents of his policy and more makers of policy themselves. Under the king's surveillance, sometimes sharp and sometimes perfunctory, they steered through Parliament measures that were essentially their own. The eighteenth century saw the evolution of the mechanism, which the

---

[2]In a highly influential work, *In Defiance of Oligarchy: The Tory Party, 1714–60* (1982), Linda Colley has argued that the party remained more cohesive and more popular than most historians have recognized and that its members' hopes of regaining national office were not wholly illusory. She rejects the contention of Evelyn Cruikshanks, put forward in *Political Untouchables: the Tories and the '45* (1979), that most Tories were secret Jacobites.

seventeenth had lacked, for amalgamating executive and legislative authority in the king's cabinet.

The roots of this process stretched back to the Restoration and can best be sketched here. The cabinet originated as an inner, secret committee of the Privy Council. Secrecy was vital, because Parliament could not call cabinet members to account unless it knew what they had done. As long as they were protected from prying eyes at Westminster, and as long as the king was able to direct them, they were servants of his will. Charles II, when told that

> He never said a foolish thing
> And never did a wise one,

answered that "my words are my own, my acts are my ministers'." But the reply was deftly misleading. He acted for himself, and so did his immediate successors. Just as he had forced the earl of Danby to act as his reluctant tool in negotiating with Louis XIV, so William III forced his cabinet to authorize unnamed persons to negotiate with Louis for unnamed ends. Ministers of the Stuarts had no doubt about who determined policy.

William began his reign by drawing cabinet members from both parties, but in his last years he preferred to take them from whichever party held a parliamentary majority. His reasoning was merely that government could function more effectively, and with less legislative interference, if it had a solid base of support than if it depended on segments of both parties. By the end of his reign, however, with Parliament at its most obstreperous, it interfered with a vengeance: It attacked the whole cabinet system as a device for subverting parliamentary supremacy. The Act of Settlement of 1701 barred the cabinet from offering secret advice to the sovereign and provided that after Anne's death cabinet members should also be barred from the House of Commons. These two provisions would have made the experiment unworkable. Prohibiting ministers from advising the crown privately would have ended their usefulness to it. Excluding them from the Commons would have destroyed the essential characteristic of the modern cabinet, that it is an executive body selected from and based in Parliament. Both provisions were soon repealed, however, and the cabinet continued its unplanned evolution.[3]

The Hanoverian accession opened a new phase of development. The principle that cabinet members — both peers and commoners — should be drawn from the majority party lost its meaning as soon as only Whigs found favor, and the rise of factions within that prevailing party left the king leeway in choosing his ministers. He had to assure himself that his appointees commanded the support of a sufficient number of factions in

---

[3]One relic of the Queen Anne era was a requirement, not ended until 1918, that every member of the House of Commons appointed to high ministerial office could not assume his post until he had returned to his constituency so that voters could register their approval by reelecting him.

the Commons to carry on his government. As matters turned out, he could leave this problem largely to the men of his choice. The conduct of administration became a matter of manipulation, bargaining, and influence, which the Whig politicians soon developed into a fine art. Understanding how they did so — in other words, how the Hanoverian political system worked — demands some understanding of the structure of the House of Commons.

The knights of the shire, the two members representing each county, were elected at large by those who held freehold property worth forty shillings a year. Powerful local families, as time went on, learned to control most of the elections by adjusting differences and balancing interests so as to present only two candidates, whom the voters were expected to return and usually did. These county members had to hold land worth £600 a year and therefore belonged to the well-to-do gentry, but they composed less than a quarter of the House. The majority comprised borough representatives.

A parliamentary borough was any town to which the sovereign had accorded one or more representatives. But "town" was often a euphemism, for boroughs ranged from great cities to decaying hamlets. The way in which they had been apportioned at the beginning of Parliament in the Middle Ages had reflected, in a rough and ready fashion, the distribution of urban wealth and population at that time. Yet during the eighteenth century, although population patterns shifted, the apportionment of parliamentary seats did not. The disparity between intention and reality widened. Tiny villages might send two members to Parliament, growing industrial towns none.

Although the qualification for voting in the boroughs varied as widely as their size, in almost all of them the electorate was small. Only three had more than 4,000 voters, most had fewer than 500, and several as few as a dozen. In England as a whole, approximately one adult male in seven possessed the franchise. The fact that a candidate did not need to be a resident enhanced the possibilities of influencing an election in such tiny constituencies. If a candidate had landed property worth £300 a year, he might stand for any borough, and he did not have to look far to find one where the voters would return whoever offered them the most. Offers included bribes and favors to individuals, paying for public improvements in the town, and promoting the borough's interests in the kingdom's capital.

If the candidate did not personally possess the wealth or influence to meet the terms demanded, he needed only to discover a patron who wielded so much influence over the voters of a particular borough that at election time he, in effect, reached into his pocket and pulled out one or both members. In the case of such a "pocket borough," the candidate scarcely needed to lift a finger. "Your seat in the new parliament is at last absolutely secured," Lord Chesterfield wrote his son in 1754, "and that without opposition or the least necessity of your personal trouble or appearance." A patron had been found, and "he brings you in with himself at his surest borough." The wheedling and bargaining that preceded

Canvassing for Votes   A painting by William Hogarth. *(The Granger Collection)*

such an agreement were often difficult, but the election itself became a mere formality.

As the century wore on, patronage evolved into a highly developed system. A Whig aristocrat, usually a peer who sat in the House of Lords, would work through agents and friends to gain and maintain control of a group of boroughs. Such a large landlord might build up what was known as his "interest," a group of members of the House of Commons who owed him their seats and who generally followed his advice. Four or five territorial magnates, pooling their resources in the cabinet, could command a substantial bloc of votes in the Commons, and many of the remaining votes they needed would come to them because they held office. The king, one of the greatest landholders in the country, had a borough "interest" of his own to put at his ministers' disposal. As his agents, they had a variety of other ways in which to influence votes in the Commons.

A key to this influence came with the Septennial Act of 1716, which extended the life of any Parliament from a maximum of three to a maximum of seven years. Not until after the American Revolution was a Parliament dissolved before the end of its legal term, and the reason is apparent. From the viewpoint of members of the Commons and their patrons, elections cost time and money and so were to be avoided. (Whereas 156 English and Welsh seats were contested in the election of 1722, only 66 were fought in 1757.) From the perspective of the cabinet, a long interval between general elections made it easier to build up a dependable phalanx of government supporters.

Some votes went almost automatically to any administration in power. Many army and navy officers sat in the House of Commons, and so did placemen, who would now be called civil servants. These groups rarely voted in opposition — officers because they had their eye on promotion, placemen because they themselves constituted a part of government. The forty-five Scottish M.P.'s, chosen by electorates even smaller than those of England, almost invariably supported the government of the day. In return for such support, Westminster tended to leave the management of day-to-day government in Scotland in the hands of one or more of the leading Scottish noblemen. Other members responded to more indirect influence: a relation who hungered for a bishopric or a colonial governorship, or even peerage, or merely a job as postmaster or customs collector. The king remained the source of promotion, honors, offices, and cash: His ministers could barter his favors for political support.

Their "interests," combined with the king's influence, could never secure a working majority, however. For that, the government always had to obtain substantial assistance from the independent members, those who were beholden to no one in office and voted as they pleased. They are sometimes called the Country party, as distinct from the ministerial or Court party, but the phrase misleads, for they constituted even less of a party in any meaningful sense than the pre-Hanoverian Whigs and Tories. For the most part, such independents sought no office for themselves; they concentrated instead on advancing the needs of their localities and on such national questions as they deemed important. Merchants and financiers concerned with the government's commercial policy or country gentlemen intent on keeping down the land tax, they became a force in the House of Commons that no cabinet could neglect for long and stay in office.[4]

Thus a ministerial majority, like an electoral majority in a borough, developed from careful bargaining and arrangement. Critics called the system corrupt, but a majority of the oligarchs came to take for granted that this was how government worked. The chief ministers, the embryonic cabinet, who depended on the monarch for appointment and on Parliament for tenure in office, preferred to call the deal-making system "influence" rather than "corruption," and they deemed such influence necessary for government to function.

The Tories had become too small and suspect a party to provide the formal, organized opposition that the modern British political system

---

[4]For a fuller analysis of the composition of Parliament, see Chapter 1 of W. A. Speck, *Stability and Strife: England 1714–1760* (1977), and for an understanding of its operations, see P. D. G. Thomas, *The House of Commons in the Eighteenth Century* (1971). In *Voters, Patrons and Parties: The Unreformed Electorate of Hanoverian England, 1734–1832* (1990), Frank O'Gorman contends that eighteenth-century elections provided a greater opportunity for popular involvement than has generally been assumed.

requires. In a world in which all the ambitious were Whigs and in which the new dynasty stood as the symbol of Whiggism triumphant, loyalty to the monarch — if not enthusiasm for him — was incumbent on all. Ministers were still the servants whom the king chose to carry out his policy. They were fair game in debate, but only on specific measures; to attack them on principle, because they were ministers, would have been tantamount to attacking the throne. Although when they fell from power they might criticize the succeeding administration, they did not seek to overthrow it. What is formally known today as "Her Majesty's loyal opposition" can be both loyal and in opposition because the crown no longer plays a personal role in government. The Hanoverians did play such a role and hence could not have such an opposition.

Once every generation, however, opposition was able to assume a kind of dynastic loyalty. The reason derived from an odd family characteristic of the Hanoverians: Each sovereign in turn became, sooner or later, bitterly estranged from his heir, the Prince of Wales. George I and his son George were at loggerheads as long as the father lived; George II and his wife quarreled furiously with their firstborn, Prince Frederick, whom the Queen once described as "the greatest ass and the greatest liar and the greatest *canaille* [scoundrel] and the greatest beast in the whole world." George II outlived his son only to find himself at odds with his grandson, the future George III. A generation later, George III in turn was made miserable by his eldest, the prince who eventually became George IV. This repetitive antagonism of monarch and son exerted a political impact. Malcontents could rally around the heir to the throne, as long as he opposed his father, and attack the royal ministry in the name of royalty-soon-to-be. The king was the setting sun; those who championed the prince were likely, when the sun set, to become the ministers of the new reign. Meanwhile they could be both loyal and in opposition.

Another trait of the first two Georges had major political repercussions. Both men were at least as devoted to the electorate of Hanover as they were to the kingdom of Great Britain. George I accepted the throne from a sense of duty to his house, not from love of the island. "His views and affections were singly confined to the narrow compass of his Electorate," said Lord Chesterfield. "England was too big for him." George II spoke English, unlike his father, but with a marked German accent; in his heart he was equally German and longed to escape the cares of British kingship. "I am sick to death of all this foolish stuff," he once burst out, "and wish with all my heart that the devil may take all your bishops, and the devil take your ministers and the devil take the parliament, and the devil take the whole island — provided I can get out of it and go to Hanover."

Both kings spent part of each year in their electorate, strove to safeguard its interests, and expected their British ministers to provide the means to meet this goal. This expectation posed a new kind of problem. For the first time since the Middle Ages, except for the brief Dutch connection brought by William III, Britain had a territorial stake in Europe.

The location of Hanover made it far more vulnerable and difficult to defend than the Dutch Republic. It lay across the lower Elbe and Weser, the two great rivers stretching from central Europe to the North Sea; to the east loomed the rising power of Prussia, on the west the Dutch and Austrian Netherlands and France. Hanover was directly or indirectly involved in every struggle for power in that part of the continent. With every burgeoning crisis, the great question was how far Britain would involve itself.

That question, arising over and over again, emphasized the equivocal position of the king's ministers. They were responsible to him as well as to Parliament and therefore faced a dilemma whenever Hanoverian and British interests conflicted. Sacrificing the first cause to the second would never be forgiven at court; sacrificing the second to the first would never be forgiven at Westminster, where the independent country gentry cared not a whit about the electorate and pounced on any hint that the Hanoverian tail was wagging the British dog. For half a century, the problem of how to coordinate tail and dog would plague successive ministries.

Local Government

Just as the aftermath of the Glorious Revolution had enabled members of England's ruling class — aristocrats and landed gentlemen — to play a continuing role at the parliamentary level, so it confirmed their domination of local government. The central government, except in the person of excise collectors and of wartime impressment gangs, was far removed from the day-to-day concerns of most Britons. Most important were the local aristocrats, landed gentlemen, and Anglican clergymen who had been commissioned as Justices of the Peace.[5] More than one hundred of these J.P.'s were active in the average county at any given time. Selected in the name of the monarch by the Lord Chancellor (a member of the cabinet and a peer), they possessed powers limited by statute, but they resided in the county in which they exercised both judicial and administrative responsibilities. They received no salary; their reward came from the status the position conferred, the power it enabled them to exercise, and the feeling it gave them that they indeed "kept the peace" in their portion of the kingdom.

Acting alone, a Justice of the Peace could order a vagrant to be whipped and a disorderly person put in stocks. He could fine a baker who shortchanged his customers, a hawker who lacked a license, and anyone who hunted and fished illegally. Most significantly, he could demand a recognizance of good behavior (in the form of a specific sum of money)

---

[5]The most authoritative modern account is Norma Landau, *The Justices of the Peace, 1679–1760* (1984). The author suggests that in the course of the century the J.P.'s were gradually changing from "patriarchs" (prominent individuals concerned with their neighborhood) to "patricians" (men who had a sense of themselves as a collective governing group).

from persons he thought likely to act in a riotous or criminal manner. Acting together with one or more fellow J.P.'s in their division of the county — in "Petty Sessions" — Justices of the Peace oversaw parish affairs and approved the parish poor rate and highway rate. Because most J.P.'s also served as commissioners of the land tax and the window tax, they assessed those as well. Acting in pairs, J.P.'s licensed alehouses and decided disputes about which parish was legally obligated to assist a pauper. Every three months, most of a county's J.P.'s assembled in a meeting known as Quarter Sessions. There they made decisions concerning the maintenance of bridges and the upkeep of the county jail and houses of correction. They also licensed grain merchants and dealers in poultry and dairy products as well as the chapels set up and the teachers employed by religious dissenters. On occasion, J.P.'s still set maximum wage rates and the official price of bread. They were not merely influential in nominating parish officials such as churchwardens, overseers of the poor, surveyors of highways, and constables, but they could also indict such officials for failing to carry out their duties. The freeholders, tenant farmers, and artisans who held such parish offices were formally elected by the parish vestry, in theory the assembly of all householders. In a minority of England's parishes, this custom exemplified village democracy in action; in a majority, the influence of local landed gentlemen prevailed.

Finally, the Justices of the Peace at Quarter Sessions presented cases of rape, riot, assault, fraud, and "leaving bastards in ditch" to a grand jury for indictment. If the jury found the case valid, the accused were tried by a petty (twelve-man) jury. Disputes over rights to landed property and crimes that involved the possibility of capital punishment (such as murder) were tried before the royal judges who traveled to the county seat twice a year to serve as a court called the Assizes. Although local J.P.'s could themselves be tried before Assize judges for failing to abide by the law, such occasions were rare. J.P.'s were therefore largely free both of administrative supervision from above and of popular control from below. At both the local and the national level, the political structure of the day was hierarchical in nature and often contradictory in detail. Procedures rested as much on local convention as they did on either logic or administrative or judicial symmetry. Yet this form of local government had come to be taken for granted. It was relatively cheap and relatively effective.

Years of Instability (1714–1722)

Although historians have often described the Hanoverian succession in 1714 as marking the onset of a new era, a number of years passed before King George I felt truly secure on his new throne. Indeed, his coronation had scarcely ended before Jacobite sentiment rekindled. The victorious Whigs fanned the flames with their vindictiveness: When George's first Parliament met, in the spring of 1715, its Whig leaders attacked Lord Bolingbroke and his colleagues, purged Tory henchmen from office throughout the country, and so convinced many Tories that rebellion provided the only alternative to political extinction. By summer, unrest had spread widely. Jacobite mobs rioted in the west country, the midlands, and the north; rebellion brewed in Scotland. Local magistrates did nothing to stop the disorders or to enforce the measures taken by the government. Central authority seemed to crumble. Eight months of Hanoverian rule, wrote the Prussian minister to London, had done more for the cause of James Stuart, the Pretender, than had four years of Tory predominance under Queen Anne.

But James, like his father, was badly served. He himself had been exiled from France to Lorraine after the Treaty of Utrecht, and at that distance he had no power. His cause depended entirely on daring leadership in Britain, and this luxury he did not enjoy. Bolingbroke, who had the best chance of rallying the Tories to action, was no more capable of seizing the moment than he had been the year before. At the height of the crisis, he bolted across the Channel and took service with the Pretender, and no one of stature replaced him. Risings in the west country melted away; royal troops seized Oxford. Only in the north of England, where great landlords could still rouse their tenantry in a lost cause as they had in the days of Elizabeth, did a sizable number of "Jacks" turn out to fight for "King" James.

Their chance of success hinged on Scotland, the focus of rebellion. Since 1707, successive British ministries had abolished the old Scottish Privy Council, undermined the privileges of the established Presbyterian kirk, and imposed a new malt tax. The unpopularity of the union, combined with the magic of the Stuart name, might have touched off a national rising if James himself had been on hand. Even without him, some 10,000 men took up arms against a force of only 3,300 royal troops. But the Jacobites again lacked a competent leader. They failed to join hands with their friends across the border and marched aimlessly to and fro until the Pretender finally arrived, just after Christmas 1715. By then his cause had flagged, and he was not the man to revive it. "Throughout his life he was, like his grandfather Charles I, a great gentleman, but the virtues of a great gentleman are not by themselves sufficient to regain a lost throne."[6] After six weeks of wandering in the Highlands, more and more the fugitive and less and less the king, James VIII of Scotland and III of England, as he called himself, vanished into the exile's limbo from which he never returned.

The failure of the rising, known to history as the Fifteen (although it actually did not end until 1716), secured the Hanoverian succession at a small price in lives. A few victims, ranging from aristocrats to humble sergeants,

---

[6]Sir Charles A. Petrie, *The Jacobite Movement: The First Phase, 1688–1716* (1948), p. 195. This and its companion volume, subtitled *The Last Phase, 1716–1807* (1950), are a convenient and sympathetic history of Jacobitism. Bruce Lenman, *The Jacobite Risings in Britain 1689–1746* (1980), is a helpful one-volume account. The most comprehensive survey of the Jacobite subculture has been provided by Paul Kleber Monod in *Jacobitism and the English People, 1688–1788* (1989).

MUG-HOUSE RIOT.

The Mug-House Riot   In July 1716, a London tavern (in which ale was sold in mugs) that served as the headquarters of loyal supporters of the new Hanoverian dynasty was attacked and gutted by a Jacobite mob shouting, "No Hanover, No King George." The mayor had to call in troops to put down the rioters. *(Mary Evans Picture Library)*

were executed for form's sake. Most leaders either were pardoned or fled before they could face trial; a few were tried and condemned and then vanished mysteriously just before their executions, to reappear in France. The rank and file of the Scottish rebels dissolved into the obscurity from which they had come and kept the cause alive among some of the Highland clans. In England the spirit of rebellion ebbed even more quickly.

In the years after the Fifteen, the economy prospered until it produced in 1720 a financial crisis that struck at the foundations of the new regime. This lurid episode, known as the South Sea Bubble, was, on the surface, nothing more than an orgy of speculation and bribery that ended in the worst stockmarket crash in British history. Under the surface, it presented a political danger of the first order that threatened to bring down the government, if not the throne itself. The crisis was averted, however; Robert Walpole came to power. During the next twenty years, under his guidance, the dynasty became so firmly established and the political world so well systemized that the tumults of midcentury — foreign war and another Jacobite invasion — could not shake the house of Whiggism.

In 1720 that house was still under construction, however, and the bursting of the Bubble shook it badly. The South Sea Bubble deserves to be seen as an example not merely of individual skullduggery and of popular self-delusion but also of the growing pains of a commercial economy. The stock mania resulted in part from the lure of trade with exotic parts of the world. As the accompanying graph demonstrates, the monetary value of trade with the continent ranked far above trade with Asia or the Americas, and according to modern economic historians, domestic trade

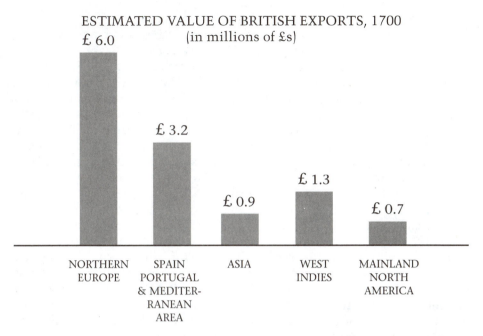

ESTIMATED VALUE OF BRITISH EXPORTS, 1700
(in millions of £s)

£ 6.0   £ 3.2   £ 0.9   £ 1.3   £ 0.7

NORTHERN
EUROPE

SPAIN
PORTUGAL
& MEDITER-
RANEAN
AREA

ASIA

WEST
INDIES

MAINLAND
NORTH
AMERICA

Adapted from Charles Wilson, *England's Apprenticeship, 1603–1763* (1965), p. 162.

had far greater value than all the foreign trade added together. These facts, however, in no way diminished the intoxication with a commercial El Dorado in distant lands.

Because the supply of gold and silver coins could not keep up with the demands of an expanding commerce early in the century, businessmen increasingly transacted their trade by letters of credit, bills of exchange, and other forms of paper money. A still unusual form of business organization, the joint-stock company, also gained importance. In the age of Elizabeth I, a handful of such companies, run by and for the privileged few, had monopolized the kingdom's trade with Russia, the Levant (the eastern Mediterranean), and India. By the beginning of the eighteenth century, the joint-stock principle offered an attractive method of obtaining money for an array of projects. The stocks and bonds that such companies issued to raise capital constituted in turn a relatively new form of property, which investors could buy and sell more readily than land. The "stock-jobbers" who marketed such securities, although they earned the blame of those who made foolish investments, clearly served a need. Because the law was slow to take cognizance of the changing methods of the commercial world, the promoters and investors of the South Sea Bubble era joined a game that did not yet have clear rules.[7]

---

[7]The story is told in careful detail in P. G. M. Dickson, *The Financial Revolution in England* (1967). In *The South Sea Bubble* (1960), John Carswell evokes the spirit of popular excitement.

The origins of the specific crisis stretched back to 1711, when the Tory government, which considered the Bank of England an organ of the Whig party, chartered the South Sea Company as a rival to the Bank. One of the initial purposes of the company was to trade with the South Seas (which turned out to mean the Spanish colonies in the Caribbean area). The prospect of making money there grew fabulous when Spain, as part of the Utrecht settlement, granted the Company a major concession, the *asiento*, to run for the next thirty years. The *asiento* permitted Company members to import up to 4,800 slaves a year into the Spanish colonies and to sell there, duty free, such merchandise as could fit on a single 500-ton ship accompanying the annual Spanish treasure fleet from Europe. This trade provided a wedge into the Spanish colonial market. The Company paid little attention to the limits of the *asiento* and soon cultivated a significant, if dangerous, trade in smuggled goods and in slaves.

The Company directors had less interest in trade, however, than in what they could make out of high finance. From the start, they engaged in large-scale operations connected with the public debt. The climax of these operations, and the first swelling of the Bubble, came with a coup of February 1720, in which Parliament empowered the directors to take over that portion of the national debt, more than three-fifths, that consisted of private annuities. The Company agreed to charge the government a lower rate of interest than the Treasury offered on these annuities and to sweeten the deal with a cash advance of more than £7 million.

As this gigantic payment suggests, the directors looked forward to even more gigantic profits. The operation that they had in mind was complex in detail but essentially simple: to convert the national debt into Company stock. The holders of government annuities were to be persuaded to exchange them for stock, abandoning an assured income from their old annuities for capital gains from the expected rise in market value of their new South Sea shares. Everything depended on this rise. The Company received authorization to issue more and more stock as it took over more and more of the debt, and the greater the worth of its shares, the more annuities they would buy. The scheme looked foolproof, granted the one assumption that the Company could market its stock at a price that would continue to rise indefinitely. The directors were serenely confident of this financial miracle. They had good reason: The Company was as closely tied to the state as the Bank of England was and not only monopolized the South American trade but also possessed the largest amount of working capital — some £40 million — ever amassed in England. How could investors resist?

For the first few months, they could not. Their scramble for shares drove the price to almost ten times what it had been in February, and the whole market followed the lead of the South Sea stock in a dizzy upward spiral. New companies were founded overnight to engage in enterprises both real and fanciful: they ranged from the importation of broomsticks from Germany to the setting up of a chain of pawnbroker shops throughout the kingdom. Enthusiastic investors snapped up shares in every company, for stock prices were still rising. By June, a few of the more judicious stock-owners began to sell, however, and by midsummer the market was leveling off. The South Sea directors tried to force it higher by every possible means, honest and dishonest, including loans to permit stockholders to buy more shares on credit. By then, however, the most frantic pump priming would no longer work.

The crash came in September. Foreign investors sold their shares, and six London banking houses stopped payments. The price of South Sea Company shares plummeted from 775 to 170 in just six weeks; paper fortunes vanished; those who had bought on credit faced ruin. Worse still, the ministry and the court had involved themselves to the hilt: The directors had been lavish in their bribes to the influential and had not neglected even the king's mistresses. The public, disillusioned with its dream of riches, cried for retribution, but almost no one in the government had clean hands. Parliament reassembled in an ugly mood.

The door opened for Robert Walpole. A seasoned politician, he had been in and out of office for years, but at the moment he held a relatively minor post. He had not foreseen the crash and, like almost everyone else, had lost money in it. He had had no shady dealings with the Company, however, and he possessed a clear idea of what had to be done and the adroitness to get it done.

He had two objectives: To avert panic until investors regained their confidence in what was still an essentially sound economy. To prevent public anger, focused in the House of Commons, from destroying the government and perhaps even the dynasty. In both aims Walpole succeeded. He proposed a scheme for salvaging what was left of the South Sea Company with the help of the two remaining giants of finance, the Bank of England and the East India Company. Although the plan was never implemented, it gave time for the market to recover, for people to realize that they could still make money in sane ways. Walpole did not prevent a parliamentary inquiry, but he managed to keep it within discreet bounds. While the directors' estates were being confiscated and a few ministerial victims thrown to the wolves, the key figures in the government and court were saved from awkward questions. The skill with which Walpole unwound the South Sea Company's tangle of financial fact and fantasy won the admiration both of the king and of "the City" (the kingdom's leading financiers, whose institutions clustered within the original boundaries of London). Ultimately his efforts helped reconcile even the competing interests of land and trade. After the Bubble, the prevalent mood of commercial expansion and economic innovation admittedly gave way to greater caution: The Bubble Act of 1720 forbade all joint-stock companies not authorized by royal charter, and many a landed gentleman vowed to invest in real estate in the future rather than in the stock market. Overseas trade continued to expand, though more slowly, and in the 1720s and 1730s, the annual value of British exports grew by one-third, and the value of imports by one-fifth.

Luck also had a hand in Walpole's rise to power. Lord Stanhope, George I's chief minister since 1717, defended himself so vigorously against charges linking him to the South Sea fiasco (in a House of Lords debate in February 1721) that he burst a blood vessel and died. Walpole detested his principal remaining colleague and rival, the rancorous Lord Sunderland, but for reasons of expediency he defended Sunderland against similar charges. Although the House of Commons, by a narrow margin, voted to acquit Sunderland, George I decided to appoint Walpole in his stead. Thus in April 1721, Walpole became chief minister, and when Sunderland conveniently died within a year, a new era dawned. Politics, which for more than a generation had been so rough-and-tumble a business that no one person or group could long dominate, assumed order and form, and "the country enjoyed a stability of government such as it had not known for a hundred years."[8]

The Walpole Machine

Governmental stability derived from a fusion of the two cardinal elements required for administration: support from the king and control of the House of Commons. Walpole had a genius for handling his sovereign, but this delicate, time-consuming occupation required a blend of courage and tact. Walpole had to retain the confidence of George I — with whom he conversed in French — even as pressures from Parliament compelled him on occasion to thwart the wishes of his often suspicious monarch. At the same time, he had to do his best not to alienate the Prince of Wales, who might succeed his father at any time.

The new chief minister mastered these tasks and showed himself equally adept at handling the House of Commons. Although he could never afford to neglect the House of Lords, he recognized that the Commons had become the focus of power. For that reason, he refused a peerage and in 1726 instead became a Knight of the Garter. No commoner had received that honor in generations, but neither had a first minister who chose to stay a commoner. Sir Robert knew what he was doing. Controlling the lower house as a member of it was difficult enough; trying to manage it from the House of Lords would have been far more difficult.

The methods of control that Walpole developed and systematized remained in force for the rest of the century. The office of prime minister did not yet exist in name; Walpole's formal title was First Lord of the

---

[8]J.H. Plumb, *Sir Robert Walpole: The Making of a Statesman* (1956), p. 379. This volume and its companion, subtitled *The King's Minister* (1960), are not only a biography but a study of the period in depth. The second carries the story to 1734; the promised final volume was never published. H. T. Dickinson provides a brief but illuminating introduction to the subject in *Walpole and the Whig Supremacy* (1973). Other accounts of the Walpole era include Jeremy Black, ed., *Britain in the Age of Walpole* (1984), the surveys by W. A. Speck and Paul Langford cited earlier, and also Geoffrey Holmes and Daniel Szechi, *The Age of Oligarchy: Pre-Industrial Britain, 1722–1783* (1993).

Treasury; in that position, he controlled patronage through the appointment of customs and excise officers. From the Treasury, Walpole operated his machine. He organized a phalanx of placemen in the House of Commons. He distributed favors, honors, and preferment in order to maintain and strengthen his political control. He became the key figure, even under the jealous eye of George I, in determining promotion in the army. He exercised a tighter rein over patronage in the church than any minister had done since 1688. He filled positions in the Civil Service with men of his personal choice, not with henchmen of his henchmen. Yet there were never enough plums to go around. For every one at the minister's disposal, three or four supplicants clamored in the lines outside his doors.

Even his machine, efficient as it was, could not function without support from the independent members of the Commons, however, and Walpole wooed them assiduously — and with considerable success — throughout his years in office. Here his background boosted his success. He came from an old Norfolk family, country squires for generations, and in some ways he epitomized his breed with his hard drinking, hard riding, profanity, and womanizing. He had none of the aristocratic graces that Chesterfield extolled. During debates in the House of Commons, he would nibble on a Norfolk apple as if to emphasize his rustic origins.

Walpole was far more ambitious on behalf of himself and his children, admittedly, than was the typical squire, and in some ways he resembled an early twentieth-century American political boss, a professional in an age of amateurs. Yet this image scants the whole picture. For all his coarseness, Walpole became a connoisseur of wines and developed a sure taste in art; the collection of paintings that he amassed won fame throughout Europe. On his Norfolk estate, he built Houghton Hall, as much a monument to him as Blenheim is to Marlborough. Not a palace but a country house, austere on the outside and magnificent within, Houghton was embellished without thought of cost by the leading sculptors, plasterers, and furniture makers of the day.[9] Sir Robert, in short, embodied an odd mixture of vulgarity and sophistication.

Walpole prided himself on his Whig heritage as a champion of religious toleration and of the constitutional principles of 1689, but, as he readily conceded, "I am no saint, no spartan, no reformer." He saw himself rather as the defender of things as they had come to be. Someone had to make the creaking governmental machinery work, foster commerce, lower taxes, and buttress a shaky throne; he had supreme confidence that he was the only man for the task. Perhaps he was right. Britain needed some years of quiet in which the new dynasty could grow roots and a political system could emerge from the uncertainties of the recent past.

---

[9]Plasterers may at first glance seem out of place among sculptors and furniture makers, but English plasterwork, from the late Middle Ages through the eighteenth century, was one of the major decorative arts. For a fuller description of Houghton Hall and its contents, see Plumb, *Walpole*, Vol. 1, pp. 81–87.

The Stone Hall   Part of Houghton Hall, the elaborate country house in Norfolk that Robert Walpole built and furnished during the 1730s. *(A. F. Kersting)*

Although Walpole's predominance endured, he could never take it for granted. The first challenge came without warning in the summer of 1727, when word arrived that George I had died suddenly in Hanover. The political wolves gathered for the kill: Sir Robert's days were numbered, they believed, because a new king meant a new minister. However, they did not understand the odd little man who now took the throne. George II had led a difficult life, hated and bullied by his father and detesting him in return. He hid his loss of self-confidence behind a violent temper, a restlessness that kept him always moving and continually talking, and an almost neurotic preoccupation with the minutiae of his daily routine; he even saw his mistress at precisely the same hour each evening. His weakness made him profoundly dependent, and he became that great rarity among his fellow monarchs, one who depended on his wife. Caroline of Anspach possessed some charm and much shrewdness; her manners were deemed coarse, but her head was good enough to do her husband's thinking for him.

Caroline provided Walpole's opportunity. Soon after taking office under George I, he had marked out the Princess of Wales as the friend he needed at court. He consulted her assiduously and soon won her as his staunch ally. She helped him to survive the upheaval of her husband's accession and before long to win a place in the heart of the new king second

King George II (1727–1760) and His Queen, Caroline of Anspach Britain's second Hanoverian king remained as concerned with the welfare of the electorate as with that of the kingdom. His wife was one of the most influential queen consorts in British history. *(The Granger Collection; Hulton Getty)*

only to hers. For the next fifteen years, until his fall from office, Sir Robert was not only George II's servant and counselor but also, as nearly as anyone could be, his friend.

The Years of Stability (1727–1738)

Sir Robert was now called "the Great Man," admiringly by his friends and mockingly by his enemies. Walpole seemed to have an unchallengeable hold on royal favor and on Parliament and to stand on an eminence from which only death could topple him. Yet the appearance deceived, because the longer his ministry lasted, the more rancorous became the parliamentary critics who sought to turn the king against him.[10] They used the popular press, then in its brawling infancy, to whip up public excitement with satires, cartoons, ballads, and all the other arts that Grub Street could devise, and so bring outside pressure to bear on the closed world of Parliament. Sir Robert fought back with libel suits, stamp duties on newspapers, and with the Licensing Act of 1737, a statute that required the lord chamberlain to approve all theatrical productions. That

---

[10]Their activities are discussed in Archibald S. Foord, *His Majesty's Opposition, 1714–1830* (1964), and in B. W. Hill, *The Growth of Parliamentary Parties, 1689–1742* (1976), as well as in Linda Colley, *In Defiance of Oligarchy* (1982).

act would not be repealed until 1968. Thanks to the efforts of his critics, Walpole felt that he lived from crisis to crisis.

In 1732 he himself, quite unwittingly, provoked one that proved to be more than he could handle. It originated in his attempt to improve the tax structure, one of the few areas in which he was a genuine reformer. He wanted to reduce the land tax, partly because he believed that it unfairly burdened the country gentry, partly because he needed their support; but he could not reduce the chief source of revenue without finding a substitute. Customs and excise taxes seemed the obvious answer. This form of taxation not only increased with the growth of trade but also bore on all consumers alike, rich and poor.

Walpole had long known of the need to stimulate trade. He had helped manufacturers by reducing export duties on their goods and import duties on their raw materials; he had simplified the process by which imports destined for sale abroad passed through the country duty free. In a few categories of goods imported for home consumption, he had also experimented with shifting from customs to excise — from a duty levied on goods when they entered the country to a tax levied on them when they were released for sale. Tea and cocoa had been admitted duty free and taxed instead through the retailer, and in Walpole's opinion the experiment had proved extremely advantageous.

Excise taxes offered two advantages. In the first place, to eliminate customs duties on the goods meant to take the profit out of smuggling them, and smuggling cheated the government out of hundreds of thousands of pounds a year. In the second place, collecting a tax from retailers required an army of excise men; and the more jobs Sir Robert could provide, the greater would grow his patronage. At the beginning of 1732, he decided to reduce the land tax from 10 to 5 percent of assessed value, to reimpose a recently discontinued salt tax (thereby creating still more collectors' jobs), and to extend the excise to wine and tobacco. The proposed changes seemed sensible, but they proved explosive.

In the popular mind, customs and excise officers were corrupt tyrants. They had behind them some of the most savage laws on the statute books, which the courts interpreted in their full severity: In one case, a man was hanged merely for blackening his face, a common precaution of smugglers working at night. In a society addicted to smuggling and to excise evasion, the excise officers were detested by high and low, and the hatred mounted as law enforcement grew more rigorous. Walpole's scheme touched a match to this combustible brew; his opponents stood ready and eager to fan the flames.

For a year, while the measure worked its slow way toward a vote in the House of Commons, excitement rose to a frenzy.[11] The press did its full part; boroughs sent deputations to Westminster; riots broke out; the

---

[11]In *The Excise Crisis: Society and Politics in the Age of Walpole* (1975), Paul Langford provides a detailed account.

country seethed as it had on the eve of the Fifteen. Now, though, the pressure was on Parliament, to turn against its master and throw out his bill. Both Lords and Commons were reminded that they had better heed public opinion.

Initially Walpole ignored the danger signals and held to his course; but when Parliament reconvened after the Easter recess of 1733, which its members had spent in their constituencies, Sir Robert was amazed to find his majority melting away. At the last minute, he gave in and withdrew the bill. He survived politically, but his opponents had demonstrated the limits of his power and looked forward to further opportunities to humble "the Great Man."

Walpole survived in large part because George II and Queen Caroline had not wavered in their support, but he could no more take his sovereign for granted than he could the two houses of Parliament. Especially in the field of foreign policy, the king held strong opinions of his own, and any crisis on the continent threatened to bring on a crisis at home. Sir Robert's diplomacy was governed by a single-minded desire to preserve peace. War, he feared, would alienate the landed interest and create the opportunity for a Stuart restoration. Walpole grew almost obsessed by the threat from the Jacobites, with whose schemings he kept in touch through a wide network of spies. He had no fear that the Pretender, unaided, could raise a successful rebellion; what he dreaded was rebellion encouraged and aided by France. In that fear, future events bore him out: Britain's first war did draw in France and provoke a Jacobite invasion with French support.

At the core of Walpole's foreign policy, in consequence, lay rapprochement with France; and he had the good luck to find circumstances propitious. The death of Louis XIV in 1715 had left the throne to a boy of five, his great-grandson Louis XV, and not until 1726 did French politics restabilize after the fluctuations of a regency. In that year the young king called to power his tutor, Cardinal Fleury, a man of seventy-three, who directed policy for the next sixteen years. This aged cynic — subtle, crafty, and elusive — was poles apart from the squire of Houghton Hall, but they shared a love of power and the desire to enjoy it in peace. For more than a decade, therefore, they worked together in an implicit and uneasy partnership to prevent a major European conflagration.

One that threatened to be major broke out in 1733, the so-called War of the Polish Succession. Poland, a large but weakly governed state, was a bone of contention among the great powers. A dispute over its elective kingship brought on a brief war between Austria on one side and the Bourbon monarchies, France and Spain, on the other. France had an interest in Poland, where Louis XV's father-in-law was a candidate for the throne. Spain had no interest whatever but hoped to regain control of the Italian principalities lost to Austria in the Utrecht settlement. Britain, as Walpole saw it, had not enough concern with either Poland or Italy to warrant intervening.

King George disagreed. For all his faults, his viewpoint was more European, less insular, than Walpole's, and he recognized that a decisive

The English Colossus   Sir Robert Walpole is caricatured as bestriding the political world in emulation of the Colossus of Rhodes, one of the Seven Wonders of the Ancient World. *(Fotomas Index)*

defeat of Austria would upset the balance of power. He deeply distrusted France and, as a German prince, he had an underlying loyalty to the Holy Roman Emperor, Charles VI, also ruler of Austria. The monarch hoped to lead an army in defense of the emperor, but Walpole knew all too well that Parliament would refuse to support British intervention in Poland or Italy. Eventually George II capitulated, and Austria received no aid from Britain. Austria suffered defeat in Italy, where it lost the south to a Spanish Bourbon prince. Louis XV's father-in-law gave up his claim to the Polish throne and received in compensation the duchy of Lorraine, which would revert to France at his death. The powers finally reached this settlement in 1735, without consulting or even informing the British government. Walpole had chosen isolation at the price of being ignored.

By 1738 his troubles were mounting at home and abroad. Frederick, Prince of Wales, who did his best to justify his parents' loathing for him, had broken with them completely in 1736 and set up a court of his own, which became the focus of the opposition. In 1737 Sir Robert had lost his most valuable ally with the death of Queen Caroline. He had many peers as his avowed enemies, and under their patronage a new generation of would-be Davids were training their oratorical slingshots on Goliath. The most brilliant of these "boy patriots" was William Pitt, the grandson of "Diamond" Pitt, a merchant who had made his fortune in India and put it to work in English politics. Walpole's opponents honed their technique of embarrassing him to an art. At one moment, a handsome allowance for the Prince of Wales was moved in the House of Commons, and the minister barely managed to defeat this insult to the crown. At another, the opposition forced him to fine the city of Edinburgh for a riot in which a military officer had been lynched; the Scottish members of the House of Commons, considering the fine an insult to Scotland's national pride, turned against Sir Robert. Now by taps and now by blows, now by leverage and now by pouring acid, his enemies slowly eroded his power.

Britain and the Wider World

The opposition could not destroy "the Great Man," however, as long as the country remained prosperous and at peace. Yet Walpole found it increasingly difficult to avoid war. New sources of friction with France cropped up in America and India. The approach of a Habsburg dynastic crisis as menacing as that before the War of the Spanish Succession threatened to upset the delicate balance that the Utrecht settlement had established in Europe. A long-standing quarrel between Britain and Spain seemed ready to explode at any moment into war. For years Walpole, as he put it, had taken care to let sleeping dogs lie. Now all the dogs seemed to awake at once, and they were growling ominously.

Tensions between Britain and France in North America had roots in geography. France possessed or claimed land to the north and west of the British colonies, extending in a vast arc from the Gulf of St. Lawrence to the Gulf of Mexico, by way of lakes Ontario and Erie and the valleys of the Ohio and Mississippi. The British colonists on the Atlantic seaboard, as their numbers grew, began to press into and beyond the Appalachians in search of land and furs, trespassing increasingly on what the French considered their preserve. The struggle had already started, for the European wars of William's and Anne's reigns had had their colonial counterparts. Despite the Treaty of Utrecht, however, the Anglo-French rivalry in the New World persisted.

India provided the setting for Anglo-French friction of yet a different sort. There the leaders of the English East India Company had long jockeyed for position against its Portuguese and Dutch rivals, not as empire builders but as traders. The last thing that the Company directors had intended at first was to extend their territorial jurisdiction beyond Bombay, Madras, and Calcutta, the coastal cities that they controlled as centers for their trade with the interior. Profitable trading was possible, however, only as long as the native government maintained order. By the 1730s, the great Mogul empire was falling to pieces, and the rulers of its former dependencies on the coast competed for predominance. At the same time, the French, with their newly organized Compagnie Perpetuelle des Indes, began to make rapid inroads into the Indian market.

The next inevitable step, for both the British and the French companies, took them from trade to politics. No matter what the directors in London might say about keeping aloof from native affairs, the Englishmen on the spot knew better. They saw the local Indian rajah, to take a concrete but hypothetical example, demanding a higher price each year for maintaining the East India Company's trading privileges, and they knew that the French outbid them at court. They also knew that the rajah's nephew claimed the throne and with a small investment of British funds could probably get it. To retain the Company's trading position, its agents could scarcely resist the temptation to invest in the pretender, install him as rajah, and then protect him, once he became their client, against French efforts to reinstate his predecessor. As long as the Indians fought among themselves for power and Europeans vied for trade, the two contests were bound to mesh, and the Europeans would find themselves battling through their protégés. The stage was set for one of the great struggles in the history of imperialism, a struggle that ended years later with the ousting of the French and subordination of the native states to a trading company that became, despite its initial intentions, the paramount power of India.

In Europe, in the meantime, a more immediate problem loomed. The Habsburgs were in dynastic trouble. The emperor Charles VI faced a prospect almost as dismal as that of his Spanish cousin forty years earlier — this time not the extinction of his line but the accession of a woman. His only surviving children were daughters, and Charles well realized that a woman's inheriting a throne was dangerous when powerful and rapacious neighbors surrounded her state. He offered the rulers of those states a variety of inducements in order to secure their signatures on a document known as the Pragmatic Sanction. In return they recognized his eldest daughter, Maria Theresa, as the heir to all his hereditary dominions. He might have been better advised to guarantee his daughter's inheritance by leaving her with a full treasury and a strong army, neither of which he possessed. Europe therefore awaited his death in order to learn which king would become the first to forswear himself and plunder Maria Theresa's realm.

The Coming of War with Spain (1738–1739)

These were some of the threats to peace that confronted Walpole in the late 1730s. All of them soon materialized, but the one that first occasioned war came from quite a different quarter. As pressures built toward bloodshed in North America, India, and central Europe, Britain suddenly found itself fighting Spain. Anglo-Spanish antagonism, which was by then an old story, had such deep roots that it perhaps could not have found resolution in the long run through peaceful means; but the issues in the crisis of 1738–1739 certainly could have. Two factors, however, hamstrung Walpole's diplomacy: an opposition eager to bring him down through war, and the mutual suspicion engendered in London and Madrid by years of bickering. Both governments worked hard for compromise, because neither wanted a conflict; Walpole lacked the will to fight, Spain the means. The crushing of their efforts to keep peace illustrates how economic and political forces can frustrate the best intentions of diplomats.

Anglo-Spanish friction centered on economics, and the war proved more purely commercial than any that Britain had fought since the Dutch Wars of the mid-seventeenth century. British merchants were eager to have greater trading opportunities in the Spanish colonies of Central and South America. Spain produced only a fraction of the goods that its colonies demanded. Would the remainder come from France or Britain? The government of Philip V, if only because he was a Bourbon, looked to France, whose merchants gained an ever larger share of the legitimate trade between Europe and the Caribbean. The results of the commercial concessions that Spain had made to Britain at Utrecht back in 1713 had fallen far short of expectations, and British merchants increasingly resorted to smuggling.

The situation could only breed trouble and grievances. Spanish authorities in the Caribbean had no way to prevent smuggling except to stop every British ship that came within range and search it for contraband. Merchants hotly resented this right of search, and with reason. A captain en route from London to Jamaica on legitimate business might find himself blown off course into Spanish waters, stopped, accused of making a smuggling run for Cuba, and ruined by the confiscation of his ship. Worse still, Spanish officials did not have the money for a regular customs service and therefore licensed as a coast guard almost anyone who was willing to work on commission; such men were out for all they could get and had more interest in the value of what they seized than in the legality of the seizure.

In the early eighteenth century, legality had held small place in the Spanish Main, as the Caribbean was called. That sea was infested with pirates, and the smugglers and coast guards who warred against each other were only a short remove from piracy themselves. In the course of the 1720s, British naval captains had captured, tried, and hanged many hundreds of pirates in Atlantic and Caribbean waters.[12] When British sailors caught a Spanish patrol vessel at a disadvantage, they often gave it similarly rough handling; the Spaniards replied in kind. "It is without doubt irksome to every honest man to hear such cruelties are committed in these seas," a disgusted British admiral wrote home from Jamaica. "But give me leave to say that you only hear one side of the question. And I can assure you the sloops that sail from this island, manned and

---

[12]See David Cordingly, *Under the Black Flag: The Romance and Reality of Life Among the Pirates* (1997).

The Pirate   During the early decades of the eighteenth century, the Caribbean was filled with slave traders, privateers, smugglers, and pirates. This is how Edward English pictured a typical pirate in this woodcut of 1725. (*The Granger Collection*)

armed on that illicit trade, has [*sic*] more than once bragged to me of their having murdered seven or eight Spaniards on their own shore. . . . It is, I think, a little unreasonable for us to do injuries and not know how to bear them. But villainy is inherent to this climate."

The innocent — or at least those who protested their innocence — suffered along with the guilty. In June 1731, Captain Robert Jenkins arrived in London with cargo from Jamaica and a story to tell that curled the hair. Spanish coast guards had boarded his ship while it lay becalmed off Jamaica; they had searched it for contraband, found none, and then begun to look for cash. Three times they hanged him to his foreyard, Jenkins said, and dropped him to the deck half dead. When he continued to protest that he had no money hidden away, they cut off one of his ears, beat his first mate, and stripped his sailors of most of their clothes and his vessel of most of its furnishings. Then they let the ship go.

Such atrocity stories as this, repeated from year to year, began to do their work. West Indian traders clamored for redress; the press took up the campaign to have Britain embark on a preventive war. "No time can be more seasonable for a war with Spain than the present," one pamphleteer argued, "since we have the strongest motives to think every year will augment her revenues, her alliances, or territories." The point about revenues was spurious, the point about territories trivial: the British feared that Spain was about to claim their newly established colony of Georgia as lying within the borders of Spanish Florida. The point about alliances carried more weight: Spain was angling for a French alliance, one of Walpole's chief reasons for not wanting to fight. He feared — and events bore him out — that war against one Bourbon power would sooner or later mean war against both.

Walpole determined to defy the mounting popular clamor for war. "Are all desires," he asked the House of Commons, "proper to be gratified? Is an inflamed populace to give laws to the legislature?" Yet the parliamentary opposition pressed him hard and searched the past for source material with which to arouse Parliament. Captain Jenkins was called to tell his seven-year-old story and in doing so immortalized himself. When asked what his thoughts had been while the Spaniards cut off his ear, he answered that "he recommended his soul to God and his cause to his country."

Such words made Jenkins the hero of the hour and prompted the parliamentary opposition to accuse Walpole of having no care for the nation's honor. His only way of defending himself, short of war, was to win a tangible diplomatic victory under the watchful eyes of Parliament, "which is in this country a terrible monster," the Spanish ambassador told his government, "and is ruled by private interests under the plausible name of the public good." The situation was too explosive, the ambassador warned, for long and delicate negotiations; Parliament demanded prompt results. Walpole's diplomacy worked against a deadline imposed on it at Westminster.

If only because the Spanish fleet was in even worse shape than was the Spanish treasury, Madrid agreed to pay compensation. According to the Convention of Pardo, ratified by both governments early in 1739, Spain would pay £95,000 for illegally damaging British ships and cargoes. Opposition leaders in Parliament fumed, for they had hoped for a much larger indemnity, for a formal promise to disavow the right of search in Spanish waters, and for an abandonment of Spanish claims to the new British colony of Georgia. The settlement, William Pitt told the House of Commons, was "a stipulation for national ignominy, an illusory expedient to baffle the resentment of the nation. . . . The voice of your despairing merchants, the voice of England has condemned it; be the guilt upon the head of the adviser!" Yet the "adviser" still had the votes, and he secured Parliament's endorsement for the treaty.

Once more "the Great Man" had won, but it was his last triumph, and it was empty. As the country burned with war fever, key members of his cabinet turned against him, the king wavered, and the Prince of Wales came out as the champion of the "patriots." The final blow was struck by Madrid. First the Spanish government refused to pay the damages agreed on until it received compensation for a quite extraneous claim against the South Sea Company. Then it added a further condition: It would not pay until the British fleet withdrew from the Mediterranean. Neither party trusted the other to abide by the agreement that both had signed, and hostilities became inevitable.

In British eyes, Spain had willfully repudiated the Convention of Pardo. This accusation was what the warmongers had been praying for, a *casus belli* (justification for war). Even Walpole now had no alternative to war, for he faced a revolt within the cabinet led by his chief lieutenant, the duke of Newcastle. All of Sir Robert's diplomatic efforts had come to nothing. He still preferred peace, but now he had to relinquish either his policy or his office, and he still loved power. On October 19, 1739, the royal heralds at Temple Bar announced Britain's declaration of war. "It is your war," Walpole told Newcastle, "and I wish you joy of it."

Walpole: The Legacy

The birth of the conflict that was christened the War of Jenkins' Ear marked not only the collapse of Walpole's policy but the end of his era. Although he held on to what was left of his power for more than two years, they were a sad postscript to a proud career. War was not his element, and the period with which he is properly identified is the quarter-century before 1739, during which Britain enjoyed a time of peace, except for the brief flurry of the Fifteen, and consolidated and developed the gains of the past. In that time the nation's financial system, once it survived the South Sea Bubble, stimulated a prosperity that became the envy of Europe. The parliamentary system took on a new form, with the cabinet emerging as its central mechanism, and with patronage and influence replacing the old war of parties. Although Walpole dominated these developments, he did so less by his constitutional position than by virtue of his personality. He left behind him no tradition of one-man rule — quite the contrary. His power aroused deep and continuous distrust — witness the virulence of the opposition — and for some decades, the term *prime minister* continued to be suspect.

Sir Robert was not a prime minister in the modern sense. He was both more and less, more because no minister before or since has exercised so much power for so long or put his stamp so deeply on his age, less because he had behind him more a machine than a party. He relied on political favors more than on shared ideas to build a majority in the House of Commons, whose prestige grew under his stewardship. Unlike twentieth-century prime ministers, he also remained deeply dependent on the king and on the House of Lords. He kept his place only by endless manipulation and compromise, and at two critical moments, by surrendering the policies for which he stood. If his power was great, so was the price it exacted.

In manipulating his world, he also served it. He gave it stability, kept it at peace, furthered its prosperity. He has often been accused of debasing its standards of political morality, but the best answer to this charge is to ask which of his opponents had higher standards. Many of them proved as prosaic and cynical as he, with no greater dreams and much less shrewdness. The most that can be said for them is that by the end of the period, they sensed, as he did not, the expansive forces in the nation that pushed it to new adventure overseas.

Walpole acted as a dam to these forces, and the Spanish War broke the dam. From 1739 until 1815, Britain would become embroiled in one war after another, with never more than a twelve-year interlude of peace. Although its social structure remained relatively stable, Britain was also to be increasingly affected by demographic and economic changes at home, changes that by 1815 would transform the island into the world's foremost industrial power.

CHAPTER 5

The Winning of Empire

In 1739 Britain found itself in a war for which it was unprepared. This was no accident of the moment; unpreparedness is a recurring theme throughout British history, just as it has been in the history of the United States (at least until after World War II), and for the same underlying reason. Both nations have been island powers, strategically speaking, and as such have been immune from any massive invasion at the outbreak of war. Traditionally therefore, both denied to their armed services in time of peace the equipment, training, and thought required to keep them ready for battle. Both often bungled and suffered defeat at the start of hostilities before setting to work to create a fighting machine. Geography gave them time, as it did not give time to a land power such as France, to learn how to fight *after* the declaration of war.

The Expansion of the Conflict (1739–1740)

At the outbreak of the Spanish conflict, Britain was in an even worse state than usual. The army was negligible, the navy undermanned, and Walpole's government inexperienced and inept at military planning. Of these shortcomings, the first seemed the least important: Everyone expected the war to see a return to the Elizabethan tradition of plundering the Spanish Main, and for that lucrative occupation no great number of troops was required. Even small expeditions, however, proved beyond the capacity of the War Office, which could neither organize nor supply them effectively. Indeed, the commander of the land forces in the Caribbean quarreled violently with the chief British admiral there. That admiral, Edward Vernon, had won a dramatic victory late in 1739 by capturing Puerto Bello (a major Spanish port in what is now Panama). The triumph made Vernon a national hero, but during the next three years one amphibious operation after another collapsed in defeat, and 5,000 British soldiers fell victim to tropical disease.[1] The nation, having embarked lightheartedly on what it assumed would be a small and easy struggle, lacked the capacity to win it.

---

[1]While in the West Indies, Admiral Vernon also began the tradition of issuing to each sailor a daily ration of grog (a diluted form of rum) to drink instead of water (which could not be kept fresh on long voyages). Only in the year 1970 did the British navy abolish that custom.

This was a bad omen, for within a year a far greater struggle began in Europe. In 1740 the Habsburg emperor, Charles VI, died, and the accession of his daughter, Maria Theresa, was the signal for neighboring powers to try to partition her territories. This attempt concerned Britain, because it threatened to destroy the balance of European power. For 200 years, continental rivalries had centered on the antagonism between the Habsburg dynastic empire on one side and the reigning house of France, first Valois and then Bourbon, on the other. During the quarter-century of war that ended in 1713, the British had allied themselves with the Habsburgs in order to resist Bourbon aggression. Now Maria Theresa's troubles encouraged French ambition anew, and the British soon discovered that they could not isolate themselves from war on the continent. So they shifted their attention from the Caribbean to Europe.

France was not the first to tear up the Pragmatic Sanction and begin plundering Maria Theresa's dominions. That particular dishonor was reserved for a man known as Frederick the Great, the Hohenzollern who had just ascended the throne of Prussia. His small but relatively compact state in northern Germany, with Berlin as its capital, was entering the ranks of the great powers by virtue of its army. Prussia, as Napoleon was to say, was hatched from a cannonball. Frederick well knew that he could increase his power only at the expense of the Habsburgs, who had long been the paramount German dynasty, and he found his opportunity in the confusion in Vienna that he expected would follow the emperor's death. In December 1740 his troops marched into Silesia, the Austrian province adjacent to his own dominions. Maria Theresa resisted, and war began.

Much more was at stake than Silesia. Frederick was initiating a hundred-thirty-year struggle between Austria and Prussia over which of the two would dominate the smaller German principalities and establish in the heart of Europe a powerful and centralized German nation-state. This new theme in the power politics of Europe overshadowed for a time the older theme of Austro-French rivalry. The new war in Europe soon became mixed up with the conflict overseas. The Austro-Prussian quarrel touched off by the invasion of Silesia developed into a struggle for all of central Europe, just as the Anglo-Spanish quarrel of 1739 developed into a contest between Britain and the Bourbon powers for empire overseas. France, lured by its old ambition to expand into central Europe, was willing to ally itself with either Prussia or Austria. Britain almost automatically took the opposite side, in part to guard Hanover, in part to have a continental ally while fighting the Bourbon powers at sea and overseas. The two midcentury wars were not, like those of Louis XIV, between France and a European coalition led by Britain; they were between coalitions of fluctuating memberships. Two fundamental antagonisms remained, however: In both wars the Habsburg fought the Hohenzollern, and Britain fought France.

The Nature of Eighteenth-Century Warfare

Conflicts were conducted like business operations. Wars of religion were relics of the past; wars between nation-states or powers aspiring to become nation-states were of the future; and to a large degree, calculation and reasons of state replaced passion as the motivating force in these struggles. Each belligerent began hostilities in the hope of profit, whether in terms of trade or territory, and fought as long as fighting served its ends; then it made peace on the best terms possible and awaited another opportunity. An agrarian state like Prussia coveted new provinces, the revenues and population of which could be translated into additional army corps, while a maritime state like Britain coveted new naval bases and lucrative colonies, which could be translated into dominion of the seas. Alliances were based on expediency and might shift with circumstances, and war aims tended to be both limited and realistic.

Land warfare was rarely carried to extremes. The officer class in every European state, including Britain, was virtually synonymous with the aristocracy and had to be as long as the old regimes survived; only men dependent on the crown for their privileges and loyal to it through long tradition could be trusted to command the forces on which the social order depended. Few kingdoms possessed enough qualified aristocrats to officer a mass army, even if they had had enough money in their treasuries to equip and feed such an army. For social and financial reasons, even the military establishment of a great power was therefore small by modern standards. Governments lacked the means, even if they had had the will, to push a war to total victory — to annihilate the enemy's army, seize its capital, and dictate terms of peace. The social system imposed moderation even on war-making, humanity's most immoderate activity.

Armies were made up of soldiers who served for pay and not for love of country. Many small states hired out their troops to the highest bidder, and even in the national monarchies, few enlisted men possessed a sense of national loyalty. Such loyalty as he had was to his regiment, a loyalty that provided the first meaning of the phrase *esprit de corps*. He came from the lower classes and was often in service because the civil authorities had wanted to get rid of him —

> The youth whose most opprobrious fame
> And clear convicted crimes have stamped him soldier.

Only an iron discipline made troops out of such material, which the duke of Wellington later described as "the scum of the earth." An officer could not trust his men out of his sight for fear that they would desert, and consequently could not send them to scout and forage on their own; instead of living off the countryside, the army had to carry with it virtually everything it needed. It therefore moved at a snail's pace, always concerned for its supply lines, rarely daring to leave an enemy fortress in its rear. Campaigns were largely matters of maneuver, of threat and counterthreat, sieges begun and raised; even winning battles might bring victory no nearer.

Commanders had good reason to dread a battle because of the way it was fought. The muskets of the day were not accurate beyond fifty yards. To minimize the possibility that soldiers would accidentally kill their fellows, infantrymen were trained to advance in precise and rigid lines until they came within range, then fire a volley from the entire line, and then charge with the bayonet — while their opponents, in turn, shot at them point-blank. The effect was murderous. Casualty rates often ran between 30 and 50 percent of the troops engaged. If the survivors won a victory in the sense of driving the enemy from the field, they could rarely exploit it by rapid pursuit, which would disorder their line and expose them to counterattack. Most actions, in consequence, produced no gain commensurate with the slaughter involved, and the slaughter in itself became a defeat. The men lost were specialists, hardened by long and rigorous training, and could not be readily replaced; squandering them to no purpose was lunacy. In the words of one German military writer, battle was "the remedy of the desperate." When both sides were anxious to avoid fighting, campaigns produced results as modest as the casualty lists.

The upshot was that land warfare proved slow and inconclusive. Between 1740 and 1763, the great powers battled for fifteen years, and almost the only effect on the map of Europe was to transfer the province of Silesia from Austria to Prussia. Britain aided its continental allies with both troops and financial subsidies, but its only major accomplishment on land was to preserve Hanover for its kings. In war at sea intended to expand trade and empire, however, Britain would score more dramatic triumphs.

Naval war had, in some ways, much in common with war on land. Neither a navy nor an army could be improvised. The square-rigged sailing vessels that served as the warships of the period were costly and slow to build; sailors and naval gunners, like soldiers, were the product of long training; and the backbone of the fleet, the three-decked ship of the line that was the precursor of the later battleship, was too highly specialized and too valuable a unit of firepower to be lightly risked. Actions at sea were commonly fought between two lines, sailing on parallel or opposite courses and firing broadsides at each other like the volleys of soldiers, and the immediate results were likely to be as inconclusive as those of land battles. There the resemblances ended, however.

War at sea differed in kind from war on land. A fleet, unlike an army, did not have to stop to besiege a fortress in its path or fritter away its strength in guarding supply lines. Rather, it carried with it what it needed and could sail wherever there was blue water. Every enemy ship disabled, every base captured or put out of commission, shifted the balance in some degree and prepared the way for the next advance. Naval war was cumulative in its effect, if intelligently directed, and therefore led, in the long run, to decisive results.

The final objective of naval warfare, as the British slowly learned, was not merely to defeat the opposing battle fleet but to drive it from the sea. Ships bottled up in port were at a disadvantage: the crews grew slack from want of practice, and their captains lost their skill in maneuvering with other ships. A blockading squadron, on the other hand, because it had to stay at sea in every kind of wind and weather, tended to improve in efficiency even at the cost of damage to the ships. Hence the longer a blockade was maintained, the greater the disparity was likely to be between the passive and the active navy, and the more complete the predominance of the latter. The fruit of such predominance could well be the acquisition of every enemy possession overseas.

So much for the theory of sea power. But theory in war evolves from practice, which is a slow teacher. The British Admiralty, even when it learned the practice of blockade, had little understanding of the theory behind it. The practice was not learned until some years after the outbreak of hostilities in 1739, neglected again in the War of American Independence, and relearned in the 1790s. Another century elapsed before the theory was formulated — and then by an American.[2]

The War of the Austrian Succession (1740–1748)

In the long evolution of British strategy, the War of the Austrian Succession served as a mere preliminary, a process of trial and error, in which error predominated. The British could not concentrate on naval war as long as they had to defend Hanover against the Prussians and the French and, in 1745–1746, to resist a Jacobite uprising at home. These two factors, accentuated by governmental ineptitude, led to one of the most inconclusive struggles in British history.

The war unfolded slowly. France began to intervene on the side of Prussia as early as 1741, and Spain revived its old dream of ousting the Austrians from Italy. Several years elapsed, however, before the Bourbon powers revealed their aim: like Frederick, they hoped to partition Maria Theresa's inheritance. This aim deeply disturbed Britain, partly because Britain was already at war with Spain and much more because France intended to conquer the Austrian Netherlands, in which British interests were as closely involved as they had been at the time of the Utrecht set-

---

[2]By Alfred T. Mahan in his once-famous trilogy, *The Influence of Sea Power upon History, 1660–1783* (1890), *The Influence of Sea Power upon the French Revolution and Empire, 1793–1812* (1892), and *The Life of Nelson* (1897). These classics, which are still eminently readable, were to have a profound influence on thinking about naval strategy during the 1890s and the first decades of the twentieth century. Paul M. Kennedy, *The Rise and Fall of British Naval Mastery* (1976), provides a more recent overview as do the chapters contributed by John B. Hattendorf and Daniel A. Baugh to J.R. Hill, ed., *The Oxford Illustrated History of the Royal Navy* (1996). The characteristics of life at sea during the eighteenth century are described in G.J. Marcus, *Heart of Oak: A Survey of British Sea Power in the Georgian Era* (1975), and in N. A. M. Rodger, *The Wooden World: An Anatomy of the Georgian Navy* (1986). In terms of shipboard food and comfort, Rodger provides a distinctly upbeat assessment of a way of life that Samuel Johnson described as "being in jail with the chance of being drowned."

tlement. Not until the spring of 1744, however, did France and Britain formally declare war on one another.

The reason stemmed in great part from the political currents and crosscurrents in London. Early in 1742, in the midst of a war that he had not sought, Walpole's enemies finally drove him from office. His immediate successors found it difficult to agree on either a stable ministry at Westminster or an effective policy on the continent. Forced to triple the peacetime military budget, they hired German troops to assist Maria Theresa and safeguard Hanover. George II, acting as a German prince while Britain was still technically neutral, assumed command of an army of Austrians, Hanoverians, and Britons; and in June 1743 at the Battle of Dettingen he had the satisfaction of leading it to an unexpected victory over the French — the last time that a British monarch commanded in the field. Yet the king's triumph did not still the parliamentary outcry that he was sacrificing British interests to those of Hanover; as William Pitt protested, George was turning the nation into "a province to a despicable Electorate."

The king's ministers did not have the wit to devise a coherent offensive strategy, and France saved them the trouble by seizing the initiative. The government of Louis XV, just as Walpole had expected, revived the cause of the Stuarts and massed troops and ships for an invasion of England to coincide with a Jacobite rising. When France abandoned the plan in the face of British naval preparations, the Jacobites decided to go ahead on their own in the hope of forcing the hand of Versailles.

Their leader was no longer James, by now an aging failure, but his son, the Young Pretender. Charles Edward Stuart, "Bonnie Prince Charlie," seemed in some respects the ideal romantic hero: strikingly handsome, he had a magnetism and charm that recalled the duke of Marlborough. He lacked Marlborough's other gifts as politician and soldier, but he did possess courage and a sense of dedication. In July 1745 he sailed from France in a small ship bound for Scotland — but with London as his ultimate destination — to topple King George off his throne. When his journey began, the venture seemed hopeless, but during the next few months, the Stuart cause became a more serious threat than at any time since the Battle of the Boyne in 1690.

The Forty-Five, like the Fifteen, began with a rising of several of the Highland clans. Soon after Charles landed on the west coast of Scotland with only seven companions, he had an army of clansmen at his back. He made straight for Edinburgh and by mid-September was installed in his ancestors' palace of Holyrood. He proclaimed his father king, declared the Scottish union with England at an end, promised the Protestant churches that their possessions would not be disturbed, and pledged to end the hated malt tax. Four days later, he defeated the only force of British regulars in the country. Meanwhile, far to the south, the cold wind of panic began to blow through Whitehall: The government hastily recalled troops from the Low Countries and summoned King George from Hanover. If the Pretender had proved strong enough to invade

Charles Edward Stuart   The Young Pretender. (*Mansell/Time*)

England at once, he might have had a chance, but he waited for reinforcements until the end of October, by which time armies were massing to bar his road. He eluded them all and marched south to Derby, little more than a hundred miles from London. There he stopped, hesitated, and after bitter argument yielded to his advisers and turned back. Retreat, as he rightly feared, meant the end of his bid for a crown.

It was becoming increasingly obvious that the name of Stuart no longer wielded any magic outside the Highlands. The years of Walpole had done their work of reconciling the English and most of the Lowland Scots to the Hanoverian regime. Men might not turn out to fight for that regime, because it did not command such loyalty; but neither would they turn out to fight against it. Without the support of volunteers, the Stuart cause was doomed. Prince Charles and his advisers cared less about the presence of hostile armies than about the absence of the recruits they had hoped for; and, when they found the populace watching their march with indifference, they knew that the game was up. Such apathy provided as strong a defense for King George as his soldiers did.

The Jacobite army retreated across the border and into the Highlands, where it dwindled in the course of the winter. The end came in April 1746 when George's younger son, the duke of Cumberland, destroyed the barefoot Highlanders in a battle on Culloden Moor. The Pretender, despite a bounty of £30,000 on his head, wandered among Jacobite households on the mainland and in the Hebrides for the next five months, sometimes disguised as a woman, until in September a French ship finally managed to spirit him away. He was forced to leave his followers to the ferocious vengeance of Cumberland, who was known thereafter as "the butcher." Houses and crops were burned throughout the Highlands; 120 men were ultimately tried and executed for treason, others died in prison, and nearly a thousand were transported to the North American colonies. Some Highland chiefs saved themselves by exile, while the old clan organization was broken up by act of Parliament. The confiscated lands came under the jurisdiction of a commission of Scottish Lowland gentlemen that attempted to introduce the latest farming techniques. The clansmen were forbidden to bear arms, wear kilts, or play the bagpipes. Their leaders lost their right to administer separate law courts and to organize their dependents into private armies. During the years that followed, a system of army-built roads was extended farther into the Highlands, the speaking of the Scottish form of Gaelic was strongly discouraged, and the Highlands came to be more closely tied to the economy and society of Lowland Scotland.[3]

As for Bonnie Prince Charlie, he soon ceased to be bonnie. His wanderings after Culloden had driven him to drink. He devoted the remainder of his long life more and more single-mindedly to women and alcohol. When he died in 1788, his shadowy claim passed to his younger brother Henry, a cardinal in the Roman Church, and with Henry's death in 1807, the male line of James II was finally extinguished. Its hopes had died in the Forty-Five, and thereafter its exiled followers flitted through the capitals of Europe with nothing to do but play the game of might-have-been. "It is to no sort of purpose to talk to those people," Lord Chesterfield warned his son, "of the natural rights of mankind and the particular constitution of this country. Blinded by prejudices, soured by misfortunes, and tempted by their necessities, they are as incapable of reasoning rightly as they have hitherto been of acting wisely."

After the Jacobite movement ceased to pose a political or military danger to the British kingdom, it was transmuted, especially in Scotland, into a potent historical myth about a glorious lost cause and about a people who continued to long in vain for the return of a Stuart king who would restore a golden age of loyalty, stability, and community.[4] Yet even as the modern sense of Scottish national identity would in part draw inspiration from such romantic Jacobitism, it competed with another set of images. These harked back to the Reformation era, to John Knox and his

---

[3]In addition to Bruce Lenman, *The Jacobite Risings in Britain, 1689–1746* (1980), see the most thorough modern biography, Frank McLynn, *Charles Edward Stuart: A Tragedy in Many Acts* (1988), and a concise but reliable life, Rosalind K. Marshall's *Bonnie Prince Charlie* (1988). Equally relevant is W. A. Speck, *The Butcher: The Duke of Cumberland and the Suppression of the 45* (1982).

[4]Murray G. H. Pittock, *The Invention of Scotland: The Stuart Myth and Scottish Identity, 1638 to the Present* (1991).

Presbyterian disciples who had resisted those very Stuart monarchs in order to fashion their own independent "Godly Commonwealth."

In precipitating the Forty-Five, the Jacobites had unwittingly doomed their cause. From the viewpoint of Versailles, however, the uprising was a godsend, for it gave France the initiative in the war. When the British government withdrew its troops from the Low Countries in 1745, the French moved into the Austrian Netherlands and part of the Dutch Republic. All the subsequent efforts of the British and the Dutch failed to dislodge them. The Austrians were no help, even when Frederick, with Silesia as his prize, withdrew Prussia from the conflict. France, like Prussia, had won a substantial gain on the continent, but overseas its position was precarious. Although in India the French had captured Madras, in America they had lost the fortress of Louisbourg on Cape Breton Island. Louisbourg, the key to the St. Lawrence Valley, had been captured by an expedition from Massachusetts, supported by a squadron of the Royal Navy; and the whole of French Canada lay open to attack. By this threat, the British, in the peace negotiations, pried loose the French hold on the Low Countries.

All the belligerents by now had grown weary. The business of war offered no assurance of further profit for any of them, and they readied themselves to bargain. The peace treaty that they hammered out, signed at Aix-la-Chapelle in 1748, was remarkably inconclusive. Spain made minor gains in Italy, but as the only major change, the powers agreed to Frederick's acquisition of Silesia. He alone emerged a clear victor. Maria Theresa retained control of her other possessions, including the Austrian Netherlands. Elsewhere, the agreement reestablished the prewar status quo — the French back in Louisbourg, the British in Madras, the Austrians in their part of the Netherlands, the Dutch in the border fortresses that they had acquired at Utrecht. Britain made an almost casual peace with Spain. The *asiento* would lapse in 1750, and the chief issue that had brought on war in 1739, the Spanish right of search, was passed over in diplomatic silence. Walpole had died, but his ghost might have chuckled. Nine years of fighting — at a cost of some £80 million — had brought his country nothing.

Reversal of Alliances and Renewal of War (1748–1757)

Although the Treaty of Aix-la-Chapelle had resolved none of the rivalries among Europe's major powers, it bequeathed the kingdom several years of peace. From 1746 until 1754, Henry Pelham served as prime minister. His elder brother, the duke of Newcastle, oversaw foreign affairs while Pelham — like Walpole before him — took charge of government finance and led the ministry from the House of Commons. The Pelham ministry was composed of the "Old Corps" of Walpole Whigs, allied with former critics like William Pitt. For some years, the ministry satisfied both a large majority of the Commons and King George II. As soon as the war had ended, Pelham set about sharply reducing the size of both the army (from 50,000 to 19,000) and the navy (from 51,000 to 10,000). This shrinkage enabled him to lower the nation's annual budget by 40 percent and to cut the land tax in half.

The Pelham ministry also proved willing to disturb a number of domestic sleeping dogs. The Calendar Act of 1751, strongly pushed by Lord Chesterfield, ended the anomaly of a calendar eleven days out of line with that of most of continental Europe. Britain switched to the Gregorian calendar by decreeing that henceforth January 1, not March 25, would be the day on which a new year began, and that all Britons and British colonials would go to sleep on September 2, 1752, and wake up the next morning on September 14, 1752. Because all manner of contracts, rents, and wage arrangements had to be recalculated, the resultant outcry — "Give us back our eleven days!" — is understandable. The Gin Act of 1751 (see Chapter 3) proved more effective than previous measures to curb drunkenness in London. Lord Chancellor Hardwicke's Marriage Act of 1753 ended several generations of legal confusion by prohibiting English minors from marrying without the formal consent of their parents or guardians (and thereby averting a threat to aristocratic and gentry fortunes). The law ordered all parishes to conduct formal marriage services and to keep complete marriage registers. For the next century, the last resort for desperate English lovers remained elopement to the village of Gretna Green in southwest Scotland, where the law remained more lax. An act of 1753 to allow Jews (of whom there were in Britain fewer than 8,000) to obtain full citizenship was, however, repealed a year later because of widespread agitation against such a supposed betrayal of the Christian religion.

In India and America during these years of apparent peace, the Anglo-French rivalry remained as explosive as ever. In Europe, Austria and Prussia rested, unreconciled. France stood ready to fight again at the first promising opportunity, and before long Maria Theresa provided one. She had no intention of accepting the loss of Silesia as final, and to get it back she needed a more stalwart champion than Britain had proved to be. She began to make overtures to Versailles, to which the British government had only one possible answer — overtures to Berlin. While Austria and France had locked horns, Austria and Britain had been friendly; now that Austria and France drew together, Britain had no recourse but to turn to Prussia. This realignment of the powers, particularly in the years 1754–1756, is known as the Diplomatic Revolution.

Though startling to contemporaries, the change of partners is understandable. The War of the Austrian Succession had grown out of two distinct rivalries and had resolved neither one; they continued through a period of uneasy truce. In India the French and British companies encouraged little wars between their client rajahs, while in America the French strengthened their line of forts and trading posts from the Great Lakes to the lower Mississippi. In Europe the Austrian desire for Silesia gradually led to a much more grandiose project — a coalition of powers

Britain's Continental Allies and Enemies Maria Theresa, ruler of the Habsburg empire (1740–1780), and Frederick the Great, king of Prussia (1740–1786). *(E. T. Archive; Hulton Getty)*

to dismember Prussia. To resolve the issues left unsettled at Aix-la-Chapelle, a new and greater war was in the making, and the only question was when and where it would first erupt.

The answer proved to be in North America, where the French and British claims overlapped in the lush forests of the Alleghenies. Both sides determined to assert what they considered their rights. In 1754 an ex-surveyor and colonel of Virginia militia by the name of George Washington led a small expedition of volunteers to the Forks of the Ohio, the site of modern Pittsburgh, only to find the French established there in Fort Duquesne. Washington and his whole force were captured. News of this small debacle stirred the British government to act. In 1755 it sent troops under General Edward Braddock to seize Fort Duquesne, and a naval squadron to the mouth of the St. Lawrence to intercept reinforcements bound for French Canada. Braddock was ambushed and killed; most of the French reinforcements got through, but some were captured. This was war, real if undeclared, and within a few months it spread to Europe.

On the continent, the opening of hostilities derived as much from suspicion as from intent. Britain, drifting into conflict with France, feared for the safety of Hanover. King Frederick of Prussia feared that Maria Theresa might succeed in finding additional new allies. He was not one to wait on events, moreover; as danger enveloped him, he acted. In January 1756, he formed an alliance with Britain, and in September he invaded the German kingdom of Saxony, which he intended to add to his dominions. These moves raised against him a ring of enemies. France, which he had deserted for Britain, turned to Austria, and this Franco-Austrian combination was promptly joined by Russia. The Romanov empress, Elizabeth, detested Frederick and saw an opportunity to possess for herself eastern Prussia; for these reasons, she injected Russia for the first time into the power politics of western Europe. What came to be known as the Seven Years' War had begun. Russia, Austria, and France expected to make Prussia, the only winner in the previous conflict, the victim of the new one.

In the spring of 1756, before any formal declaration of war, France seized the initiative by attacking and capturing the Mediterranean island of Minorca and its British garrison. French armies then poured into the German states, and in 1757 they overran Hanover. For the planners at Versailles, the electorate was crucial. They accepted Britain's naval superiority as irreversible and realized that it would in all likelihood cost them a number of their colonies, but France expected to redeem this loss at the war's end. By making the return of Hanover to King George II a condition of peace, the French expected to redeem whatever losses they might suffer overseas in the short run. Maria Theresa, moreover, had promised them the Austrian Netherlands as a reward if they helped her to recover Silesia. Their strategy, in other words, was based on the lesson of the previous war: that Europe was the crucial theater and that gains there would recoup any losses elsewhere.

The Rise of William Pitt

What the French did not take into account, because they did not yet know it, was that they confronted the two greatest strategists in the period between Marlborough and Napoleon. One was King Frederick. The crisis that he had brought on himself challenged his powers as never before, and he rose to the task. Although his army ranked as the best fighting machine in Europe, it faced odds so overwhelming that a lesser man would have succumbed; even he thought at times of suicide. He lost battles and entire campaigns; he saw his troops melt away and the Russians occupy Berlin. Still he held on, always fighting, always formidable. In the end he managed to preserve — unfortunately, perhaps, for the world of the future — the Prussia that was hatching from a cannonball.

The other great strategist was William Pitt, who through the critical years of the war directed British policy.[5] Although, or perhaps because, he possessed little professional training as a soldier, Pitt had scant patience with the stolid generals of his day. He grasped military and naval problems intuitively more than rationally, often solving them by unorthodox leaps of the imagination. He had in him much of the poet and, in his arrogance and fits of nervous depression, a touch of the madman. But he also had an indomitable will, an accurate judgment of people, and above all an ability to move and inspire the nation.

In a number of respects, he anticipated Winston Churchill, Britain's leader during World War II. Pitt, like Churchill, might never have achieved leadership if the war had not begun with calamitous British defeats. The "boy patriot" who had opposed Walpole had made a name for himself by his oratory and, after Sir Robert's fall, a place for himself by his abilities. But King George, remembering Pitt's stigmatizing Hanover as "a despicable Electorate," had kept him from high office and forced him to bide his time for years in a minor position in the Pelham ministry.

The death of Henry Pelham in 1754 deprived the administration of its manager in the House of Commons and helped give Pitt his opportunity. For two more years, Pelham's brother, the duke of Newcastle, stumbled on by himself as head of the government, a position for which he was wholly unfit. He had the disadvantage of sitting in the House of Lords, but what principally disqualified him for leadership was his personality. A timid, fussy little man, he nevertheless — in the tradition of

---

[5]When Basil Williams completed his two-volume biography, *The Life of William Pitt, Earl of Chatham* (1913), Pitt was still seen as the triumphant war leader and empire-builder. More recent assessments, such as Stanley Ayling, *The Elder Pitt, Earl of Chatham* (1976), and Richard Middleton, in *The Bells of Victory: The Pitt-Newcastle Ministry and the Conduct of the Seven Years' War 1757–1762* (1985), give less credit to the often erratic Pitt. Marie Peters, in *Pitt and Popularity: The Patriot Minister and London Opinion During the Seven Years' War* (1981), emphasizes anew the importance of public opinion in his rise and fall, and Jeremy Black, in *Pitt the Elder* (1992) reminds us that, whatever his limitations, Pitt was "a hero for a country that gave that description to no other politician."

Walpole — proved an expert in the arts of political manipulation. As a minister, he was indispensable, but he lacked the fire needed to galvanize the nation in a crisis.

The war opened with defeats, not only on Minorca but in North America and India, and under these blows Newcastle was driven from office in November 1756. Pitt enjoyed enormous popularity outside Parliament, and once more, as in 1733 and 1739, the pressure of an aroused public opinion was brought to bear on Westminster. After six months of political uncertainty, King George II reluctantly agreed to a Pitt-Newcastle coalition, which remained in office for the next four years. The duke managed the patronage and the votes in Parliament; Pitt managed the war. They made an odd pair. "The Duke of Newcastle and Mr. Pitt," said Chesterfield, "jog on like man and wife, that is, seldom agreeing, often quarreling, but by mutual interest . . . not parting." They could not afford to part, for each required the abilities of the other to remain in power. Moreover, their views on the conduct of the war differed little. Although Newcastle primarily concerned himself with Europe and Pitt with the quest for trade and empire overseas, Pitt agreed that the French had to be kept militarily occupied in Europe and Hanover defended. Indeed, Pitt later boasted that "America had been conquered in Germany."

During his first year in office with Newcastle, Pitt was unable to conquer anything. In North America, an attempt to take Louisbourg failed, and the French advanced south from the St. Lawrence to threaten the Hudson valley. From India came news that in June 1756 the native ruler of Bengal had captured the British post at Calcutta; after the surrender, some forty-three members of the garrison had died of suffocation in the punishment cell of the fortress, the notorious Black Hole. In Europe during 1757, a massive British raid on the French coast, which cost £1 million, achieved nothing. In the meantime, the Austrians defeated Frederick in Bohemia, and an Austro-Russian force raided Berlin, while the French occupied Hanover. Only at the end of the year did the tide turn in Germany, when the king of Prussia, in quick succession, defeated the French at Rossbach in Saxony and the Austrians in Silesia. The Austrians recovered, but the French never did. Rossbach blunted their offensive and broke their hold on Hanover. For the next five years, they tried to regain the initiative in Germany, and their failure to do so subverted their whole strategy. Rossbach, Napoleon said years later, was the battle that started the Bourbon regime on the road to its collapse.

The Years of Victory (1758–1760)

Prussia's crisis did not end at Rossbach — far from it. In the ensuing campaigns, its enemies pressed harder and harder, until Pitt recognized that British interests required large-scale intervention. Although he steadfastly refused to commit the bulk of the British army to the continent, he did send a contingent, which at its peak came to 20,000 men, and he poured out money for hiring Germans. He furnished Frederick a yearly subsidy of £670,000 for his campaigns against the Austrians and Russians in the east and employed some 55,000 mercenaries to cooperate with the British contingent in guarding Hanover and Prussia on the west. This Anglo-German army on the Rhine, commanded by Frederick's chief lieutenant Prince Ferdinand of Brunswick, carried on the work begun at Rossbach and rendered the German war completely inconclusive for France.

In 1759 Prince Ferdinand won a battle. Out of it came a controversy that long had repercussions in Britain and that illustrates the complex interplay between war-making and politics. George II was aging rapidly. His son Frederick had died in 1751, and the heir to the throne was the king's twenty-one-year-old grandson, George, Prince of Wales, who, in keeping with the long-standing family pattern, was on bad terms with his grandfather. The commander of the British expeditionary force serving under Ferdinand of Brunswick was Lord George Sackville, a favorite of the Prince of Wales and consequently *persona non grata* to the king. Sackville was equally unpopular with his chief, Prince Ferdinand, whom he showered with advice in public and criticized in private. This tableau set the stage for the Battle of Minden.

After the Anglo-German infantry had driven the French from Minden, Brunswick ordered Sackville to deliver the *coup de grace* by a cavalry attack. Nothing happened; the moment was lost. Prince Ferdinand, furious, charged his subordinate with disobedience. Lord George answered that the orders had not been clear, but he was relieved of his command and ordered home. A beleaguered Pitt had to choose between turning on Sackville and offending the Prince of Wales, or supporting Lord George and insulting the king and Brunswick. He took the former course and sided with the king. Sackville, ostracized, demanded a court-martial, a move that at least showed courage. The notorious court-martial two years earlier of Admiral John Byng, the man who had helped lose Minorca to Spain, had resulted in his being shot on the quarter-deck of his own ship. Sackville fared better, but not much. He was found guilty of disobeying orders, declared unfit to serve in any military capacity, and disgraced before the whole army. If ever a career seemed blasted, it was his. Yet years later the Prince of Wales, as king, would entrust to this man the chief responsibility for suppressing the rebellion in America.

Minden sparked more than controversy. It was also a significant victory, even if incomplete, and one of a constellation that made 1759 a year long remembered. "I know that I can save this country," Pitt had declared in 1756, "and that no one else can." Now he was making good his words by implementing integrated strategic plans that were based on the geographical facts that Britain was an island and that France was not. Pitt exploited this advantage by relying primarily on mercenaries and subsidies to contain France in Europe while he defeated the French on the high seas and then used his army to gather in their empire.

Just as Pitt won the admiration of the House of Commons by his eloquence, so he stirred the public out-of-doors. A London philanthropist,

Jonas Hanway, was inspired to organize the Marine society in 1756 for the purpose of transforming unemployed London lads into sailors — 10,000 of them during the Seven Years' War alone. Sea power and its counterpart, a blockade of the Mediterranean and Atlantic coasts of France, formed the core of Pitt's strategy. The test came in 1759, when the French projected an invasion of the British Isles. To cover the attack, the Toulon squadron broke out of the Mediterranean for a junction with the main fleet at Brest, but it met with ruin in a battle off Portugal; the ships at Brest then put to sea for a rendezvous with the transports, only to be annihilated in a second battle. Thereafter, the remaining units of the French fleet stayed prudently in port, where the long months of inactivity undermined their crews' morale and seamanship. France lost access to the Atlantic and thus to its overseas colonies.

The effect soon made itself felt from the Ganges to the St. Lawrence. Pitt himself had little interest in India, where the Anglo-French struggle ostensibly raged between two commercial companies rather than two governments. The companies, however, had come to act as governments, in effect; they had learned to recruit sepoys, Indian troops who served under European officers, and to use them in waging full-scale war. Both sides depended on support from home, and the turning point came when Pitt dispatched a few warships to the scene. The French government, thanks to the British blockade, could send nothing equivalent, and before long the Royal Navy commanded Indian waters. This turn of events provided the opportunity for Robert Clive, the first of the great proconsuls who served the East India Company. He and his lieutenants reconquered Calcutta, seized the enemy's posts in Bengal, and by 1761 had destroyed French power in India.

Success in America was even more dramatic. In 1758 Louisbourg fell, and Braddock was avenged by the capture of Fort Duquesne; in 1759 General James Wolfe won Quebec in a brilliant campaign that cost him his life; in 1760 a fleet and converging armies took Montreal and finished the conquest of Canada. Meanwhile, far to the south in the West Indies, the British gathered French islands like ripe plums; by 1762 they had Dominica, Martinique, Guadeloupe, and St. Lucia. This seemingly miraculous surfeit of riches from all the corners of the world surpassed Britain's fondest hopes. The blockading squadrons that rode the sea in all weather off the coast of France had made it all possible.

But blockade, even though it produced such victories, did so at the price of alienating the neutral maritime states. Ships of those states could not be permitted to carry French goods under their flags and so maintain the trade between France and its empire. At the start of the war, the British government accordingly enunciated the Rule of 1756: trade closed to neutrals in time of peace was also closed to them in time of war. Because France had not hitherto permitted them to participate in the commerce with its colonies, in other words, they might not do so now. The rule was enforced not only by the British navy but also by swarms of privateers, licensed by the government to search neutral

The Death of General Wolfe   Benjamin West's gigantic painting helped transmute Wolfe, the brave soldier who had died at the moment of Britain's victory over France at Quebec (1759), into a great national hero. (*The Granger Collection*)

shipping for contraband and to appropriate for their own profit whatever they found. The right of search, which had so infuriated British merchants when exercised by Spain in Spanish waters, now occurred under the Union Jack on a vastly larger scale. The neutrals, too weak to fight, could only bide their time scheming for revenge.

Britain's victories cost the kingdom not only goodwill but also vast sums in cash. The subsidies to Prussia; the cost of the troops that guarded western Germany, of the more than 400 ships in the navy, and of combined operations overseas; the £1 million granted the colonies in America for raising their own military forces — these and other outlays sorely strained the financial resources of the kingdom. By 1760 the annual tax revenue had climbed to £15 million, more than double the figure of 1756, but expenses soared yet more quickly. Britain had to make up the difference by borrowing. The national debt rose between 1756 and 1763 from less than £75 million to almost £133 million. To Newcastle and other British leaders, such figures spelled ruin. Even Pitt realized that a nation of less than eight million people, of whom masses were desperately poor, could not pour out gold forever. But he would not make peace until he had led the country to victory, complete and final.

A Naval Triumph   A British fleet captures the Caribbean island of St. Lucia (1762). (*E. T. Archive*)

Whether he could continue to lead raised another question. His colleagues no longer followed him so obediently as they had in the dark days of the war; they began to tire of his arrogance. Pitt, moreover, now served a new king and could not count on his support. George II, who had begun by detesting his great minister but had fallen under his spell like everyone else, had died in the autumn of 1760. The accession of his grandson, as Chapter 7 will make clear, changed the whole face of politics. The new king and his advisers were in a position similar to that of the Tories fifty years before: seeking a compromise peace while the man who dominated the scene — Marlborough in 1711, Pitt in 1761 — insisted on fighting on to all-out victory. Many politicians, Newcastle among them, had ceased to believe that the kind of victory for which Pitt stood was feasible or even desirable. They preferred a compromise settlement to a triumph that might shatter the traditional balance of power. Getting rid of Pitt would be politically dangerous, but letting him have his way would be worse.

In 1761 the government learned that Spain was making ready to intervene on the side of France. Such a step seemed so foolish militarily that members of the British cabinet could scarcely credit the news. Pitt insisted on an immediate attack before the Spanish preparations were complete. His colleagues refused, but Pitt had grown too autocratic to accept their refusal. "Being responsible," he declared, "I will direct, and will be responsible for nothing I do not direct." This was the final straw. He was no longer permitted to direct, and in October 1761 he resigned.

The next few months saw a rush of events. In January 1762 the empress of Russia died. Her successor, an ardent admirer of Frederick, not only stopped fighting but also threatened to ally with him. Almost at the same moment, Spain declared war and the measures that Pitt had pre-

Robert Clive, Baron Clive of Plassey, 1725–1774   *(The Granger Collection)*

pared were carried out: British forces seized Havana, the capital of Cuba, and Manila, the capital of the Philippines. Thus in Europe Frederick was saved from the ring of his enemies and won a chance to triumph over Austria, while overseas the Bourbon powers suffered one defeat after another. The complete victory for which Pitt had worked seemed at hand.

The Peace of Paris

The new British government, however, like the courts of Madrid and Versailles, had had enough. In May 1762 the old duke of Newcastle was forced from office, and the king installed as first minister his close friend and former tutor, the Scotsman Lord Bute. George and Bute determined to make peace. They cared little about the German war and less about safeguarding the interests of their Prussian ally, who deeply resented the British desertion. In the meantime, the French, sensing Bute's eagerness for conciliation, raised their terms. The Peace of Paris of 1763 therefore brought the first good news the French had had since 1757.

Even Bute, however, could not squander all the benefits of Pitt's strategy, and in the peace Britain made enormous gains. France ceded Canada, Cape Breton Island with its fortress of Louisbourg, and all French holdings between the Alleghenies and the Mississippi except New Orleans. In the whole of North America, France retained only its rights in the Newfoundland fishery and two small islands in the St. Lawrence for drying the fish. Spain received from France New Orleans and the rest of the vast province of Louisiana, as a sop for Madrid's ill-starred intervention, and got back from Britain Cuba and the Philippines in exchange for ceding Florida and returning Minorca. Britain restored to France Guadeloupe, Martinique, and St. Lucia in the West Indies; the French also returned to India, but with only a shadow of their former power. On the surface, then, the treaty typified eighteenth-century compromise: everyone got something, and no one got enough to upset the equilibrium.

The balance of concession and counterconcession, however, was more apparent than real. The war that ended in the Peace of Paris was unlike any other in the century between 1688 and 1792, for one power emerged as the incontestable victor in the world outside Europe; and the peace settlement confirmed Britain's victory. By returning three West Indies islands to France, the British left open the question of predominance there; but in North America and India that question was settled. The French lost their empire on the American continent, for which they had struggled since the early seventeenth century, and their cession of Louisiana to Spain revealed their hopes as bankrupt. In India France's position fared little better: Even though French traders returned, the most they could do — and did for years to come — was to stir up local rulers against the British and so contribute to the series of wars through which the East India Company became the paramount power in the subcontinent. The old French empire was finished, and a century elapsed before France gained another of equal importance.

The Peace of Paris, in retrospect, became the decisive moment in the second Hundred Years' War. At that moment Britain acquired predominance over France, its only serious rival, in the struggle for dominion of the overseas world. Subsequent French attempts to reverse the verdict never came close to success. That verdict determined the future. The Pax Britannica, the oceanic peace enforced by the Royal Navy during the century between the fall of Napoleon and the outbreak of the First World War, emerged as the logical and almost inevitable outgrowth of Britain's triumph in 1763.

Success came from sea power, intelligently harnessed and directed for the first time. King Frederick, the most talented soldier of his age, had fought for seven years on land and came out where he started, with Silesia and nothing more. Britain had taken to the sea, harvested the richest plums of the mercantile world, and then almost contemptuously tossed some of them back to their former owners. The sudden revelation of strength impressed Europe in general and France in particular. Montesquieu, Voltaire, and other French writers had long admired British society in contrast to their own; now the hardheaded realists at Versailles tried to appropriate the secret of British power. In the 1760s the French attempted anew to rebuild their navy, so that when the day came for revenge, they would have the means.

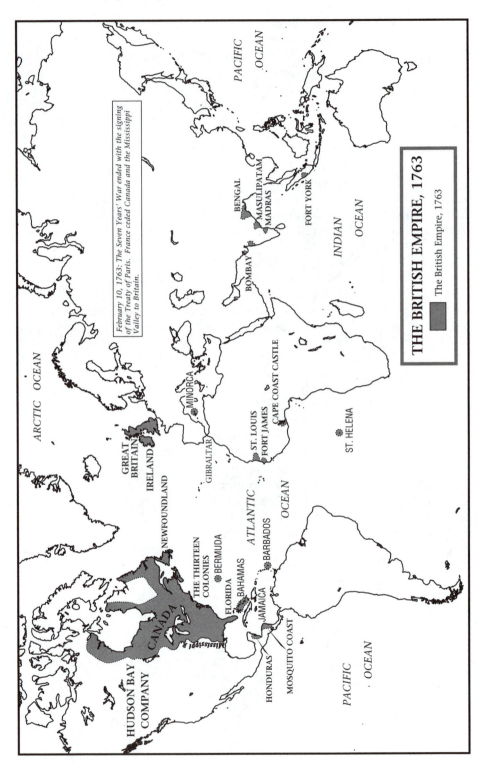

February 10, 1763: The Seven Years' War ended with the signing of the Treaty of Paris. France ceded Canada and the Mississippi Valley to Britain.

THE BRITISH EMPIRE, 1763

The British Empire, 1763

The Price of Victory

In 1763 Britain had attained a pinnacle of its history, and the prospects seemed bright. A thoughtful observer, however, looking back over the recent past and studying the example of Prussia, might have wondered whether Britain's very success did not court danger. To judge by King Frederick's experience, victory bred trouble for the victor, and the British empire now presented as tempting an object of partition as had Prussia a decade earlier. France and Spain, awaiting their opportunity, watched for the British government's first blunder.

To have avoided a misstep entirely would have taxed the wisdom of Solomon, for after the war Britain confronted a host of problems. The most immediately pressing was financial. The national debt had reached staggering proportions, and the recent acquisitions in America promised to increase it: The annual cost of protecting and administering Canada and Florida alone would come to an estimated quarter of the entire prewar budget. New sources of revenue had to be found, but where? Not by increasing taxes or customs and excise duties at home. Because these resources had already been exploited to the limits of public patience, further demands would bring political suicide for any administration. Not by levying internal taxes in the American colonies: only the colonial legislatures could legally do that. Not by asking those legislatures to tax themselves, for experience had shown that they would not respond. The only possible answer lay with some system of taxing the colonies indirectly, by customs duties and the like, to make them carry their share of the imperial burden. The rudiments of such a system had long existed, but the procedure had never been effective. To make it so, the British government would have to devise new methods, and its agents in America would have to enforce them. Increasing the revenue, in short, meant tightening imperial control from London.

Therein lay the rub. The colonists in America had always resisted control, and the situation in which they now found themselves encouraged them to be headstrong. Hitherto, if they had lost no love on the mother country, they had been unable to afford an open breach. They were divided among themselves, culturally and economically as much as geographically; this lack of cohesion had made them keenly aware of the danger from the French on their frontiers. Their need for protection had induced them to endure grudgingly the arrogance of British officers and the demands of British governors. Now the whole picture had changed. During the war, the colonists had learned a little about cooperating with one another and more about quarreling with British regulars; in addition, the Peace of Paris had freed them from their dependence on the mother country. Few of them, if any, yet dreamed of independence, but for the first time the possibility loomed. Just as Pitt had conquered Canada in Germany, he may also have lost the American colonies in Canada.

This generalization, like most in history, much oversimplifies the intricacies of cause and effect. Britain's conquest of Canada was one factor in the American problem; its financial needs were another. The two in conjunction, however, are not enough to explain what followed. To turn the American colonists' resentment into rebellion required something more, and that was ineptitude in Whitehall. If wise counsels had prevailed there, the government might conceivably have found an acceptable method of raising colonial revenue without inflaming colonial tempers. It could certainly have forgone the hope of revenue for the sake of loyalty, because events proved that the mother country was still a long way from bankruptcy. In the years after 1763, however, few wise counsels were heard. A series of short-lived ministries alternated between concession and coercion and wobbled toward disaster. Within twenty years of Britain's greatest imperial triumph was to come its greatest imperial defeat.

CHAPTER 6

Eighteenth-Century
Views of the World

One of the most fascinating and at the same time most difficult tasks that a historian undertakes is to try to see the world through the eyes of men and women long dead. It is often easier to describe the buildings in which they lived and the clothes that they wore (many of which have survived) — as well as the wars they fought and the laws their governments enacted. It is much harder to summarize not only the ideas that they professed but also their assumptions about life. They took these so much for granted that they often did not feel the need to spell them out in written form.

An additional difficulty lies in the fact that in no large society do all people think alike. Books written by such men as English physicist Isaac Newton and English philosopher John Locke are sometimes relegated to a subject called intellectual history, on the grounds that their works were presumably read by only a small elite. Yet just as the lives of millions of twentieth-century Europeans who had never directly read a book or an essay written by Karl Marx were to be affected by attempts to apply his teachings, so, too, many men and women of eighteenth-century Britain inhabited a world that was influenced, directly or indirectly, by the ideas of both Newton and Locke and, in due course, by those of French critic Voltaire and Scottish philosopher and economist Adam Smith.

The purpose of this chapter is fourfold: (1) to outline the manner in which Britain was affected by that movement of European thought known as the Enlightenment; (2) to discuss the manner in which members of both the upper ranks of society and some of the lower were educated; (3) to examine the role that religion played in the lives of people; and (4) to discuss some of the more significant writers of the first two-thirds of the century, the literary era that came to be known as England's Augustan age.

Because it is often easier to understand the world of ideas when we connect that world with particular individuals, the chapter will conclude with pen-portraits of Lord Chesterfield and Samuel Johnson, two influential Englishmen of the period. Inasmuch as both men stood out in the crowd, neither Lord Chesterfield, the articulate courtier and cosmopolitan nobleman, nor Samuel Johnson, the man who rose from an obscure provincial background to become one of London's leading writers and conversationalists, can be deemed typical of their age. Yet the (by no means identical) ways in which these men looked at their world were shared by many other people in the upper, the middle, and at times even the lower ranks of their society.

England and the Enlightenment

The cultural and intellectual world of educated Europeans in the eighteenth century, which followed the wars of religion of the sixteenth and seventeenth centuries, is usually summed up as the Enlightenment.[1] That term may be defined as the era during which *philosophes* — the contemporary European term for inquirers into the ways of man and nature — came to examine almost every facet of the world around them seeking relatively simple, yet fundamental, "natural laws" comparable to those mathematical equations by which Isaac Newton had explained the workings of the cosmos. The *philosophes* revered the human mind, regarding it as a torch that could cast a beam into any deep and complex cavern and in the course of time reveal every crevice. In the words of the age's most famous poet, Alexander Pope (1688–1744):

> Nature and Nature's laws lay hid in night
> God said Let Newton be! and all was light.

Newton, building on the work of earlier scientists, had discovered the formulae that described the revolution of the earth and planets about the sun, and his findings had superseded complex ancient and medieval theories. Newton's younger associate, Edmund Halley (1656–1742), mathematician and cartographer as well as inventor of a deep-sea diving bell, went on to apply Newton's theories to comets, whose long elliptical paths he was able to calculate. In 1705 he confidently predicted the return in 1758 of the comet that he had first observed in 1682. Some years after Halley's death, the comet (which now bears his name) appeared as predicted, as it has on three other occasions since — the latest in 1986. In the eighteenth century, other men sought to become the Newtons of the social or economic world, to dispense with ancient superstitions, substitute the natural for the fanciful, and supplant outmoded dogma with the power of human reason.

---

[1] The eighteenth-century world of ideas is the subject of Peter Gay, *The Enlightenment: An Interpretation*, 2 vols. (1967, 1970). R. W. Harris, *Reason and Nature in Eighteenth Century Thought* (1968), concentrates on the overall British scene. David Daiches (and collaborators) provides an excellent brief introduction to Scottish developments in particular in *A Hotbed of Genius: The Scottish Enlightenment, 1730–1790* (1986). See also Jane Rendall, *The Origins of the Scottish Enlightenment, 1707–1776* (1978), Richard B. Sher, *Church and University in the Scottish Enlightenment* (1985), and Alexander Broadie, ed., *The Scottish Enlightenment: An Anthology* (1997).

Newton's compatriot John Locke had taken several giant steps toward applying reason to both government and education. In his *Two Treatises on Government*, he had sought to justify human government on the basis of reason rather than dogma. He argued that people ought to obey government not because of habit or religious sanction but out of self-interest, for only by creating a government could they protect their lives, their liberty, and their property. The governments that they set up had to justify themselves in turn on the basis of reason, for it was presumed that a contract existed between the governed and the governors for the benefit of the former. When governments, such as that of James II, did not abide by this contract, they could and should be supplanted by others that did. Although many architects of the Revolution of 1688–1689 preferred to believe that the hand of Providence had determined the outcome of that series of dramatic episodes, eighteenth-century thinkers increasingly came to see government as an institution to be fashioned and as necessary refashioned by human beings. Certainly the creators of the American republic (see Chapter 8) would borrow heavily both from Locke and from the eighteenth-century French *philosophe*, Baron Montesquieu.

In his *Essay Concerning Human Understanding*, Locke had outlined similar axioms in the area of human psychology. Human beings are not born, he wrote, with a host of innate ideas; rather, at birth our minds are blank slates to be filled by experience — by sense impressions and by reflections on those impressions. In *Some Thoughts Concerning Education*, a book giving aristocratic and gentry families advice on bringing up their sons, Locke argued that the primary purpose of education was to teach a child by degrees to follow the dictates of reason rather than of instinct or passion. Such education, Locke explained, was most effectively carried out in an atmosphere that favored kindness and encouragement as opposed to the all-too-frequent pattern of shouting and whipping.

The implications of Locke's psychology seemed optimistic: If one could improve the environment in which human beings were educated, one could make the next generation better than the one that had gone before. One could emphasize the potentialities of human beings rather than their limitations, their possible achievements in this world rather than the "original sin" that, according to traditional Christianity, deferred ultimate happiness to the world to come.

To the leading exponents of the eighteenth-century Enlightenment throughout Europe — Voltaire, Diderot, and Condorcet — Newton and Locke served as "founding fathers" of reform. In England itself, they became the bastions of the status quo. As the Whig party had transformed itself within half a century from a quasi-revolutionary opposition group to a pillar of respectability, so the ideas of Newton and Locke during the same short period lost many of their radical implications and became the conventional wisdom of the day. The English, unlike the French, could claim to have limited arbitrary royal power, to have established an independent judiciary, and to have begun to tolerate a diversity of religions; these achievements bred complacency throughout English society. Thus, as we have seen in Chapter 4, Robert Walpole prided himself on being a Whig, but in most respects he had no desire to become a political reformer. The Royal Society, which had stood at the forefront of scientific experimentation in the late seventeenth century, inspired less innovation in the eighteenth. Analogously, young gentlemen at the universities of Oxford and Cambridge merely socialized for several years and dipped into books at their leisure. Even though university faculty members may have been more tolerant toward intellectual diversity than were some of their seventeenth-century forebears, they did not regard it as the prime function of a university to expand the horizons of human knowledge, and they largely ceased to impose examinations on their students. As the historian Edward Gibbon recalled in his *Autobiography*, the Oxford dons of the 1750s "supinely enjoyed the gifts of the founder [but] from the toil of reading, or thinking, or writing, they had absolved their conscience."

In eighteenth-century England, there was no national system of either elementary or secondary education. What did exist was a hodgepodge of town grammar schools, ancient endowed schools such as Eton and Westminster, religiously inspired charity schools (to educate some of the poor), and private schools supported solely by the tuition payments of students' parents. Truly well-to-do families employed private tutors. We may infer the quality of the weaker elementary schools from a sign placed in 1776 over the doorway of such a Cambridgeshire establishment: "Reding, Riting and Spelin taught according to the rules of Grammer — and caer taken of their Morels at 6d a week." Literacy statistics for the century are elusive, but among the laboring poor, probably little more than a third of the men and a fifth of the women could read and write. Among artisans, shopkeepers, and self-employed tradesmen and their spouses, more than four in five could read and write and also keep account books. Literacy was almost universal among members of the aristocracy and the gentry.[2] Many of them indeed shared a growing appetite for reading material of every sort, both for instruction and recreation — novels, newspapers, and monthly periodicals, the first of which, *The Gentleman's Magazine,* was founded in 1731.

Scotland and the Enlightenment

Whatever the breadth of English literacy, it was in Scotland rather than in England that the seeds of the European Enlightenment germinated most visibly. Scotland's independent Parliament in 1696 had directed every parish to appoint and support a schoolmaster out of local taxes. And for several generations, the universities of Edinburgh and Glasgow flourished as centers of learning, displaying far greater vitality than did Oxford or Cambridge.

After the Act of Union, Scotland was no longer a distinct political entity, and numerous Scots — including novelist Tobias Smollett, surgeon

---

[2]See David Vincent, *Literacy and Popular Culture, 1750–1914* (1989).

Science as Entertainment   This lithograph by Thomas Rowlandson portrays an eighteenth-century chemistry lecture. (*Hulton Deutsch*)

John Hunter, and diarist and biographer James Boswell — found fame and sometimes fortune in London. Edinburgh, however, although it had ceased to be the capital of a separate kingdom, remained the chief center of culture for most Scottish aristocratic and professional families; they found London too distant and too expensive a mecca. Although Scotland's seventeenth-century Presbyterian kirk had earned renown for its censorious rigor, the leaders of the Scottish Enlightenment took advantage of the less dogmatic temperament of the emerging kirk leaders, the Moderates, and transformed their old political capital into a new cultural capital, "the Athens of the North."

Edinburgh was to be inhabited by virtuous citizens, well grounded in the tolerant Christian humanist values taught at Glasgow by the Irish-born Francis Hutcheson and taking pride in a vision of a cosmopolitan Britain that would accomplish what neither England nor Scotland could manage separately. While the University of Glasgow shone in mathematics and philosophy, Edinburgh developed the best medical school in the English-speaking world. Adam Smith, professor of moral philosophy at Glasgow, laid down the principles of the modern study of economics as a separate social science, and Adam Ferguson of Edinburgh became "the father of modern sociology." Joseph Black, who taught at both Glasgow and Edinburgh, laid many of the foundations of modern chemistry and was the first person to isolate carbon dioxide in the laboratory. Perhaps the most original of all eighteenth-century thinkers was David Hume, who followed up Locke's theories of human knowledge in so rigorous a fashion as to cast doubt not merely on the fallacies and superstitions of past ages but also on the assumptions and methods of reasoning of his fellow philosophers. Hume's skepticism, which seemed to undermine the very basis of the prevailing belief in a benevolent deity that ruled the world by means of natural laws, cost him appointments to the chair of philosophy at both Edinburgh and Glasgow. His fellow exponents of "the Scottish Enlightenment" defended Hume's right to hold unorthodox views, however, and he went on to apply his skills as a master of English prose to writing a history of England. Like his fellow Scot, William Robertson — a long-time moderator of the Church of Scotland's General Assembly who also wrote about Europe in the sixteenth century and the Spanish settlement of the Americas — Hume provided a model of careful and undogmatic historical scholarship.

The Role of Religion

Educated people in England and Scotland continued to view the world from a Christian perspective; they thought it proper for most people — especially the poor — to attend church regularly. For many Enlightenment leaders, however, the God who had been an overwhelming personal reality to both Puritans and Cavaliers was fading into the abstraction of deism, "more a polite bow to the unknown than an act of faith." They branded any personal experience of the deity as emotional "enthusiasm" and dismissed it as bad form.

Most clergymen of the Church of England, however, adhered to a theology more complex and biblical than simple deism, and the Church remained the kingdom's largest and wealthiest institution. With its two archbishops, its twenty-four bishops (each located in a cathedral town and administering a staff of hundreds), and its ten thousand parishes, the Church presented an imposing facade. Yet the available evidence suggests that, as religious passions cooled during the century's early decades, the number of church services offered also declined. Once church attendance was no longer enforced with fines or even with corporal punishment, the percentage of regular attenders decreased, until in most parishes such faithful followers came to constitute a distinct minority of the population. Yet the Church remained very much involved in marking the rites of passage of its parishioners — baptism, confirmation, marriage, and burial. Although belief in witchcraft may have persisted at the village level, the land's religious and political leaders had become skeptical, and in 1736 Parliament removed the crime of witchcraft from the English statute book.[3]

A majority of clergymen may have been both university educated and pious, but many of them came to believe that a weekly worship service

---

[3]See Keith Thomas, *Religion and the Decline of Magic* (1971) and Ian Bostridge, *Witchcraft and Its Transformations, c. 1650–1750* (1997).

and occasional visits on request to sick parishioners sufficed to earn them their (legally enforced) tithes. Just as bishops were nominated by prime ministers and named by the monarch, so was a majority of the parish clergy named by the local squire. In 1717, when the state suppressed convocations (church assemblies), the bishops and the clergy lost the opportunity to consult on matters of common concern and to see themselves as a distinct and impressive corporate entity. Although the Church of England continued to embody the kingdom's dominant faith, in their Sunday sermons its clergy came to put less emphasis on burning conviction or biblical prophecies and miracles than on uprightness, benevolence, and sober good sense. Passionate denunciations of the devil gave way to moralistic homilies. One of the most influential critics of the evils of the age was neither a writer nor a churchman but the painter and engraver William Hogarth, many of whose pictures, such as *Gin Lane* and *Beer Street*, were intended not merely as deft pictorial satire but as graphic moral tales.[4]

The Augustan Era in English Literature

If the general acknowledgment that the universe operated according to discoverable natural laws could inspire some eighteenth-century thinkers to search for similar laws in the social sciences, it persuaded others that life on earth was already natural and reasonable, if one would but ask the right questions. As Alexander Pope wrote in his "Essay on Man":

> All nature is but Art unknown to thee;
> All Chance, Direction, which thou canst not see;
> All Discord, Harmony not understood;
> All partial Evil, universal Good:
> And, spite of Pride, in erring Reason's spite,
> One truth is clear, WHATEVER IS, IS RIGHT.

Such an attitude could indeed lead to an inner tranquility that expressed itself outwardly in good manners and good form. To be civilized meant to be free of the passions, religious as much as political, that had convulsed the past; and good form was the mark of freedom. A gentleman's or gentlewoman's goal, it seemed, was no longer to be saved but to keep calm:

> Void of strong desire and fear,
> Life's wide ocean trust no more;
> Strive thy little bark to steer
> With the tide, but near the shore.

---

[4]In a number of books, especially *English Society 1688–1832* (1985), Jonathan Clark has argued that a majority of recent historians has underestimated the significance of the Church of England in molding eighteenth-century society. The most comprehensive modern survey is provided by Gordon Rupp in *Religion in England, 1689–1791* (1986), a volume in the *Oxford History of the Christian Church*. The mid- and late-eighteenth-century Methodist and evangelical reaction against Anglican sobriety and complacency is taken up in Chapter 10.

Thus prepared, thy shorten'd sail
Shall, whene'er the winds increase,
Seizing each propitious gale,
Waft thee to the port of Peace.

This almost complacent serenity appears over and over again in the literature of the era, many of whose writers modeled themselves on those of the golden age of ancient Roman literature identified with the reign of the Emperor Augustus. This quasi-classical flowering is therefore often referred to as Augustan. The savage satire and political pamphleteering of Queen Anne's reign gave way to a quieter mood in which even satire lost its barb. It is true that the embittered Irishman Jonathan Swift published *Gulliver's Travels* in 1726, but this attack on the human race was as exceptional as it was masterly. A much more typical satire, mixed with light nonsense, was *The Beggars' Opera*, by John Gay, which appeared the following year and took the country by storm. This featherweight comedy (for it is not an opera) is peopled with highwaymen, jailers, pickpockets, and their womenfolk, all talking and behaving like — and busily poking fun at — the gentry. A father, for instance, asks his newly wed daughter,

"Had not you the common views of a gentlewoman in your marriage, Polly?"

"I don't know what you mean, sir."

"Of a jointure,[5] and of being a widow."

"But I love him, sir: how then could I have thoughts of parting with him?"

"Parting with him? Why that is the whole scheme and intention of all marriage articles. The comfortable state of widowhood is the only hope that keeps up a wife's spirits."

This is not great comedy; John Gay's fondest admirers would scarcely rank him with the Elizabethans. In one respect, however, he has an advantage over them for readers of today: He is completely intelligible. Little more than a century had passed since Shakespeare's death, and in that time the English language had changed. It had lost its wealth of metaphor and simile, and its elaborate sentence structure, and at that price had gained in lucidity.[6] Georgian England conversed and wrote in a prose that had already taken on its modern form.

---

[5] A settlement that the wife received on marriage and retained in her widowhood.

[6] For comparison with the prose of *The Beggars' Opera* take this passage from *Much Ado About Nothing*, written at the close of the sixteenth century:

"I can tell you strange news that you yet dreamt not of."

"Are they good?"

"As the event stamps them: but they have a good cover; they show well outward. The prince and Count Claudio, walking in a thick-pleached alley in my orchard, were thus much overheard by a man of mine: the prince discovered to Claudio that he loved my niece your daughter, and meant to acknowledge it this night in a dance; and, if he found her accordant, he meant to take the present time by the top and instantly break with you of it."

The age was essentially prosaic, and a poet such as Alexander Pope won notice less for soaring love lyrics than for heroic couplets that displayed his literary technique, his wit, and his wisdom. Many an oft-cited twentieth-century aphorism turns out to have originated in one of Pope's poems or essays:

> Who shall decide when doctors disagree?
> A little learning is a dang'rous thing.
> To err is human, to forgive, divine.
> For fools rush in where angels fear to tread.
> Hope springs eternal in the human breast.

As Pope himself observed,

> True wit is nature to advantage dressed,
> What oft was thought but ne'er so well expressed.

Some of Pope's dicta, admittedly, would have pleased neither the Victorians nor their twentieth-century successors. For example,

> Men, some to business, some to pleasure take;
> But every woman is at heart a rake.

As the eighteenth-century began, a number of English and French writers were still waging "the battle of the books" between "the ancients" and "the moderns." The first group argued that the classical Greeks and Romans had achieved an excellence in all fields of endeavor —especially literature and the arts — that had yet to be surpassed. The second group insisted that, in science and philosophy at least, "the moderns" had the upper hand. By the middle of the century, a belief in gradual but definable human progress was becoming increasingly widespread among the educated.[7] All English gentlemen continued to share a knowledge of the Roman classics, however, and at times they poured out their knowledge in a flood of Latinity that drowned the meaning of the English. They give the impression that they were dressing up their prose with Latin just as poets dressed up their verse with figures of speech. Lord Chesterfield, who was as fond as anyone of invoking the Romans, recognized at least that they did not belong in business correspondence. "Carefully avoid all Greek or Latin quotations," he cautioned his son, "and bring no precedents from 'the virtuous Spartans,' 'the polite Athenians,' and 'the brave Romans.' Leave all that to futile pedants. . . . There is an elegant simplicity and dignity of style absolutely necessary for good letters of business; attend to that carefully."

Chesterfield, like many of his contemporaries, was obsessed with style. He insisted on it in writing, and he insisted on it in living. His *Letters to His Son* are a rambling, discursive exposition of what he deemed a

---

[7]See David Spadafora, *The Idea of Progress in Eighteenth-Century Britain* (1990).

gentleman's proper style of life.[8] In them he revealed a great deal about the values and concerns of his world, and a survey of that world may suitably proceed with a glance at what he had to say. The letters preach an egoism as cold as Machiavelli's; repetitive and often trivial, they never probe the depths of experience. For Chesterfield has a narrow vision: He sees only the surface, the outward form, the style; but he sees with the eyes of a hawk, and he is completely honest.

The World of Lord Chesterfield

Philip Stanhope, fourth earl of Chesterfield (1694–1773), belonged to one of the political dynasties of the period. He was a diplomat, a cabinet member, a friend and patron of French and British writers, and a voluminous author himself. His life bore out his conviction that "any man of common understanding may, by proper culture, care, attention, and labor, make himself whatever he pleases, except a good poet." His primary concern, however, was not with politics or diplomacy or literature but with being a gentleman. Here, by his own rigorous standards, he succeeded. His success did not extend, however, to his illegitimate son Philip, to whom he addressed his letters. The boy had in him a touch of boorishness, which his father tried for more than a decade to eliminate by sage admonitions. What mattered to Chesterfield was that he failed; what matters to posterity is that, in failing, he expressed his concept of what a gentleman should be.

The essence of the concept was to be pleasing. "You had better talk trifles elegantly to the most trifling woman than coarse, inelegant sense to the most solid man; you had better return a dropped fan genteelly than give a thousand pounds awkwardly; and you had better refuse a favor gracefully than to grant it clumsily. Manner is all, in everything; it is by manner only that you can please, and consequently rise." The central rule of life, therefore, was never to impose yourself on those around you or try to make them admire you, but always to cater to their tastes and interests in order to buttress their self-esteem. "Those whom you can make like themselves better will, I promise you, like you very well."

This creed is obviously based on pure, if sophisticated, egoism. The *Letters*, complained Samuel Johnson, "teach the morals of a whore, and the manners of a dancing master." But Chesterfield's writings reveal something else as well: a love of form for its own sake. The earl had an almost physical aversion to those who lacked the graces of good breeding

---

[8]A selection of the letters has been published in the Everyman series, and Oliver H. G. Leigh edited them in full and sumptuous form for the Navarre Society, 2 vols. (1926). The best biography remains Samuel Shellabarger, *Lord Chesterfield and His World* (1951). The era became noted for its assiduous letter writing, much of it designed for ultimate publication. The most prolific and famous of all correspondents was Horace Walpole (1717–1797), for whose epistolary output see W. S. Lewis et al., eds., *The Yale Edition of Horace Walpole's Correspondence*, 48 vols. (1933–1983).

Lord Chesterfield (1694–1773) His letters to his son provide a guide to "the age of aristocracy." *(National Portrait Gallery, London)*

and admitted frankly that he cared more for the clothing of ideas than for their intrinsic worth. Awkwardness was for him the sign of worthlessness. He was honest enough to suspect that he might be wrong, but he resented the suspicion and did all he could to keep from putting it to the test. "If a speaker should ungracefully mutter or stammer out to me the sense of an angel, deformed by barbarisms and solecisms or larded with vulgarisms, he should never speak to me a second time if I could help it."[9]

This worship of form was amoral, because it permitted any kind of dissimulation as long as it came gracefully garbed. Religious belief, for example, was important for the simple reason that society did not trust freethinkers; therefore a wise atheist would pretend to a belief that he did not hold. Chesterfield deemed women a much more important case in point, for they also required a gentleman to pretend. Although they were only grown-up children, they played a crucial part in the school of good

---

[9]Such fastidiousness was far from universal; otherwise Samuel Johnson, whose manners were notorious, would never have exercised the dominion that he did over the literary world. A tribute to Johnson by a friend provides the commonsense rebuttal of Chesterfield's position: "To reject wisdom because the person of him who communicates it is uncouth and his manners are inelegant — what is it but to throw away a pineapple, and assign for a reason the roughness of its coat?"

manners; "the concurrence of the two sexes is as necessary to the perfection of our being as to the formation of it." A man must flatter and humor women and, because they always suspect that they are being dallied with and crave to be taken seriously, must give them the impression that he is opening his innermost secrets to them. "Weak men really do, but wise ones only seem to do it."

Chesterfield judged females to be only a little more gullible than males. Although he lived in an age of rationalism, he had no illusions about the role that reason plays in governing human conduct. "Those who suppose that men in general act rationally, because they are called rational creatures, know very little of the world, and if they act themselves upon that supposition will nine times in ten find themselves grossly mistaken." Everyone is a blend of reason and passion and appetite; no two blends are identical, and each contains weaknesses that are waiting to be manipulated. All that is required of the manipulator is to address himself to the whole man, heart as well as head, and he will find the weak spots soon enough.

Such insights became Chesterfield's recipe for success in the drawing room as well as in the House of Commons. He had been a member of the lower house before inheriting his earldom and had soon lost his awe of its members. "I discovered that, of the five hundred and sixty, not above thirty could understand reason; . . . that those thirty only required plain common sense dressed up in good language; and that all the others only required flowing and harmonious periods, whether they conveyed any meaning or not, having ears to hear but not sense enough to judge." This discovery he carried with him to the House of Lords; he believed that it accounted for his high reputation as a parliamentary orator.

His gloomy view of human intelligence did not, of course, extend to himself or those he loved. He was an educated man, grounded in the classics, fluent in modern languages, and knowledgeable in history and in what would today be called political science. Like most other aristocrats and well-to-do squires, he sent his son to the continent for a Grand Tour that lasted for a number of years, to acquire not only polish but also information. Over and over again, he enjoined Philip to keep up his French, improve his German, learn Italian and someday Spanish, and study the ways and institutions of the countries through which he traveled. A favorite injunction was *approfondissez*, get to the bottom of things: "Learn if you can the *why* and the *wherefore*." This insistence on learning, like the insistence on good manners, had a practical purpose, for Philip was being trained for the diplomatic corps. But the rigor of the training shows that his father, the apostle of the graces, set equal store by a well-stocked and disciplined mind.

Because most people did not have such minds, in Chesterfield's opinion, they were often wrong. He was strongly averse, however, to telling them so and viewed their mistakes with an almost supercilious pity. "The blindness of the understanding is as much to be pitied as the blindness of the eye; and there is neither jest nor guilt in a man's losing his way in either case. . . . I may as well expect that every man should be of my size and complexion as that he should reason just as I do. Every man seeks for truth, but God only knows who has found it."

Chesterfield obviously believed that he had found as much of it as he needed for using others to his advantage. He would have said that he had taken thoroughly to heart Pope's famous couplet:

> Know then thyself, presume not God to scan;
> The proper study of mankind is man.

The matters that the earl scrutinized included, as Pope had advised, his own nature, about which he thought he was as clear-sighted as about the rest of humanity. "I know myself (no common piece of knowledge, let me tell you); I know what I can, what I cannot, and consequently what I ought to do. . . . My only remaining ambition," he confided to Philip, "is to be the counsellor and minister of your rising ambition. Let me see my own youth revived in you; let me be your mentor, and with your parts and knowledge, I promise you, you shall go far."

Yet what counsel did he actually have to give? Learn the facts; *approfondissez*. Learn to think. Above all, learn to charm men and women in order to manipulate them, for without well-mannered manipulation, learning and thinking are profitless. This was no creed to fire the mind, let alone the heart. It focused entirely on superficialities, as Chesterfield would have been the first to admit, and for that very reason he considered it the only realistic guide to life. "The world is taken by the outside of things, and we must take the world as it is; you nor I cannot set it right."

If Chesterfield lacked the spirit of scientific inquiry and the relative optimism that inspired many Enlightenment *philosophes*, he shared their cosmopolitanism, their religious skepticism, and a faith in his own (if only his own) powers of reason.

The World of Samuel Johnson

Although their life spans overlapped and they even met on a few occasions, Samuel Johnson (1709–1784) grew up under circumstances very different from those of Lord Chesterfield. The son of a poor bookseller in the small Staffordshire town of Lichfield, Johnson managed to spend thirteen months at Oxford University. He could not afford to stay longer, however; and after working for a time as a schoolmaster in a village near Lichfield, he decided in his late twenties to move permanently to London. There he sought to raise himself from both poverty and obscurity by the power of his pen. For several years, Johnson composed (and in part invented) parliamentary debates for *The Gentleman's Magazine*, based on notes gathered by visitors to the House of Commons. Because the House of Commons officially barred published accounts of its debates as a "breach of privilege," he disguised his chronicles as reports from "the Senate of Lilliput."

Oliver Goldsmith, James Boswell, and Dr. Samuel Johnson at the Mitre Tavern   The records that he kept of conversations at London taverns enabled Boswell to fashion his remarkable biography of Johnson. *(The Granger Collection)*

Johnson went on to write poems, biographies, and essays, and in 1755 brought forth his masterly dictionary of the English language. Although not the country's first lexicographer (an occupation he defined as that of "a harmless drudge, that busies himself in tracing the original, and detailing the signification of words"), he was the most conscientious and the most brilliant man ever to have set himself such a task. Further, he was the first to illustrate his definitions with tens of thousands of quotations drawn from the works of Britain's greatest writers. Johnson's professed purpose was to explain the English language in such a manner that "its purity may be preserved, its use ascertained, and its duration lengthened." In spite of Britain's successes in war and in colonization, at midcentury the English language was spoken by, at most, twelve million people around the world. As the new *Encyclopedia Britannica* complained in its 1773 edition, "it is less known in every foreign country than any other language in Europe."[10] In the British Isles themselves, only three-quarters of the people spoke English as their sole language. The others spoke Irish Gaelic, Scottish Gaelic, or Welsh as their first or only language.

Along with his friend and one-time student, David Garrick (1717–1779), the leading actor and theater manager of the day, Johnson was as responsible as any other individual for establishing William

---

[10]Cited in Langford, pp. 306–307.

Shakespeare's reputation as England's greatest national playwright and poet. Garrick produced numerous successful revivals of neglected Shakespeare plays, acting in them in a far more naturalistic manner than had been common on the English stage. He remained willing, it is true, to tamper not only with the bard's words but also with his plots — even going so far as to provide *King Lear* with a happy ending. Johnson, in the meantime, had published a new edition of Shakespeare's plays (1765) in which he persuasively defended the bard against continental critics who had accused Shakespeare of having neglected the ancient Greek rules of drama. By then Johnson's services to literature had earned him a generous pension from King George III, and there followed honorary degrees first from Trinity College, Dublin (the sole Irish university), and later from Oxford. These academic distinctions caused him to be generally known as "Dr. Johnson."

By the 1760s, Johnson also enjoyed growing recognition as a conversationalist who held forth night after night in a London tavern on almost any subject under the sun. Neither Johnson's ungainly manner and appearance nor his slovenly dress seemed to disturb the members of his informal Literary Club, which from 1764 on met weekly at the Turk's Head Tavern for food, drink, and talk. Its members included Joshua Reynolds, the portrait painter who in 1768 became the first president of the Royal Academy; David Garrick; Edmund Burke, the youthful parliamentarian; and the yet more youthful James Boswell. Boswell had just arrived from his native Scotland to prepare for a legal career — "Much may be made of a Scotchman," declared Johnson, "if he be *caught* young." Boswell found even greater satisfaction, however, in the self-imposed task of writing down verbatim lengthy snatches of Johnson's conversation, jottings that he later used to fashion the most remarkable biography of the age.[11]

Another member of Johnson's club was the poet and playwright Oliver Goldsmith, who dedicated his best-remembered play, *She Stoops to Conquer* (1773), to Johnson. In Goldsmith's words, Johnson demonstrated that "the greatest wit may be found in a character, without impairing the most unaffected piety." Johnson, whose outlook on the world was often tinged with melancholy, was a staunch supporter of the Church of England and devoted the greater part of his Sundays to studying the Bible and to personal meditation. His Christian faith and his adherence to a strict moral code went hand in hand with a hard-headed devotion to common sense. The philosopher and bishop, George Berkeley, had set forth the theory that the physical matter that formed the universe was not real but only an image in the human mind. On one occasion, Boswell

---

[11]Boswell's biography, *The Life of Samuel Johnson, LL.D.*, was first published in 1791. As edited and annotated by George Birkbeck Hill and revised by L. F. Powell, it is available in a six-volume edition (1934–1964). Of the modern biographies of Johnson, that by W. Jackson Bate (1977) is the most detailed, and that by John Wain (1974) constitutes the most readable introduction. Boswell's own extraordinary diary, rediscovered in the 1920s and 1930s, has been edited and published in thirteen volumes (1950–1989).

remarked to Johnson that Berkeley's theory was difficult to believe but impossible to refute. With great alacrity, Johnson struck his foot against a large stone: "I refute it *thus.*"

On another occasion, an associate told Johnson and Boswell that he was about to set up a school on his estate but that he had been warned that education might make his tenant farmers and laborers less industrious.

> JOHNSON: No, Sir. While learning to read and write is a distinction, the few who have that distinction may be the less inclined to work; but when every body learns to read and write, it is no longer a distinction. A man who has a laced waistcoat is too fine a man to work; but if every body had laced waistcoats, we should have people working in laced waistcoats. There are no people whatever more industrious, none who work more, than our manufacturers; yet they have all learned to read and write. Sir, you must not neglect doing a thing immediately good, from fear of remote evil; — from fear of its being abused. A man who has can- dles may sit up too late, which he would not do if he had not candles; but nobody will deny that the art of making candles, by which light is con- tinued to us beyond the time that the sun gives us light, is a valuable art, and ought to be preserved.

> BOSWELL: But, Sir, would it not be better to follow Nature; and go to bed and rise just as nature gives us light or withholds it?

> JOHNSON: No, Sir; for then we should have no kind of equality in the partition of our time between sleeping and waking. It would be very dif- ferent in different seasons and in different places. In some of the north- ern parts of Scotland how little light is there in the depth of winter!

When Oliver Goldsmith put forth the notion that the prevalence of luxury had caused the degeneration of England's people, Johnson took is- sue once more:

> Sir, in the first place, I doubt the fact. I believe there are as many tall men in England now, as ever there were. But, secondly, supposing the stature of our people to be diminished, that is not owing to luxury; for, Sir, consider to how very small a proportion of our people luxury can reach. Our soldiery, surely, are not luxurious, who live on six-pence a day; and the same remark will apply to almost all the other classes. Lux- ury, so far as it reaches the poor, will do good to the race of people; it will strengthen and multiply them. Sir, no nation was ever hurt by luxury; for, as I said before, it can reach but to a very few. . . .

By background and by temperament, Johnson was a Tory rather than a Whig. As he often explained, "The first Whig was the Devil," and in his *Dictionary,* Johnson defined Whig simply as "the name of a faction," whereas a Tory was "one who adheres to the ancient constitution of the state, and the apostolical hierarchy of the Church of England." Although he lived into an age in which an increasing number of people sought in- stitutional reform in church and state, Johnson accepted the world as it was. He had risen to become one of the most eminent men of his day, and he claimed many others as friends. Gruff and curmudgeonly as he often appeared, he demonstrated compassion on a personal basis by using much of his limited income to support in his household a group of hapless pensioners and by assisting several other unfortunates whom he encountered in the London streets he had come to know so well.

On the continent, the Enlightenment became a program for fundamental and potentially revolutionary reform, but Samuel Johnson represented numerous eighteenth-century Britons for whom their land had already undergone its share of revolutions. He was not averse to innovation, but for the most part he accepted and justified his country's institutions as he found them. Less skeptical and less concerned with outward manner than was Chesterfield, he approached the world with his own distinctive brand of robust common sense. Both Chesterfield and Johnson lived in a time and place generally regarded as inegalitarian and sometimes violent, but fundamentally stable (at least for those Britons who were not fighting wars abroad or on the high seas). Such stability was to be rocked repeatedly during the final decades of the century.

PART THREE

FORCES OF CHANGE
1760 to 1789

THE IRONWORKS AT COALBROOKDALE
(Mary Evans Picture Library)

CHAPTER 7

The Age of George III

Although the transition from the reign of George I to that of George II in 1727 had — as a result of Walpole's political skill — resulted in continuity rather than change, the accession of the youthful King George III in 1760 opened a new and controversial political era. Not only did the new king's personality put its stamp upon the reign, but his actions also gave rise to a historical dispute that has endured into our own time. Was George III, as some of his contemporary critics suggested and as several Victorian historians felt certain, an ambitious man who sought in unconstitutional fashion to restore to the monarchy powers and responsibilities that his predecessors had let slip into the hands of ministers whose primary loyalty lay with Parliament? Was he the tyrant and enemy of free institutions that he is depicted to be in the American Declaration of Independence? Or was he a victim of the propaganda spread by his enemies? Was he rather a public-spirited and conscientious man eager to use the accepted constitutional practices of his day in order to advance not his personal interests but those of his nation?[1] Any attempt to provide even tentative answers to these and related questions requires an analysis of both the personality of the new monarch and the political problems that beset his reign.

The Character of the King

The future George III became the immediate heir to the throne in 1751 at age twelve, when his father Prince Frederick died, and he was educated to

---

[1] The late-nineteenth-century hostile Whig tradition is exemplified by the writings of Sir George Otto Trevelyan in works such as *The American Revolution*, 2nd ed., 4 vols. (1905–1912). Sir Lewis B. Namier was responsible for a major reevaluation in the late 1920s in *The Structure of Politics at the Accession of George III*, 2nd ed. (1957) and *England in the Age of the American Revolution*, 2nd ed. (1961). Richard Pares provides a balanced assessment in *King George III and the Politicians* (1957). The historiographical controversy is the subject of Herbert Butterfield, *George III and the Historians* (1957), and E. A. Reitan, ed., *George III: Tyrant or Constitutional Monarch?* (1964). Ian R. Christie, *Wars and Revolutions: Britain, 1760–1815* (1982), and Paul Langford, *A Polite and Commercial People, 1727–1783* (1989) touch on all aspects of the era. John Brooke, *King George III* (1972), the most reliable modern biography, may be supplemented with Christopher Hibbert, *George III: A Personal History* (1998).

become a king. His somewhat rakish father left George a remarkable political testament that urged him to resist "the perverseness and bad example of the times," to be pious, to practice personal economy and reduce the national debt, and as "an Englishman born and bred," to win the love of his people and the respect of foreign powers. "I shall have no regret," Frederick concluded, "never to have worn the Crown if you do but fill it worthily." Frederick's widow, Princess Augusta, was at least as eager to have her son fit for the position that he was destined to occupy. As a result, she kept him cloistered in the schoolroom and deprived him of the company of people his own age, most of whom, she declared, "were so ill educated and so very vicious that they frightened her." George grew into a shy, moody, and lonely boy, and it was not until Lord Bute became his mother's political adviser and his personal tutor in 1755–1756 that George found a friend, a confidant, and an affectionate substitute father. Twenty-five years older than George, the third earl of Bute was a penurious Scottish nobleman with a large family. He had read widely and possessed a worldly air of wisdom, but except for four undistinguished years as a representative Scottish peer in the House of Lords, he had no immediate experience in British politics.

As tutor to the future king, Bute set forth high political ideals, and in his schoolboy essays young George reflected Bute's teachings. "We stand in debt for our liberty and religion to the success of 1688," he wrote, and he went on to exalt freedom of speech as "not only the natural privilege of liberty but also its support and preservation." He studied and wrote about earlier "corrupt" eras in the history of England, but he assured his tutor that "no good and great Prince born in a free country . . . will ever despair of restoring his country to virtue, freedom, and glory, even though he mounts the Throne in the most corrupted times. . . ." In a firm yet friendly manner, Bute discouraged George's infatuation with the youthful Lady Sarah Lennox: It would not do to marry a commoner who was a close relative of several major politicians. In a spirit of conscious self-sacrifice, George gave way.

At the same time, Bute taught George to see himself as chief executive in fact as well as in name. Like William III in his best years, George hoped to rule through ministers of his choice and a cooperative Parliament. This seemed to be an ambition that he could realize within the existing system; all he had to do was repossess the means of influencing Parliament that his predecessors had largely delegated to the politicians who had ruled for them. In fact, however, his concept of his role struck at the assumption of the previous forty years that the reins of government should be held by the Walpole Whigs and their successors, such as the duke of Newcastle. For half a century, the Whig oligarchs had governed, on the condition, when necessary, of deferring to the monarch's wishes and prejudices; they and not he had acted as the prime policymakers. A monarch who was prepared to consider members of all parliamentary parties and factions, including erstwhile Tories, as possible ministers and to guide policy himself posed a profound threat, a threat so dire that some thought the king's actions unconstitutional. Yet they had a weak case. Constitutional theory, as distinct from previous practice, was more on his side than theirs; he was the source of the influence and patronage that they had so long used to manipulate Parliament. The means by which they had hitherto governed, with tacit royal consent, were precisely the means by which the new king expected to place his personal stamp on the government of the realm. The Whig leaders were not at first prepared to fight back by seeking to alter the structure of the House of Commons— with its rotten boroughs and its placemen. Nor were several of them prepared to acquiesce readily in the king's rule. The result was a decade of tension and instability, from 1760 to 1770, followed by twelve years in which George largely had his way —and lost the American colonies.

The king's former tutor was instrumental in starting him on this disastrous course. He obviously possessed personal ambitions as well as grandiose ideals, and he was jealous of the leading ministers of the day. He therefore imbued George not only with the desire to restore his "much loved country to her ancient state of liberty . . . again famous for being the residence of true piety and virtue" but also with the misleading impression that his grandfather had become the veritable prisoner of a bevy of knavish politicians and that Bute alone was a pure spirit in what George described as "the wickedest age that ever was seen." Most of his subjects exulted in the extraordinary military triumphs engineered by the most successful war minister in British history, but the new king saw the world about him through quite different spectacles. He possessed a profound and admirable sense of duty but no practical experience in government. He found it more difficult to deal with flesh-and-blood human beings than with lofty but abstract ideals.

Soon after mounting the throne, he issued a royal proclamation asking his people "to preserve and advance the honour and service of Almighty God, and to discourage and suppress all vice, profaneness, debauchery, and immorality." The wicked, whatever their social rank, were to be held in contempt, the good to be distinguished by "marks of our royal favour." George did his best to practice what he preached. In 1761 he married Princess Charlotte of the German principality of Mecklenburg-Strelitz, a plain but intelligent and vigorous seventeen-year-old who familiarized herself quickly with the English language and the English environment. The young couple set an example of surprisingly simple domesticity in their large drafty palaces, and they made their way to the coronation ceremony in sedan chairs rather than in an elaborate gilded carriage. They felt happiest in rural surroundings, and from the 1770s on, the king went to London for government business but preferred to live at Windsor, where in the role of country squire he could supervise his model farms and mingle with ordinary people. He liked hunting and was an excellent horseman; even in his fifties, after a long day in London, he would ride the twenty miles back to Windsor. In the

King George III as Family Man   The king, Queen Charlotte, and the first six of their fifteen children as painted by John Zoffany in 1770. The boy sitting on the extreme left is the future King William IV, the boy standing next to him the future Prince Regent and King George IV. *(Reprinted by permission of Her Majesty the Queen)*

morning he would himself light the bedroom fire and spend an hour in his study before breakfast, a frugal meal because he was fearful of growing fat. Prayers in the royal chapel would follow. George took religion seriously. When a preacher sought to ingratiate himself by delivering a sermon highly flattering to the king, George rebuked him by saying, "I go to Church to hear God praised and not myself."

Though in his own eyes he was a friend to humanity at large, he felt ill at ease on public occasions. It took him many years to become accustomed to the levees and drawing room soirees that constituted so important a part of the royal routine. He enjoyed both theater and opera but preferred a quiet evening at home — where he could play the flute while Charlotte accompanied him on the harpsichord — to an elaborate palace function. He favored barley water over brandy, and at court he abolished Sunday dancing and tried to limit gambling. One of his favorite hobbies was book collecting, and he eventually amassed some 65,000 volumes. He also took a keen interest in astronomy and became the patron of William Herschel, the discoverer of the planet Uranus; the king ordered the largest telescope of the day built for Herschel's use. Though theirs was a marriage of diplomatic convenience, George and Charlotte became deeply devoted to one another, and in due course she presented him with fifteen children. Royal mistresses were banned

William Herschel's Telescope Built in 1775 under the patronage of King George III. *(The Science Museum, London)*

from the court of George III, and no evidence exists that the king ever fathered an illegitimate child. He sponsored the founding of the Royal Academy as an exhibition site and as a training school for British artists. He had definite ideas, moreover, as to what sorts of paintings were proper, and he much preferred compositions that portrayed Britain's historic military heroes to pictures of nude women reclining on divans. Analogously, he enjoyed the theater, but he deplored the "extreme immorality" of the comedies of the Restoration era. In several respects, the king and queen were Victorians in a pre-Victorian age, and some of their subjects made fun of the piety, the prudery, the penchant for economy, and the general dullness of the court. Those who did not were all too likely to suspect the king's political designs. It was only in the later 1780s and the 1790s, after his active reign was more than half over, that King George III's personal qualities truly won the admiration and even the affection of his people.

Even if George, before he ascended the throne, had been on excellent terms with his grandfather and his grandfather's ministers, the transition from a king of seventy-seven to one of twenty-two would have had a profound impact. Not only youth but also upbringing distinguished the new ruler from his predecessor. Privately George had denounced Hanover, "that horrid electorate," in as vigorous a fashion as might any Whig politician, and in his own hand he inserted in the draft of his speech to his first Parliament the words, "Born and educated in this country, I glory in the name of Britain." Whigs long suspicious of Hanoverian influence applauded such a sentiment. So did the Tory squires who had felt alienated from national politics for two generations and London Tories such as Samuel Johnson. Johnson found admirable the piety, the political ideals, and the generosity of King George III, who in 1762 offered him, as England's leading man of letters, the generous pension of £300 a year for life. A few years later the king deliberately sought Johnson out in order to ask his opinions about the state of literary life in Britain. When Johnson said of himself that he "thought he had already done his part as a writer," the king replied, "I should have thought so too, if you had not written so well." This, Johnson afterward declared, was a compliment "fit for a King to pay. It was decisive." The king's favor spurred Johnson not merely to embark on his last major literary work, *The Lives of the Poets*, but also to write a number of pamphlets defending the policies of George III's ministries during the late 1760s and early 1770s.

The Politics of the 1760s

Not all of his subjects were equally pleased with either King George III or his ministers. Many objected in particular to the speed with which the king advanced the fortunes of his Scottish friend, Lord Bute. The latter was suspected of all manner of evil designs—such as wishing to remove from office the leading Whig politicians, including the duke of Newcastle, who had served in high office for the greater part of four decades.

By March 1761 Bute had been installed as one of the two secretaries of state. In October Pitt resigned, and in May 1762 Newcastle followed suit. George III had not removed either man, for both had departed on questions of policy, but the king had wanted to see them go, unaware that any successors might have trouble managing Parliament without the support of both the greatest orator of the day and the most experienced dispenser of patronage. Bute now became First Lord of the Treasury, and, although the House of Commons gave overwhelming approval to the Peace of Paris, he soon found himself embroiled in difficulties. An excise tax on cider, which his ministry felt compelled to impose to balance the budget, was denounced as an example of Scottish tyranny seeking to deprive the English of their liberties. The London populace, which had made a hero of Pitt, pelted Bute's carriage with mud and attempted to overturn it. The blue ribbon of the garter, which the king had conferred on him, was derided in a London street ballad:

> O Bute! If, instead of contempt and of odium
> You wish to obtain universal eulogium,
> From your breast to your gullet transfer the blue string
> Our hearts are all yours at the very first swing.

The cider tax passed, but Bute had become so fearful for his personal safety that in April 1763 he resigned. Parliamentary politics were not his métier. He would have happily remained the power behind the throne (and was suspected of being precisely that for many years to come), but George gradually became disillusioned with his "dearest Friend." After 1766 they corresponded no longer.

Bute's resignation returned government to English politicians and began a long period of ministerial instability. George Grenville, a Whig of the old school, followed in Bute's position for two years (1763–1765). Although they agreed on policy, the king never learned to like the minister's self-righteousness and verbosity. "When he has wearied me for two hours," the monarch complained, "he looks at his watch to see if he may not tire me for an hour more." George resented Grenville's attempt to monopolize all patronage appointments to gain parliamentary support, even lofty appointments in the army and the Church that the king considered above politics. In 1765 he replaced Grenville with the marquis of Rockingham, whose ministry proved weak. In the summer of 1766, George tried bringing back the one great figure of recent British politics to steer the government out of its doldrums. Still the great orator of his age, whenever William Pitt spoke, he "carried with him unpremeditated," in Chesterfield's words, "the strength of thunder and the splendor of lightning." He enjoyed enormous popularity in the country, and even the Americans looked up to him. Yet his ministry proved a failure. At its start he undercut his position by accepting a peerage and becoming earl of Chatham. Chesterfield expressed the amazement of the political world that any consideration could have induced Pitt to withdraw from the House of Commons, "which procured him his power and which could alone insure it to him, and to go into that hospital of incurables, the House of Lords." Greater wonders were to come. By December 1766, a severe mental depression gripped the new Lord Chatham and kept him a recluse for the next two years. In his absence, the cabinet disintegrated into quarreling factions. In 1768 Chatham gave way to his former lieutenant, the duke of Grafton, who proved more devoted to his racehorses and his mistress than to public business. After two years the duke's lackluster ministry fell apart.

Grafton's successor, who remained in office for the next twelve years, was Lord North, at first glance the ideal man to implement royal policy. He was easygoing and conciliatory, without long-range plans and uncommitted to any faction, a seasoned politician though not yet in his forties, a superb debater, and deft in managing the House of Commons.[2] His startling ugliness was counterbalanced by charm and wit, but under a polished surface, he struggled with a deep self-distrust. The king's search for an ideal minister had brought him almost more than he had bargained for: a servant who found it painfully difficult to counter the king's views and who turned to him not only for guidance but also for willpower. North consulted his monarch four or five times a week, and George was pleased to find himself

---

[2]To find Lord North in the lower house instead of the upper is confusing, but so are British titles. North was not a peer and hence did not sit in the House of Lords. He was the heir to an earldom, and the eldest son of a duke, marquis, or earl was—and still is—called lord as a courtesy during his father's lifetime. Both Peter D. G. Thomas, in *Lord North* (1976) and Peter Whiteley, in *Lord North: The Prime Minister Who Lost America* (1996), provide relatively sympathetic appraisals.

involved in the day-to-day direction of policy to a degree not known since the days of William III. Had times been as stable as forty years before, North might have lasted as long as Walpole did, but John Wilkes and his supporters at home, and the colonists in America, had raised a host of issues that made it all but impossible to let sleeping dogs lie once more.

The Case of John Wilkes

The 1760s saw wobbling not only at the ministerial level. They also gave rise to a development that aroused much more attention in Britain than did colonial discontent and had almost as much importance for the future. The ineptitude of successive ministries brought the whole parliamentary system into disrepute and, for the first time since the seventeenth century, awakened the force of political radicalism. Divisions within Parliament expanded the influence of public opinion outside its doors, and much evidence suggests that the "political nation" — especially in London and in numerous provincial cities — had grown larger than the formally enfranchised parliamentary electorate. Mid-eighteenth-century printing presses could not easily produce more than 3,000 newspaper copies a day; but by the 1760s, London had four daily papers and ten triweekly papers, as well as prestigious monthlies like the *Gentleman's Magazine.* By then, any sizable provincial town could boast at least one newspaper of its own, and each year thousands of political pamphlets rolled off the presses as well. People who could not afford their own paper might borrow their neighbor's or read it in a coffeehouse or tavern. The prime purpose of most papers and pamphlets seemed to be to complain about the government of the day. As Lord North lamented, "Libels, lampoons, and satires, constitute all the writing, printing, and reading of our time."

The remarkable, if not estimable, man who for some years came to personify this mood of popular protest was John Wilkes, who for many years kept the world of Westminster in turmoil. He was as ugly, charming, and witty as Lord North, but there the resemblance ended; Wilkes, even in a period of lax morals and little faith, had a notorious reputation as a rake and blasphemer. If the fear of God was not in him, neither was the fear of man. He began by attacking the king's ministers and ended by hammering at the king himself and the whole constitutional structure on which royal power rested.

Marriage to a wealthy heiress had made it possible for Wilkes, the son of a distiller, to set himself up as a country squire and in 1757 to gain election to the House of Commons, where he became a protégé of Earl Temple, Pitt's brother-in-law. In 1762 Temple enabled Wilkes to become the owner and editor of a weekly paper, the *North Briton,* which catered to a lower-middle-class London audience; its tone was violently antigovernment, anti-Bute, and anti-Scot. "How far," asked France's Madame de Pompadour, "does liberty of the press extend in England?" "That," Wilkes replied, "is what I am trying to find out." In successive issues of the *North*

Briton, Wilkes broadly suggested that Bute was the lover of the king's mother and had bribed the House of Commons to approve the Treaty of Paris. In Number 45 of the journal, Wilkes denounced as a lie the passage in the king's speech to Parliament that characterized the peace as "honorable to my Crown and beneficial to my people."

Grenville had Wilkes arrested on a general warrant (an order issued by a secretary of state that named no names). In this case, the document demanded the arrest, for seditious libel, of all concerned in the publication of the *North Briton* and the confiscation of all their papers. Such exercise of executive power was reserved for emergencies, and its legality was doubtful. So was the question of whether a Member of Parliament could be sent to prison for libel. Nevertheless, Wilkes was sent to the Tower of London. When granted a court hearing on a writ of habeas corpus, he dramatically made himself the symbol of English freedom: "The liberty of all peers and gentlemen and, what touches me more sensibly, that of all middling and inferior set of people, who stand most in need of protection," he told the judge, "is in my case this day to be finally decided upon: a question of such importance as to determine at once whether English liberty shall be a reality or a shadow." The court freed him on the ground that a Member of Parliament was privileged. He then sued the responsible secretary of state, protesting that general warrants were not authorized by English law. The judges eventually ruled in Wilkes' favor, and he recovered £1,000 in damages.

This attack on the Goliath of officialdom made Wilkes such a popular hero that the Grenville ministry dared not leave him alone. When, in

John Wilkes: The English Radical as Seen in 1764 by a Supporter and by a Critic   Engraving based on a painting by Robert E. Pine; etching by William Hogarth. *(Library of Congress; reproduced by courtesy of the Trustees of the British Museum)*

defiance of the advice of his aristocratic patrons, Wilkes personally re-published the libelous articles, the government counterattacked. It induced the House to deny that its privilege covered libel and exposed in the House of Lords *The Essay on Woman,* an obscene parody of Pope that Wilkes had written in part and had printed for private circulation. He now stood open to prosecution both for obscenity and for his earlier libel in the *North Briton.* Early in 1764 he fled to France and consequently was expelled from the House of Commons, convicted *in absentia* of libel, and outlawed. Four years later he returned, unrepentant and unafraid, and promptly stood for election to Parliament for the county of Middlesex, an electorate made up largely of London shopkeepers. He canvassed as an independent man persecuted by a costly and inefficient government. When one voter told him, "I'd rather vote for the Devil," Wilkes quipped: "Naturally, but if your friend is not standing, may I hope for your support?" He won the election but almost immediately thereafter was imprisoned under his old sentence for libel. He proved more dangerous, however, in prison than at liberty. Mobs rioted outside his windows; troops were called in, fired on the crowd, and killed several people, an action that resulted in coroners' juries bringing verdicts of murder against the military.

These events unfolded during a time of economic distress in London: weavers, sailors, hatters, tailors, and coalheavers all intermittently involved themselves in strikes. Such discontented workers were ever ready to cheer Wilkes, not because he advocated a specific economic program but because, like them, he thumbed his nose at what a later generation would call "the establishment." The London clubs of shopkeepers and tradesmen who supported Wilkes took pride in the notion of "independence" from the pressures that aristocratic patrons or clients had often imposed on them. When the threat of revolution raised its head in the London atmosphere, however, moderate opinion rallied to the government, then headed by the duke of Grafton. In 1769 the House of Commons quashed Wilkes's election only to see him reelected once more for Middlesex. After the House of Commons again refused to seat Wilkes, he won yet a third by-election. On this occasion, the House of Commons formally declared Wilkes's opponent, who had received a fifth of the votes, to be the legal member. The defenders of expulsion took their stand on the ground that Wilkes was deliberately flouting the will of the House of Commons, which had in the seventeenth century successfully asserted, against crown and law courts alike, the right to control its membership and to resolve electoral disputes. The opponents of expulsion, with Wilkes's eager encouragement, took their stand on the ground that the House was purposefully undermining the freedom of voters to choose their own representatives.

While the issue was still in dispute, Wilkes became involved in a related question: Was the House of Commons a private club whose debates could be kept secret, or was it a public institution whose debates might be reported openly in the press? Such disclosure had hitherto been intermittent, and in 1771 several London printers were charged with having violated parliamentary privilege by publishing transcripts of debates. Wilkes,

An Election Riot in Middlesex (Greater London) in 1768   John Wilkes's protracted effort to enter the House of Commons prompted intermittent public violence. *(Mary Evans Picture Library)*

who was by then a London alderman, saved them from arrest, but the government ultimately decided, on the king's advice, to "have nothing more to do with that devil Wilkes."[3] Although the House of Commons continued to reserve the right "to exclude strangers," the reporting of debates soon became customary and newspapers printed them with impunity.

The Radical Impulse

In due course, Wilkes rose to be lord mayor of London. When a new general election took place in 1774, he was again chosen M.P. for Middlesex. On this occasion he was quietly permitted to take his seat. Although he gradually faded from the public stage, his followers, who in 1769 had organized the Society of Supporters of the Bill of Rights, set in motion what became a continuous radical tradition in British politics. In their rhetoric they often harked back to the "Country" Opposition of Walpole's day: they sought more frequent parliamentary elections, lower taxes, and an end to political "corruption." Yet they focused their concern less on the welfare of landowners than on the so-

[3]*That Devil Wilkes* (1930) is also the title of an informative biography by Raymond Postgate. Peter D. G. Thomas has provided a balanced and scholarly modern account in *John Wilkes: A Friend to Liberty* (1996). George Rudé's *Wilkes and Liberty* (1962) analyzes the social and economic background of Wilkes's supporters, while John Brewer's *Party Ideology and Popular Politics at the Accession of George III* (1976) sets the Wilkite movement in a broader national context. Ian R. Christie, *Wilkes, Wyvill and Reform* (1962), links Wilkes with subsequent radical reform movements.

cial status and financial well-being of urban merchants and shopkeepers. They initiated a pattern of organizing, petitioning, pamphleteering, and distributing symbolic badges, medals, and rings that would be emulated time and again in the decades to come. They appealed not only to Londoners but to English people at large to sign petitions upholding Wilkes's cause and asking the king to dismiss his "evil and pernicious counsellors." Their organization reflected and encouraged a widespread sense of disaffection with the government of the day, which seemed to be imposing the burden of taxation primarily on city dwellers. They disliked the king, feared Bute, and considered Parliament corrupt and a potential tool of the royal will. Wilkes's judicial battles helped to arouse distrust of the executive and of a legislature that, by denying Wilkes his seat, seemed determined to remain a self-perpetuating oligarchy. Wilkes's supporters borrowed from the American colonists the theme of "no taxation without representation" and applied it to the mother country itself. The campaign for the right of the press to report parliamentary debates was elevated into a struggle for the lowliest artisan's right to knowledge of public affairs.

Organizations such as the Supporters of the Bill of Rights and the analogous Constitutional Society learned how to collect funds for political purposes. Over time they also formulated a radical program of reform. Its demands were all political: the abolition of rotten boroughs, a broader franchise, more frequent elections, members of Parliament specifically pledged to abide by the wishes of their constituents, and the protection of the individual against executive or legislative persecution. A decade later, such radicalism was to manifest itself far from London in the so-called Yorkshire movement, headed by the Reverend Christopher Wyvill, which petitioned in favor of strict governmental economy, parliamentary elections each year (or, at the very least, every three years), and the addition of one hundred independent county M.P.s to lessen the influence of the magnates who controlled the rotten boroughs.

A considerable number of Members of Parliament who were not officeholders played with such reform ideas and supported some of Wilkes's causes. One M.P., Edmund Burke, then secretary to the marquis of Rockingham, set forth his *Thoughts on the Present Discontents* in 1770. Burke put forward the controversial notion that the key to good government lay not in a ministry above party but in organized parties, groups of individuals working together to implement policies on which they agreed. This notion appealed rather more to the out-of-power Whigs of the day than did the notion of altering the entire constitution. Party organization and loyalty would undermine the king's initiative by restricting his means of influencing Parliament, but it would leave the system intact. Although major electoral reform was to be postponed for another sixty years, the agitation personified by Wilkes served as the first significant sign of revolt. Some of the unenfranchised grumbled at their betters, and a strengthening network of public opinion outside Parliament, and even outside London, grew critical of a government that could act high-handedly and with doubtful legality. Although only a few self-professed Radicals won election to Parliament and to local government office during the 1770s and 1780s, such agitation called into question the whole idea of an exclusive governing club, composed of a sovereign, his ministers, and the Lords and Commons, that could ignore the will of even the few who voted in elections. The king's threat from above to the constitution of the club proved transitory, but a popular threat from below grew intermittently stronger over the years until it inspired the upheaval of 1832.

CHAPTER 8

The Loss of Empire

The American colonies in general, and New England in particular, had always been difficult to govern. Colonists had quarreled with British officials, civilian and military, and above all had resented British efforts to regulate their commerce. As early as the 1670s, English ministers were complaining to the king that the New Englanders "do not conform themselves to the laws, but take a liberty of trading where they think fit," and that the question to be faced was "what degree of dependency that government will acknowledge to his Majesty." Ninety years later, the question was still unanswered; indeed, during those years it had scarcely been confronted.

The American Problem

Most British leaders had been too much absorbed with domestic and European affairs to appreciate how rapidly their overseas colonies were growing in population, in wealth, and in self-confidence. As Adam Smith observed in 1776, "there are no colonies of which the progress has been more rapid than that of the English in North America." Yet between the 1680s and the 1750s most of the royal ministers cared little about America and knew less; and they had few experts to advise them. The Colonial Office did not yet exist, and until 1768 no single member of the cabinet was charged with American affairs. The only knowledgeable body was the Board of Trade, created in the reign of William III to supervise colonial commerce and the relationship of the various governors with their legislatures; but the board could not act except by recommendations to the cabinet or Parliament. The British government, although it reserved for itself the right to decide imperial matters, found it difficult to develop a coherent policy.

Neither was it able to implement effectively the policies that it did develop, because its agents in America were unreliable. Customs collectors were notoriously lax, and the few who disapproved of smuggling enough to bring cases to court were likely to see them thrown out by local juries. Governors were in no position to exert royal authority. Most of them were pulled between the need to obey the crown, which appointed them, and the need to placate their assemblies, which paid their salaries.

When royal policy and local opinion were at odds, the governor was in a dilemma; but the assemblymen had the whip hand. "I must," said a governor of New York in the 1740s, "either come into their measures — which by doing it may forfeit my governorship — or starve." The constitutional problem was analogous to that in Great Britain before the evolution of the cabinet: the various colonial executives were not responsible to their legislatures but depended on them for money, and no legal mechanism existed for resolving a quarrel between the two branches of government. As long as this situation endured, real reform of the imperial system was out of the question.

Ideas of reform were under discussion in London during the Seven Years' War (1756–1763) and by 1763 they had coalesced into something of a policy to be applied to two very different areas. One was the wilderness west of the Alleghenies, still populated only by Indian tribes, that France had ceded in 1763; the other was the settled colonies of the seaboard. In the West the essential problem was how to keep the peace, while in the East it was how to raise the money needed for keeping that peace.[1] Requiring the colonists to help pay for their own defense seemed only reasonable. Britain had emerged from the Seven Years' War with a vastly enlarged national debt, and it has been estimated that during these years the average colonial paid one penny in taxes for every fifty pence paid by the average British taxpayer at home.

The British government was convinced that strict limits had to be imposed, if possible from London, on white settlement of the wilderness. Otherwise colonial land hunger would continually stir up the hornets' nest of Indian wars, niggardly and irresponsible colonial assemblies would give no help in restoring order, and the resultant demands on the British army and exchequer would become prohibitive. The remedy was to close the frontiers to settlers and police the area with British garrisons at strategic points. The need for such patrolling was demonstrated in

---

[1]For a helpful study of the first problem see Jack M. Sosin, *Whitehall and the Wilderness: The Middle West in British Colonial Policy, 1760–1775* (1961). There have been innumerable studies of both the deeper roots and the more immediate catalysts of the conflict that broke out in 1775. Most historians of recent decades have given chief emphasis to a deepening sense among American colonials that their constitutional rights as British subjects were being undermined. See, for instance, the classic account by Lawrence Henry Gipson, *The Coming of the Revolution, 1763–1775* (1956). In *Ideological Origins of the American Revolution* (1967), Bernard Baylin shows how both sides came to see themselves as victims of a conspiracy. In a revisionist study, *The Language of Liberty, 1660–1832: Political Discourse and Social Dynamics in the Anglo-American World* (1994), Jonathan Clark pays special heed to the religious dimension: The English were primarily Anglican, the colonials Protestant dissenters. *Empire or Independence, 1760–1775: A British-American Dialogue on the Coming of the American Revolution* (1976) by Ian R. Christie and Benjamin W. Labaree remains a concise and balanced overview. These events are placed in broad context in P. J. Marshall, ed., *The Eighteenth Century* (1998), Volume II of *The Oxford History of the British Empire*.

1763–1764 by a widespread Indian rising known as Pontiac's Rebellion. It was suppressed, the military posts were strengthened, and a royal proclamation forbade white settlement in the wilderness. What remained to be seen was whether the seaboard colonies could be made to pay for the garrisons and to respect the proclamation.

They would clearly do neither of their own free will. To secure a fixed revenue from them, Whitehall had to devise some form of indirect taxation that was both legal and enforceable. The question of legality was open even in Britain, where many shared Pitt's opinion that the powers of the imperial Parliament over the colonists did not include "that of taking their money out of their pockets without their consent." Even if this could be done legally, it could not be done safely, for an enforceable system was necessarily one controlled from London, and any tightening of imperial authority was dangerous. It meant curtailing what the colonists had come through long usage to regard as their rights. If the British used the navy to strengthen the hand of the customs collectors, they would attack the colonial "right" to smuggle. If they transferred the prosecution of smugglers from colonial courts to their own Admiralty courts — the only way in which they could secure convictions — they would assail the colonists' idea of judicial process. If they found the means to give each royal governor the financial independence needed to carry out the king's commands, they would deprive the colonial assemblies of one of their most cherished weapons. Money could not be raised, in other words, without raising as well a host of issues — economic, legal, and political. Once those issues came to the fore, as they did in the 1760s, they ultimately proved impossible to resolve by peaceful means.

The Decade of Wobbling (1761–1770)

During the eighteenth century the Atlantic Ocean had served as a highway — for goods, immigrants, books, and ideas — as well as a barrier, and as the decade began, most inhabitants of Britain's North American colonies still took for granted their membership in the British empire. Consistent pressure on the colonies might therefore have proved effective, but the administrations of the 1760s could not maintain consistency. Ministers did not stay in office long enough to learn from experience how ignorant they were of colonial realities, let alone to become knowledgeable; they came and went as the Whig old guard struggled to resist royal influence and the king struggled to assert it by choosing his own servants. The American issue played a part in this conflict, but one that was more often exploited for partisan purposes than considered on its merits.

The events of the decade therefore left a fatal mark on the empire. The question of imperial revenue was gradually converted into a constitutional issue, in which the colonists' appeal to their rights and liberties as the king's subjects became an overt challenge to the authority of the crown in Parliament. Grenville opened this Pandora's box, first by readjusting import duties in America and tightening the methods of collecting them, then by imposing the notorious Stamp Act of 1765. The act required the purchase of government stamps for a variety of paper articles, from newspapers to legal documents; the money so raised was to go toward defraying the expenses of the military garrisons. The best political forecasters, in America as well as in the mother country, had no inkling of the storm that the act would provoke — resolutions from colonial assemblies, a general congress to petition for redress, mobbing of those who distributed the stamps, a boycott of British goods. The American issue dominated British politics when Grenville fell, and the Rockingham ministry had to decide whether to retract or face the threat of civil war. British opinion was as much aroused as that of the colonists in America, but far more divided. The division expressed itself in Rockingham's solution: to repeal the act. In order to muster enough votes for repeal, however, he added a declaratory act that reaffirmed the authority of Parliament to tax the colonies. As one critic dryly remarked, the ministers "have relinquished the revenue but judiciously taken care to preserve the contention."

This was the situation that Chatham inherited in 1766. In the two years that he left the government leaderless, matters went from bad to worse. His chancellor of the exchequer, Charles Townshend, followed a policy of his own, one designed to buttress royal authority by a series of integrated measures — strengthening customs collection, adding new duties on imports into America, and using the resultant revenue to free governors and other officials from dependence on the colonial assemblies. The colonists regarded this as a revival of the policy behind the Stamp Act, in a more effective and therefore more dangerous guise, and reacted accordingly. The Massachusetts assembly took the lead in denouncing the Townshend duties as taxation without representation and was promptly dissolved by the governor; but the Boston mob, not he, had effective power, and soon he could no longer govern. British ministers took the only possible course short of evacuating the province: They ordered in troops. Then, as if to cloud the whole issue, in 1769 Grafton's ministry retreated on the financial question and repealed all the Townshend duties except a symbolic levy on tea. Again, as in 1766, Parliament relinquished the revenue but preserved the contention.

Few on either side of the Atlantic were yet thinking of one extreme solution, independence, or of the opposite extreme solution, to hold the empire together by force of arms. By the time Lord North took office in 1770, however, the quarrel had grown so bitter that a mutually acceptable compromise anywhere between the extremes was probably out of the question. This impasse was the fruit of the decade of wobbling.

The Coming of War (1770–1775)

In the eyes of some Britons, by 1770 rebellion at home seemed almost as likely as rebellion in the colonies. North had no thought, however, of yielding to the radical critics. His central purpose was to allow the crown to exercise the powers that it rightfully possessed according to his concept

Lord North   The prime minister as portrayed in a painting by Nathaniel Dance. *(The Granger Collection)*

of Whig theory — to permit the king to guide policy through ministers who depended on his favor as well as on the support of a majority of members of Parliment. His supporters in the House of Commons included a group of members who came to be known as "the King's Friends."

A critic of the government, who signed his fiery newspaper articles with the pen name Junius, called attention to the danger of such a course. "One particular class of men," he wrote, "are permitted to call themselves the King's Friends, as if the body of the people were the King's enemies. . . . Edward and Richard the Second made the same distinction between the collective body of the people and a contemptible party who surrounded the throne. The event of their mistaken conduct might have been a warning to their successors." If Junius's readers had forgotten the deposition and murder of those two late-medieval English kings, he went on to remind them of the more recent past. Now that the royal prerogative was being exercised *through* Parliament, he declared, it was even more dangerous than when the Stuarts had exercised it against Parliament; and the remedy would surely be the same. King George, "while he plumes himself upon the security of his title to the crown, should remember that, as it was acquired by one revolution, it may be lost by another."

Junius, like so many who use the past for predicting the future, was disappointed in his expectation; George did not provoke revolution at home. He did, however, provoke a bitter struggle there, one that influenced the coming revolution in America. His attempts to control Parliament and his ministers' attempts to retain Parliament's control over the colonies were necessarily interrelated: Those who opposed one tended to oppose the other and to see in American resistance the best hope of maintaining the British constitution as they had come to define it. Chatham was indeed to compare the American colonies to the biblical Samson: "America, if she falls, will fall like the strong man; she will embrace the pillars of the state, and pull down the constitution along with her."

North had no more intention of subverting the constitution than he had of reforming it. It was not his desire to rouse popular passions on either side of the Atlantic, and in the early 1770s the crisis in America again seemed only a small cloud on the horizon. Grafton's repeal of the Townshend duties appeared to have soothed contention with the colonies, but the impression was deceptive. Troops still garrisoned Boston, after all, and the one remaining duty, that on tea, remained in place. North soon persuaded himself that he could do even more to ease colonial tensions. The East India Company, which was beset by temporary but serious financial difficulties, was compelled by law to ship its tea to England for reexport to America; if it were permitted instead to ship directly from the Orient, the reduced cost of transportation would more than offset the surviving and symbolic duty on tea. The Americans would then buy cheaper tea and in the process be painlessly taxed. This seemed to be the way to kill three birds with one stone — to make a profit for the East India Company, to conciliate the colonists by lowering the price of tea, and to induce them to accept the principle of indirect taxation. The proposal was well intentioned, but it led straight to war.

North, like most of his predecessors, was ignorant of colonial realities. Cheaper tea threatened not only the powerful smuggling interest in America but also legitimate dealers, who would have to dispose of their unsold stocks at a loss. Far more important, the colonists were quite able to discern the principle of taxation at stake, even if they saved money in the short run. Tea had become a symbol in London. In December 1773 it also became a symbol in Boston, when raiders dressed as Indians boarded the East India Company ships and dumped their cargoes into the harbor. The Boston Tea Party meant open defiance, and the quarrel entered a new phase. Few had foreseen the challenge, fewer still had desired it; but, once it was made, Lord North's government decided that it had no alternative but to meet it.

Events marched fast to a climax. What the colonists called the Intolerable Acts remodeled the charter of Massachusetts and closed the port of Boston to all shipping until the colony paid compensation for the tea. These actions had to be backed by force, and the only available troops were those that had been fortifying the wilderness. Ever since 1768 they had been moving eastward to curb the growing discontent on the seaboard, and now London had to find another way of keeping peace among the Indians and — the other side of the same coin — excluding the land-hungry colonists. Its solution was the Quebec Act of 1774, which had a dual purpose: to detach the French Canadians from their southern neighbors by concessions to Roman Catholicism, and to give control of the wilderness to the only authority on the spot that had shown some aptitude for the job, the government of Quebec. The move intensified antagonism in the thirteen colonies, which again felt themselves encircled on the north and west by their old enemies, the French.

The Intolerable and Quebec acts, like so many measures issuing from London in those years, constituted a policy that looked good on paper but had no solid foundation. A realistic policy is one that can be implemented, but the means of implementation did not exist. The French Canadians, even if they had the will, lacked the power to police the wilderness, just as the handful of British troops in Boston lacked the power to coerce Massachusetts. And Massachusetts, it soon became clear, was not alone in its intransigence. In September 1774 representatives of all the colonies except Georgia met in the First Continental Congress to coordinate means of resistance. Now that North's government had taken the strong line in words, the logic of events forced it to back up those words.

That logic the cabinet would not see. General Thomas Gage, commander-in-chief in America and governor of Massachusetts, insisted that he needed an army. He was in a panic, the ministers concluded, and really required only a few stalwart subordinates to strengthen his nerve. Consequently, they sent him, along with a handful of soldiers, three major generals — William Howe, John Burgoyne, and Henry Clinton —all destined to play crucial parts in losing the war that London still hoped to avoid. When the three landed in Boston in May 1775, that war had already begun. Because Gage's unsuccessful attempts to seize the colonists' gunpowder supplies at Lexington and Concord had raised an impromptu army against him, he was cooped up in the peninsula of Boston. In June the rebels occupied an adjacent peninsula, from which their guns could have made the town untenable. General Howe, sent to dislodge them, showed as much stupidity as courage in leading his troops directly against their breastworks; by the time he won the Battle of Bunker Hill, it had cost him almost half his force. These "banditti," as British officers called the enemy, knew how to shoot.[2]

The Civil War (1775–1778)

In the aftermath of Bunker Hill, royal authority crumbled throughout the colonies. Royal governors either took refuge on shipboard, where the

---

[2]Jeremy Black has provided an overview of the struggle that began at Lexington and Concord in *War for America: The Fight for Independence, 1775–1783* (1992). Other relevant studies are by Piers Mackesy, who argues in *The War for America 1775–1783* (1964) that the military conflict was winnable by the British, by William B. Willcox, *Portrait of a General: Sir Henry Clinton in the War of Independence* (1964), and by Franklin and Mary Wickwire, *Cornwallis: The American Adventure* (1970). Charles Royster appraises American attitudes toward the conflict in *A Revolutionary People* (1979).

The Battle of Lexington   The scene on Lexington Common, April 19, 1775, as depicted in an engraving done the same year by Amos Doolittle. *(The Granger Collection)*

navy could protect them, or fled home to England. The war thus opened with a massive British defeat, much as the American Civil War, eighty-six years later, would begin with a massive Union defeat: In both cases, the rebels secured, in one stroke, control of virtually the entire area of rebellion. Lord North's government, like President Lincoln's, had to reverse a verdict already rendered, by attacking the enemy on their own ground, evoking support from those who were loyal but cowed, splitting the rebellion into parts, and extinguishing it piecemeal. The only possible British road to victory was to take the offensive and drive it home.

Britain began with major advantages. The available British army, though small, was an effective fighting machine. The notion that rebel minutemen and militia, fired by the Spirit of '76, could stand up to British regulars in a pitched battle in the open is one of the myths about the war. Britain had vastly greater financial resources than the colonists, as well as a functioning governmental system, in contrast to the improvised and discordant authorities in the states and the Continental Congress. Last and perhaps most important, for the first three years the Royal Navy had unchallenged command of the coast. The British were consequently able to blockade, to move their troops by sea faster than the rebels could move theirs by land, and to attack when and where they pleased.

But they also labored under a host of difficulties. The most insidious was financial. If in order to win the war and maintain that victory, the British had to garrison all major American cities, the ultimate cost would far outrun the sum that they had vainly sought to extract in colonial taxes before the war began. An empire held by force alone would not be worth holding. London therefore felt compelled to seek some form of compromise peace, and hence to combine military pressure with conciliation. Yet a general instructed to fight with one hand and negotiate with the other was unlikely to perform either task very well. There existed, furthermore, no real basis for negotiating. If, on the one hand, the British gave up their claim to ultimate authority, they would give up what they were fighting for. If, on the other hand, they refused to surrender effective authority, they would preclude any compromise. The outbreak of hostilities, in short, plunged the British government into an apparently insoluble dilemma.

There was also uncertainty as to how the war should be waged most effectively. The effort to relieve the burden of the British taxpayer by increasing colonial revenue had brought on the rebellion, which Britain could not quickly suppress without adding greatly to the tax burden to support a large army and navy. The various groups of the opposition in Parliament were at best lukewarm about the war, and a steep rise in taxes was unlikely to make the conflict more popular at home. Yet a war conducted in too economical a fashion not only might drag on for months or years but also might increase the risk of foreign intervention. France and Spain were waiting to learn whether the rebellion was serious enough to offer them a reasonable chance for revenge on Britain.

Although Lord North was far from an ideal war leader, in the short run King George III imbued his government with a sense of determination, and Lord North held his cabinet together and raised the necessary funds. Neither of the two cabinet ministers immediately responsible for the conduct of the war was truly equal to the task, however. The earl of Sandwich was First Lord of the Admiralty, the civilian head of the navy. Lord George Germain, in the recently created post of secretary of state for the American colonies, made himself the civilian head of the army. Between them they provided a gift without price to the American cause.

Lord Sandwich, a rake and a former friend of John Wilkes, had had long experience in naval administration. It had taught him, however, neither strategic sense nor how to discover and promote fighting admirals; he contented himself with humdrum ideas and timorous commanders. Germain, the American secretary, had taken a new name since the Seven Years' War: He was none other than the Lord George Sackville who had been court-martialed and cashiered from the army after the Battle of Minden.[3] The officers who now served under him remembered his past disgrace, and he did little to earn their respect. His principal talent in directing military operations consisted of evading responsibility for the plans that he suggested. He had slightly more taste than Sandwich for aggressive strategy but no more gift for finding aggressive commanders. Both men played favorites and spread government factionalism throughout the armed services.

---

[3]For Germain's disgrace, see Chapter 5. In *The Insatiable Earl* (1993), N. A. M. Rodger argues that Sandwich's poor reputation at the Admiralty merits reconsideration.

Since generals and admirals were gentlemen even before they were officers, many of them did not scruple to put their personal dignity or political opinions ahead of their professional duty. Some refused to serve because they disapproved of the ministry or the war or both; others served so halfheartedly that they were suspected of "opposition principles," which meant sympathizing with the enemy. Commanders frequently asked to resign. If the government felt compelled to let them do so, they were likely to reappear at home, often as members of Parliament, to air their caustic criticisms. The oligarchy was a house divided, and the division ran from London to the army's headquarters and the admiral's quarterdeck.

By the spring of 1776, the British government had come to recognize that the leaders of the American rebellion were both more popular and more determined than first thought, and it made plans accordingly. Because not enough British troops were available, the government augmented them — as it had during the Seven Years' War — with mercenaries from various German states, whom the Americans lumped together under the hated name of Hessians. General Howe, who had replaced Gage as commander-in-chief in the autumn of 1775, was now provided with a force of some 30,000 men, the largest that Britain had ever sent overseas, and was supported by a strong fleet under his older brother, Viscount Howe. Their target was New York. Boston, threatened by artillery that the Americans had captured at Fort Ticonderoga and had carried across New England, had already been evacuated. In the coming campaign, the Howes intended to seize Manhattan as a base for controlling the lower Hudson, while General Guy Carleton, the governor of Canada, advanced south from the St. Lawrence by way of Lake Champlain to the upper Hudson. Their strategy thus aimed to cut New England off from the rest of the rebel colonies.

General George Washington, the new American commander-in-chief, decided to defend Manhattan by installing his army on the island. The decision should have been fatal to him, for his troops were hopelessly inferior to their opponents in quality and numbers, and Lord Howe's ships commanded the surrounding water. Keeping in mind the lesson of Bunker Hill, General Howe dreaded risking his precious regulars in battle; he was more concerned with gaining territory than in destroying the enemy force. Part of that force was destroyed in August 1776 in the Battle of Long Island, however, and Howe then maneuvered Washington out of New York, into Westchester, and eventually across the Hudson, all without serious bloodshed. Meanwhile a small American flotilla on Lake Champlain, improvised by the energy of Benedict Arnold, had turned back Carleton's advance from Canada. This development was scarcely the way to achieve a quick decision.

The rebel army, almost in spite of its commander, remained intact; the king's army, thanks primarily to its commander, won an island and lost the best chance it would ever have of winning the war. The results of the campaign reflected little glory on either side; yet by December 1776, British victory seemed only a matter of time. Having surrendered lower

New York and New Jersey, Washington's remnant of an army had been driven into Pennsylvania. To protect his new gains, Howe had established posts, manned by Hessians, along the Jersey shore of the Delaware; he was too confident, however, to be cautious, and it never occurred to him that Washington could be dangerous. Although Washington himself thought that the game might well be up, he had one more play. On Christmas night he ferried his ragged troops across the Delaware and captured the Hessian garrison of Trenton. On January 2, 1777, the British counterattacked and pinned him against the river, but during the night he slipped away to Princeton, destroyed a British force there, and vanished into the New Jersey hills. This was a different Washington from the general of the previous summer. In little more than a week, he had revived a dying cause and so changed the face of the war.

The British remained undeterred, however, by their small taste of defeat. Their main forces were unimpaired, and for the summer campaign of 1777 they planned an even greater effort — in two parts. One was an advance from Canada to the upper Hudson under the command of General Burgoyne, the dapper soldier-playwright known as Gentleman Johnny. The other part should have been, according to all the dictates of common sense, a move by Howe with the main army from New York up the Hudson to meet Burgoyne, but it was nothing of the sort. Sir William (the commander-in-chief had recently been knighted) determined instead to leave only a small detachment on Manhattan under his second in command, Sir Henry Clinton, and take the rest of the army by sea to the Chesapeake for an attack on Philadelphia. Burgoyne, he airily supposed, could look after himself. Germain agreed; instead of listening to warnings that such dispersion of force was stupid, he adopted Howe's and Burgoyne's mismatched plans without a thought for their incongruity.

Howe's campaign proved a thorough success. Washington failed to defend Philadelphia just as he had failed to defend New York, and by late autumn his defeated army was forced into winter quarters at Valley Forge. Meanwhile, however, the British suffered a disaster on the Hudson that outweighed their gains in Pennsylvania. Burgoyne's invasion ignored the fundamental requirements of supply: As he advanced southward, his communications with Canada stretched to the breaking point, and he could not establish contact with New York by way of the Hudson; an American army stood in his path, and American forts barred the river. By early October, he was marooned at Saratoga, unable to continue, to retreat through the wilderness, or to subsist where he was. Clinton, on Manhattan, learned of his plight and made a desperate effort to fight his way upriver to save him. The odds were insuperable, however, and Burgoyne was by then beyond help. On October 17, 1777, he surrendered.

Saratoga proved decisive, not in America but in Europe. For some time the court of Versailles had given the Americans surreptitious aid and watched their progress with calculating eyes: Would the rebellion provide the opportunity for revenge that the French had craved since 1763? Even if it did, would intervention be wise? "The spirit of revolt, wherever it breaks out," said one of Louis XVI's chief ministers, "is always of dangerous example." Ministerial policy, nevertheless, moved steadily if hesitantly toward intervention; Burgoyne's surrender provided only the final inducement. The rebels by then had demonstrated their ability to maintain themselves, and the chance of recouping French prestige by helping them seemed to outweigh the menace of their ideas. In March 1778, Versailles therefore announced the signing of a treaty of alliance with the infant United States.

The World War (1778–1783)

French intervention changed the whole character of the struggle. What had started as a civil war fought on the American seaboard became a world war, fought from India to the Caribbean.[4] In 1779 Spain joined France, thereby leaving Britain for the first time facing a coalition without an ally of its own. The crux of the fighting shifted from land to sea. There the British, thanks to the revival of the French navy, confronted formidable opposition in their task of guarding the outposts of empire and supporting the armies in America. Their best chance of victory lay in reviving Pitt's earlier strategy of blockade in European waters, but the numerical odds made this task far more difficult than it had been twenty years before. Success hinged on whether daring and skill could compensate for too few ships of the line.

The first months after the French announcement proved that daring, and even clear thinking, were in short supply at Whitehall. The Admiralty permitted the French Mediterranean fleet to sail across the Atlantic without either warning or reinforcing its own naval forces there. Instead the cabinet dispatched a commission to America to negotiate peace at almost any price short of independence, and it commanded the army to evacuate Pennsylvania and retreat to New York by sea. Incredibly, it did not bother to alter this plan when it learned that a French fleet was arriving off the coast. The government did everything possible, in short, to arrange for failure. It told the Americans, by the retreat from Pennsylvania, that its peace overture stemmed from weakness; also, it told those Americans who remained loyal to Britain that it could not consistently protect them. It ordered the army to sea, in vulnerable transports, when enemy ships of the line were in the offing. It did nothing to forewarn, let alone forearm, the responsible commanders.

Since Sir William Howe had recently resigned, the army was in the hands of Sir Henry Clinton. Although a far more contentious and difficult person than the easygoing Howe, Clinton was fully his equal as a

---

[4]H. M. Scott's *British Foreign Policy in the Age of the American Revolution* (1990) places British diplomatic failures and successes in a broad context, and Paul W. Schroeder's *Transformation of European Politics, 1763–1848* (1994) provides a comprehensive interpretive overview of Britain's place in the European and world balance of power.

**General William Howe
(1729–1814)** He served
as Commander-in-
Chief of the British
army in North America
from 1775 to 1778.
(Hulton Getty)

tactician and far abler as a strategist. Sir Henry's naval colleague was still
Lord Howe, who was waiting for his successor's arrival from England before following his brother into retirement. The admiral's presence was a
lucky accident: He was the one competent naval chief who served in
America during the war. He and Clinton between them saved what was
left of the British position.

Sir Henry took liberties with his instructions. He marched the army
overland to New York, engaging Washington en route in an inconclusive
battle, and joined Howe and the fleet at New York just when the French
arrived off the harbor. The enemy commander refused to attack in the
face of Howe's naval dispositions and sailed off instead to capture a
British post in Rhode Island. Howe thwarted him there, by a mixture of
determination and good luck, and soon afterward the French left for the
West Indies. While the campaign had produced no gain for either side, the
British were left in possession of New York and Rhode Island. The Americans contemptuously rejected their peace overture. The commissioners,
with such little dignity as they could muster, sailed home from their
fool's errand.

The next year, 1779, brought equally inconclusive results. Clinton
planned an elaborate campaign around Manhattan, which came to nothing because his promised reinforcements did not arrive from England in
time. The French fleet reappeared, this time off Georgia, which the British
had recently garrisoned, and was repulsed in an attack on Savannah.
Meanwhile Clinton gathered his meager strength for a new move. He felt

convinced that the British could win the war only by organizing support from the American loyalists, or Tories. Although thousands of American loyalists had joined the British army, Britain had not found it possible to support loyalist civilians consistently in either New England or the middle colonies. The one area believed to have a sizable loyalist population, as yet untapped and unassisted by the British, was the South, and there Clinton decided to go. In order to obtain the necessary troops, he evacuated Rhode Island, leaving the British nothing in the North except Manhattan, and on Christmas Day he sailed with his army for South Carolina. He thereby opened the phase of the war that ended at Yorktown.

Although plausible strategically, Clinton's decision to go south represented a dangerous gamble. It forced him to divide his forces between New York and the Carolinas at a time when enemy sea power might cut his waterborne communications. He knew that the Admiralty could not or would not confine the French to European waters and prevent their sending fleets overseas. The most it would do, when such a fleet sailed, was to detach what it hoped was an equivalent squadron, in what it hoped would be sufficient time, to what it hoped was the point of danger.

Clinton opened his campaign for South Carolina with a brilliant victory in May 1780, when he surrounded and captured Charleston and its garrison. Immediately afterward, however, he learned that another French squadron, this time accompanied by troops, was about to establish a base in Rhode Island. The news, which came to him from Benedict Arnold, who was already planning to betray the colonists' cause, necessitated Sir Henry's returning at once to New York. He had to turn over the southern operations to his second in command, Earl Cornwallis, whom he neither liked nor trusted. The earl was popular in the army and as brave as he was ambitious. However, he also had a headstrong nature and no more strategic sense than a charging bull; to leave him in virtually independent command invited trouble.

Clinton and the naval chief who had succeeded Howe, Admiral Marriott Arbuthnot, returned to a summer of frustration at New York. First they learned that the French had landed troops in Rhode Island, commanded by the Comte de Rochambeau. Then, when the admiral left to reconnoiter the enemy position in Narragansett Bay, he and Sir Henry spent two months quarreling about their next step. In the end they did nothing. Next came the climax of Benedict Arnold's conspiracy to betray West Point, the new fortress guarding the Hudson. The colonists discovered the plot by accident and captured and hanged Clinton's emissary and close friend, John André. Arnold escaped to New York and was commissioned a British brigadier general. Although Clinton thus acquired one of the ablest commanders on either side, he could never make good use of him because Arnold was distrusted. British regular officers had little love for loyalists as colleagues and none at all for a turncoat.

In December, nevertheless, Clinton gave Arnold command of an expedition to the Chesapeake. The progress of the southern campaign necessitated establishing a post on the bay, where a small body of troops supported from the sea could cut overland communications between Washington's army in the North and American forces in the Carolinas. Arnold established himself at Portsmouth, Virginia; in March 1781, he was almost captured there in a combined attack by Washington and the French fleet from Rhode Island. The latter suffered defeat at sea at the hands of Admiral Arbuthnot, and the Franco-American operation collapsed; but seven months later, the allies repeated it on a larger scale against Cornwallis.

By the spring of 1781, Cornwallis was turning his eyes toward Virginia, for he had had more than enough of campaigning farther south. After securing what he thought was control of South Carolina in 1780, he had embarked on an offensive through the back country of North Carolina, where, out of touch with the sea, he had to live off the countryside and hence had to move his army from place to place. He could never stop long enough in any one area to organize loyalist support and so consolidate his gains. He could only strike blows in the air, like Burgoyne on his march to Saratoga; and the earl faced a far abler opponent than Gentleman Johnny had met. Nathanael Greene, the American commander in the South, had a gift for winning campaigns by retreating. Cornwallis chased him to the border of Virginia, defeated him in battle in March 1781, and then, desperate for supplies, fled to the coast. His retreat left Greene free to move against South Carolina, which he promptly did. Instead of following him, the earl marched with the wreck of his army to join Arnold in Virginia.

This foolhardy decision endangered all that the British had won in the South, deepened their commitment to the Chesapeake, and for the first time brought Cornwallis within striking distance of the Franco-American forces in the North. Lord Cornwallis had moved his force to Virginia without consulting his superior, General Clinton, who was furious but who failed to exert leadership because he feared that the government was grooming Cornwallis to succeed him. For the remainder of the campaign, the British army in North America possessed neither strength of command nor sense of purpose.

In August 1781, Cornwallis grudgingly obeyed an order from Clinton to establish a post at Yorktown. By that time the British forces had divided into three widely separated contingents: in South Carolina, at Yorktown, and on Manhattan. Greene threatened the first, and Washington and his French ally, Rochambeau, had the choice of attacking the second or the third. They chose Yorktown, which they proceeded to capture by one of the most brilliant combined operations of the eighteenth century.

The campaign's success rested on French sea power. Admiral de Grasse, who had recently reached the West Indies from France with a fleet that outnumbered the British West Indian squadron, now offered to bring his entire line of battle to the Chesapeake. Washington and Rochambeau eagerly accepted. They prepared to march overland to Virginia, while the small French squadron at Rhode Island sailed to join

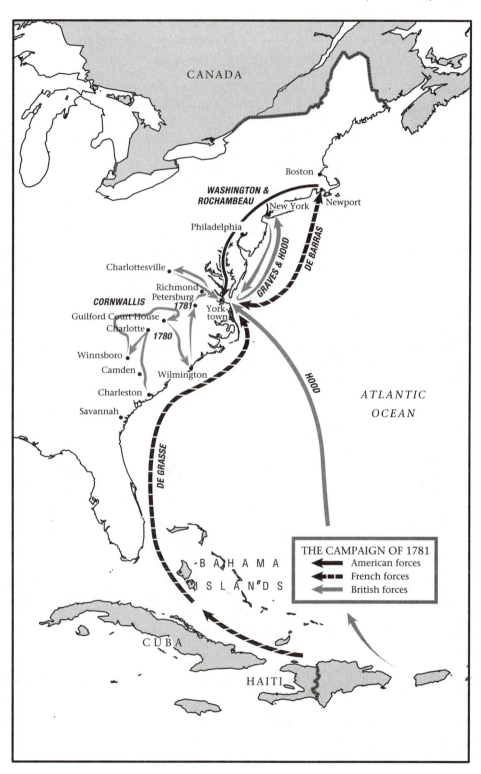

CANADA

Boston

**WASHINGTON &
ROCHAMBEAU**

New York   Newport

Philadelphia

GRAVES & HOOD

DE BARRAS

Charlottesville

Richmond
Petersburg
CORNWALLIS
1781
Guilford Court House   York-
Charlotte   town
                  1780
Winnsboro
Camden
          Wilmington
Charleston
Savannah

HOOD

ATLANTIC

OCEAN

DE GRASSE

B A H A M A

I S L A N D S

C U B A

HAITI

THE CAMPAIGN OF 1781
━━▶ American forces
▪▪▪▶ French forces
━━▶ British forces

de Grasse and give him an overwhelming superiority. French ships would close the mouth of the Chesapeake and cut off Cornwallis from Clinton's army at New York, thus sealing his fate.

De Grasse sailed from the West Indies at the beginning of August. Admiral Sir Samuel Hood followed him with what he thought — quite mistakenly — was an equivalent force, to join the much smaller British squadron at New York. The two squadrons joined forces to sail at once for the Chesapeake. At the entrance of the bay, the British admirals experienced a nasty shock: French ships came out to meet them in a seemingly endless line. Badly outnumbered, the British fleet nevertheless attacked. Tactically the resultant battle was indecisive, but it had a momentous strategic effect. The British fleet fell back on New York and left Cornwallis to his fate.

The earl still had several weeks of grace before the enemy army arrived from the North to besiege him. In that time, he might have escaped, but instead he did nothing except appeal to Clinton for help. At the beginning of October, the siege began. Cornwallis made one abortive effort to break out; then on October 17 — four years to the day since Burgoyne's capitulation at Saratoga — he asked for terms; and on October 19 he surrendered. After all his marching and countermarching through the Carolinas and Virginia, he had allowed himself to fall into a trap, and his behavior in it had been, as Washington said, "passive beyond conception." That passivity brought the war in America to a close.

Disunion at Home

The British now sought peace with their former colonies not because they lacked the means to continue the fight but because they no longer had the will. For many months before Yorktown, war weariness had been growing. Not since the news of Charleston had Britons tasted real victory, and troubles pressed in four separate areas closer to home: Ireland was in turmoil; in Yorkshire a new movement for political reform was being organized; in Parliament itself, North's opponents boldly attacked the power of the crown; and London suffered the worst riots of the century.

Three generations of ascendancy in Ireland had imbued the Protestant Anglo-Irish landlords with a strong sense of self-confidence; they had built large manor houses in the countryside and splendid townhouses in Dublin. The government in London continued, however, to appoint their rulers and to manage their Parliament. Several decades of relative sectarian peace had made them less fearful of their Roman Catholic tenants and neighbors. In the words of Henry Grattan (1746–1820), the eloquent leader of the "Patriot" party in the Irish Parliament, "the Irish Protestant could never be free till the Irish Catholic had ceased to be a slave." And so in 1778, the Irish Parliament — with the strong support of Lord North's government — modified the onerous penal laws. Roman Catholics once again could own land and bequeath and inherit it on the same terms as Protestants. The goal of the "Patriots" was to obtain a greater degree of self-government for Ireland. In part they were emulating the American rebels, in part they were responding to the economic problems that the war had caused them. It had prevented them from exporting textiles or foodstuffs to North America and to France. After the Bourbon powers entered the war and London withdrew much of the army ordinarily stationed in Ireland, the Anglo-Irish leaders organized a volunteer force to defend the island against a possible enemy invasion and against American privateer John Paul Jones, who was capturing ships in Irish waters. Yet the army of eight thousand volunteers proved a double-edged sword: At a time when Irish merchants threatened a boycott of British goods, on the American model, the volunteer force could undermine British authority as readily as it could uphold it. Irish leaders such as Henry Grattan now sought freer trade as well as greater legislative independence, and they obtained substantial concessions. In 1780 the British government opened the colonial and the Mediterranean trade to Irish merchants. In 1782 the ministry that succeeded Lord North's repealed Poynings' Law, the centuries-old statute that had maintained Britain's right to pass laws that bound Ireland and to amend those passed by the Dublin Parliament. Britain also acknowledged the independence of Irish courts. The monarch retained the right to veto acts passed by the Irish Parliament, but for the time being, only the monarch and the lord-lieutenant of Ireland (who served both as Irish chief executive and as a member of the British cabinet) continued formally to link Ireland with Great Britain.[5]

In the closing years of the war, North's parliamentary critics increasingly risked accusations of lack of patriotism. The true patriot, they insisted, opposed an unnecessary and unsuccessful war. They revived talk of the excessive power of the crown over the House of Commons and of ministers who fashioned majorities by corrupt means. In distant Yorkshire, squires inspired by the Anglican clergyman Dr. Christopher Wyvill organized county committees linked by a general assembly to petition Parliament on behalf of a reform program similar to that of John Wilkes in the 1760s. Their plan featured lower taxes, annual parliamentary elections, and the addition of one hundred independent county members to the House of Commons. North's opponents in both houses, little as many of them liked such proposals, drew encouragement from the discontent. In April 1780, a defiant House of Commons endorsed John Dunning's resolution "that the influence of the Crown has increased, is increasing, and ought to be diminished." Lord North seemed on the ropes, but there was no widely acceptable substitute; the influence of the king remained sufficient to keep him in office.

---

[5]J. C. Beckett provides a useful summary of these events in Chapters X and XI of *The Making of Modern Ireland,* 2nd ed. (1981). R. B. McDowell furnishes a detailed modern account in *Ireland in the Age of Imperialism and Revolution, 1760–1801* (1979).

The most violent example of domestic discord in 1780 also had indirect ties to the war. To encourage the enlistment of Scottish and English Roman Catholic soldiers, Lord North's government had permitted the passage in 1778 of a Roman Catholic Relief Act. Those Catholics who took an oath of loyalty to the king were permitted not merely to serve in his army but also to purchase and to inherit land. Meanwhile, an old English statute, no longer enforced, that made Roman Catholic priests and schoolmasters subject to life imprisonment, was also repealed. Parliament accepted these limited measures of toleration with little debate or fanfare, but within two years they aroused a groundswell of "No Popery" fears. By the spring of 1780, a group known as the Protestant Association held rallies petitioning for the repeal of the act of 1778. The organization was led by the eccentric younger son of a Scottish duke, the twenty-nine-year-old Lord George Gordon, who had long dreamt of spearheading a popular cause. When Parliament refused an immediate hearing to Gordon's anti-Catholic petition with its supposed 120,000 signatures, the crowd assembled outside the Palace of Westminster began to jostle peers, bishops, and some commoners. Within hours the "Gordon Riots" had spread throughout the metropolis. Five days later, according to one observer, "London offered on every side the picture of a city sacked and abandoned to a ferocious enemy."

Although religion clearly provided a pretext for many of the apprentices, petty criminals, and thrill seekers who were drawn into the riot, a pattern of sorts emerged in the destruction that ensued. First the rioters targeted the Roman Catholic chapels attached to the houses of foreign ambassadors; burning and looting then spread to the section of the city occupied primarily by Irish immigrants resented for their willingness to work for lower wages than English laborers earned. Next the mob attacked the homes of well-to-do Catholics, such as the owner of one of the city's largest distilleries, and the homes of public figures favorable to the Catholic cause or active in attempts to suppress the uprising. The rioters also burned the Blackfriars Bridge tollbooths, at which those who crossed the Thames had to deposit half a penny each time. They stormed and set afire Newgate Prison and set free hundreds of prisoners. In the days that followed, they attacked other prisons as well, along with the homes of two symbols of authority: William Markham, the archbishop of York, and Lord Mansfield, the Lord Chief Justice. The crowds made a bonfire of Mansfield's unique legal library.

City magistrates soon lost all control of the situation. They hesitated to instruct the army to shoot, lest the rioters sack their homes in turn. The tide turned only after the king spurred Lord North's government to take a stand and after the attorney general formally ruled that army commanders had the right to use force whenever they witnessed lawbreaking. After the army fired on rioters who were trying to attack the Bank of England and the London homes of Lord North and the archbishop of Canterbury, the violence soon died down. Some Britons blamed the French, others the Americans, and yet others the leaders of the parlia-

The Gordon Riots (1780)   *Top:* The anti-Catholic petitioners march to the House of Commons on the afternoon of June 2; *bottom:* Newgate Prison is set aflame four nights later. *(Reproduced by courtesy of the Trustees of the British Museum; The Granger Collection)*

mentary opposition for having plotted the riots, but no evidence came to light that anyone had deliberately planned the outburst. One youthful parliamentary critic of the ministry, Charles James Fox, insisted that he, for one, would "much rather be governed by a mob than by a standing army," but most of his colleagues disagreed. Even those members of Parliament most eager to oust North and most accustomed to speak in the name of "the people" were horrified by the consequences of popular frenzy. On this occasion even John Wilkes sided with the forces of order. The half-mad Lord George Gordon spent several months in the Tower of London but was ultimately found innocent of high treason. Of some 160 rioters who were eventually brought to trial, twenty-five of these went to the gallows — for an outburst that had killed more than 300 Londoners and injured many hundreds more.[6]

The Gordon Riots failed to topple Lord North's government, but the American war at long last did. In 1780 the neutral maritime states formed an armed league to enforce against the Royal Navy their right to trade where they pleased; even Britain's old friend, the Dutch Republic, had been goaded into entering the war against the British. The king's prestige was sinking and his adamant refusal to consider American independence was increasingly regarded as folly. The news of Yorktown provided the last straw. North's government staggered on for a few more months, with the opposition in full cry. In March 1782, the House of Commons resolved that offensive war in America should end; a few weeks later North resigned. The king prepared to abdicate but then thought better of it. His policy had been repudiated, however, as had his ability to govern only through ministers who had gained his personal approval. Defeat in America led to the decline of royal initiative at home.

The Peace Settlement

In September 1783, the former combatants signed peace treaties at Paris and Versailles. Britain acknowledged the independence of the United States and its sovereignty as far west as the Mississippi; Florida and Minorca were ceded to Spain, and minor possessions in the West Indies and Africa to France. The French had the satisfaction of witnessing the apparent breakup of much of the British empire, but Anglo-French naval warfare had been too indecisive to justify major French territorial gains at the peace table. The outcome constituted a triumph for the new United States but not for France. The French acquired little prestige, a burden of debt, and the virus of revolutionary ideas.

Although American independence necessarily created a schism in the old British empire, it did not mark such a complete break with the mother country as it appeared to at the time. In the fifteen years after the

---

[6]The story of the Gordon Riots is vividly recounted in Christopher Hibbert, *King Mob* (1958). Hibbert's account may be supplemented by Part III of George Rudé, *Paris and London in the Eighteenth Century* (1973).

peace treaty, 1783–1798, Anglo-American trade doubled. The tradition of hostility between the two countries, born of the war and soon to be nourished by a second war in 1812, lasted for another century. Yet during that time, the United States grew to nationhood within a framework of British power. The Royal Navy, after the War of Independence even more than before, controlled the egress from Europe and discouraged European states from gaining new footholds on the American continent. The United States was consequently free to expand westward without hindrance and, when the time became ripe, to acquire land from Florida to Louisiana and from Texas to California that France and Spain had formerly claimed. Expanding northward was another matter. Canada long remained a temptation to the growing republic and after 1814 sparked periodic crises in Anglo-American relations. The very fact that the crises did not lead to war, however, indicates that they were no more than surface turbulence.

Underneath that turbulence, the United States and Britain had more in common than either one cared to acknowledge. Between the Canadian frontier and the West Indies, Britain had no vital interest. London never seriously considered reconquering the former colonies or encircling them on the west as France had once tried to do, and it had no intention of permitting a rival to subjugate them in its stead. British command of the Atlantic acted as a largely inadvertent but highly effective barrier against European interference in America. Indeed, it insulated the United States from outside dangers so effectively that the fledgling nation grew into a great power without possessing, except during its Civil War, the large army and navy that were the hallmarks of other great powers. The British did not only acknowledge a new republic in 1783, but, quite unintentionally, they also took on its protection as it steadily inched its way westward into the thinly populated space that stretched to the Pacific. Just as the failures of the Royal Navy contributed to the birth of the new nation, so did the power of that navy serve as America's mainstay in childhood and adolescence.

CHAPTER 9

The Coming of Industry

The years between the beginning of the American and the French revolutions — 1775 to 1789 — witnessed a notable quickening in the pace of economic change. Such change in European history may be discerned from the tenth century on: in international trade fairs, the growth of medieval cities, the beginnings of transoceanic commerce in the fifteenth and sixteenth centuries, and the development of medieval and early modern textile weaving, shipbuilding, and coal mining. Yet alterations in technology and methods of production came so imperceptibly that the average person rarely had the sense of being propelled from one economic world to another. Britons who were born in the 1750s or 1760s and who lived into the 1830s, however, were acutely aware of change, so much so that historians have dubbed the era the Industrial Revolution.

Although that revolution involved no single event that corresponds to the Battle of Lexington or the fall of the Bastille, the metaphor has stood the test of time. It is a capsule description of the process by which new methods of production and new sources of power enabled a given worker to produce an ever greater quantity of goods and through which a largely agricultural society transformed itself into one composed primarily of producers of manufactured goods and providers of services. In the course of the nineteenth century, the quantity of goods and services provided per person grew fourfold. There was no precedent for the development of such self-sustaining growth: The process has been compared to an airplane that slowly gathers speed on the runway until it takes off and flies.[1]

The purposes of this chapter are to outline some of the explanations that have been advanced as to why the first such "takeoff" took place in Great Britain and to call attention to both the characteristics and the consequences of industrialization during the late eighteenth and the

---

[1]Although W. W. Rostow's *The Stages of Economic Growth* (1960; 3rd ed., 1990) has been criticized in detail, his concept of "takeoff" has won widespread acceptance. In the course of the 1970s and 1980s, several historians, such as N. F. R. Crafts in *British Economic Growth During the Industrial Revolution* (1985), contended that the rate of overall growth during the late eighteenth century and the early nineteenth century was too gradual to merit the word "revolution." Their arguments are disputed in turn in the essays by Joel Mokyr and David Landes in Joel Mokyr, ed., *The British Industrial Revolution: An Economic Assessment*, 2nd ed. (1998).

early nineteenth centuries. First, however, we must examine the demographic conditions of the age.

The Eighteenth-Century Population Explosion

Traditional accounts of the Industrial Revolution present the rapid growth of population in the British Isles as a plausible byproduct of economic growth. Demographic historians of our day have grown skeptical of that assumption. For one thing, they have realized that the mid-eighteenth-century onset of rapid population growth preceded rather than followed industrialization. For another, they have noted that population rose dramatically in other parts of Europe as well. In Ireland such growth took place in a society that was scarcely industrializing at all. The late-eighteenth-century population explosion appears to have been the third period of significant growth during a thousand years of European history. The first, during the twelfth and thirteenth centuries, was followed by a decline in the fourteenth and fifteenth as a result of repeated epidemics of bubonic plague. The second period of population expansion, from the late fifteenth to the early seventeenth century, was followed by another century-long period of stagnation or even of decline.

The hard data on which population estimates rest tend to become less reliable the further into the past that demographers venture from 1801, the year of the first national census. Ever since the era of Henry VIII, however, Anglican parish clerks had recorded baptisms, marriages, and deaths, but many parish registers have not survived, and not all have proved equally reliable; the births of the unbaptized and the deaths of non-Anglicans often went unrecorded. The most elaborately plotted modern estimate,[2] which makes careful use of surviving parish registers, postulates that the population of England increased by 14 percent between 1701 and 1751, by 50 percent between 1751 and 1801, and by almost 100 percent between 1801 and 1851 (a half-century for which reliable census data do exist).

Historians agree far more on the reality of this growth than on the reasons for it. Some have argued that the mid-eighteenth-century upturn, during an era of relatively cheap and plentiful food, may have stemmed from the fact that the average English woman married two to three years younger than her forebears and had more children.[3] The manner in which the population continued to grow in the last decades of the eighteenth century and during the first half of the nineteenth appears to have had less to do, however, with a modest rise in the birthrate than with a significant

---

[2]E. A. Wrigley and R. S. Schofield, *The Population History of England, 1541–1871: A Reconstruction* (1981). But see the review in the *Economic History Review* of August 1982 by M. W. Flinn, whose own work, *The European Demographic System, 1500–1820* (1981), places the English experience in broader context.

[3]E. A. Wrigley, "The Growth of Population in Eighteenth-Century England: A Conundrum Resolved," *Past & Present* (February 1983).

The First Vaccination   In 1796, Dr. Edward Jenner (1749–1823) pioneered the process of immunizing against the often deadly disease of smallpox by innoculating an eight-year-old boy with cowpox. *(Hulton Getty)*

fall in the death rate. But why did it fall? An earlier generation of historians called attention to the end of the "gin mania," better food, greater use of soap, and superior medical care. More recent scholars have cast doubt on the reality of such improvements, at least for the mass of the population, until well into the nineteenth century. The "gin mania" probably had not affected all of Great Britain. Eighteenth-century medical advances may have made some people more comfortable but appear to have prolonged few lives; the practice of "bleeding," a remedy that only the well-to-do could afford, clearly did more harm than good, and hospitals were as likely to spread infections as to cure them. The rapid growth of cities was as likely to create public health problems as to solve them.

Part of the answer may lie in the greater availability of food and more specifically in the introduction into the British diet of the potato, which Adam Smith characterized as "being peculiarly suitable to the health of the human constitution." The potato clearly stimulated Irish population growth and may have done so in England and Scotland as well. Part of the answer also may lie in the widespread practice of inoculation against smallpox. Though the actual injection of smallpox virus was more dangerous than the method of vaccination developed by Dr. Edward Jenner in the 1790s, inoculation had by then prevented the death of thousands of Britons from one of the most dangerous diseases of the age; the others included typhus, dysentery, influenza, whooping cough, and cholera. As a result of the taming of smallpox, the disappearance of bubonic plague from the British Isles after its last major outbreak in the 1660s, and the declining virulence of other infectious diseases for reasons still unclear, epidemics no longer wiped out cumulative increases in population. The consequent survival of just a few more infants per thousand people per year does much to explain the dramatic increase in population over three generations.

The process of industrialization may therefore have had little to do with the first stirrings of the eighteenth-century population explosion. Yet it had a great deal to do with the fact that, during the decades that followed, an era of decreasing mortality was not again followed by a period of rising mortality. Instead, a two-century-long process now generally known as the demographic transition gradually worked itself out. During these years, a wide gap opened between a still-high birthrate and a distinctly lower death rate. Before the process began in the mid-eighteenth century, birthrates and death rates ranged between thirty and forty per thousand per year. Birthrates reached high levels despite the fact that the poor were encouraged to marry late or, if they worked as domestic servants or army recruits, not at all. Death rates were high because a majority of children failed to reach adulthood. A woman who lived to the age of forty-five might produce eight children in the course of a typical marriage, but only two or three of them could expect to survive infancy or childhood. By the time the demographic transition ended in Britain and much of Europe in the mid-twentieth century, both birth and death rates had dropped to between ten and twelve per thousand per year. The average life expectancy had soared to sixty-five or more (rather than twenty-five to thirty), and parents of only two children might feel reasonably sure that both would reach adulthood.

A growing rather than stagnating population can provide industrialists with workers for their factories and with consumers for their products. However, a population growing too quickly can, as twentieth-century third-world experience has demonstrated, handicap rather than encourage the accumulation of investment capital and the utilization of labor-saving devices. The population of late-eighteenth-century Britain was expanding at the rate of 1.5 percent per year, fast enough to encourage industrial development but not so fast as to overwhelm it. A change of methods in production helps to explain how the Britain of the early nineteenth century managed to feed, house, and clothe twice as many people as it had a century before. Changes yet more dramatic might be required if individual living standards were to improve significantly while the number of people continued to expand.

Industrialization: The Prerequisites

Historians may never resolve the problem of which factor triggered the eighteenth-century economic takeoff. They do agree, however, that a number of conditions had to be present to make possible the onset of industrialization: A supply of natural resources; a system of agriculture flexible enough to feed an increasing proportion of workers divorced from the land; a market sufficiently large and accessible to make the concentration of industry and large-scale division of labor worthwhile; the necessary capital to finance both the new industries and the roads and waterways on which products were transported; a social structure flexible enough to allow individuals to shift their occupation; a growing demand for mass consumer goods by people eager to emulate those above them on the social ladder; and a social environment favorable to technological innovation and new enterprises.[4]

The natural resources most important for industrialization were coal and iron, and Great Britain was blessed with sizable deposits of both. Their location — in northeastern England, the Midlands, South Wales, and lowland Scotland — did much to determine the geography of industrial growth. At the same time, the British Isles completely lacked what proved a highly significant natural resource for its rapidly growing textile industry: raw cotton, soon to be imported in increasing quantities from the American South.

A British population that doubled between 1750 and 1821 obviously required twice as much food to keep pace with mid-eighteenth-century dietary standards. During the late eighteenth and early nineteenth centuries, more land was brought into grain production, and the methods of improvement outlined in Chapter 3 — planting of turnips and clover rather than leaving arable land fallow, greater use of fertilizer, improved drainage — came into extensive use. A principal technique for promoting more efficient production was the enclosure of the open fields in which the strips of different owners and tenant cultivators had intermingled since time immemorial. Much land had already been enclosed by mid-century, and between the 1750s and the 1780s, most of the remaining open fields suitable for grain growing were also enclosed. During the 1790s and the early decades of the nineteenth century, most of the remaining waste or marginal lands were enclosed as well.[5] Hundreds of private acts of Parliament empowered commissioners to cut through the tangle of property rights and, in effect, to redistribute the land to its owners in compact rather than scattered parcels. The result could benefit all who held valid title, though the expenses of enclosure (such as legal fees and the cost of hedge planting) tended to fall more heavily on the small landholder than the large. Cottagers without legal title to the land lost their traditional right to pasture pigs, cows, and geese on the manorial common, which their betters had appropriated.

> The law locks up both man and woman
> Who steals the goose from off the common,
> But lets the greater felon loose
> Who steals the common from the goose.

---

[4]Until recently, historians seem to have been more concerned with the consequences than with the origins of the Industrial Revolution, but M. W. Flinn provides a compact introduction to the subject in *Origins of the Industrial Revolution* (1966), as does Peter Mathias in Part I of *The First Industrial Nation*, 2nd ed. (1983). See also the essays in the same author's *The Transformation of England* (1979) and Harold Perkin's stimulating essay, "The Social Causes of the Industrial Revolution," in his book *The Structured Crowd* (1981). In his revisionist study, *Continuity, Chance and Change: The Character of the Industrial Revolution in England* (1988), E. A. Wrigley places renewed emphasis on the natural resources that made possible a "mineral-based energy economy."

[5]Michael Turner provides a helpful brief introduction in *Enclosures in Britain 1750–1830* (1984).

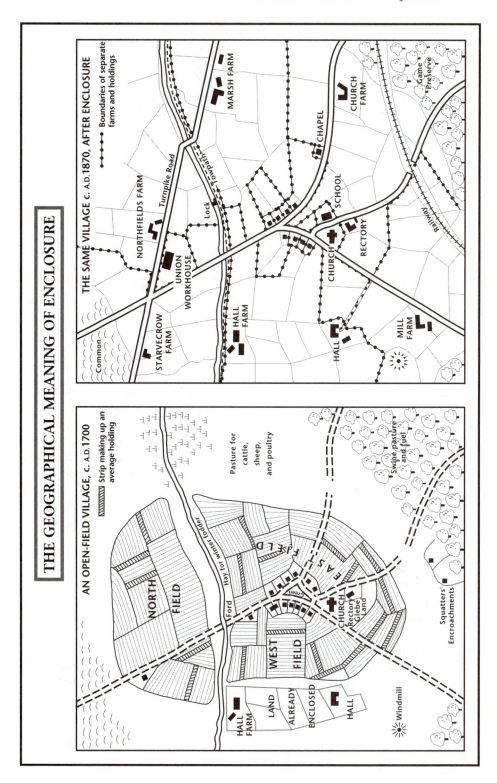

THE GEOGRAPHICAL MEANING OF ENCLOSURE

THE SAME VILLAGE c. A.D. 1870, AFTER ENCLOSURE

•••• Boundaries of separate farms and holdings

AN OPEN-FIELD VILLAGE, c. A.D. 1700

▨ Strip making up an average holding

A related phenomenon was going on in the Scottish Highlands, where landlords found sheep raising a much more profitable use of land than growing oats or other grains. The result was the notorious "Highland Clearances." Some landlords encouraged their displaced tenants to become kelpers — that is, to gather and dry seaweed; the resulting potash was used in the manufacture of soap and glass. Deprived of their plots of land, however, some of these farmers drifted into cities like Glasgow while many others emigrated to North America or Australia.[6] In the long run, in England enclosure increased the size of landholdings and concentrated them in fewer hands. Enclosure also undoubtedly helped make agriculture more efficient: The average yield per acre for English wheat, fifteen bushels in 1750, almost doubled to twenty-seven a hundred years later. For several decades, however, the amount of food grown in Great Britain did not increase as quickly as did the number of mouths prepared to eat it, and the occasional bad harvest led to genuine dearth. Outside the Highlands, no mass depopulation of rural areas occurred before the middle of the nineteenth century; as the number of people grew, however, so did the number of landless laborers, and their lives remained bleak. They worked long hours for little return, with scant hope of improving their lot; in times of distress they had to rely on the goodwill of the local overseers of the poor. Increasingly the children of such laborers strove to better their status, either in London or in a growing number of factory towns.

At a time when transportation by water remained far more economical than by land, Great Britain had an invaluable advantage in being an island. Adam Smith once estimated that eight men sailing a ship between Edinburgh and London could transport as large a load as fifty wagons, pulled by four hundred horses and driven by one hundred men, could carry overland. By midcentury, 1,000 miles of river had been made navigable so as to supplement the coastal seas; between 1760 and 1800, a network of 3,000 miles of canals was constructed so as to link coal mines to ports and factories to customers. By 1790, canals connected London, Bristol, Birmingham, Liverpool, and Hull, as well as Scotland's Edinburgh, Glasgow, and Dundee.

Joint-stock corporations, each authorized by a separate act of Parliament, built most of the canals, and local turnpike trusts that were granted the authority to collect a toll from each driver constructed or improved hundreds of roads. The typical eighteenth-century main road had been impressive only in name — the "king's highway." In fact, it was usually no more than a strip of cobblestone flanked on each side by dirt tracks. Each parish had the responsibility to maintain its roads, but according to one pamphleteer, the condition of most roads resembled "what God left them after the Flood." In contrast, as Lord Byron observed in *Don Juan,*

---

[6]The most comprehensive and judicious account is Eric Richards's *A History of the Highland Clearances,* 2 vols. (1982, 1985).

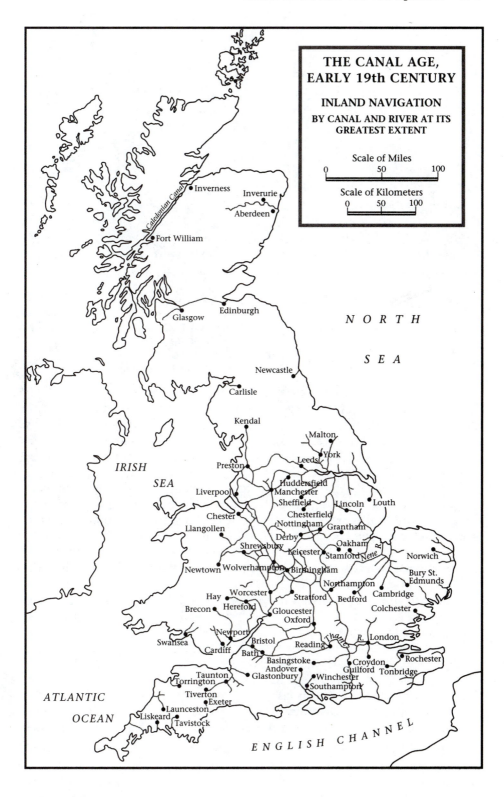

THE CANAL AGE,
EARLY 19th CENTURY

INLAND NAVIGATION
BY CANAL AND RIVER AT ITS
GREATEST EXTENT

Scale of Miles

0   50   100

Scale of Kilometers

0   50   100

The Canal Age.   Canal boats such as the Paddington-Uxbridge Packet (1801) moved people as well as goods. *(Bettmann/Corbis)*

What a delightful thing's a turnpike road!
So smooth, so level, such a mode of shaving
The earth, as scarce the eagle in the broad
Air can accomplish, with his wide wings waving.

Merchants concerned with speed and reliability of service shipped goods by road, and by the 1760s wagons lumbering along major turnpikes carried loads of up to four tons each, the legal maximum. People traveled by road also, and with increasing speed. Whereas it took a stagecoach four-and-a-half days in 1754 to travel from Manchester to London, by 1788 the time had shrunk to twenty-eight hours.

Although canals and turnpike roads expanded the large domestic market for manufactured goods, eighteenth-century Britons did not overlook the potential market beyond the seas. A midcentury boom in overseas trade that gave way to stagnation in the 1760s and 1770s — in part because of the American War of Independence — was followed by a new era of growth, as the value of British exports doubled during the final fifteen years of the century.

Industrialization required not merely a large and accessible market; it also needed capital. Funds could derive both from profits on land — which some landowners invested in canals and mines rather than in the enlargement of country houses — and from profits in commerce. The capital needs of the early factory owners were relatively modest, and in the course of the century more money was invested in roads, bridges, and canals than in factory buildings. Many late-eighteenth-century captains of industry plowed back much of their profits into the family business; others depended on a growing number of country banks to lend them operating capital.

The process of industrialization had noneconomic roots as well. A social environment that encouraged rather than discouraged innovation was essential, and the Royal Patent Office, which issued fewer than a dozen patents a year during the first half of the century, granted 36 in 1769, 64 in 1783, 107 in 1802, and 250 in 1825. Although widespread complacency accompanied the Enlightenment in England, numerous people in England as in Scotland welcomed the inventions. Audiences in British towns found entertainment as well as education in the lectures and experiments conducted by traveling scientific enthusiasts. Groups such as the Society for the Encouragement of Arts, Manufactures, and Commerce (1754) awarded prizes to successful inventors, and even Parliament occasionally voted its thanks in monetary terms. Though a considerable gap often separated popular mechanics from theoretical science, it was as an instrument maker for the University of Glasgow that James Watt, the inventor of the first rotary steam engine, learned his trade.

Equally important to the British industrial takeoff, the social environment favored the entrepreneur who was prepared to put new inventions to work and to mobilize capital and labor in novel forms of organization. English society, hierarchical as it was, proved sufficiently adaptable to permit the wealthy merchant to buy a country seat and to have his children intermarry with the squirarchy; a fledgling industrialist might hope to do the same. Protestant dissenters, moreover, who constituted less than 3 percent of the midcentury population in England, provided as many as half of the more notable inventors and entrepreneurs of the Industrial Revolution. Thus a tiny number of Quaker families furnished many of the big names in British banking and business — the Gurneys, the Lloyds, the Frys, and the Cadburys among them. Part of the reason may have lain in the relatively high quality of education provided by dissenter academies, part in a custom of mutual support within a small religious community, and part in the drive to excel economically in a society that tolerated religious minorities but did not grant them full social equality.

Entrepreneurs, whatever their religion, lived in a society in which many internal economic restraints had fallen into abeyance. British guilds wielded less power than those on the continent, though sometimes they exerted enough influence to persuade industrialists to set up shop in rural areas outside guild control. A relatively new industry like cotton could therefore develop more rapidly than an old guild-dominated industry like wool. No tariff barriers or chartered monopolies existed within Great Britain, a circumstance that helps to explain why Adam Smith made free enterprise a formal philosophical condition for economic prosperity in his *Inquiry into the Origins and Nature of the Wealth of Nations* (1776). It was "the highest impertinence" for kings and ministers "to pretend to watch over the economy of private people." Let them cease imposing restrictions on commerce and industry, he argued, and limit themselves to providing for the national defense, the administration of justice, and the construction of large public works beyond the powers of individuals.

The British government was by no means isolated from the process of eighteenth-century industrialization, but it played a more passive role than have numerous twentieth-century governments in seeking to foster economic change. The tariffs that it levied — in accordance with mercantilist assumptions — did provide protection from foreign competition for certain industries, such as cotton, linen, and shipbuilding. Although patent laws might hamper economic growth by granting temporary monopolies to successful inventors, they also gave publicity to new ways of doing things and a financial incentive to those who wished to support industrial research. The Bubble Act of 1720 tended to confine industrial undertakings to individual owners or partnerships. The government's ability to keep relatively stable the value of the pound sterling aided economic growth as did the standardization of weights and measures, the erection of innumerable milestones and signposts, and the standardization of the time of day throughout the kingdom. Admittedly, the state could have done more to provide the small-denomination coins that manufacturers needed to pay wages to their workers; it could also have imposed a minimum of public services on rapidly growing industrial towns. Yet despite occasional rioting, it did foster a general sense of internal security in which enterprises could develop. The legislation that made the parish responsible primarily for the poor who had been born there tended to restrict the mobility of labor, but the Poor Law itself provided a safety net of sorts to those who fell victim to economic change.

Industrialization: The Process

The availability of natural resources, the expandability of farm production, the presence of a sizable market and investment capital, a social environment favorable to innovation, and a government that served as a benevolent policeman — all these conditions help to account for the late-eighteenth-century industrial "takeoff." The process itself is difficult to grasp, however, because almost every change influenced and was influenced by every other.[7] Take coal and iron and steam, for example. By the mid-eighteenth century, the depletion of forests threatened to extinguish the iron industry, but then innovators found an effective way to smelt iron with coal rather than wood. One visitor compared the new ironworks at Coalbrookdale to "an immense Theatre, lighted only by the Streams of Light which rise from the Furnaces . . . the Craters of the

---

[7]Recent overviews are provided by Pat Hudson, *The Industrial Revolution* (1992), and in the essays included in Patrick K. O'Brien and Roland Quinault, eds., *The Industrial Revolution and British Society* (1993). Two somewhat older works retain great value: Phyllis Deane, *The First Industrial Revolution*, 2nd ed. (1979), and T. S. Ashton, *The Industrial Revolution, 1760–1830*, rev. ed. (1964). *How the West Grew Rich: The Economic Transformation of the Industrial World*, by Nathan Rosenberg and L. E. Birdzell, Jr. (1986), seeks to place the entire phenomenon in a much longer and far broader geographical context.

burning Mountains."[8] In the meantime, coal miners were deterred by water leaking into the mines, and the deeper the mines were dug, the worse the problem became. The solution, as we shall soon see, proved to be steam pumps, which were eventually transformed into steam engines. Thus steam helped to provide coal for the iron foundries, which in turn provided the metal for steam engines, while the coal mines supplied fuel for the foundries and engines alike. Coal production increased from 3 million tons in 1700 to 10 million tons in 1800 and 25 million tons in 1830 (three-quarters of all the coal then mined in Europe), and the number of blast furnaces grew from fewer than 20 in 1760 to 372 in 1830. The three industries grew in such intimate relationship with each other that describing any one by itself is impossible.

Nevertheless, we can understand the process of change most easily by concentrating on a single industry. The best focus is not coal or iron or steam engines or even the wool trade, which had so long dominated the nation's economy, but an upstart — the manufacture of cotton cloth. Largely because it was a newcomer, the cotton trade took an early lead in the race to industrialize and kept that lead for generations.

Cotton cloth of a sort had been manufactured by hand since the late seventeenth century in Lancashire, on the western slope of the Pennines. The availability of water provided the primary reason the industry grew up in that rural part of Britain: The prevailing winds from the Atlantic with their burden of rain, which make the west coast one of the wettest parts of the island, ensured both a reliable source of waterpower in the Pennine streams and a moist atmosphere in which the fragile cotton threads could be worked without breaking. Lancashire therefore became the cotton kingdom, with Manchester its capital and Liverpool its port.

The earliest incentive to cotton manufacture came with cloth imported by the East India Company, which caught the fancy of the British public. The Company, intent on protecting its market from domestic competition, allied itself with the wool trade, which wanted no rival textile industry. Early in the century, these powerful vested interests secured legislation to discourage domestic cotton manufacture; the industry throve, however, in spite of laws that soon became dead letters. The early years of the cotton trade went far to determine its character. It attracted men of daring, who were tough and unconventional and ready to seize every opportunity for increasing their output. They had to be adventurers to make headway against the conservative woolen interest, which the state had monitored and cherished for centuries. They were self-made men, nurtured on open and even cutthroat competition, who wanted from the government neither regulation nor protection. By the 1780s, they were already showing the spirit of what would become Victorian free enterprise.

---

[8]Kenneth Morgan, ed., *An American Quaker in the British Isles: the Journals of Jabez Maud Fisher, 1775–1779* (1992), p. 264.

Cotton producers also began to challenge the economic predominance of wool. By now they had most of what they needed to increase production — market, capital, labor, and a food supply. The principal obstacle was technological: Machines were not available for the entire manufacturing process, which at some stages was held to the snail's pace of the hand laborer. Just as a chain is no stronger than its weakest link, so the output of cloth can grow no faster than the slowest operation involved.

The revolution in the cotton trade entailed the progressive mechanization of four main operations: harvesting and transporting the cotton; combing its matted fibers and spinning them into thread; weaving the thread into cloth; and finishing, bleaching, and dyeing the cloth for market. The first major improvements occurred in weaving, and their introduction revealed a basic characteristic of industrialization: Accelerating the slowest operation removes that bottleneck and speeds up the whole manufacturing process, but only up to the point where some other operation becomes a new bottleneck. The focus of improvement therefore shifts from one to another and back again in a never-ending battle for more output.

At the accession of George II, when the cotton trade had still been confined to the workers' houses, the bottleneck had been weaving. The invention of an improved shuttle by John Kay in 1733 increased the productivity of the looms until four spinners were required to keep one weaver in thread. Spinning then became the bottleneck, and inventors tackled the problem of a spinning machine. By the time of the American Revolution, two such machines driven by waterpower — one the brainchild of James Hargreaves and the other of Richard Arkwright — were in common use. The devices were far too expensive for domestic workers, and even capitalists could afford them only if they kept them in continuous operation; they therefore put them in factories, to which the workers came around the clock in shifts. Before the end of the century, hand laborers were an anachronism in cotton spinning, and the factory system was well established. Whereas it had taken a hand spinner a thousand hours to produce 22 pounds of cotton yarn, the operator of a Hargreaves "spinning jenny" needed fewer than 400 hours. Further improvements cut the time to 20 hours by 1830 (and to less than one hour by the end of the twentieth century).

Weaving again became the bottleneck, but here progress was much slower. The hand loom, as improved by Kay, was vastly more complex than the spinning wheel; years passed before an effective machine was devised to replace the loom. In the interim, the hand weavers became the aristocrats of the trade; for the very reason that they could not keep up with the output of the new spinning mills, their services were everywhere in demand. Their days were numbered, however. Manufacturers clamored for inventions, and inventors grew ever more adept. Before the end of the Napoleonic Wars, the power loom was in operation for all but the finest cloths, and weaving was in transformation as spinning had been.

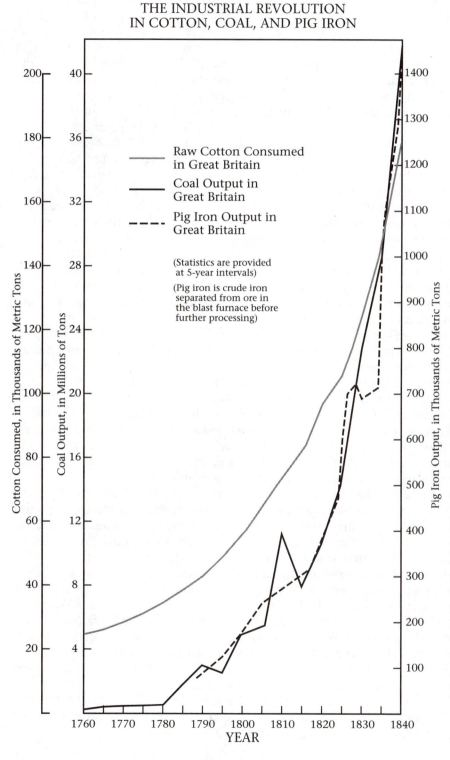

THE INDUSTRIAL REVOLUTION
IN COTTON, COAL, AND PIG IRON

Raw Cotton Consumed
in Great Britain

Coal Output in
Great Britain

Pig Iron Output in
Great Britain

(Statistics are provided
at 5-year intervals)

(Pig iron is crude iron
separated from ore in
the blast furnace before
further processing)

Cotton Consumed, in Thousands of Metric Tons

Coal Output, in Millions of Tons

Pig Iron Output, in Thousands of Metric Tons

YEAR

Cotton and pig iron statistics adapted from Brian Mitchell, ed., *European Historical Statistics, 1750–1970* (1975), pp. 391–392, 427–428. Coal output estimates adapted from Sidney Pollard, "A New Estimate of British Coal Production, 1750–1850," *Economic History Review* (May 1980), p. 229.

Mechanizing these two operations stimulated change elsewhere. For example, bleaching the cloth created a temporary bottleneck, but by 1800 chemists had managed to reduce the time needed for bleaching from several months to a few days. For a time the demand for raw cotton exceeded the supply. The old methods of harvesting proved inadequate until the New England inventor Eli Whitney provided the answer with his cotton gin, which separated the fiber from the seeds. Raw cotton then poured into Britain in ever increasing quantities: fewer than 8 million pounds a year in the 1770s; 37 million in the 1790s; 100 million in 1815; 250 million in 1830, by which time the cotton industry employed 500,000 people. By then men and women all over Britain had become accustomed to wearing relatively cheap and washable clothes made of cotton, and cotton yarn and cloth constituted 40 percent of the total value of British exports. Thus, by the strange ramifications of cause and effect, the needs of Lancashire mills in the 1790s contributed to an American invention, which in turn furthered the spread of cotton growing in the southern states and the concomitant strengthening of slavery — and so to the Civil War of 1861.

In Britain the transformation of the cotton trade had intimate links with other changes in industry, of which the most dramatic was the harnessing of power. Until the reign of George III, available sources of power for work and travel had not increased since the Middle Ages. There were three sources of power: animal or human muscles; the wind, operating on sail or windmill; and running water. Only the last of these was suited at all to the continuous operating of machines, and although waterpower abounded in Lancashire and Scotland and ran grain mills as well as textile mills, it had one great disadvantage: streams flowed where nature intended them to, and water-driven factories had to be located on their banks, whether or not the location was desirable for other reasons. Furthermore, even the most reliable waterpower varied with the seasons and disappeared in a drought. The new age of machinery, in short, could not have been born without a new source of both movable and constant power.

The source had long been known but not exploited. Early in the century, a pump had come into use in which expanding steam raised a piston in a cylinder, and atmospheric pressure brought it down again when the steam condensed inside the cylinder to form a vacuum. This "atmospheric engine," invented by Thomas Savery and vastly improved by his partner, Thomas Newcomen, embodied revolutionary principles, but it was so slow and wasteful of fuel that it could not be employed outside the mines for which it had been designed. In the 1760s, James Watt perfected a separate condenser for the steam, so that the cylinder did not have to be cooled at every stroke; then he devised a way to make the piston turn a wheel and thus convert reciprocating into rotary motion. He thereby transformed an inefficient pump of limited use into a steam engine of a thousand uses. The final step came when steam was introduced into the cylinder to drive the piston backward as well as forward, thereby increasing the speed of the engine and cutting its fuel consumption. At long last the new source of power was fully harnessed.

An Early Nineteenth-Century Coal Mine   A Watt steam engine (near the center of the picture) is used to raise the coal out of the mine. Women workers pick stones out of the coal while horse-drawn carts, donkeys, and wheelbarrows are used to transport the coal. *(Walker Art Gallery, Liverpool)*

Watt's steam engine soon showed what it could do. It liberated industry from dependence on running water; the factories did not have to go to the streams when power could come to the factories. The engine eliminated water in the mines by driving efficient pumps, which made possible deeper and deeper mining. The ready availability of coal inspired William Murdoch during the 1790s to develop the first new form of nighttime illumination to be discovered in a millennium-and-a-half. Coal gas rivaled smoky oil lamps and flickering candles, and early in the new century well-to-do Londoners grew accustomed to gaslit houses and even streets. Iron manufacturers, who had starved for fuel while depending on charcoal, also benefited from ever increasing supplies of coal; blast furnaces with steam-powered bellows turned out more iron and steel for the new machinery. Steam became the motive force of revolution, as coal and iron ore were the raw materials. Matthew Boulton, Watt's partner in manufacturing steam engines at the great Soho Works near Birmingham, well understood the importance of his product. "I sell here, Sir," he proudly remarked to James Boswell, "what all the world desires to have — *power*."

By 1800 more than a thousand steam engines were in use in the British Isles, and Britain retained a virtual monopoly on steam-engine production until the 1830s. Steam power did not merely spin cotton and roll iron; early in the new century, it also multiplied ten times over the amount of paper that a single worker could produce in a day. At the same time, operators of the first printing presses run by steam rather than by hand found it possible to produce a thousand pages in an hour rather than thirty. Steam also promised to eliminate a transportation problem not fully solved by either canal boats or turnpikes. Boats could carry heavy weights, but canals could not cross hilly terrain; turnpikes could cross the hills, but the roadbeds could not stand up under great weights. These problems needed still another solution, and the ingredients for it lay close at hand. In some industrial regions, heavily laden wagons, with flanged wheels, were being hauled by horses along metal rails; and the stationary steam engine was puffing in the factory and mine. Another generation passed before inventors succeeded in combining these ingredients, by putting the engine on wheels and the wheels on the rails, so as to provide a machine to take the place of the horse. Thus the railroad age logically, almost inevitably, sprang from what had already happened in the eighteenth century.[9]

At the close of that century, industrialization was in only its initial stages. Canals were being built and roads improved; coal mining, iron manufacture, and the cotton trade boomed; and in some industrial processes, such as cotton spinning, machines were replacing hand labor, steam engines were replacing waterpower, and the factory system had gained a firm foundation. However, industrialization affected only certain areas of the economy as yet, and much of what the Victorians took for granted still lay far in the future in 1800. Steel, in contrast to iron, was a luxury because it could not yet be cheaply produced. The stationary steam engine exhibited limited efficiency, and a practical locomotive and steamship had not yet been perfected. Weaving, even in cotton, was done predominantly on the handloom. Not until the 1790s were machines first used to spin woolen yarn as they had earlier been employed to spin cotton yarn. Well into the nineteenth century, therefore, even with bustling examples of innovation on every side — in the blast furnaces of Birmingham, the collieries of South Wales and Northumberland, the mills of Lancashire — the wool weavers of Yorkshire and East Anglia went their old ways undisturbed. They had almost as little to do with the industrial world rising around them as the gentry of Jane Austen's novels. And yet industrialization had already unleashed vast new economic resources that would help Britain to finance more than two decades of war and grow stronger in the process. In 1815 the nation emerged with a power felt throughout the world.

The Social Consequences

Historians have viewed the Industrial Revolution as everything from an economic triumph that made Britain, for a time, the most influential country in the world to a social disaster that fastened "the curse of Midas" and "the moral atmosphere of the slave trade" on society and

---

[9]See Asa Briggs, *The Power of Steam* (1982).

that in the process wrought "suffering and the destruction of older and valued ways of life."[10] The disagreement stems in part from the fact that for some historians "the Industrial Revolution" refers to anything that happened in Great Britain between, say, 1760 and 1830, whereas for others, it involves only those conditions directly affected by the growth of industry — and many aspects of British society clearly had not come under such influence, even by 1830.

The most obvious consequence of industrialization was the growth of large factory towns such as Manchester, the cotton capital; Liverpool, which was rapidly becoming the nation's second port; and Birmingham, the chief center for metal wares. Such communities all grew from villages into large cities in the course of a few decades in an unprecedented manner. Greater London's population numbered 959,000 by 1801 and 1,685,000 thirty years later. Cities that expand so rapidly tend not to develop civic amenities and the necessary public services at a comparable pace, and many a factory town became a drab and smoky entity where redbrick rowhouses stretched mile after mile about the town center.

Factory organization required not merely a high degree of division of labor — found on occasion in domestic industry but rarely in farming — but also a clear-cut separation of roles and functions among employers, foremen and employees. In the course of a generation, a few skilled craftsman or retail merchants transformed themselves into the owners of enterprises employing as many as a thousand people. Some pioneer industrialists saw themselves as benevolent paternalists and their workforce as an extended family, but in other cases employer/employee relations grew coldly institutional. For the first generation of working people, factory life also demanded psychological adjustment. The mill whistle and the factory clock exerted a type of discipline and an emphasis on punctuality for which the eighteenth-century church bell provided

---

[10]The first two quotations come from J. L. and Barbara Hammond, *The Rise of Modern Industry* (1925), one of several frequently reprinted volumes that portray the lower classes almost solely as victims rather than as beneficiaries of industrialization. The third quotation comes from E. P. Thompson, *The Making of the English Working Class* (1963), a compendious attempt to see the Industrial Revolution from the vantage point of the articulate or semiarticulate artisan and laborer. Enlightening as it is, the evidence fails to confirm the book's thesis: that by 1830 there existed a single quasi-revolutionary English working class. Nor do Thompson and his disciples explain how a nation whose population was tripling in size during less than a century could house, clothe, and feed so many more people while preserving its old "moral economy" and retaining its old artisan traditions. Another "pessimist" is E. J. Hobsbawm, the author of *Industry and Empire* (1968). The first volume of J. H. Clapham's *An Economic History of Modern Britain*, 3 vols. (1930–1938), and the books by Ashton and Mathias cited earlier, take a far less gloomy view of the social consequences of industrialization. In *The Origins of Modern English Society, 1780–1880* (1969), Harold Perkin provides a thoughtful overview. In recent decades, most historians have become less persuaded of the centrality, as a motive force in history, of social class divisions based on economic roles. One of the skeptics is David Cannadine; in *Class in Britain* (1998), he charts the different and often contradictory ways in which the concept has been used and abused in the course of the past three centuries.

no precedent. Factory owners perpetually fined workers for arriving late or drinking on the job. Once independent artisans now had to follow the rhythms of a machine. Even though the factory operative was paid better and more regularly than the worker in domestic industry or the rural laborer, such an advantage may not have provided sufficient recompense. Furthermore, although industrialization enhanced the opportunities of skilled artisans, such as mechanical engineers, it devalued the traditional skills of others, such as the hand-loom weavers, who were demoted in both status and well-being once the power loom had been perfected.

In a factory atmosphere, a sense of class consciousness began to develop among some workers, though not among all. Francis Place, the London tailor who became a noted political reformer in the 1820s, complained indeed in 1834 of the tendency to jumble together, "as the 'lower orders,' the most skilled and the most prudent workmen with the most ignorant and most imprudent labourers and paupers, though the difference is great indeed, and indeed in many cases will scarcely admit of comparison." Most factory workers could read, and at least a bare majority could write.[11] Large workplaces thus fostered the exchange of ideas and, on occasion, the formation of trade unions. Writing about the cotton industry in the 1820s, one observer took note of this sharpening of wits among factory operatives: "from being only a few degrees above cattle in their scale of intellect they became Political Citizens."

For the social reformers of the 1830s, child labor in the factories constituted the darkest blot on the face of the new industries. In the cotton mills, such labor was common; in 1835, 40 percent of the mill workers were under eighteen, 16 percent under thirteen. Some children worked there because, as pauper orphans, they had been apprenticed by their parish overseers; a majority were employed because their parents found the children's wages, which were paid to the parents, a useful and often necessary addition to the family income. Whether it took place on the farm, in the workshop, or in the factory, child labor was not, of course, a nineteenth-century novelty but an ancient tradition being adapted to new circumstances. Reformers found the presence of women workers as troubling as that of children of both sexes and feared the danger to morals as much as to health. Yet many young women found factory work a liberating experience. It freed them either from the supervision of parents in the overcrowded cottages in which lace making, glove making, straw plaiting, and similar domestic industries were still carried on, or from the authority of master and mistress in domestic service.[12]

---

[11]See E. G. West, "Literacy and the Industrial Revolution," *Economic History Review* (August 1978).

[12]See Clark Nardinelli, *Child Labor and the Industrial Revolution* (1990), and Ivy Pinchbeck, *Women Workers and the Industrial Revolution* (1930). In *The New Industrial Woman* (1995), Deborah Valenze concerns herself primarily with the manner in which some eighteenth-century women workers in farm and workshop found themselves marginalized by the industrializing economy.

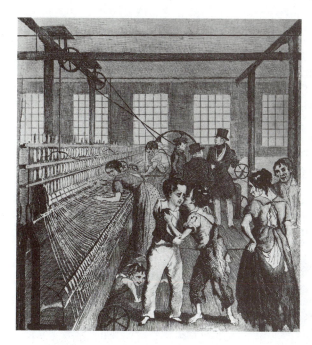

Child Labor in a Cotton Mill (1839) An engraving, by an unknown artist, entitled "Love Conquers Fear." *(Mansell/Time)*

The new industrial system did not solely drive the cycles of boom and depression that characterized the nineteenth century. The eighteenth century had also known such fluctuations, determined by the abundance or paucity of the most recent harvest. Indeed, the size of the harvest continued to exert a major impact well into the nineteenth and even the twentieth century. Mass unemployment and the collapse in bankruptcy of an enterprise employing hundreds of people were, however, phenomena far more visible in an industrial society than in the largely rural one that it displaced. In times of distress, workers' discontent grew highly vocal and sometimes violent. Thus in 1792, a group of hand-loom weavers burned down the first Manchester factory to install Cartwright's power loom. Several years elapsed before the next power loom was set up.

Although the available statistics cannot quantify relative happiness or unhappiness, they do measure the wages earned and the prices paid both for food and for the slowly increasing number of consumer goods, such as cotton clothes, pots and pans, dishes, tableware, and clocks. Such figures reveal that over the last three decades of the eighteenth century and the first five decades of the nineteenth, the average standard of comfort of the lower ranks of British society improved — not rapidly, not steadily, and not uniformly among all wage earners; but on balance, the supply of food, clothing, and shelter was greater (for a much larger population) after the Industrial Revolution than before.[13]

---

[13]The evidence is summed up by M. W. Flinn in "Trends in Real Wages 1750–1850," *Economic History Review,* August 1974, pp. 395–413.

This tendency did not operate, however, during the war period (see chapters 11 and 12), when the government harnessed the kingdom's growing resources for military rather than domestic purposes. In the years 1793–1815, the position of the average wage earner stagnated or in some cases deteriorated.

The era of the Industrial Revolution was thus a complex one that involved a unique historical "takeoff" into self-sustaining economic growth, the utilization of steam power and new forms of industrial organization, a rapid growth of population, a widespread reorganization of agriculture, and a generation accustoming itself to the discipline of the factory whistle. At the same time, the novel experience of rapid population growth and such perennial phenomena as the alternation of good harvests and bad and the fluctuation of peace and war continued to influence the manner in which human beings lived. As Thomas Ashton has concluded,

> If harvests had been uniformly good; if statesmen had directed their attention to providing a stable standard of value and a proper medium of exchange; if there had been no wars to force up prices, raise rates of interest, and turn resources to destruction, the course of the industrial revolution would have been smoother, and its consequences would not have been, as they are, in dispute.[14]

---

[14]*The Industrial Revolution*, pp. 107–108.

CHAPTER 10

A Pause Between Storms

One characteristic of the 1780s was a quickening in the pace of economic change. Another was a widespread concern on the part of voluntary organizations with a variety of humanitarian causes. Yet another was a growing parliamentary interest in political and administrative reform, an inclination that reached a climax in the early 1790s when the French revolutionaries imposed a choice on English reformers: were they to regard the French as models for emulation or as prophets of disaster? Until the Revolution in France was well under way, however, concern with reform aroused more ripples than storm waves on the surface of an era of relative calm. With the partial exception of debates over the future government of India, the great issues of the immediate past had been settled: the Bourbon powers had tried and failed to regain what they had lost overseas in 1763; the problem of how to govern the thirteen American colonies no longer existed; the king's attempt to dominate the ministry had ended with North's resignation; and after two years of ministerial uncertainty, a balance of power between the sovereign and the leading parliamentarians had been in essence restored.

By the 1780s, in London and in Britain's provincial towns alike, the number of individuals who claimed status in the middle ranks of society seemed to be expanding even more quickly than the overall population, and the heads of an increasing number of families involved in commerce, manufacture, and law claimed the right to affix the titles "Mr." and "Mrs." in front of their names. They experienced both the burden of paying the poor rates and the satisfaction of living in houses displaying carpets on the floors and brass locks attached to hardwood doors. To the extent that they could afford to do so, provincial families emulated London fashions and patterns of polite behavior. Yet the essentials of eighteenth-century social structure had not changed, and like the country houses of the magnates, its foundations appeared solid.

The Great Landlords

For the families of most of the peers of the realm, and for other large landowners (who might have to make do with titles such as "baronet" or "knight" and who were therefore ineligible to sit in the House of Lords), life could be a delight. Society for them moved with a seasonal rhythm from town to country and back again, congregating in London for the winter when Parliament met, dispersing in summer to its members' country estates. In the dog days of July and August, no one of fashion wanted to be in town and, least of all, in Parliament; men's light summer clothing had not yet been dreamed of, and the heat of Westminster could be intolerable. In winter, on the other hand, the great country houses were likely to be frigid; most of them were designed for grandeur rather than warmth, and the wood that burned in their monumental fireplaces made little impression on the chill of the rooms. Town houses, smaller and more compact, were better suited to cold weather. Yet convention, as much as nature, helped determine that yearly cycle of urban and rural life, a cycle that would continue until the early twentieth century. Thus did Lord Byron satirize the customs of his fellow aristocrats:

> 'Tis perhaps a pity
> When nature wears the gown that doth become her
> To lose those best months in a sweaty city,
> And wait until the nightingale grows dumber,
> Listening debates not very wise or witty,
> Ere patriots their true *country* can remember —
> But there's no shooting (save grouse) till September.

Comfort and hunting were not the only reasons for the exodus from London. Britain's rulers had roots in the countryside as deep as their grandfathers', but they had also grown more urbane, both figuratively and in the literal sense of becoming habituated to the city. That metropolis, with its slums as well as fashionable West End squares, continued to grow; by 1801 it comprised close to one million people. Most of its medieval gates had been torn down. The numbering of houses had begun and was soon made mandatory, thus simplifying the task of postmen who carried letters from one end of town to another for a penny. Gentlemen who strode along London's paved streets were now less likely to wear swords than to carry umbrellas. To a greater degree than ever before, London had become the cultural capital of the kingdom. This is where the great musical concerts were held, where the most exciting theatrical performances took place, where the most imposing paintings were exhibited, and where books were published in ever increasing numbers. Taste in high culture was no longer dominated by a handful of royal or aristocratic patrons but by a broader public of purchasers and organization members.[1]

Although they lived in London for a season each year, the great English landlords remained countrymen at heart. The high social position they retained in their localities was tied not only to their economic role as rent collectors but also to the influence they continued to wield both on local

---

[1] See John Brewer, *The Pleasures of the Imagination: English Culture in the Eighteenth Century* (1997).

government and on parliamentary elections. Yet they tended to be less earthy than the blue-blooded country bumpkins of Walpole's day, for time had eroded their provincialism. Many of them had been polished in youth by the Grand Tour, and they kept up their knowledge of Europe through frequent travel; they spoke and read French as a second language. Even though they might regard foreigners with the scorn of Samuel Johnson or the humor of novelist Laurence Sterne, their opinions were likely to be based on firsthand experience, and they sometimes achieved a level of sophistication that would have delighted Lord Chesterfield. At heart they were still uncompromisingly English; on the surface they were cosmopolitan.

Their taste had improved, and the change shows most clearly in the monuments that they built to celebrate their own grandeur. A typical example, just as Blenheim Palace typified an earlier period, is Kedleston Hall in Derbyshire, largely the work of the famous Scottish architect and decorator Robert Adam. A comparison of the façades of the two structures demonstrates that they have much in common: They are symmetrical, in that the flanking wings are balanced on each side of the central building; and there is a rhythmic alternation of such decorative motifs as columns and pilasters, round-arched and square-headed windows. But there the resemblance ends. Vanbrugh's work at Blenheim reveals an almost obsessive concern with variety and mass. The design has so many constituent parts that it is a busy jumble, and the elaboration of obelisks on the skyline looks like the headgear of a crowd of overdressed dowagers. Adam, by contrast, achieved his effect through restraint. The flanking wings are subordinated to the central block, though tied to it by the repetition of window motifs; the columns are concentrated on a single point of emphasis, and the moldings of doors and windows and stringcourses are set off against unadorned stonework. The silhouette is clean against the sky. Kedleston, though on a smaller scale than Blenheim, is equally monumental but much quieter. It is self-assured, where the other is self-assertive.

A great house such as Kedleston served as a hub of county society. Guests came and went continually, to stay for a meal or a weekend or a month; hospitality was mixed with business. The selection of local candidates for Parliament, the choice of a new vicar or Justice of the Peace, the planning of an enclosure act or of how to pull down a cabinet minister were discussed and often settled over the after-dinner port and madeira. The country house, in other words, was more than a building or even a way of life; it was a political institution that endured as long as the governing class endured. The leaders of that class, unlike their counterparts in eighteenth-century France, did not draw away from the countryside to the court in order to win favors from the king. Courtiers they were in season, and adept at scrambling for governmental plums, but they were never mere courtiers. The sources of their power and the centers of their lives lay in their counties, and above all in their estates.

No estate of any size could be maintained without a vast number of servants. Horses and carriages, the only means of conveyance, required an army of stable boys and grooms; a similar army of parlor maids wielded

Blenheim Palace: The Main Entrance   The work of John Vanbrugh during the 1710s. *(Mary Evans Picture Library)*

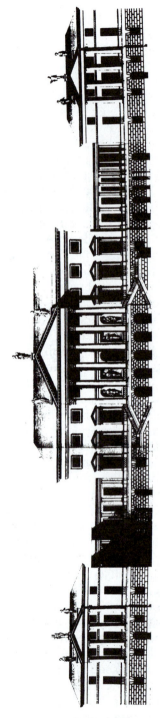

Kedleston Hall, Derbyshire   The work of Robert Adam in the mid-1760s. *(Columbia University)*

the dusters and polishing cloths and brooms that provided the only means of housecleaning. The formal garden, by then very much in vogue, needed a staff of its own. A kitchen large enough to serve twenty or thirty guests, and body servants to attend to their needs, meant an additional horde of cooks, scullery maids, footmen, valets, and lady's maids, each with status and functions strictly defined by custom, and all presided over by the head butler and housekeeper, the monarchs of the world below stairs. It was a world that the gentry took for granted but on which their whole way of life depended. These servants were by modern standards poorly housed, overworked, and underpaid. Yet they gained from the advantages, and were compelled to abide by the restraints, of a paternalism from which workers in industry were beginning to escape. For the time being, indeed, the Industrial Revolution scarcely affected their way of life.

The Religious Revival

The surface calm of the 1780s was ruffled not merely by economic change but by an increasingly widespread revival of religious feeling. In the late 1730s, a new outburst of Christian faith had come from a small group of Anglican clergy, and by the 1780s their work was having a profound impact on the working classes and affecting other groups in English society as well. No movement could have been more unexpected, either in its origin or its impact. As suggested in Chapter 6, the eighteenth-century Church of England was in several respects an institution in the doldrums. Not only had its gospel been rationalized and diluted to fit an increasingly secular age, but also its clergy concerned themselves more with teaching sober good sense in this world than with arousing fears about salvation in the next. Although they preached that charity to the poor was part of Christian duty, they felt little concern for the poor themselves. Neither, for that matter, did the small groups of religious dissenters who had survived into the second half of the eighteenth century. Organized Christianity was primarily of and for the propertied classes, as it had been since the Restoration. Its leaders felt no special sense of mission toward those growing up in the London slums, and new parish churches were not being built in the rapidly growing industrial towns.

The Church of England was not completely absorbed, however, with being respectable. A few of its members still held to the concept expressed by its famous seventeenth-century archbishop, William Laud. The Church, as Laud had envisaged it, embodied the whole of society — in Saint Paul's phrase "the Body of Christ." The institution embraced rich and poor alike, and salvation through Christ was open to all the faithful rather than limited, as the Calvinists held, to a narrow circle of the elect. This Anglican concept survived, if dimly, amidst the intellectual torpor of the one-time stronghold of Laudianism, the colleges of Oxford. Out of Oxford came the beginnings of a spiritual revolution.

The Great Evangelist   John Wesley began his career as a Methodist preacher during the 1730s as a missionary to American Indians in the British colony of Georgia. *(The Granger Collection)*

On a May evening in 1738, John Wesley, a former fellow of an Oxford college and a High-Church Anglican clergyman, had an overwhelming experience. "I felt my heart strangely warmed, I felt I did trust in Christ, Christ alone, for salvation; and an assurance was given me that he had taken away *my* sins, even mine, and saved me from the law of sin and death." Wesley became convinced that everyone to whom this experience of conversion came was saved, and that everyone to whom it did not come, no matter how good or pious, was in a state of damnation. He determined, therefore, to open human hearts so that God might invade them — to preach hellfire on the one hand, repentance and salvation on the other. His words brought a startling message to a rationalistic age, for it implied that God was not a set of precepts or an abstraction but a Person concerned with redeeming every one of his children.

Wesley thus set into motion an evangelical revival of religion. He and his companions, a small group called Methodists, began to carry their gospel to all who would listen. They traveled from parish to parish, asking and sometimes demanding to be heard from the pulpit. They held out to their listeners the choice of heaven or hell, Christ or Satan, and denied them the comfortable middle ground between belief and unbelief. They preached with a passion and crude power that left some convulsed with repentance, others with anger. The workings of grace, which the Methodists hailed, more skeptical Christians stigmatized as mania, and this clash of views could not be arbitrated. The parish clergy, understandably enough, resented the itinerant missionaries who troubled their peace, and they began to bar them from their pulpits. The Methodists then took to the highways and byways, speaking wherever they could gather a crowd. They still considered themselves Anglican clerics, but when their church excluded them, they found their congregations out-of-doors.

Their greatest preacher was George Whitefield. He reached the hearts of the humble, and they gathered in the hundreds, thousands, and even tens of thousands to hear him. A man of passion and intuition, not logic, Whitefield cared as little for theological niceties as for the disapproval of his bishop. His one overmastering purpose was to save souls, wherever and however he could reach them; indeed he, more than anyone else, transformed Methodism from a revival within the established church into a mass movement outside it. John Wesley was deeply reluctant to accept this transformation. He had an almost superstitious reverence for Anglican ritual and usages, and if he could have had his way, he would never have left the ecclesiastical fold. But that fold had little respect for him and his followers, and they were gradually but inexorably forced out of it.

Two worlds were in conflict. One was the cool and decorous world of the established clergy and the society to which they ministered, a society much influenced by Enlightenment ideas. The other was the mental world of the lower classes with its evil spirits, spells, and omens; its magic charms and cures; and its lingering fear of witches. The Methodists appealed to that world with their talk of miracles and demonic possession and redemption open to all. These ardent spiritual egalitarians took at face value Christ's teaching about rich and poor, and some of the rich therefore suspected them of being social as well as religious firebrands. "Their doctrines," wrote an irate duchess, "are most repulsive and strongly tinctured with impertinence and disrespect towards their superiors, in perpetually endeavoring to level all ranks and do away with all distinctions. It is monstrous to be told that you have a heart as sinful as the common wretches that crawl the earth." The duchess and her ilk would have nothing to do with the new movement for the very reason that the common wretches embraced it.

By the 1780s Methodism was virtually a separate denomination. Wesley, in many ways the most conservative of revolutionaries, was forced reluctantly to ordain his own clergy and — in the fledgling United States but not in Britain — even to consecrate his own bishops. In organizing his flock, he showed an administrative genius at least equal to his power to touch human hearts. His followers were mostly uneducated, imbued with what the era called "enthusiasm," and convinced that they were inspired by the Holy Ghost; hence they faced the danger of falling apart, like the Puritans before them, into numberless splinter groups. Yet Wesley held them together. Tactfully and patiently and firmly he imposed on them an ecclesiastical structure and so gave a cohesion and corporate discipline to his movement that Puritanism had lacked. Methodist life featured music — the fervent hymns composed and written by John Wesley and his brother Charles, one of the finest lyric poets of the age. It also provided rituals, festivals, education, and entertainment, and for many lowly born laymen, it presented an opportunity to exert leadership. By the time Wesley died in 1791, Methodism had clearly become a force to be reckoned with.[2]

The institution that had cast out the Methodists was soon affected by them. The Church of England, unreceptive as it was to change, still considered itself Christian, and it could not remain impervious to the new evangelism. Before the end of the century, a leaven began its work in many Anglican rectories and even some episcopal palaces. It showed itself in a heightened emphasis not only on the experience of individual conversion and Bible reading but also on the social implications of the Gospels. An "evangelical movement" — focusing on salvation by faith in Christ and on the authority of scripture — gained ground within the established church, just as Methodism gained ground outside it. A similar spirit could be sensed in two of the old dissenting denominations, the Congregationalists and the Baptists, and also within the established Presbyterian Kirk of Scotland. In the course of the next sixty years, those religious forces coalesced to help alter the whole tone of British society.

Humanitarian Movements

"We live in an age when humanity is in fashion," declared Sir John Hawkins in 1787. The evangelicals were indeed influential in spurring a number of changes in attitude and behavior — changes that were to be brought about not necessarily by act of Parliament but by personal example and by private charitable organizations.

In the judgment of evangelical converts such as William Wilberforce, what Britain required most of all was a change of behavior. Accordingly, he helped to found the new Society for the Reformation of Manners.[3] That organization derived much encouragement from the example of piety and simplicity set by King George III and Queen Charlotte — though not from the example set by their sons — and it applauded the Royal Proclamation of 1787 against vice. The monarch urged magistrates to punish all persons operating public gambling houses, profaning the Lord's Day, or publishing "loose and licentious" books. Gradually the aristocratic code of the Georgian era, with its emphasis on reason and de-

---

[2]Four valuable modern accounts are Bernard Semmel, *The Methodist Revolution* (1974); David Hempton, *Methodism and Politics in British Society, 1750–1850* (1984); Stanley Ayling, *John Wesley* (1979); and Henry D. Rock, *Reasonable Enthusiast: John Wesley and the Rise of Methodism* (1989).

[3]The movement for reform of manners during the late eighteenth and early nineteenth century, and its successes and setbacks, is well described in Maurice J. Quinlan, *Victorian Prelude* (1941) and in Ford K. Brown, *Fathers of the Victorians* (1961).

tachment and the Chesterfieldian graces, yielded to the more earnest Christianity of the Victorians.

True, during these years some children, such as London chimney sweeps and parish orphans sent off to work in textile mills with their unfenced machinery, endured base cruelty. Yet others became the object of philanthropic concern. "Let the subject be never so poor," insisted philanthropist Jonas Hanwey, "humanity and religion do not therefore change their nature; and we ought no more to suffer a child to die for the want of the common necessaries of life, though he is born to labour, than one who is the heir to a dukedom."[4] Evangelicals such as Hannah More took a particular interest in establishing charity schools for children. In the course of the 1780s and 1790s, more than a thousand Sunday schools were founded to teach reading, scripture, piety, and drill to children who might otherwise have had no formal education at all. Hannah More and other authors who devoted themselves to writing stories for children tried to replace old-fashioned tales like those about Cinderella and Little Jack Horner with useful knowledge. They also sought to make it possible for more young people to read the Bible, which new evangelical societies such as the Church Missionary Society and the British and Foreign Bible Society printed in increasing numbers. The missionary impulse, dormant in the Church of England and in Scotland during much of the eighteenth century, revived both within the British Isles and overseas as the century closed.

A number of evangelicals also showed sympathy toward a prison reform movement. Either capital punishment or "transportation" to distant colonies remained the preferred eighteenth-century antidotes to serious crime; however, by the middle years of the century, imprisonment for debt had become common, and prisons were increasingly used to hold convicts until the determination of a final punishment. During the 1770s and 1780s, prison reform became the special province of John Howard, a Protestant dissenter whose experiences as a French prisoner of war in 1756 persuaded him to devote his life both to the study of prison conditions and to the advocacy of a program of reform: the provision of adequate food, water, and fresh air, as well as an end to the indiscriminate herding together of men and women, children and adults, hardened criminals and first offenders. As high sheriff of Bedfordshire, he had the authority to put such proposals into effect. The purpose of punishment, argued reformers like Howard, was less to exact society's vengeance than to deter and even rehabilitate criminals by accustoming them to discipline and hard labor as well as giving them time for repentance in a well-ordered and closely supervised environment. An act of 1779 therefore renamed the new prisons penitentiaries. The emphasis on corporal punishment diminished, and the same statute formally abolished the practice of branding convicts.

---

[4]Cited in Roy Porter, *English Society in the Eighteenth Century* (1982), p. 284.

Unfortunately the new prisons did not live up to expectations. The money to build and maintain them fell short, and they soon became overcrowded. It was difficult, moreover, to find enough dedicated prison warders. Most Britons of the 1780s, therefore, continued to regard "transportation" as the proper punishment. Now that convicts could no longer be sent to the North American colonies, authorities sought a new destination. The voyages of exploration and scientific discovery that Captain James Cook had conducted in the South Pacific during the 1760s and 1770s provided an answer.[5] Cook had charted the coast of New Zealand and had both explored and claimed on behalf of Britain the fertile southeast coast of Australia. There, at Botany Bay in 1788, a British penal colony was founded. The new colonizers, who blithely ignored the claims of the aborigines already on the scene, had several overlapping and in part contradictory purposes: to found a new European empire in the southern hemisphere and to set up a prison colony that would rid Britain of criminals, rehabilitate as many of them as possible, and deter future criminals by the fear that they too would be exiled to harsh conditions on the opposite side of the globe. For some years free settlers were discouraged by the presence of convicts, but Australia held out the promise of almost free land. By the 1820s, voluntary immigrants had come to outnumber convicts by a ratio of five to one. As a system of punishment, "transportation" would not end, however, until the 1860s. Convicts subject to "transportation" often endured harsh lives, but in due course most were emancipated and many became successful landowners in their own right. The system may well have proved more successful in rehabilitating criminals abroad than in deterring potential offenders back home.[6]

A reform movement into which many evangelicals (as well as Quakers and Methodists) threw themselves even more vigorously than into the treatment of crime at home was that of opposition to the slave trade abroad — as a first step toward the eventual abolition of slavery within the British empire and the wider world. Slavery had existed in Africa since time immemorial, and for several generations, most Britons had taken for granted the trade whereby English shippers sent

---

[5]The purpose of Cook's voyages had not been to seek out a new penal colony but to chart unexplored coastlines, discover unknown islands, find plants unfamiliar to Europeans, and demonstrate that careful hygiene and the regular consumption of citrus fruits would safeguard sailors on long voyages from the scourge of scurvy. On returning from one voyage in 1771, expedition naturalists unpacked more than 1,000 new species of plants, 500 fishes, 500 bird skins, and more than a thousand drawings and paintings of exotic places and peoples. It was also Cook's purpose, as a monument to him testified, "to spread Civilisation and the blessings of the Christian faith among pagan and savage tribes. . . ." Cook was killed by Hawaiian natives in 1779. See J. C. Beaglehole, *The Life of Captain James Cook* (1974), and David A. Pailin, *Attitudes to Other Religions: Comparative Religion in Seventeenth- and Eighteenth-Century Britain* (1985).

[6]Robert Hughes has provided a dramatic and comprehensive account in *The Fatal Shore* (1987).

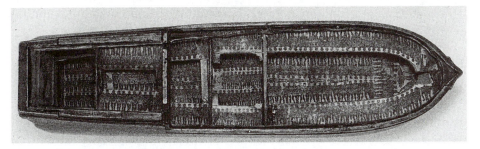

Wilberforce's Model Slave Ship   The anti–slave trade crusader used the model as a propaganda tool — to demonstrate to his parliamentary colleagues how 300 or more slaves could be crowded into a 130-ton vessel. *(Wilberforce House, Kingston-upon-Hull City Museums and Art Galleries)*

vessels to the West African coast in order to exchange textiles and manufactured goods with native chieftains for black slaves, whom they would transport to the Caribbean and to mainland North America. During the middle years of the eighteenth century, the port of Liverpool had come to dominate a trade that involved the annual dispatch of thirty thousand or more human beings across the Atlantic Ocean. By the 1780s, more than a million and a quarter Africans had been shipped to Jamaica, Barbados, and the smaller West Indies "sugar islands" to serve as plantation laborers; and almost three hundred thousand had been unloaded and sold on the North American mainland. On the mainland the black population grew, but in the one-crop sugar islands, undernourishment and disease shrank a slave population that could be maintained only by continued imports. The trade had proved both moderately profitable and dangerous: The net profit per voyage averaged 10 percent, but one voyage in three brought no gain whatsoever. By the 1780s, the anti–slave trade organizers, joined by William Wilberforce, had become a powerful pressure group. It mobilized public opinion in growing provincial cities like Manchester by organizing a large-scale petitioning campaign that appealed to women as well as to men. The campaign leaders criticized not only the horrors of the "middle passage" for the enslaved victims (of whom 10 to 20 percent perished at sea) but also the hazards that the trade posed for British sailors. Of every ten crewmen who left Liverpool, two were likely to die by accident or of some tropical disease, three were likely to jump ship, and only five would return to their home port. The slave trade, Thomas Clarkson insisted in 1788, was not the nursery but the graveyard of the British navy.

The anti–slave trade movement had won initial encouragement from the Somerset case of 1772, in which Chief Justice Mansfield had ruled definitively that a slave brought to England by a West Indies planter was automatically free because the laws of England did not sanction slavery. Although the anti-slave trade lobby did not gain a parliamentary triumph during the 1780s, it did transform a state of affairs long taken for granted into a subject of keen controversy; both the West Indies planters and the Liverpool merchants found themselves thrown on the defensive.[7]

The religious revival clearly helped to alter standards of behavior and influenced questions of public policy. It may also have strengthened Britain in two ways for the coming wars against France. First, it helped turn members of the lower ranks of British society against the avowed atheism of the French Revolution. Secondly, it helped inculate in them a sense of order and discipline antithetical to the spirit of revolutionary violence.[8] Clearly, Wesley's own political inclinations were Tory rather than radical; he sought inner conversion, not political revolution. Yet, however many listeners Wesley and other Methodist leaders may have inspired by their open-air sermons, there were, at the time of Wesley's death, no more than 130,000 formally committed Methodists in an England and Wales of more than 8 million people. By itself, therefore, the Methodist movement could hardly have inoculated the British people against French revolutionary propaganda. What it obviously did was to give many ordinary people not only an assurance of salvation but the opportunity to exercise leadership. During the nineteenth century, after Methodism had divided into at least three sects, many a self-confident young Methodist found it possible to move from the role of lay leader in his chapel to that of trade-union organizer or aspiring politician. In nineteenth-century Wales, Methodism was to become the dominant religious force.

Pitt and Reform

Although some Englishmen thought of reform as religious conversion and change of heart, and some as the legislating of proper behavior, others worked for the reform of the constitution. After the American Revolution, the parliamentary opposition added three laws to the statute book

---

[7]See Roger Anstey, *The Atlantic Slave Trade and British Abolition, 1760–1810* (1975); David Eltis, *Economic Growth and the Ending of the Transatlantic Slave Trade* (1987); and Philip D. Curtin, *The Atlantic Slave Trade: A Census* (1969). In *Capitalism and AntiSlavery* (1986), Seymour Drescher demonstrates how broadly based the anti–slave trade and antislavery movement became from the 1780s on. In "The Somerset Case and the Abolition of Slavery in England," *History* (February 1994), William R. Cotter underlines the significance of the legal decision. The subject is placed in broad context by Hugh Thomas in *The Slave Trade: The History of the Atlantic Slave Trade, 1440–1870* (1997).

[8]William E. H. Lecky, *A History of England in the Eighteenth Century,* 8 vols. (1878–1890), Vol. 3, pp. 145–146; Elie Halévy, *England in 1815,* Vol. 1 of *A History of the English People in the Nineteenth Century,* 2nd ed., 6 vols. (1949), pp. 424–426. Lecky's monumental work is by now antiquated. Yet he was a talented historian writing in a leisurely age, and his volumes contain a wealth of information, lucidly presented, on every aspect of the period. Halévy was a French scholar who knew British history better than most Britons. His treatment of the nineteenth century is as exhaustive as Lecky's treatment of the eighteenth, and his judgments are always interesting and often provocative. In our own time, E. P. Thompson, in *The Making of the English Working Class* (1963), has interpreted Methodism as fundamentally conservative, but see Eric Hobsbawm, "Methodism and the Threat of Revolution" in *Laboring Men* (1964).

designed to lessen the influence of the crown — the executive branch of the government — on the makeup of the House of Commons: The new legislation disenfranchised customs and excise officers, ruled government contractors ineligible for election to Parliament, and abolished numerous sinecure positions through which the ministry had long influenced members of the House of Commons. These measures exerted some effect: They helped to persuade future ministries to give political rewards in the form of honors rather than of patronage positions and also to replace gentlemanly amateurs with professional civil servants. What did yet more to curtail royal influence was the emergence of a leader who proved so knowledgeable and conscientious an administrator that the king was increasingly willing to leave day-to-day details in his hands.

In December 1783, after a year and a half of ministerial turmoil following the fall of Lord North, the king called on William Pitt, the second son of the earl of Chatham, to head his government. Already a seasoned politician at the age of twenty-four, Pitt had a gift for using the support of the crown without becoming its tool. He also proved a superb administrator who had as shrewd a head for finance as Walpole himself and a greater taste for experimenting. The experiments primarily involved attempts to liberalize commercial policy, as well as measures to improve Britain's antiquated fiscal system. That system, at the end of the War of the American Revolution, seemed in dire straits; the national debt stood at £240 million, sixteen times the government's annual revenue. Even peacetime budgets remained unbalanced, and over half of each year's income was paid out in the form of interest payments on the debt.

In his commercial policy, Pitt was influenced by Adam Smith, the pioneer Scottish economist, whose *Wealth of Nations* had publicized the doctrine that unfettered private enterprise generally operates to the public good. The wealth of a nation rested on the production of consumable goods, Smith argued, and the way to increase production was to leave each producer of goods or services "free to pursue his own interest his own way." Furthermore, the machinery of governmental regulation created over the years ought to be dismantled, and state interference be limited to those areas, such as education and public works, that could not be supported by private capital alone. Because Smith also emphasized national defense and hence sea power, he commended the Navigation Acts that were designed to encourage the British merchant marine at the cost of foreign competitors. With this exception, nonetheless, he believed that the rule in commerce, as in industry, should be uninhibited competition. His book laid the foundations of early-nineteenth-century "classical economics," with its doctrines of laissez-faire at home and free trade abroad. Pitt, though he was a practical politician rather than a theoretical economist, stood ready to experiment in accordance with Smith's teachings.

The first experiment, to reduce tariffs between Britain and Ireland, proved unsuccessful. The Dublin Parliament had recently regained a high degree of legislative independence and the right to export Irish glass and woolen goods to Great Britain and the British Empire. Pitt hoped to

William Pitt the Younger Addresses the House of Commons   Detail of a painting by Karl Anton Hickel. *(The Granger Collection)*

continue the process of conciliation by agreements that would amount to a commercial union. But a complex of forces worked against him. Now that Irish manufacturers had begun to recover from the doldrums of the early Hanoverian era, conservative British industrial interests dreaded to see the domestic market flooded with Irish goods. Pitt's political opponents made the most of these fears and also stirred the apprehensions of the Irish that commercial union would subvert their newly won political autonomy. The prime minister abandoned his measure, and a significant opportunity to improve Anglo-Irish relations was lost.

Pitt remained undiscouraged. In the following year, 1786, he opened negotiations for a treaty with France to effect a mutual reduction of tariffs. This overture to Britain's oldest, most inveterate, rival showed both his courage and his clear-sightedness. "To suppose that any nation can be unalterably the enemy of another," he said, "is weak and childish. . . . It is a libel on the constitution of political societies, and supposes the existence of diabolical malice in the original frame of man." He had to contend with the "weak and childish" not only in Parliament but also among leaders of the older industries, such as the wool trade, that protection had nourished. Such industrialists formed a pressure group, known as the General Chamber of Manufacturers, to impress on the business world that the principle behind the treaty was one of "serious and awful importance . . . comprehending a prodigious change in the commercial system of this country."

Nevertheless, Pitt found influential allies among leaders in the new industries, who believed, as he did, that the treaty would benefit both sides. France exported primarily such products as wine, they argued, which did not compete with British manufactured goods; an agreement between the two nations would be mutually profitable and would usher in an era of good feeling. When Pitt succeeded in concluding the agreement, known from the name of his chief negotiator as the Eden Treaty of 1786, the point was illustrated by a jingle celebrating the occasion.

> May kingdom 'gainst kingdom no more be at spite;
> For both 'twere much better to trade than to fight;
> And whilst mutual friendship and harmony reign
> Our buttons we'll barter for pipes of champagne.

Pitt's economic reforms were not confined to the Eden Treaty; in fact, those he made at home proved more important because they lasted longer.[9] He attacked smuggling by reducing and simplifying import duties, and he increased the government's revenues by extending the excise (as Walpole had tried and failed to do) to tobacco, wines, and other articles on which smugglers had hitherto made their profit.[10] He improved the tax structure, abolished numerous sinecures, established a Consolidated Fund in which all revenues were deposited and from which all governmental expenses were paid, and created the so-called Sinking Fund, which he hoped would eventually yield enough interest to pay off the public debt. Although this last experiment failed, the others met with success. Pitt did more than anyone else in the eighteenth century to curb bureaucratic fraud and bring order and efficiency into the finances of the state, and he accomplished his goals in the nick of time. Although such reforms bore little relation to the work of either the new manufacturers or the humanitarian reformers, Pitt, like them, was strengthening the nation for the ordeal to come.

In other areas Pitt's efforts at improvement were halfhearted and unsuccessful. In 1785 he proposed reforming the House of Commons by gradually abolishing a number of rotten boroughs. When he encountered strong parliamentary opposition and found that even his eloquence could not arouse a lethargic public, however, he abandoned his measure. Three years later, he championed the movement led by his close friend, William Wilberforce, to wipe out the slave trade throughout the empire. Pitt denounced the trade as a "noxious plant . . . under whose shade

---

[9]The Eden Treaty vanished, like much of the rest of the eighteenth-century world, in the explosion of the French Revolution. Between 1785 and 1793 Pitt made numerous unsuccessful attempts to secure similar treaties with other powers; see John Ehrman, *The British Government and Commercial Negotiations with Europe, 1783–1793* (1962), and, for all aspects of the domestic and foreign policy of those years, see Ehrman's three-volume *The Younger Pitt* (1969, 1983, 1996). Derek Jarrett, *Pitt the Younger* (1974), provides a stimulating brief introduction to the man and the era. L. G. Mitchell's *Fox* (1992) is a lucid and scholarly account of Pitt's great political rival.

[10]For Walpole's failure to extend the excise, see Chapter 4.

**Charles James Fox
(1749–1806)** William
Pitt's great parliamentary
rival in the late eighteenth
century. *(The Granger
Collection)*

nothing that is useful or profitable to Africa will ever flourish or take
root." Yet he had no wish to stake the future of his ministry on the measure; when it failed to attract a parliamentary majority, he let it drop. Pitt
was no crusader. The stability and continuity of his ministry meant more
to him than did a campaign for causes that the king and a majority of the
House of Commons found unappealing.

Pitt's character stood squarely at odds with that of his great rival,
Charles James Fox. Fox, who had entered Parliament a decade before Pitt,
had become one of the most vocal of North's opponents during the American war and one of the most inveterate enemies of royal influence.
George III had developed a strong animosity toward Fox's father, a leading politician of the early 1760s, and he readily transferred that dislike to
the son. Fox, in turn, spoke in private of the king as a "blockhead" and
even as "Satan," and he insulted the king publicly by proposing a toast to
"His Majesty — the People." The king detested Fox in turn not merely
because of his politics and reputation as a rake, but also because his
friendship with the king's eldest son, the Prince of Wales, seemed to encourage that young man's rebellion against parental authority. For a time
in 1782 and 1783, the king felt compelled to accept Fox as a minister; but
thereafter, for more than two decades, royal influence kept Fox out of of-

fice. On a number of public issues, Pitt and Fox thought alike: They both believed that the American war had been a mistake; they wanted to reform Parliament, end the slave trade, and conciliate the Irish; they were experts in the thrust and parry of debate and had earned renown as powerful orators. Their personalities differed sharply, however. Pitt wrapped himself in a lofty and austere virtue and never unbent except to a few intimates. He saw himself as a professional administrator, hard-working and incorruptible, who won from his contemporaries vast respect and little love. Fox was just the opposite. He embraced great causes, often with more passion than wisdom; he loved conviviality; he drank and gambled excessively and with gusto; he threw himself into the political battle with everything he had and yet retained enough sense of humor to feel unembittered when victory time and again eluded him. Although in his long career he never achieved more than momentary power, he may have garnered more affection than any other man in the history of Parliament. He was big, both in girth and in personality, and what a friend called his "negligent grandeur" left its mark on the age.

Empire in India

One of Pitt's major achievements was to find an answer to the question of how to govern India. Ever since the Seven Years' War, that dilemma had increasingly plagued British politics, as the East India Company had become more and more deeply involved in the affairs of the native princes. Political involvement remained as far removed as ever from the intent of India House, the Company's headquarters in London, for the directors still focused their interest on trading, not governing. Yet their own servants forced their hands. The men on the spot realized that only by assuming political power could they safeguard trade, and they carried on the process begun during the Seven Years' War of transforming the Company into a sovereign state. By the time Robert Clive left India in 1767, the Company had establishments at Bombay on the west coast and Madras and its environs on the southeast coast; and, most important, it had become the paramount power in Bengal, the area around Calcutta in northeastern India. There it held extensive territory and controlled, through native puppets, the revenue of the entire province. Bengal formed the cornerstone of the empire that India House was somewhat reluctantly acquiring.

The government at home could not long remain indifferent to events. Company officials, Clive among them, returned home with great wealth gained by dubious means. These "nabobs," strutting their way through British society, aroused both anger and envy — anger because they were accused, often with good reason, of having shamelessly exploited the natives; envy because the golden fruits of exploitation seemed reserved for only those servants of India House who demonstrated both the willingness to take risks in India and the luck to survive their stay there. Two factors combined, in other words, to attract the attention of Parliament: the moralist's desire to ensure at least some minimal standards of good government in Bengal, and the politician's desire to share in the Company's vast and growing patronage.

Lord North attacked the problem in his Regulating Act of 1773, the first clear assertion of Parliament's supremacy over India House. The act created a governor-general in Bengal, gave him authority over Bombay and Madras, provided him with a council, named the governor-general and the councillors for the next five years, and settled on them handsome salaries to be paid by the Company. This attempt to solve the problem had serious drawbacks. It made the directors of the Company responsible for agents whom they had not chosen. Moreover, it set up a governor-general only to limit his powers and to give him but a single vote in a governing council of five. The arrangement proved so cumbersome that only a genius could have made it work at all.

The Company's service produced such a man. For the next twelve years, Warren Hastings, one of the great proconsuls in the history of empire, served as governor-general. During the crisis occasioned by the American War of Independence, when Britain fought with its back to the wall and the French stirred up trouble throughout India, Hastings almost single-handedly saved the Company and extended its power. His chief enemy was neither French nor Hindu but one of his own councillors, Philip Francis, a man with vast ambition and a program of his own. The Company should continue to rule Bengal, Francis believed, without responsibility for justice or effective administration or anything but moneymaking, and should leave the rest of India to its own devices. Hastings, in contrast, felt convinced that the Company must become the paramount power in the whole subcontinent, ruling directly in Bengal through a governor-general with centralized authority, and indirectly elsewhere through princely dependents and allies. In Hastings's view, the Company must slowly permeate the whole complex of native institutions with British concepts of justice and good government. Francis worked to limit British responsibilities, Hastings to create a new order.[11]

Hastings persuaded his colleagues, by methods less than scrupulous, to agree to his policies; consequently, in 1780 Francis left for home to engineer his revenge. By then Hastings was at war against a coalition of princes in central India who, induced by French intrigue and their growing fear of the Company, decided to do what they had never done before: unite to drive out the British. They almost succeeded. Hastings's small

---

[11]Even Hastings was far from envisaging the way in which the new order would develop. For a vivid sketch of him see Philip Woodruff, *The Men Who Ruled India: The Founders* (1954), pp. 122–132. This volume, the first of two, deals with the period from 1600 to 1858; it is an unorthodox collection of portraits of men who served the Company, famous and obscure, good and bad, by an author who, prior to Indian independence, had himself had a distinguished career in the Indian civil service. He became familiar at first hand with the kinds of problems that his predecessors had faced, and he describes them with a freshness and professional appreciation that most historians lack.

armies of sepoys — Indian natives employed as soldiers — were overwhelmingly outnumbered, and he was so desperate for money that he resorted to what his enemies regarded as high-handed extortion. Yet by a mixture of hard fighting and shrewd diplomacy, he managed to break up the coalition, and the advent of peace in Europe saved him in the nick of time from a French naval threat. By 1784 his work was done, and in India the position of the Company had grown stronger than ever before.

But in Britain its position came under attack. Recent events had made clear that North's Regulating Act left room for great irregularities, and rumor painted Hastings as a monster of rapacity. India House was split by factions, each of which had parliamentary support; also, the quarrels in London had their parallels in Bombay, Madras, and Calcutta. Both the Company and its governor-general needed surveillance by the state, but how would this be achieved? If the Company lost all power to appoint officials in India, who would appoint them? The obvious answer lay in the crown. However, Whig politicians like Fox, who had long fought the king's influence, had no intention of giving him such a vast increase in patronage. For Parliament itself to appoint, as it had in 1773, would turn the Company's service into a grab bag for politicians.

It was difficult also to come up with a way of ruling India that did not make use of an autonomous governor-general. Whigs like Charles James Fox might dislike the idea of concentrating power in a single executive, but government by council had proved ineffective. Such a governor-general would have to have considerable leeway also because of the difficulty of communication; on occasion it took as long as a year to send a dispatch from London to Calcutta and to receive a response. Even if Hastings himself might deserve to be called to account, the power of his office could not be impaired.

Pitt met the problem by dividing authority at home between the Company and the government and by demarcating the relationship between London and Calcutta. His India Act of 1784 created the pattern of British rule for the next seventy-four years and proved as much a constitutional landmark as Hastings's governorship had been a political landmark. In essence the new system established a partnership between the Company and the state: The former continued to direct commercial affairs, and the latter took responsibility for governmental affairs. A board of control, composed in part of cabinet ministers, was set up in London; to it the Company directors submitted proposals for political or military action, and from it they received their orders. The Company appointed all officials except the highest, but the board had power to remove them. The crown named the governor-general, to whom Bombay and Madras were subordinated, and he was soon made commander-in-chief and empowered to override his council. The plan thus established a mixed authority. The Company retained a sphere of action and its patronage, the government assumed responsibility for Indian administration, and the governor-general acquired the executive authority that he needed.

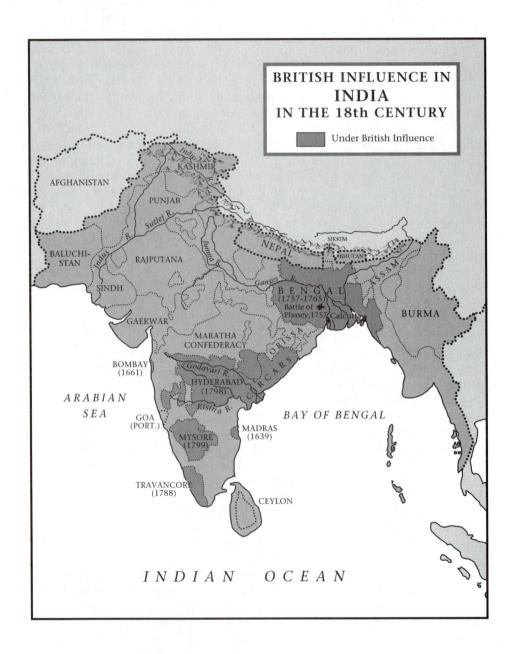

BRITISH INFLUENCE IN
INDIA
IN THE 18th CENTURY

Under British Influence

Although the India Act shaped a new future, it also tried to perpetuate the past by clauses that condemned territorial conquest and intervention in the affairs of the native states. Hastings correctly interpreted these as reflecting on his policy, so in 1785 he resigned and came home. Three years later he was impeached for misconduct as governor-general. Philip Francis had poisoned the minds of Edmund Burke and others in Parliament, until they saw in Hastings the epitome of all the evil, extortion, and ruthlessness that had stained British rule for generations. He was the scapegoat more than the epitome, for he had committed fewer and more venial sins than most of his predecessors while fighting against heavier odds, but even he was not above reproach. For seven years his trial dragged on, draining his fortune, until at last he was acquitted on every count.

He deserved vindication, but his impeachment was more significant than the rights and wrongs of the charges against him. For many years the conduct of the Company's servants had troubled even the tough consciences of British politicians, who were coming to realize slowly and grudgingly that political authority in India entailed responsibilities to the governed. The state, now that it had assumed the authority, could not in honor shirk the responsibilities and join in the game of exploitation. Burke persuaded himself that Hastings had done exactly that and should be called to account for it. "I impeach him," he said in closing his indictment, "in the name of all the commons of Great Britain, whose national character he has dishonored. I impeach him in the name of the people of India, whose laws, rights, and liberties he has subverted. . . . I impeach him in the name and by the virtue of those eternal laws of justice which he has violated."[12]

The charge was as intemperate as the oratory suggests, and the victim unfairly selected, but the underlying idea was valid. A principle cannot be judged by the use to which it is put, for good causes frequently lead to mistaken persecutions. Burke, for all his partisan blindness, could at least see that the crown, in assuming a new role, had also acquired a new duty — to provide a framework of order within which the Indians could enjoy their "laws, rights, and liberties."

The India of the nineteenth century was already beginning to take shape. Britain, on the way to becoming the major power of the subcontinent, was developing a form of rule that was at best paternalistic but that remained in essence dictatorial. Although such a concept of sovereignty might seem anachronistic at the end of the eighteenth century, Hindus and Moslems were unacquainted with representative institutions or with constitutional curbs on executive power. British rule significantly improved the prospects for peace on the subcontinent and therefore a lessening of oppression and bloodshed. In due course, it also reduced governmental inefficiency and corruption.

As Indians adapted to the British and the British to them, the effect on both sides was profound. The new rulers from the west broke out of

---

[12]In *Edmund Burke and India: Political Morality and Empire* (1997), Frederick G. Whelan assesses the conflicts of principle involved in Burke's impassioned political campaign.

A Briton in India   He is seen wearing Indian dress, smoking a hookah (a pipe attached to a long flexible tube), and watching an exhibition by Indian dancing-girls. *(India Office Library/The Bridgman Art Library, London)*

the constitutional traditions of their own land and adopted a form of autocratic paternalism that appeared to work in an alien culture. In the course of the nineteenth century, as British influence spread, they continued to learn by trial and error, even as some Indians in turn began to learn from them novel ideas about liberty and parliament and nationhood, ideas that were in due course to undermine that same British rule.

British dominion rested from beginning to end on the Indians themselves. They provided the sepoys, the soldiers of the army, by which first the Company and then the British crown acquired military predominance — thereby making India the outstanding example in modern history of a country subdued, administered, and policed by its own inhabitants on behalf of rule by a foreign state. The importance of the sepoys, however, did not end there. They eventually became the means of British expansion outside India, and even a factor in the power politics of Europe. Until the First World War, Britain never maintained at home a military force comparable with those of its European rivals, but in India it did; and the Indian army strengthened Britain's hand in international affairs. Danger to India or to the Indian sea routes always touched a sensitive nerve in London, for a threat to the raj was a threat to the heart of Britain's imperial position.

When Hastings was acquitted, much of India had not yet come under direct or even indirect British control. However, the elimination of the

French and the weakening of the princes had prepared the way. Even though those old enemies were not yet ready to admit defeat and crises aplenty lay ahead, the means of weathering crises lay at hand in the sepoys and in a workable system of government. Moreover, a new sense of responsibility, in London and Calcutta, ensured that the worst exploitation had ended and that in the future, power would be used soberly. The foundations of the nineteenth-century empire were securely laid.[13]

Conclusion

The 1780s foreshadowed in many other respects the world of the nineteenth century. The nature of government was changing: Pitt was modernizing the fiscal system and experimenting with new economic policies; and the king, as his prime minister gained firmer control, was gradually yielding the center of the political stage. Great aristocrats still dominated local and national affairs from their country palaces and the House of Lords and had reached the peak of their sophistication and splendor, but it was the splendor of approaching sunset. Land no longer provided the primary source of wealth. Iron and coal and steam and cotton textiles — as well as commerce, banks, and insurance companies — were creating a new class of plutocrats, who might soon demand greater political and even social recognition. Some of them were already challenging the traditional concepts of economic policy. The relative cohesiveness of the eighteenth-century ruling class was beginning to give way, and intermittent tension between landed gentlemen on the one hand and commercial and industrial magnates on the other anticipated the political readjustment to come in the later 1820s and the 1830s.

This readjustment was delayed for almost half a century by Britain's wars against the French Revolution and Napoleon. For the better part of a generation, a relentless military crisis preoccupied the nation, so that domestic reform, whether of Parliament, the Poor Law, or trade policy, took a back seat. Yet the need grew steadily more urgent as the population expanded and the pressures of war both spurred and distorted the process of industrialization. That development was lopsided, and it spawned all manner of new problems and tensions. When the country emerged from twenty-two years of fighting in 1815, its economy and society were badly askew, and those who had led the nation to victory abroad found themselves compelled to adapt to the forces of change at home.

---

[13]C. A. Bayly, *Imperial Meridian: The British Empire and the World, 1780–1830* (1989), sets these events within a broader context.

PART FOUR

WAR AND ITS AFTERMATH

1789 to 1830

WELLINGTON AT THE BATTLE OF WATERLOO (1815)
(Hulton Getty)

CHAPTER 11

The Struggle Against the French Revolution

On the afternoon of May 6, 1789, King Louis XVI opened the first session of the French Estates-General to be held in 175 years. Unable to raise the funds that his government required and beset by critics, the monarch hoped to rally representatives of the nobility, the clergy, and the third estate (the middle classes and others) to support the regeneration of his kingdom. Events soon moved far beyond the expectations of the king, and within the next three years most of the institutions of the French *ancien régime* were either altered dramatically or abolished altogether. The king's government may have been bankrupt, but France possessed the money, the people, and the ideas to fashion a new order for itself and for much of the continent. By the autumn of 1789, the medieval Estates had been converted into the National Assembly, and Paris, the center of radicalism, had captured from Versailles the legislature and the royal family. Three years later, France had become a republic, waging war against Austria and Prussia. French troops had thrown back the enemy armies and were pouring into northern Italy, central Germany, and the Low Countries. The Revolution had Europe in its grip.

French Revolutionaries and British Reformers

The British were slow to realize what the upheaval meant. At its start, different observers interpreted it in diverse ways; patriots predicted the disintegration of Britain's most dangerous rival, reformers the conversion of absolutism into a parliamentary system molded on that at Westminster. Both groups looked on in complacent approval. Only the radicals felt enthusiastic, for they dreamed that the collapse of one regime of privilege would usher in a new day of freedom for all people. This dream was given enduring expression by the young William Wordsworth, for whom the French appeared as the heroes of humanity:

[A] people from the depth
Of shameful imbecility uprisen,
Fresh as the morning star. Elate we looked
Upon their virtues; saw, in rudest men,
Self-sacrifice the firmest; generous love,
And continence of mind, and sense of right,
Uppermost in the midst of fiercest strife. . . .
Bliss was it in that dawn to be alive,
But to be young was very Heaven!

In his exclamatory way, the poet voiced a sense of human kinship widespread among intellectuals of the period. Such thinkers took an interest in the rights of all people, not merely the English or the French or the Germans. It was this cosmopolitan interest, reflected in the acts and words of the National Assembly, that gave the early phase of the Revolution its appeal outside France. The Assembly spoke of the powers inherent in one particular people, as Thomas Jefferson had spoken earlier in the Declaration of Independence; but both used terms so ultimate that they could apply to every people. The American proclamation of popular sovereignty had been a faint and distant challenge to the privileged orders of Europe; the French proclamation was a trumpet at the gates.

We can see the supranational character of the ideas enunciated by the National Assembly most clearly by contrasting them with the ideas enunciated by Parliament in the Glorious Revolution. The contrast lies in the language of two constitutional documents drafted exactly a hundred years apart: the English Bill of Rights of 1689 and the French Declaration of the Rights of Man and the Citizen of 1789. The Bill of Rights opens with a recitation of past history, then declares illegal certain practices of King James that have violated the "undoubted rights and liberties" of his subjects and of Parliament; it then settles the crown on William and Mary. The document is a terse, prosaic bit of lawmaking, intended to remedy specific grievances of the English and provide for the future of the monarchy, not to theorize about the nature of humankind. The French Declaration, on the other hand, speaks to the world in sweeping terms. "The ignorance, neglect, or contempt of the rights of man," it begins, "are the sole cause of public calamities and of the corruption of governments." Those rights, which are liberty, property, security, and resistance to oppression, belong to all people by virtue of their being citizens and can be limited only by law that is applicable to everyone and is made by the citizens through their representatives; without such law society has no constitution. Unlike the Bill of Rights, the Declaration is not primarily legislative, but a manifesto of political philosophy that has no limits of time or place.

Wordsworth was not alone in believing that the Revolution represented the dawn of universal freedom. People prominent in many walks of life shared the young poet's enthusiasm. Charles James Fox, the leader of the opposition in Parliament, hailed the fall of the Bastille as the greatest and best event in history. Leaders of the new industry, such as James Watt and Matthew Boulton, shared such sentiments. Joseph Priestley, an eminent chemist as well as religious leader, wrote to a friend that "I feel myself becoming all French, both in chemistry and politics." Priestley, a nonconformist, detested the established Church of England and consequently applauded the revolutionaries' assault on the French equivalent, the Roman Catholic Church. He believed that "the time is approaching when an end will be put to all usurpation in things civil or religious, first in Europe and then in other countries." Many dissenters shared his views and saw in the Revolution their best hope of full religious emancipation.

In the autumn of 1789, Richard Price, a well-known nonconformist minister, published a sermon in which he adapted to the British scene the philosophy of the Declaration of the Rights of Man. "A king," he declared, "is no more than the first servant of the public, created by it, maintained by it, and responsible to it. . . . His authority is the authority of the community; and the term *Majesty*, which it is usual to apply to him, is by no means *his own* majesty, but the *Majesty of the People*." King George and those who governed under his aegis derived their power from the people, to whom they were answerable and by whom they could be ousted for misconduct. This was the logic of the Declaration of Independence, of the National Assembly, and, Price believed, of the future. The light of liberty that had first appeared in the freeing of the English colonies in America was now "reflected to *France*, and there kindled into a blaze that lays despotism in ashes, and warms and illuminates *Europe!* Tremble, all ye oppressors of the world! . . . Restore to mankind their rights; and consent to the correction of abuses before they and you are destroyed together."

Burke and the New Conservatism

Such fire-breathing made members of Britain's governing class uneasy. Some of them did not know precisely why, because as Whigs they considered themselves friends of liberty. They were soon given reasons, however, when Price's sermon evoked a refutation from the leading political theorist of the day. Edmund Burke had strongly opposed coercing the American colonies, but he refused to agree that the French Revolution was an extension of the American upheaval. To his mind France was busily subverting everything on which social order depended, and Price's implication that Britain should follow suit drove him to answer. Burke's rebuttal was more than mere polemic, more even than is suggested by its title, *Reflections on the Revolution in France.* He went beyond reflection on a particular revolution to a consideration of the basic questions that it raised about the relationship of the citizen to the state. His treatise left its mark on all later conservative thinking.

Burke was no slave to the status quo. He recognized the truth of the old adage that times change and we change with them; indeed, he had made his name as a reformer, but he insisted that reform must not be the means of eliminating the good with the bad. He was too much pervaded by a sense of the past to be a revolutionary. The social organism was for him

French "Liberty" and British "Slavery"   The Frenchman suffers his supposed freedom while the well-fed Englishman complains about his "enslavement" to those who govern (and pamper) him in this depiction by the English cartoonist H. Humphrey in 1792. *(Mansell/Time)*

not a thing of the moment, to be reconstituted according to the dictates of abstract philosophy; it was the product of a slow and infinitely complex process of historical development, "a partnership not only between those who are living, but between those who are living, those who are dead, and those who are to be born." The revolutionary would dissolve that partnership and destroy that organism in the hope of creating something better in its place. The French appeared to be abolishing useful institutions for the sake of an untried future, and their faith that human reason alone could construct a political utopia impressed Burke as madness.

Their watchwords, liberty and equality, left him unmoved. Liberty in itself was no virtue: As he dryly pointed out, if we permit individuals to do as they please "we ought to see what it will please them to do before we risk congratulations. . . ." The liberties of the English were not their abstract rights as members of the human race, but special privileges acquired and passed down to them by their forebears, privileges that did not include, as Price contended, any right of the people at large to choose or change their governors. As for equality, it was a dangerous myth. In any society some are always at the top, some at the bottom; and those who try to level the hierarchy do not equalize but merely turn the social order topsy-turvy. To grant power to the unpropertied masses would turn them against the propertied few in a scramble for spoils and in the end would give each of them an infinitesimal share in the plunder of the wealthy.

A government subservient to the popular will, as expressed through universal suffrage, would head for disaster, Burke argued, because wise public policy cannot be determined by the simple arithmetic of counting votes. He saw the French revolutionaries in their zeal for abstract liberty and equality busily tearing down all intermediate corporate bodies — guilds, provinces, churches — that stood between the individual and the state. The result of wiping the slate clean, he warned, would be to leave the individual defenseless against the power of the all-encompassing state that might speak in the name of, but that could never be controlled by, the public.

Burke thus attacked the first principle of the French Revolution — that sovereignty resides in the entire body of citizens and is perfectly expressed in the law that their representatives make. The people may claim for themselves the *power* of governing, but, he said, that does not give them the *right* or the *capacity* to govern. "Government is a contrivance of human wisdom to provide for human *wants*," and such wisdom comes only from long ages of experience. No individual or group has a right to flout experience and destroy a constitution that has taken centuries to build, for no one has the wisdom to create a better one from whole cloth. Although the rationalists argue that they have such wisdom, their "new conquering empire of light and reason" is an illusion. In Burke's judgment, they misconceived the very nature of society and government. Burke revered history as the medium of divine creation, and his religious convictions ran as deep as those of Whitefield or the Wesleys. He saw in the social order and in humanity's historical heritage the handiwork of God and regarded those who would jettison it as infidels. Although many of Burke's initial readers regarded his assessment of the implications of French revolutionary doctrines as overly fearful, he provided his generation with an underlying philosophy with which to defend their threatened world.

By the time his work appeared late in 1790, the upheaval in France was dividing British public opinion. Events were forcing Britons to examine what they believed and to take a stand on the issue of reform. Many stood with Burke. Others, such as Charles James Fox, insisted that true Whiggism was dedicated to the cause of liberty and that the Revolution, whatever its mistakes and even its crimes, was furthering that cause. These factions were relatively moderate, but on each side extremists cropped up. To the right of Burke were the arch conservatives, who identified all reform with treason. To the left of Fox were outright republicans, who sent addresses and delegations to the National Assembly in Paris and worked to promote French principles at home. A contemporary thus parodied the views of one of these Francophiles:

> Whatever is in France is right;
> Terror and blood are my delight;
> Parties with us do not excite enough rage;
> Our boasted laws I hate and curse,
> Bad from the first, by age grown worse;
> I pant and sigh for universal suffrage.

Edmund Burke (1729–1797) and Thomas Paine (1737–1809)   In the 1790s and for decades thereafter, Burke and Paine were the rival prophets of conservatism and radicalism. *(Library of Congress)*

The most famous of the republicans was Tom Paine. He had already made a name for himself in 1776 with his fiery pamphlet, *Common Sense,* in which he supported the American Revolution. Now he threw his heart into backing the French. He answered Burke in 1791 by publishing *The Rights of Man,* an uncompromising attack on the whole nature of Britain's oligarchical society. Paine gloried in the very abstractions that Burke had sought to undermine. He called on his fellow Britons to throw off the shackles of the past and to follow the French example in order to construct, on the basis of "the natural rights of man," a completely egalitarian democratic state. For Paine, monarchs were no more than the descendants of robber chieftains; no one was more noble by birth than another. Parasitical courtiers, placemen, pensioners, and unnecessary soldiers and sailors riddled society; if they were eliminated, the nation might save £4 million a year in taxes. In Part II of his work, Paine outlined a "welfare state" program of children's allowances, old-age pensions, and tax-supported elementary schools for which such savings might be used. The pamphlet, both provocative and inexpensive, enjoyed an enormous circulation — some 200,000 copies in two years — among artisans and small tradesmen. During the next half-century, it wielded a greater impact on British popular radicalism than any other work. The government immediately responded by indicting Paine for seditious libel. He fled to France, where he was first elected to the legislature and then condemned as an enemy of the Revolution whose virtues he had so ardently extolled. Barely escaping the guillotine, he spent his final years in the United States.

The first individual to answer Burke, however, had been not Paine but one of the most remarkable women of the age. Mary Wollstonecraft had penned *A Vindication of the Rights of Man* late in 1790 and followed it a year later with her pioneering manifesto *A Vindication of the Rights of Woman*. In the latter work, she sought to expand the implications of Enlightenment thinking so as to encompass women as well as men. She therefore argued against an interpretation of "nature" in which men figured as law-giving teachers and women as their well-behaved pupils. "It is a farce to call any being virtuous whose virtues do not result from the exercise of its own reason. This was Rousseau's opinion respecting men; I extend it to women." In her judgment, men and women shared the same canons of morality and therefore merited the same type of education, the same economic opportunities, and the same political rights and responsibilities. In 1797 Wollstonecraft married William Godwin, a fellow political radical and the author of *Political Justice* (1793). Godwin's book challenged the social conventions of the age and anticipated the ultimate disappearance of all governments in the interest of human liberation and "the right of private judgment." Mary Wollstonecraft's often tempestuous life ended in September 1797 when she died of an infection contracted during childbirth. The child, Mary Godwin, survived and in due course became the wife of the poet Percy Bysshe Shelley as well as an author in her own right.[1]

The fear of a popular rising in Britain, which underlay the government's prosecution of Paine and other political radicals, proved unfounded. The common people were as much divided as were their governors. Agitators wandered the country, preaching that a republic lay at hand and that all property would be apportioned equally; in some areas, mobs rioted against the established order. In other areas, though, demonstrators protested against the reformers. Among these, the most prominent victim was the theologian and pioneer chemist Joseph Priestley. In 1791 his house in Birmingham, which contained his manuscripts and scientific instruments, was sacked and destroyed; three years later, like Paine, he found refuge in the United States. The old days of embittered factions, political trials, and forced exiles seemed to have returned.

The War in Europe (1793–1797)

For almost four years after the outbreak of the Revolution, Pitt tried to keep peace at home and abroad. He hoped to contain the agitation of domestic radicals without resorting to stringent repression and to

---

[1]Relevant biographies include Eleanor Flexner, *Mary Wollstonecraft: A Biography* (1972); William St. Clair, *The Godwins and the Shelleys: The Biography of a Family* (1989); and David Freeman Hawke, *Paine* (1974). For Burke see Alfred Cobban, *Edmund Burke and the Revolt Against the Eighteenth Century*, 2nd ed. (1960); Carl Cone, *Burke and the Nature of Politics*, 2 vols. (1957, 1964); and Conor Cruise O'Brien, *The Great Melody: A Thematic Biography and Commented Anthology of Edmund Burke* (1992), a study that emphasizes Burke's Irish background and concerns. F. J. Lock has published volume I (1730–1784) of a comprehensive new biography, *Edmund Burke* (1999).

avoid a conflict with France that would undo all the progress he had made in financial retrenchment. But by November 1792, his second hope was fading. War had broken out between the French revolutionaries and the rulers of Austria and Prussia. Using the Austrian Netherlands (modern Belgium) as a base, Austrian and Prussian armies had begun a march toward Paris, only to be forced into retreat by French troops, who proceeded to overrun the Austrian Netherlands and menace the Dutch state immediately to the north. In Paris the monarchy had given way to a republic and the National Assembly to a new legislature, the Convention, that was increasingly dominated by its most radical element, the Jacobins. The Convention had proclaimed that "France will grant her help to all peoples who desire to recover their liberty." The Jacobins, as the only judges of who these desirous peoples were, could use the proclamation as a basis for conquering all of their European neighbors.

The British were familiar with this kind of threat. Since the days of Marlborough, they had fought French expansion into the Low Countries, into Germany, and across the Alps. French armies presented no less a threat under the new tricolor of the Republic than under the Bourbon lilies. Pitt had no desire to fight the Revolution while it remained within the frontiers of France, as Austria and Prussia had done, yet no responsible British prime minister could sit by while the French established their hegemony in western Europe. The Convention had launched an idealistic conflict, spiced with the hope of territorial aggrandizement. The government in London, which cared little about the ideals but a great deal about the aggrandizement, was being drawn into a struggle to defend the old balance of power.

In February 1793 France declared war on Britain, the Dutch state, and Spain, and so added them to a coalition that already included Sardinia, Prussia, and Austria — a ring of enemies that would have done credit to Louis XIV. Their aims, in which even Pitt now acquiesced, were to despoil France of border provinces and overseas colonies and to reimpose on the French people the regime that they had shaken off. They intended to crush French power along with French ideas; if they had succeeded, as Fox said, they would have given "all the kings of Europe a perpetual guarantee against all peoples who might be oppressed by them in any part of the world."

The allies seemed to have every chance of succeeding. The War of the First Coalition, on the face of it, should have crushed the Revolution in its infancy. The bureaucratic and military system of the Bourbons lay in ruins; factions in the Convention struggled for power and for their own lives, under the periodic threat of the Paris mob; the royalists of northwestern France had taken up arms in a counterrevolution. Yet a nation that seemed to be disintegrating won the war with ease. By 1795 the French Republic ruled by the Jacobins and a "Reign of Terror" gave way to a less radical regime, the Directory. That same year the regime conquered the Dutch, and Prussia and Spain agreed to make peace. Only Sardinia,

Austria, and Britain continued to fight. In 1796–1797 a young French general from Corsica, Napoleon Bonaparte, eliminated Sardinia and Austria in a whirlwind campaign in northern Italy's Po Valley. Britain was left alone. France annexed Belgium, turned the Dutch into a satellite republic, extended its eastern frontier to the Rhine, and dominated northern Italy. What the Bourbons had dreamed of, the Directory achieved.

The military force that the Revolution generated in France deserves explanation, or it remains as mysterious as it was to its victims. French armies, first under the Republic and then under the Directory, defied all the rules and advanced from triumph to triumph, producing an unprecedented military overturn. Yet their victories gave only a taste of what was to come. Small wonder that contemporaries were bewildered. They could not grasp the fact that a military revolution, growing out of the political revolution within France, was giving rise to a new kind of warfare.

The War of the First Coalition saw conflict between two kinds of society, and their armies mirrored the contrast between them. Those of the *anciens régimes* were products of a world sharply divided between the privileged and unprivileged: Officers were gentlemen; common soldiers were a mere rabble, creatures to be insulated from contact with civilians, their needs supplied by the commissariat, and controlled by rigorous discipline.[2] An army thus moved and fought under a tight rein, and its leaders' premise that they could not trust individual soldiers to act on their own affected both tactics and strategy.

This premise disappeared in France as a result of the Revolution. When the Jacobins had to improvise a military system in 1792, they called the country to arms in a *levée en masse,* in itself a major act of revolution. A new kind of army arose, which had to fight in a new way if it was to fight at all. The army was huge and was composed largely of recruits who had little training but great enthusiasm. Because these citizen soldiers were numerous and ill trained, they were expendable, for the government could draw on the manpower of the nation to replace them in short order. Because they were enthusiastic, they did not need to be tightly controlled to prevent desertion. They could forage on their own; the army therefore needed to carry fewer supplies, moved at a speed that its opponents could not match, and even more important had the capacity, which its enemy lacked, to exploit a victory to the full. These raw troops were formidable.

The nature of battle changed to match the changed fighting man. The French relied on mass more than specialized training, on fervor more than discipline, and they could afford much heavier losses than the enemy. French soldiers soon learned how to utilize their advantages on the battlefield, flowing around the static lines of regulars and turning their opponents' retreats into routs. Battle began to yield them rich dividends. It ceased to be "the remedy of the desperate" and became the means of winning a campaign, a province, an empire. The old days of limited war

---

[2]For a discussion of eighteenth-century warfare, see Chapter 5.

for limited ends were over: The Jacobin military revolution had opened almost unlimited possibilities of conquest.

The Impact of War at Home

These conquests, which began toppling the old order on the continent, staggered the ruling classes in Britain and forced them, though slowly, to mobilize the nation's resources as never before. In the days of Queen Anne, the government had spent some £5 million per year for military purposes, and in the era of the elder Pitt it had spent £15 million; the expenses of the quarter-century of war that began in 1793 would average £40 million per year. No government could raise such sums without unprecedented taxation and a huge increase in the debt. The amount derived from customs and excise duties — the normal source of revenue for the state — quadrupled during the war years, and that derived from the land tax doubled. Even so, these sums proved insufficient; therefore, in 1797 Pitt persuaded Parliament to impose an income tax on those who earned more than £60 a year. All these taxes combined failed to match expenses, however, so that by the time the war was over, Britain had tripled its national debt.

The needs of war distorted the development of the economy in other ways. For shipbuilders and munitions makers, the war constituted a boon; for overseas merchants, the vicissitudes of the conflict closed some traditional avenues of trade and opened others. Consumer industries such as brewing were handicapped by high excise taxes, while the construction of roads, canals, and ordinary houses was severely curtailed by a sharp rise in interest rates. In 1797 the Bank of England stopped redeeming its pound notes in gold on demand, an action that spurred an inflationary trend already well under way. Eighteenth-century Britons had grown accustomed to price fluctuations resulting from the harvest, but these ups and downs tended to average out over the years, and long-range price stability had been the rule. The inflation of the 1790s came therefore as a shock.

Wartime inflation and the meager harvests of 1794 and 1795 accentuated the problem of poor relief. In 1795 in the Berkshire village of Speenhamland, the Justices of the Peace initiated a novel form of aid for workers whose wages had not kept up with rising prices. Their wages were supplemented with contributions from the poor rates, in accordance with a sliding scale tied to the price of bread. The so-called Speenhamland system came to be applied in much of the country during the decades that followed; it helped to triple poor rate expenses by the end of the Napoleonic Wars. The system has earned praise for its humanity and drawn condemnation for its high cost and its tendency to deter employers from raising wages and laborers from working harder. Whatever the limitations of such methods of relief, the working poor received some measure of protection in a period of critical economic distress; the cost was the price of assuaging what might otherwise have ended in explosive

The British Butcher   By 1795 wartime food prices had shot up rapidly, and the cartoonist's sardonic advice to the poor workman is, "Since you can no longer afford bread, buy meat instead!" *(The British Museum)*

discontent. At a time when much of Europe was torn by revolution spreading outward from France, most British laborers remained loyal to a society that, for all its shortcomings, strove to keep them alive.[3]

In the early years of the war, Britain's rulers felt far from certain of that loyalty, however. They saw in every critic of the status quo a Francophile conspirator, and their alarm infected the government and the judiciary. Any attempt at change was treated with suspicion: A motion to reform Parliament, for example, which had won 174 votes in the House of Commons in 1785, mustered only 41 when it was reintroduced in 1793. Pitt's ministry, reflecting this changed mood in the ruling class, began to adopt repressive measures. Aliens came under severe restrictions in 1793, and the government was authorized to expel them at its discretion. From 1794 to 1801, habeas corpus was suspended, so that suspects could be — and were — held in prison for years without trial. In 1795 the Treasonable Practices Act broadened the law of treason to cover any writing or utterance that incited the populace to contempt of the sovereign, the authorities, or the constitution. In the same year, the Seditious Meetings Act required the license of a

---

[3]J. D. Marshall, *The Old Poor Law, 1795–1834* (1968), provides a succinct introduction to the subject.

magistrate for any gathering of more than fifty persons; this drastic interference with freedom of assembly broke up most of the radical clubs that had flourished since 1789. Freedom of the press was as drastically curtailed: stamp duties forced cheap newspapers out of business, and printers were held strictly accountable for publishing anything that displeased the government. The rights of the citizen, in short, no longer included the right even to grumble at the established order.

The judges enforced the new legislation with a rigor of their own. Pitt's ministry was especially nervous about Scotland, where a widespread movement had developed in the early 1790s urging a parliamentary reform program: equal representation, frequent elections, and the right to vote for all adult males. After the war began, the ministry charged the leaders of this movement with sedition, and for a crime no more serious than advocating a change in the laws, they were found guilty and sentenced to seven to fourteen years' "transportation." On occasion English jurymen proved more independent, as they showed in 1794 by acquitting the shoemaker Thomas Hardy and eleven other leaders of the London Corresponding Society who were being tried together for high treason. According to the indictment, their plea for parliamentary reform had been no more than a pretext for inspiring "rebellion and war" against the king and his ministers. Even when such prosecutions failed, they dampened the ardor of the more radical of British groups sympathetic to French Jacobinism.

Many members of the middle and lower ranks of British society had not found French Jacobinism attractive in the first place — if only because it was French and therefore foreign. By the tens of thousands, they joined loyalist Societies for King and Constitution. The longer the conflict with revolutionary France lasted, the more did the loyalists celebrate George III as the symbol of his nation's will to resist, as "the Father of his People," and as the champion of an ancient tradition holding the fort against French revolutionary upstarts. George III was lauded as an honest and philanthropic head of state and as a conscientious and genial family man as well. In the words of John Wesley, "He believes the Bible . . . he fears God . . . he loves the Queen."[4] Such loyalists happily assisted local magistrates throughout the country in unearthing what they considered proof of sedition. Spies and informers earned rewards for turning up lurid tidbits. Voluntary snoopers gathered "evidence" from gossiping servants, disgruntled peasants, drunken innkeepers, and other similarly reliable sources. Fear of the traitor and the foreign agent ran rampant.

Fear, however, was only one factor that united the country behind its government. Religious motives also contributed to the growing hostility to the Revolution. The Jacobins in Paris were moving not only toward greater radicalism but also toward more and more open atheism, and they were thereby alienating all British Christians. John Wesley's political inclinations had been conservative from the start, and the Methodists

---

[4]See Marilyn Morris, *The British Monarchy and the French Revolution* (1998).

in particular, with their sizable lower-class membership, discovered in Jacobinism the figure of the anti-Christ. The antipathy toward France that ordinary people had long felt now intensified with mistrust and religious antagonism. In the grip of such emotions, most Britons willingly followed the lead of their rulers. Bad harvests and sharp rises in prices might lead to occasional localized riots, but a majority accepted the idea that only a traitor would want to remold the established order. The various reform movements of the 1780s and early 1790s collapsed or were dispersed or forced underground for a generation to come.[5]

Pitt's belief that, in time of all-out war, domestic reform had to be postponed and civil liberties temporarily restricted won the support of many of his erstwhile parliamentary critics. The Whig party divided between the followers of the duke of Portland, who cooperated with Pitt and some of whom in 1794 joined Pitt's cabinet, and the followers of Charles James Fox. Fox continued to oppose the war against the French Revolution and to insist, in the teeth of misrepresentation and obloquy, that the true strength of the nation lay in the citizen's freedom to think, speak, and criticize. Year after year he flayed the government with all the power of his oratory, even at the price of political ostracism. Although he may have exaggerated the devotion of the French revolutionaries to representative government and civil liberties, he kept alive such ideals in Britain. The Tories of the immediate post-1815 era would trace their political heritage back to William Pitt. The Whigs who returned to power in 1830 were to see themselves as the political descendants of Charles James Fox.

The Naval Conflict (1793–1797)

France's triumphs on land in the War of the First Coalition had no counterpart at sea. The Revolution that put new power into the hands of France's generals did not help its admirals, for their problem was different in kind. Although they too had numerous and enthusiastic recruits, they could not re-create the old Bourbon navy on revolutionary lines. The reason was simple. The square-rigged ship of the line, the mainstay of the fleet, was so complex that her crew needed years of training in discipline and seamanship before it became an effective fighting instrument, let alone a smoothly functioning part of a squadron. A general

---

[5]Albert Goodwin, *The Friends of Liberty: the English Democratic Movement in the Age of the French Revolution* (1979), provides a sympathetic and detailed narrative account of the reformers whom the British government feared as revolutionaries. In *Threats of Revolution in Britain, 1789–1848* (1977), Malcolm Thomis and Peter Holt evaluate the significance of those threats. In *Riots and Community Politics in England and Wales, 1790–1810* (1983), John Bohstedt examines the nature of the popular outbursts that did occur. Ian R. Christie's *Stress and Stability in Eighteenth-Century Britain* (1985) provides a judicious assessment of the reasons that the Britain of the 1790s did not succumb to revolution. The essays in H. T. Dickinson, ed., *Britain and the French Revolution, 1789–1815* (1989), summarize the fruits of recent scholarship.

might fashion an army out of inexperienced men and officers promoted from the ranks; an admiral who put to sea with ships so manned invited disaster. Factors that made military innovation possible and successful did not apply to war under sail.

From the beginning of hostilities, in consequence, Britain had the wherewithal for naval predominance; but Pitt's ministry had so many military priorities that it frittered its resources among them. It sent one expeditionary force to the Austrian Netherlands, another to aid the Dutch, a third to the Mediterranean, and a fourth to attack French islands in the West Indies. It also promised the king of Prussia enough financial aid to pay for an army of 60,000 men. By 1795, however, all three British expeditionary forces had been driven off the continent, and its soldiers in the West Indies were dying by the thousands of yellow fever. The aid to Prussia failed to arrive in time. Only British power at sea remained beyond challenge throughout the War of the First Coalition. In 1793 Britain had half again as many serviceable ships of the line as the enemy, with far better crews. British naval administration, by comparison with that of the French, was a model of efficiency. Yet Britain's admirals had no clear idea as to how to take advantage of their naval superiority. They were still governed by the notion that a battle should be fought between two parallel lines of ships firing at each other, and such tactics were likely to prove inconclusive.[6] Nor was the British fleet used to impose a complete blockade on the major French ports. In winter British vessels were brought home to protect them from storms, and enemy ships were permitted to come and go as they pleased. British naval predominance was consequently used to little purpose while it lasted; and it did not last long.

In 1797 the First Coalition against France collapsed, so that after the French government had rejected Pitt's compromise peace feelers, the British were left to fight alone. At sea they now faced the same ring of enemies that had nearly ruined them in the War of American Independence. France had gained the Dutch navy by conquering the Netherlands, and it had bullied Spain into alliance. Faced with these combined fleets, the British were forced on the defensive and withdrew their naval squadron from the Mediterranean Sea. Soon mutiny in their navy and rebellion in Ireland added to their troubles. Their worst crisis in the whole quarter-century of war came in the years 1797–1798, when they confronted the most serious peril they would face until the dark days of 1940–1941.

They might not have weathered that crisis if the new generation of admirals rising to high command had not contained, at long last, some men of genius. One of the best of the new school was Sir John Jervis, the commander-in-chief of the fleet that had withdrawn from the Mediter-

---

[6]For a discussion of traditional naval tactics, see Chapter 5. The best modern overview is provided by G. J. Marcus in *The Age of Nelson: The Royal Navy, 1793–1815* (1971). See also John Creswell, *British Admirals of the Eighteenth Century: Tactics and Battles* (1972), and Michael Duffy, *Soldiers, Sugar and Seapower: The British Expeditions to the West Indies and the War Against Revolutionary France* (1987).

ranean. A cold, awesome disciplinarian, Jervis also had a fighting spirit. In February 1797, he encountered off Cape St. Vincent, the southwestern tip of Portugal, a large Spanish fleet sailing to join the French and cover an invasion of the British Isles. Jervis, outnumbered by almost two to one, attacked with a confidence that was justified in the event. At the decisive moment of the battle, one of his officers, who commanded the smallest ship in the line, left his post without orders and interposed his vessel between the divided segments of the enemy to keep them from uniting; he then boarded and captured two of the huge Spanish vessels. Jervis acknowledged this bold initiative in his subordinate, who had flouted the time-honored principle of holding the line and had thereby converted an indecisive action into a triumph. London soon buzzed with the officer's name: Horatio Nelson.

The Battle of Cape St. Vincent shattered a Franco-Spanish plan to invade Britain, and in the autumn of 1797 a defeat of the Dutch fleet ended the threat from that quarter. Between those two victories, however, the Royal Navy had to surmount a momentous danger in its own midst. In April mutiny broke out in the Channel Fleet at Portsmouth and soon spread to the squadrons guarding the Thames against the invasion momentarily expected from Holland. For weeks the nation was stripped of its defenses. The spirit of disaffection seemed suddenly to infect everyone, and even the army was suspect.

The mutiny had far less to do with French revolutionary ideas than with the frustrations of men tried beyond endurance. Sailors ranked among the roughest and toughest members of the king's service. Some had been forced into it by the press gangs that roamed English port towns in search of likely victims; some were foreigners, others Irish. Although the great majority grudgingly accepted cramped quarters, poor food, and a ferocious discipline, they finally rebelled against their rate of pay. At a time of rapid inflation, merchant marine wages had risen to four times the naval rate, and even soldiers had recently received a small raise. Sailors, however, were paid what they had been for more than a century, and even those payments were often late. Many sailors had families to feed, and those families now faced starvation.

The Admiralty had ignored a number of petitions from the Channel Fleet, and on Easter Sunday, 1797, the men took matters into their own hands. They politely pushed their officers aside, seized the ships, and then waited for the government to redress their grievances. The Admiralty for once acted with speed and good sense; the First Lord hurried to Portsmouth and conceded the substance of the men's demands, subject to parliamentary approval. The crisis seemed resolved. But the mutineers' taste of power proved intoxicating. Parliament acted too slowly for them, and they again took over the ships. The contagion spread to the fleets at Plymouth, Yarmouth, and the Nore, off the mouth of the Thames, and paralyzed the navy.

When Admiral Adam Duncan sailed from Yarmouth to watch the Dutch coast, all but two of his ships deserted him. With those two, the indomitable old man took up his blockading station. To keep the enemy from attacking him, he signaled over the horizon to his nonexistent fleet. For some days his bluff succeeded, until one by one his mutinous ships rejoined him, for the Admiralty had managed to pacify all the malcontents except those at the Nore, where trouble persisted for weeks. When supplies to the fleet were cut off, the mutinous sailors retaliated by seizing every ship that tried to reach or leave the port of London. Eventually, however, they acknowledged the futility of their defiance, which the public regarded as treason, and by the middle of June the last resistance at the Nore fizzled.

Twenty-nine ringleaders were executed and others variously punished, but the men in general profited from what they had done. They had taught their superiors a salutary lesson: that obedience could not be taken for granted. Sailors were human beings, and if driven too far they would, like the Frenchmen they despised, assert their rights. The most pressing of their grievances were redressed and the worst abuses remedied. Slowly but surely, conditions in the fleet began to improve, and with them morale, until within a few years the Royal Navy became the finest fighting force that Britain had ever possessed.

The Egyptian Expedition (1798)

In the spring of 1798, many signs pointed to another imminent French invasion of England, the one unconquered enemy. General Bonaparte, fresh from his triumphs in Italy, commanded an army massed on the Channel coast of France, where the ports bustled with preparation. Pitt called the people to arms, and thousands of volunteers responded; plans were made for laying waste to the coastal countryside and fortifying every tenable point. "The nation had not yet learnt to know its own strength or its resources," wrote a foreign observer. "The government has taught it the secret and inspired it with an unbounded confidence almost amounting to presumption."[7] Presumption indeed it was, for yeomanry armed with fowling pieces would have provided no match for Bonaparte's veterans.

But the Corsican had no desire at that time to attempt invasion, which he knew would be suicidal as long as the Royal Navy held the Channel. His preparations served as a disguise for a quite different plan — to attack Egypt. By invading this dependency of the Ottoman Empire, he hoped to expand French influence in the Near East and to make the route to India via the Suez isthmus the preserve of French merchants. Eventually he hoped to march toward India itself. The Directory supported him with an enthusiasm born of self-interest; his success would

---

[7]Quoted by Arthur Bryant, *The Years of Endurance, 1793–1802* (1942), p. 228. This is a vivid and lively account of the first phase of the war. See also Clive Emsley, *British Society and the French Wars, 1793–1815* (1979), chapters 10 and 11 of Ian R. Christie, *Wars and Revolutions: Britain, 1760–1815* (1982), and J. E. Cookson, *The British Armed Nation, 1793–1815* (1997).

bring wealth and glory to a shaky regime, and his failure would rid it of a general who was becoming too popular for comfort. In May, Bonaparte sailed from Toulon for Alexandria.

His Egyptian expedition supplied the first sign that his genius, dazzling as it was, had a serious limitation. No leader in history had greater gifts for commanding an army or organizing and administering a state, but Napoleon was inferior to many of his pedestrian contemporaries in his understanding of sea power. He expected to establish on the Nile a base for operations against other parts of the Near East, but that base would depend on waterborne communications with Europe. If those communications were cut, his army would sooner or later be imprisoned between sea and desert. He was acting on the assumption that Britain would not or could not regain control of the Mediterranean — an assumption that proved fallacious.

Pitt realized that Britain could not make headway alone and that its best chance of creating a new coalition lay in reasserting British naval power in the Mediterranean. He had consequently weakened the fleet at home, despite the possible threat of invasion, in order to reinforce the squadron at Gibraltar under Admiral Jervis — now Lord St. Vincent in honor of his victory — and to permit him to reenter the inland sea. St. Vincent thereupon sent most of his battle line to join Nelson, who was cruising off Toulon to observe the French preparations. The Royal Navy resumed a blockade in force.

On May 19 Bonaparte sailed from Toulon, convoyed by thirteen ships of the line. On June 6, Nelson, joined by his reinforcement, set off in pursuit with thirteen ships of the line and one heavy frigate but without light frigates for scouting. On June 22, he learned that the French had captured Malta from the Knights of St. John, who had long possessed it, and had then sailed eastward. He guessed that their destination was Egypt and in a fever of impatience, set sail to overtake them. On the night of June 22, Nelson unwittingly passed the French fleet in the darkness and, on reaching Alexandria, found to his chagrin no signs or rumor of the French. Immediately he left to hunt along the Syrian coast. As Egyptian observers watched his sails disappear over the eastern horizon, they saw other sails rise from the sea to the west. Bonaparte had arrived; sheer luck had saved him for his future.

He landed his army, crushed native resistance, and soon secured himself in the mastery of Egypt. Yet his fleet was far from safe. The coast offered it no refuge, no fortified harbor like Toulon's. In the meantime, Nelson spent several weeks searching the eastern Mediterranean in vain for Napoleon. "The Devil's children," he lamented, "have the Devil's luck." Late in July, learning that the French had gone to Egypt after all, he closed in. On the afternoon of August 1, Admiral Nelson and his captains, whom he called his band of brothers, sighted the enemy fleet moored in Aboukir Bay. Here, near the Nile Delta to the east of Alexandria, the French admiral had anchored his ships in a line. Shoal water to port seemed to preclude attack from that side, and only the starboard batteries were cleared

Nelson at the Battle of Trafalgar *(The Granger Collection)*

for action. The wind blew from the sea, and the British ran before it as they bore down on the enemy van. Their tension reached a fever pitch. They knew that their chief was determined on victory at any cost. "If we succeed," asked one of his captains, "what will the world say?" "There is no *if* in the case," Nelson answered. "That we shall succeed is certain; who will live to tell the story is a very different question."

The enemy had almost as many ships as the British and larger ones; thus the only hope of complete success lay in concentrating fully on one part of the French line after another. Nelson gambled on having enough room to pass between the line and the shoals without running aground; his five leading ships got through, by superb seamanship, and anchored on the west side of the van while the rest of the fleet assaulted the other side. Darkness fell, and the battle raged on. Nelson himself was dazed and disabled by a flying splinter, but his captains knew their job. The French, caught between two fires, could reply to only one because their port batteries were useless. Their ships in the van surrendered one by one. The attack moved on to the center, where their huge flagship caught fire and blew up with a glare that lighted the bay and a shock felt for ten miles. All night the cannonading waxed and waned until both sides grew too exhausted to man the guns. At dawn two enemy ships at the rear of the line slipped their anchors and escaped to sea, the lone survivors of thirteen. No conflict

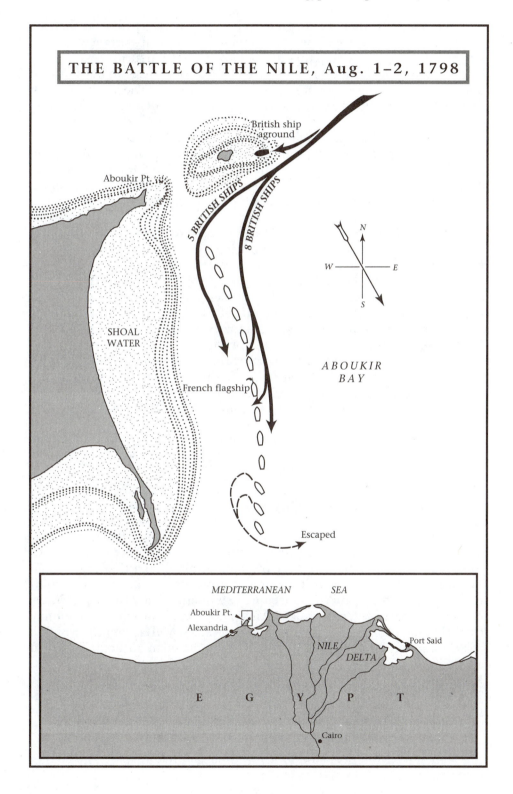

THE BATTLE OF THE NILE, Aug. 1–2, 1798

British ship aground

Aboukir Pt.

5 BRITISH SHIPS

8 BRITISH SHIPS

N

W — E

S

SHOAL WATER

ABOUKIR BAY

French flagship

Escaped

MEDITERRANEAN SEA

Aboukir Pt.

Alexandria

NILE

Port Said

DELTA

E G Y P T

Cairo

between fleets of comparable strength had ever before produced such an overwhelming victory. Nelson's novel approach to naval warfare was to attempt to destroy every ship that he could reach. He pursued this aim with whole-souled concentration, undeterred by fear of damage to his ships, of casualties in his crews, of wounds or death for himself. The kind of victory that he sought justified all losses. His goal in battle, like Bonaparte's, was enemy annihilation; and at the Nile he achieved it.

His triumph had far-reaching repercussions. The Corsican and his army were cooped up in Egypt, the prisoners of his miscalculation. In the spring of 1799, he tried to break out by moving into Syria to attack the Turks, who had declared war on him, but his grandiose dreams of emulating Alexander the Great evaporated before the city of Acre, when a small British squadron captured his siege artillery and used it to strengthen the Turkish garrison. The French were repulsed, the invasion collapsed, and Bonaparte fell back on Egypt. For the first time in his career, he had, thanks to sea power, met defeat.

In August 1799 he and his staff sailed for home in two frigates. He evaded British cruisers and in early October landed in France, where the populace received him as a savior. His skillful propaganda had magnified his triumphs and concealed his underlying failure, whereas back in France the government of the Directory had become increasingly unpopular because of its inability to procure a permanent peace with its neighbors. In November Bonaparte overthrew it and established the Consulate, with himself as First Consul; and where he was first, no one else was second. The Revolution had come full circle. It had destroyed a decrepit absolutism only to create in its stead an efficient one: a military dictatorship.

The War of the Second Coalition (1799–1801)

The Egyptian expedition impressed the French people, thanks to Bonaparte's skill in advertising himself, but it did not impress the rest of Europe. The other powers saw in it the long-awaited sign that France had overreached itself. Most Britons and many continentals saw its ambitions as insatiable: France had occupied Switzerland and the Papal States before Bonaparte's departure for Alexandria and had extracted money from them to pay for his expedition; it had seized Malta from the Knights of St. John, whom Tsar Paul, the half-insane Russian autocrat, regarded as his particular protégés; it had infiltrated the German states and the Kingdom of the Two Sicilies, the feeble Bourbon power in southern Italy. The French nation was undermining the political structure of the continent, but Europe needed some indication of France's weakness to rekindle armed opposition.

The Battle of the Nile provided such an indication. In its aftermath, the French position in the Mediterranean began to collapse. The British seized Minorca, which they had lost in 1783, and so regained their base for blockading Toulon. Their troops strengthened the fragile Bourbon hold on Sicily; their fleet encouraged a revolt on Malta and blockaded its French conquerors. This reversal of fortune, together with a British subsidy large enough to pay for a Russian army of 45,000 men, persuaded Russia and Austria that the time had finally come to overthrow the Revolution. By the spring of 1799, they were allied with Britain in the Second Coalition.

At first the allies swept everything before them. A Cossack general, Alexander Suvorov, stormed through Italy; the Austrians defeated the armies of the Directory in Switzerland and Germany; a French fleet that had ventured into the Mediterranean retreated ignominiously; rebellion again broke out in western France; and an Anglo-Russian expeditionary force invaded the Dutch Netherlands. In that summer of 1799, with Bonaparte still in Egypt, the French empire tottered. A concerted push might well have brought it down.

The allies lost their opportunity once more, however, because of mutual mistrust. The eruption of Suvorov into Italy disturbed the Austrians, who had no desire to see the peninsula pass from French to Russian dominance. They rejoiced when he was transferred to Switzerland, and they failed to support him there. Anglo-Russian cooperation in the Dutch Netherlands fared little better, and the expedition failed dismally. By autumn the French had suppressed rebellion at home and regained control of the Netherlands, Switzerland, and western Germany. The Austrians held Italy, but at the price of infuriating Tsar Paul. In the autumn he withdrew from the war, just as Bonaparte seized the reins in Paris.

The next two years proved disastrous for Britain. The First Consul justified his coup d'état to the French people by dealing promptly with the Austrians, in a campaign that broke their grip on Italy and forced them, in February 1801, to make peace. Meanwhile Bonaparte had courted and won the favor of the mercurial tsar, whom he persuaded to turn against Britain and put an embargo on its ships; Russia also joined Sweden, Denmark, and Prussia in a new League of Armed Neutrality, like that of 1780, to enforce its members' right to trade as they pleased. This defiance of Britain's blockade revealed how low its stock had fallen. The British had been deserted by their allies; their navy had done nothing of moment since the Battle of the Nile except force the surrender of Malta; their troops had been ferried around the coasts of Europe on a series of pointless and fruitless expeditions. For the moment, all plans to defeat the French on land had collapsed.

During these same years, however, the British fleet grew stronger than ever before. Between 1795 and 1800 it made ready for its central task of blockade by conquering what had hitherto been its most lethal enemy: scurvy. The disease is caused by a deficiency of vitamin C, found in fresh fruits and vegetables, both of which were lacking in the sailor's diet. Prolonged cruising without some source of this vitamin had long meant that scurvy would decimate the crew. Although nothing was known about vitamins, since the early seventeenth century lime juice had been recognized as an antiscorbutic, or corrective of scurvy. During the War of the Austrian Succession, a way had been found to concentrate and preserve the juice, and the voyages of Captain Cook had given further proof of the value of citrus fruits and juice. In 1795 the Admiralty at last ordered a regular issue of lemon or lime juice on every ship; over the next twenty years, it would distribute 1.6 million gallons.[8] The measure virtually eliminated the disease in the navy. British sailors, who came to be known popularly as "limeys," could remain healthy at sea for indefinite periods; admirals no longer had to replace the ships of a blockading squadron with ships fresh from home but could hold their station month after month. The result was a dramatic increase in naval power.

The navy had also relearned the techniques of effective blockade. The tactics were extremely arduous, but Lord St. Vincent, now in command of the Channel Fleet, enforced them with a ruthless disregard for wear and tear on ships or men. He cruised in all weather and seasons off the western approaches to the Channel, where he communicated by frigates with smaller squadrons patrolling the exits from the French port of Brest; if the enemy dared to come out, one of these detachments would summon help from the main fleet. The enemy did not dare. Their ships of the line were penned into the harbor of Brest like helpless sheep, and the First Consul's repeated orders to put to sea were not obeyed. He was learning one more lesson in the uses of sea power.

By the spring of 1801, Bonaparte had devised a plan for circumventing that power through the League of Armed Neutrality. If the Baltic states combined their navies against Britain, they would pose enough of a threat so that the Channel Fleet, to meet it, would have to relax its stranglehold on Brest. Whitehall, however, had no intention of waiting passively for this plan to mature. The keystone of the neutral coalition was Denmark, and Pitt resolved to demonstrate to the Danes, and so to their would-be allies, the futility of their designs. In deep secrecy he prepared to deliver an ultimatum to Copenhagen, backed by what Nelson called "the best negotiators in Europe" — twenty ships of the line.

The Admiralty entrusted the mission to the aging and unimaginative Sir Hyde Parker, but it had the good sense to name Baron Nelson of the Nile his second-in-command. Nelson had done almost nothing since his victory except acquire a glamorous mistress. He had returned home with her and her complaisant husband and had broken with his own wife and been snubbed by the king; his career seemed bankrupt. Whatever the shortcomings of Nelson's private life, however, in a crisis the Admiralty wanted his talents.

The Danes rejected the ultimatum. The only way to coerce them was to destroy their fleet, moored in Copenhagen harbor under strong shore defenses, and Parker was most reluctant to do so. To conquer the enemy,

---

[8]Kenneth J. Carpenter, *The History of Scurvy and Vitamin C* (1986).

Nelson had first to conquer his superior; this he did, and he received permission to attack as he pleased. But in the middle of the battle, Parker, watching from a distance, lost his nerve and signaled the ships to retire. They could not have done so if they would, and Nelson would not let them. He put his telescope to his blind eye and said that he saw no signal. His coy disobedience might have earned him a court-martial; instead, after he had battered and bluffed the Danes into submission, he was empowered to sail to St. Petersburg to negotiate with the Russians. Tsar Paul had been assassinated. His successor, Alexander I, agreed to reopen his ports to British trade and admit the Royal Navy's right of search.

The League of Armed Neutrality had dissolved at the touch of force, and the British had made it clear that they could control the Baltic at will. Meanwhile they had reemphasized their power in the Mediterranean by landing an army in Egypt to begin the reduction of the French garrison there. The long arm of their sea power now reached around Europe from the Gulf of Finland to the mouth of the Nile. Although Britain was once more alone and France had grown stronger than ever before, the effective limit of French ambitions was the water's edge.

The Irish Crisis (1797–1801)

By the time the operations that he had planned in the Baltic and in Egypt came to fruition, Pitt was no longer in power. After having held office for almost eighteen years, he had been unseated by a complex of developments growing out of the Irish problem. He had tried and failed to resolve that problem in time of peace, and almost inevitably it returned to plague him in time of war. The pattern repeated itself over and over in British history, from the days of Elizabeth I to the days of Lloyd George: Irish grievances went unredressed until Britain had become embroiled in conflict at home or abroad, when a significant number of the Irish seized their opportunity for making trouble. They revolted against Elizabeth during her war with Spain. They rebelled against Charles I on the eve of civil war in England and went on fighting until Cromwell crushed them. They rose in the cause of James II as King William launched his struggle with France and again were crushed. They threatened revolt when Britain had its back to the wall in the War of American Independence, and at that time the Irish of the Protestant Ascendancy succeeded in winning both economic and political concessions. Yet many of the Irish felt far from satisfied, and in the 1790s the story unfolded once again.[9]

The legislative "independence" that they had acquired in 1782 was proving illusory. Even by British standards, the Irish Parliament was

---

[9]Chapters 13, 14, and 15 of J. C. Beckett, *The Making of Modern Ireland, 1603–1923*, 2nd ed. (1981), provide an excellent survey of the events of these years. The details may be found in G. C. Bolton, *The Passing of the Irish Act of Union* (1966). The efforts of the United Irishmen to harness French aid are recounted by Marianne Elliott in *Partners in Revolution* (1982) and *Wolfe Tone: Prophet of Irish Independence* (1989).

corrupt, and old religious tensions were reviving. Although Grattan's Parliament had restored the right to vote to Presbyterians and the right to hold land and to become lawyers or schoolmasters to Roman Catholics, a small Anglican clique continued to dominate the Irish executive. This clique, which was appointed by and dependent on the British government, had grown adept at manipulating a legislature to which it owed no constitutional responsibility.

The 1780s had witnessed economic growth in Ireland, but the French wars disrupted that growth. Presbyterians and Roman Catholics alike soon agitated once more for reform. Pitt, wishing to conciliate upper-class Catholics, secured for them in 1793 the right to vote for members of the Dublin Parliament, though not the right to serve as members themselves; the bogy of a legislature dominated by Catholics terrified most Protestants. The radicals of Ulster were beyond conciliation: Their Society of United Irishmen, headed by a charismatic young Protestant lawyer named Theobald Wolfe Tone (1763–1798), wanted to transform the island into a nonsectarian democratic republic similar to France or the United States. They hoped to transcend thereby all the differences of religion, ethnicity, and economic well-being that had hitherto divided the emerald isle.

The means to do so seemed ready at hand, and their emissaries assured the French government that the Irish, if supported by French troops, would chase the British into the sea. At the end of 1796, a strong French expedition, accompanied by Wolfe Tone, eluded the British blockade and appeared off the Irish coast. A storm prevented the soldiers from landing, but their enterprise stirred wild excitement in Ulster. There the United Irishmen had set up their own military organization and armed thousands of peasants with muskets and pikes. Their newspaper, the *Northern Star*, hailed the ideals of the French Revolution at the same time that it sought to "revive and perpetuate the ancient music and poetry of Ireland." Fearful of full-scale rebellion but short of regular troops, the Dublin government sent an army of yeomen and militia to harry the northern province. In search of arms, they burnt down houses, tortured suspected traitors, and destroyed the printing press of the *Northern Star*. Most of the remaining leaders of the United Irishmen were seized in Dublin early in 1798.

After the dispersion of the United Irishmen, the dream of a revolutionary nonsectarian Ireland faded, and the next temporarily successful rising took place in Wexford, in southeastern Ireland; it was led in large part by Roman Catholic priests. The Wexford rebels regarded the Protestants in general as their enemies — to be attacked, plundered, and even murdered. The "boys of Wexford" might have secured a more permanent success if the French had attempted to aid them. The Pitt ministry assumed, indeed, when it heard of Bonaparte's departure from Toulon, that the French *were* headed for Ireland; but they sailed off to Egypt instead. By the time a few French troops did land in Ireland in late August, the Dublin government had crushed the Wexford rebellion, and the French invaders were rounded up within a few weeks. In late September a somewhat larger French force was intercepted off the northern Irish coast. Wolfe Tone was captured, sent to Dublin, tried by court-martial, and found guilty. He committed suicide in prison.

The events of 1798 had destroyed the fragile union of rebellious Protestants and Catholics. An "Orange Order" (in memory of William of Orange) had been founded in 1795 in order to safeguard the Protestant Ascendancy in Ireland; and in the aftermath of the predominantly Roman Catholic revolt of the summer of 1798, many Irish Protestants had come to see a reviving Catholicism as a more dire threat than the continuing connection with Britain. The Irish executive in Dublin seemed to have only one policy: to use the local Irish yeomanry and militia (supplemented by troops from Britain) to repress rebellion or potential rebellion wherever it raised its head. For Prime Minister William Pitt back in London, such a policy was not good enough. Pitt was no Cromwell, and he had no desire to govern Ireland with a permanent British army of occupation. In any case he could not afford one during a European war. He determined to find a more lasting solution, which meant one that would be acceptable to Catholic Ireland — and therefore unacceptable to Dublin Castle. His troubles were just beginning.

His solution had two integrally connected parts. One part entailed a political union of Ireland and Great Britain, akin to the union of England and Scotland in 1707, with a single Parliament in which the Irish would have proportional representation. The other involved Catholic emancipation — in other words, the admission of Roman Catholics to the newly enlarged Westminster Parliament. They could not feasibly be admitted to the existing Dublin Parliament, as he had discovered, because the Protestant interest feared their domination. At Westminster they would form a small and unthreatening minority in a legislature overwhelmingly Protestant, but they would have a voice in government. The scheme had great advantages for both sides. All denominations of Irishmen who met the electoral qualifications would for the first time have members of Parliament of their own choosing, commercial barriers between the two countries would disappear, and the British would be rid of a governmental system that was artificial, antiquated, and unworkable. But the scheme could succeed only as a whole. Neither half by itself was viable: Protestant Ireland would never accept emancipation without union, and Catholic Ireland would never accept union without emancipation.

Pitt decided to tackle the two halves of his problem separately — to achieve first the legislative union of Ireland and Britain and then Catholic emancipation. Union met little resistance in Britain but much in Ireland, where the Dublin Parliament understandably hesitated to pass an act that would end its own existence. Pitt's Irish agents emphasized the continued threat from the French and a widespread outbreak of agrarian crime as arguments in favor of union, and they persuaded wavering Irish members of Parliament with peerages, honors, and simple bribes. The mass of the Irish population had no strong feelings about a debate that involved the small politically active minority. Most Dubliners, many large landowners, a majority of the members of the Orange Order lodges, and Henry Grattan were hostile. Ulster Presbyterians were cautiously favorable, as were the Roman Catholic bishops and a majority of politically active Catholic laymen, all of whom welcomed the prospect of Catholic Emancipation. In February 1800, the Irish House of Commons approved the Act of Union by a vote of 158 to 115. By summer both the British and the Irish parliaments had approved the measure, which went into effect at the beginning of 1801. Twenty-eight Irish peers, elected for life, and four Irish bishops took their places in the British House of Lords, and a hundred Irish members in the House of Commons.[10] The union established virtual free trade between the two countries, along the lines that Pitt had tried and abandoned in 1785. The cross of St. Patrick was superimposed upon those of St. George and St. Andrew to form a new flag, the Union Jack, symbolizing the United Kingdom of Great Britain and Ireland.

The symbolism was hollow. Although the union with Ireland in 1800 resembled that with Scotland back in 1707, notable differences existed as well. Even more markedly than Scotland had differed from England, so early nineteenth-century Ireland differed from Great Britain — economically, socially, religiously, and linguistically (for the Irish form of Gaelic, rather than English, remained the mother tongue of more than half its people). Rather than doing all in their power, moreover, to promote a true union of peoples, successive British governments preferred to look upon the Act of Union as the final solution to an ancient problem. Although the two judicial systems were largely coordinated and all remaining economic barriers were scheduled to lapse within two decades, the continuation (under Protestant Ascendancy influence) of a separate British executive and administrative staff in Dublin served as a reminder that London still thought of Ireland as a half-alien dependency.

Pitt did attempt to keep the other half of his bargain as well — to open the new Union Parliament and most administrative posts to professing Roman Catholics. He discovered to his dismay, however, that even some of his cabinet colleagues continued to resist Catholic Emancipation. Most important of all, so did the king. That obstacle turned out to be insurmountable. Supporters of the old order in Dublin and London adamantly objected to any concessions to Catholics, and they could readily appeal to a now-centuries-old British tradition of identifying national liberty and prosperity with steadfast resistance to "Popery." In this respect, King George III reflected the attitudes of his people. At his coronation, the monarch had taken an oath to uphold the supremacy of the established Anglican Church; he believed, as he had long insisted to Pitt, that to permit Catholics in Parliament would violate that oath. "I shall

---

[10]The act allowed an Irish peer, if not elected by his fellow peers to the House of Lords, to stand for election to the House of Commons from a British constituency. This provision accounts for the continuance of titled Irish members in the lower house, some of whom, such as Lord Palmerston, were to play prominent roles in nineteenth-century politics.

reckon any man my personal enemy," he said, "who proposes any such measure." He was in an excitable frame of mind, which threatened to lapse into the insanity that had already attacked him twice during his reign.[11] The king's stubbornness provoked a major crisis. The cabinet refused to press for emancipation, and Pitt was impaled on the horns of a dilemma. Because he could not fulfill, but would not repudiate, the assurance that he had given the Irish Catholics, he took the only honorable course and submitted his resignation. The king reluctantly let Pitt go, after extorting from him the promise that while his sovereign lived, he would not reopen the Catholic question.

Pitt had staked his ministry on an equitable solution to the Irish problem, and he had lost. Whether the Act of Union would permanently have satisfied a majority of the politically involved Irish, even with Catholic Emancipation, remains disputable. In any event, after two decades of relative quiet, a new generation of Irish national leaders would come to mourn the loss of their separate Parliament, however imperfect it had been. For Roman Catholic leaders, Pitt's failure to exact Catholic Emancipation would provide the grievance around which Daniel O'Connell during the 1820s would build the first modern Irish nationalist mass movement. What Pitt had intended as part of a larger reconciliation of peoples came to be looked back on as no more than a British contrivance. With a different king on the throne, the union might have begun under happier auspices. In practice, the Act of Union turned out to be less the permanent answer to "the Irish Question" than the end of one chapter and the beginning of another.

The Peace of Amiens (1802)

Pitt's resignation came at a time when the country's will to fight had reached a low ebb. Twice Britain had joined coalitions to stop French aggrandizement, and twice it had seen them disintegrate. Now the kingdom was on its own again, and it could no more hope for victory on land than France could at sea. After eight years of war, the burden of the national debt was staggering; it had more than doubled since 1793 and stood at over £530 million. Prices were rising faster than wages, so that by 1800 some farm laborers received in real wages less than half of what they had obtained at the start of the war. Trade and industry were booming, it is true; between 1796 and 1800 the value of British exports and imports increased dramatically. The harvests of 1799 and 1800 proved unusually poor, however, and in a number of towns rioters insisted that farmers reduce the price that they sought for their grain. "Peace and Large Bread or a King without a Head" read one anonymous placard. People whose income had been fixed by prewar contracts had cause for

---

[11]Most of the king's recent biographers attribute his illness not to psychological stress but to a hereditary physical disease, porphyria, about which nothing was known at the time. See Ida Macalpine and Richard Hunter, *George III and the Mad Business* (1968).

complaint, as did those hardest hit by wartime excise taxes and the new income tax. Continuing the war seemed pointless, when rich and poor alike longed to be free from the burden of what promised to be an interminable conflict. Their views were summed up by an admiral in the blockading squadron off Brest, who wrote that "nothing good can ever happen to us short of peace."

If Pitt had remained in office, he might have opened peace negotiations, but he would not have conducted them as his successor did. The new prime minister, Henry Addington, was an amiable nonentity unversed in foreign affairs, who had the gentleman's illusion that Bonaparte would behave like a gentleman. All began smoothly. The First Consul was ready to negotiate; he needed a breathing space to consolidate his position at home, to organize France's conquests and satellite states, and to create an effective navy. But his need did not make him easy to deal with. First he bullied London into an armistice that removed the pressure of blockade; then he haggled over terms for months, using bluff, threat, and deception, and ended by driving a hard bargain. In March 1802 the peace treaty was signed at Amiens.

The British people rejoiced wildly, but they had little to rejoice about. The government had returned virtually everything conquered overseas to France and its satellites, the Netherlands and Spain; it had agreed to restore Malta to the Knights of St. John under a flimsy international guarantee, and to evacuate both British and French troops from Egypt; and it had done nothing to secure British trade with Europe. Most humiliating of all, London had accepted the First Consul's haughty insistence that the affairs of Germany, Switzerland, and Italy were not subject to negotiation; in those areas he considered his will to be sovereign. For him the peace represented a substantial, though short-lived, triumph. He ceded nothing of moment, marked out western Europe as his preserve, and regained access to the world overseas. The French people hailed this success by making him First Consul for life, and he now began to call himself Napoleon.

The Peace of Amiens marked the end for Britain of what turned out to be only the first half of a very long war. The kingdom had entered the conflict in 1793 with little idea of how its armed forces should be used, with public opinion deeply divided, and with no overriding purpose to steel its will. Pitt had hoped that, after a quick victory, Britain would be able to help restore the continent's prewar frontiers. When that hope faded, he had made abortive efforts to negotiate peace with the Directory, and he favored renewing the negotiations with Bonaparte. For Pitt the war was not ideological but essentially defensive, to curb the expansion of France rather than destroy it as a power or undo the Revolution. The British public, by and large, took a similar view.

Yet over the years, Pitt had come to see, more clearly than many of his contemporaries, the scale of the threat inherent in French aggression. Shortly before his resignation, he was asked in Parliament to define his war aims without the qualification of any *but*'s or *if*'s. "In one word," he answered, security, security against a danger the greatest that ever threatened the world. . . . Peace is most desirable to this country. *But* negotiation may be attended with greater evils than could be counterbalanced by any benefits which would result from it. And *if* it afford no prospect of security, *if* it threaten all the evils which we have been struggling to avert, *if* the prosecution of the war afford the prospect of attaining complete security, then I say that it is prudent for us not to negotiate. These are my *but's* and my *if's*. This is my plea, and on no other do I wish to be tried by God and my country.[12]

The Peace of Amiens did not make the British secure, for Napoleon had no intention that they should be. Instead it ended their hope of finding security as long as Bonaparte ruled western Europe. For the British the uncertain phase of the war, with its periodic gropings for a settlement, was drawing to a close. During that phase, they had slowly and painfully learned how to use their strength, particularly their sea power, but had not recognized the need to defeat the Napoleonic regime outright. In the second phase, which opened in 1803 and lasted with one brief intermission until 1815, an early abortive attempt to negotiate peace would arise. Thereafter, however, the British would settle down to the job of destroying the French empire, whatever the effort might cost and however long it might take.

This later phase, like the previous one, was replete with military stupidity, bright chances lost, allies defeated. Yet in it the British harnessed their power as never before and exerted it with greater and greater effect. When Napoleon rejected his opportunity to make a lasting peace with them, he evoked a force that contributed, perhaps more than any other, to driving him step by step down a long road. That road led from Paris to Moscow, from Moscow to Leipzig and Elba, and from Elba to Waterloo and St. Helena.

---

[12]Winston Churchill, just after he became prime minister in May 1940 at the start of Britain's great crisis in the Second World War, dealt with the same question of war aim, and his words bore a striking resemblance to Pitt's. "You ask, what is our policy? I will say: It is to wage war . . . against a monstrous tyranny, never surpassed in the dark, lamentable catalogue of human crime. That is our policy. You ask, what is our aim? I can answer in one word: Victory — victory at all costs, victory in spite of all terror; victory, however long and hard the road may be; for without victory, there is no survival." Winston S. Churchill, *The Second World War*, Vol. 2 (1949), p. 22.

CHAPTER 12

The Napoleonic Wars

Although many Britons accepted the Peace of Amiens at face value, members of the Addington Ministry remained skeptical about Napoleon's long-term intentions, and they had good cause. In the immediate aftermath of the signing of the treaty, he drastically restricted British trade with his dominions, tightened his control of the Netherlands and Italy, transformed Switzerland into a satellite, sent French agents to stir up trouble in India and Ireland and even to survey British ports, renewed his active interest in Egypt, and brushed aside all protests as impertinent. Addington's government, by the standards of traditional diplomacy, might claim compensation for the buttressing of French power in Europe; and the First Consul's continuing interest in Egypt made a British naval base in the Mediterranean vital. Addington decided that Britain would compensate itself by holding on for the time being to the island of Malta. Napoleon was furious. "Woe to those who do not respect treaties," he burst out at the British ambassador. "They shall answer for it to all Europe." For his own treaty violations, he saw no need to answer.

Bonaparte spurned several last-minute efforts to resolve the quarrel by compromise, and in May 1803 the British government renewed the war. The First Consul's impatient inflexibility defeated his own ends. He wanted peace in order to prepare for more effective war, particularly at sea, and had ordered a 50 percent increase in ships of the line. With the shipyards of the Low Countries, France, and northern Italy at his command, he might have gained this great increment within another year or two. By provoking the British before he was ready, he enabled them to reestablish a blockade that he was powerless to break. His naval plans gradually evaporated, and with them his dreams of reconquering Egypt and moving against India, and even his hope of retaining a colonial empire.

The renewal of the war had an immediate impact on the United States. In 1800 France had regained from Spain by treaty the territory of Louisiana, which the French had ceded in 1763. This vast tract had indeterminate frontiers, but it stretched from the Mississippi to the Rockies and from the Gulf of Mexico to Canada. The prospect of its passing from the frail hands of Spain into the grip of the First Consul roused angry excitement in the United States. Napoleon realized that he could not reassert French control without war against the United States and that he

262

could not fight such a war if the British closed the Atlantic to him; their navy insulated the young republic from his power. As soon as he understood that Britain was about to renew the struggle, he concluded that Louisiana was as worthless to him as it was valuable to the Americans, and he offered to sell it to them for fifteen million dollars, a sum that he added to his military budget. In May 1803, just when London declared war, he completed the transaction. Thus the United States, with the quite inadvertent help of the British government and navy, almost doubled its territory.

The War at Sea (1803–1805)

Napoleon now resolved to destroy Britain, and he had only one sure way to do so — to invade. The prerequisite was the same for him as it had been for the Spaniards in 1588 — to secure control of the Channel. Unless he had control, invasion was out of the question. A few regiments might get across under cover of night or fog, or by rowboats in a calm that immobilized sailing ships. But to supply his troops when they landed, he had to concentrate in the Channel a fleet strong enough to beat back whatever the British brought against it and to hold its position until the invaders had crushed resistance ashore. The Spanish Armada had failed, but Napoleon was not accustomed to failing. He was approaching the zenith of his career, for in 1804 he had himself proclaimed emperor of the French; and his one sure way to secure his empire was by breaking the islanders' will to fight.[1]

While awaiting his chance for a naval concentration, he prepared small craft and drilled the soldiers that they would carry. The shipyards of western Europe were mobilized and turned out a flotilla of some 2,000 flat-bottomed boats, propelled by sail and oar, to ferry the elite of the French army across thirty-odd miles of water from Boulogne to the beaches of Kent. As the boats reached completion, they moved, under protection of shore batteries, to the points of concentration near Boulogne. There Napoleon massed 100,000 superbly trained men, the *Grande Armée* with which the emperor subsequently overawed the continent. However, that army, fine as it was, could not march on the water, or be carried in boats, until the French navy controlled the Channel.

Mastery for six hours, Napoleon said, would make him master of the world. Presumably he recognized this boast as grandiloquent nonsense, for by the spring of 1804, he faced formidable British defenses on land as well as at sea. Addington had strengthened the nation both in

---

[1]For works dealing with Britain's role in the Napoleonic Wars see, in addition to those cited in the previous chapter, Carola Oman, *Britain Against Napoleon* (1942), Richard Glover, *Britain at Bay: Defense Against Bonaparte 1803–14* (1973), Christopher D. Hall, *British Strategy in the Napoleonic War 1803–1815* (1992), and Arthur Bryant, *The Years of Victory, 1802–1812* (1945), the sequel to the same author's *The Years of Endurance, 1793–1802* (1942).

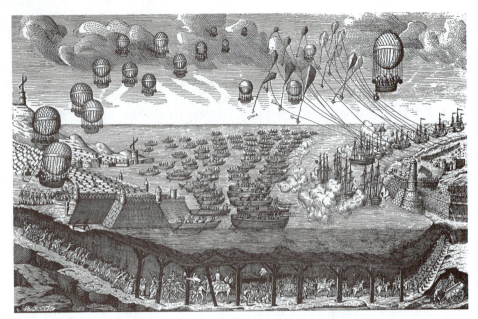

A Fanciful French Plan to Invade England in 1805 — by Tunnel, Sea, and Air   *(The Mansell Collection)*

finance —by collecting the income tax more efficiently — and in man-power. More than 400,000 volunteers underwent training, prepared to supplement a regular army and militia of 180,000 men. Light vessels and fortifications protected the coast. Women were expected to tend the fires at home even as men fought for their country abroad, and the Napoleonic Wars would harness the efforts of British women as in no previous world conflict. They organized to collect shoes and clothing for the troops; they subscribed to the London-based Patriotic Fund; and they sewed flags and banners and presented them publicly to the vol-unteer regiments. Most British women had been deeply shocked by the grisly public execution of Queen Marie-Antoinette and by the manner in which the leaders of the French Revolution exalted the creed of obe-dience to the state above that of devotion to the family. For many of them, the wars with France therefore became a conflict justified by the need to safeguard their own lives and the security of their households.[2]

Despite his efforts to prepare his homeland, most politicians could not visualize Addington as war leader, and in the spring of 1804 Pitt re-turned as prime minister to oversee the final preparations for the ex-pected invasion. The southeastern counties were denuded of any supplies that invaders might use, and the ministry laid plans for defending the Midlands if London fell. The island was a tough nut to crack, and Napoleon could not have cracked it without weeks — let alone six

---

[2]See Chapter 6, "Womanpower," in Linda Colley, *Britons* (1992).

hours — of undisputed naval control. British admirals determined to use their blockading prowess to keep the enemy's vessels in port.

The newly crowned emperor was prepared to challenge that blockade. His naval forces for this purpose were superficially imposing: Spain had recently joined France in the war; and the Dutch, Spanish, and French fleets, if they could combine, were roughly equal to the British in numbers though in nothing else. It became Napoleon's strategy to combine as many of these scattered fleets as possible while luring the British fleet from the Channel.

In the spring of 1805, when the final campaign opened, the combatants had arrayed their forces as shown on the accompanying map. The main French fleet, twenty-one ships of the line, was cooped up in Brest by Admiral Cornwallis, cruising in the western approaches to the Channel with twenty-five of the line; Admiral George Keith, with eleven, guarded the Channel itself. A minor French squadron at Rochefort and Franco-Spanish contingents at El Ferrol and Cadiz were contained by small British forces. The French Mediterranean fleet at Toulon, eleven of the line under Admiral Pierre Villeneuve, was watched by Nelson with thirteen. Although the impending campaign focused on the Straits of Dover, the naval elements involved were dispersed along the whole coast of western Europe.

Napoleon hoped to have his fleets escape from port, elude their British pursuers, and then converge secretly on the Channel while the British hunted them blindly across the ocean. If a French fleet threatened the West Indian islands on which the "nation of shopkeepers" set such store, then the British fleet would have to chase after it. The French would join forces in the Caribbean before their enemy arrived and then double back to the Straits of Dover to convoy the invading force. Britain would be conquered while its fleet was half a world away.

This daring and imaginative plan rested on the unwarranted premise that both the Royal Navy and the French navy would play the role that Napoleon had assigned to them. When ships rode idly at anchor month after month, as most French vessels were condemned to do, sailor morale deteriorated. The emperor assumed that his orders would galvanize these men into breaking out of their long confinement and that they would then cross the Atlantic for a precisely timed rendezvous in the Caribbean and return in a victorious armada sweeping up the Channel to Boulogne. It was a glittering dream.

The wonder is that any part of it materialized. In January 1805 the Rochefort squadron escaped to the West Indies, waited for support that did not arrive, and then returned in May with nothing accomplished. The main fleet at Brest stayed prudently in harbor. In March, Villeneuve did get out of Toulon, evaded Nelson, and set off in turn for the Caribbean. None of the other contingents that he expected met him there, and when he learned that Nelson was in hot pursuit, he doubled back to Spain. So did Nelson. Napoleon's chief purpose in the campaign, to combine his three fleets, had failed. Nevertheless, Villeneuve's fleet had grown to

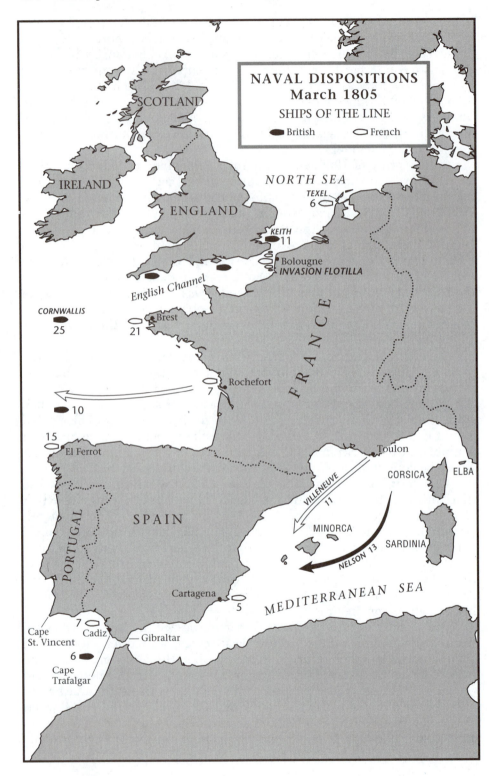

NAVAL DISPOSITIONS
March 1805
SHIPS OF THE LINE
● British   ◯ French

SCOTLAND

IRELAND

ENGLAND

NORTH SEA

TEXEL
6

KEITH
11

Bolougne
INVASION FLOTILLA

English Channel

CORNWALLIS
25

21 ● Brest

F R A N C E

Rochefort
7

● 10

15
El Ferrot

Toulon

CORSICA   ELBA

VILLENEUVE
11

MINORCA   SARDINIA

NELSON 13

SPAIN

P O R T U G A L

Cartagena
5

Cape
St. Vincent   7 Cadiz

Gibraltar

MEDITERRANEAN SEA

6 ●

Cape
Trafalgar

formidable size, thanks to French and Spanish ships that joined him, and after refitting in Spain and gathering additional ships, the admiral put to sea in a forlorn effort to reach the Channel. He felt deeply discouraged, and he complained about bad masts, bad sails, bad officers, and bad seamen. In August he simply gave up and returned to the port of Cadiz. When some weeks later news reached the inactive Villeneuve that Napoleon was about to deprive him of his command, he felt impelled to make one last gesture. On October 19, 1805, the Franco-Spanish fleet of thirty-three ships put to sea and headed south.

At dawn on October 21, it sighted Nelson's blockading force, twenty-seven ships of the line. In the darkness far to the west lay Cape St. Vincent, where Nelson had first made his name; to the east the surf rolled against the cliffs of Cape Trafalgar. The British approached from the west with a light wind behind them; as they drew near, Villeneuve reversed course and headed back for Cadiz. "We know only one maneuver, to form line, and that is just what the enemy wants us to do." Villeneuve's judgment proved accurate: Nelson did intend to tear that line apart. The admiral divided his force into two divisions, one to break through the allied rear and his own to break through the center. Signal flags proclaimed Nelson's order of the day, "England expects that every man will do his duty." A sailor allegedly retorted: "Does the old bitch think we shan't?"

Battle was joined at noon and raged for the next four hours, but the outcome was never in doubt. Early in the action Nelson was mortally wounded, and he died at the moment of victory. Partly in consequence, the British did not achieve a triumph of annihilation as they had at the Nile, but they did break the back of French sea power. They captured or destroyed roughly half of Villeneuve's fleet; thereafter Napoleon had no force of any consequence except the squadron at Brest, which dared not venture out. Numerous minor naval skirmishes broke out during the decade that followed, and by the time the war had ended, the British had sunk or captured more than 1,100 enemy vessels. For the rest of the war, however — in fact for most of the next hundred years — the British were free not only from threat of invasion but from any serious challenge at sea. Their power extended as far as the tides ran. After Trafalgar they used their naval preponderance to contain and destroy Napoleon, and after Waterloo they used it to maintain the Pax Britannica throughout the maritime world.

The War of the Third Coalition (1805–1807)

Napoleon's attempt to invade Britain did not end at Trafalgar; it had ended months before. Since the spring of 1805, he had realized that he faced a renewal of the continental war: His expansion in Germany and Italy threatened to alienate Sweden, Russia, and Austria; and British diplomacy had begun to bring them into alliance against him. The emperor waited until late August to see whether Villeneuve's fleet might

Pitt and Napoleon Carve Up the Globe   A cartoon by George Cruikshank (1805). *(Mansell/Time)*

yet open the Channel to him, and then, deciding that it would not, he turned to a campaign on the Danube. Two months before Trafalgar, he had tacitly admitted the bankruptcy of his naval plans; the battle itself was a postscript to their failure.

Napoleon's genius and army had reached their peak, however, and he launched the greatest offensive of his career. He marched from the Channel to the Danube, like Marlborough a century before, with a speed that his enemies thought impossible. On the day before Trafalgar, he captured an Austrian force of 60,000 men. He pressed on to Vienna, occupied it, and in December moved north to annihilate an Austro-Russian army at Austerlitz. Austria for the third time made a humiliating peace, and the Russians fell back toward their frontiers.

In London, during these catastrophes, Pitt was dying; the strain of the war years had worn out his frail body. When the news of Austerlitz reached him, he recognized what it meant: The old map of Europe, he said, would not be needed for another ten years, a prophecy that was fulfilled almost to the day. He died in January 1806, murmuring, "My country, how I leave my country!" Although he did not leave it triumphant, he did leave it indomitable. It was sufficiently united, thanks in great part to his leadership, so that it carried on the struggle for the next nine years without a single leader of his stature.

The next administration had an optimistic name, the Ministry of All the Talents, which at last included those of Charles James Fox. The talents were largely wasted, however. Fox promptly put to the test his long-standing sympathy for the French Revolution, and for Napoleon as its heir, by opening peace negotiations. Napoleon encouraged them with one hand, and with the other tightened his grip on Europe. Even Fox became disillusioned. The French, he concluded, did not want peace and were not to be trusted; they "fly from their word." Then, in September 1806, Fox died, only nine months after the death of his lifelong rival, Pitt. Peace negotiations lapsed completely soon thereafter.

In his brief tenure of office, Fox did achieve one aim that had been as dear to him over the years as the cause of peace. Just before his death, he secured the consent of Parliament to abolish the slave trade throughout the empire, and the measure formally became law in the spring of 1807. Although slavery itself remained legal in Britain's colonies for another quarter-century, and only the importation of slaves was forbidden, this prohibition was recognized at the time for what it was — a crucial step in abolishing the whole institution of slaveholding. The statute was not the work of Fox alone. For nearly twenty years, William Wilberforce had waged the parliamentary campaign for abolition, and in the country at large — as noted in Chapter 10 — the cause had won the support of a powerful lobby of petitioners. But Fox led the final phase of the battle, and the victory that he assured before he died is a fitting tribute to his indomitable spirit.

The Ministry of All the Talents, which did not long survive the loss of Fox, resigned in the spring of 1807. It failed in its central task, for it neither made peace nor showed any talent for making war. Although Pitt's successors continued his policy of subsidizing continental allies, thereby making Britain "the paymaster of Europe," they had no greater success than he in integrating Britain's efforts, by land or sea, with those of its major allies, Russia, Prussia, and Austria. Consequently, Britain exerted a negligible strategic influence on the War of the Third Coalition, and by 1807 that conflict was drawing to a close in a peculiarly threatening way. In the previous autumn, Prussia had joined Russia against the French emperor, who was more than a match for them both; in June 1807 he defeated them with finality. Prussia was conquered, and Russia was ready to come to terms.

Napoleon met the young Tsar Alexander, who found him dazzling; a series of interviews between them produced the Treaty of Tilsit. This settlement, signed in July 1807, was a landmark in the Napoleonic Wars. It forged an alliance between the two emperors, by which they divided the whole continent into French and Russian spheres of influence. Prussia was temporarily reduced to impotence, and Austria was in eclipse. The emperor of the French had become emperor of the West, dominating Germany and Italy; and in the east the tsar ruled the only other remaining great power. "What is Europe, where is it," Alexander exclaimed to Napoleon, "if it is not you and I?" Though melodramatic, for the moment he was right.

The two sovereigns bound themselves at Tilsit to cooperate in any war that either might undertake in Europe. As a result, when the British refused to come to terms, Alexander changed sides and turned against them. By now he detested them, and they had given him cause: In the recent war, they had done nothing effective to aid him, either by arms or subsidies, and had even seized some of Russia's merchant ships. To his proud and mercurial temperament, the only answer was to join Napoleon and bring Britain to its knees.

Once more the islanders stood alone, with no hope of creating another coalition like those of the past. They seemed to have only enemies left in a Europe more solidly united against them than ever before. The climactic phase of the struggle was beginning, and it brought into sharp relief both the strengths and the shortcomings of British society. One source of strength was industrialization, which was advancing at a forced pace under the impetus of war: The British supplied the continent with much of its manufactured goods, and even their enemies felt compelled to buy from them. War also stimulated the enclosure movement, as did the rising population that had to be fed; even bad harvests did not halt the increasing productivity of the land. Foreign imports had to supplement domestic foodstuffs, however, because the British by now insisted on their coffee, tea, and sugar. Their merchant marine, despite the best efforts of French privateers, retained the lion's share of the European carrying trade. Mines, factories, farms, and ships created the wealth that the government converted, by taxation and borrowing, into the sinews of war.

An admiring German observer wrote,

> A nation that by her activity and the genius of her citizens manufactures its numberless articles of merchandise infinitely finer, in much superior workmanship, in far more exquisite goodness than all other nations without exception, and that is able to sell them infinitely cheaper, owing to her admirable engines, her machines, and her native coal; a nation whose credit and whose capital is so immense as that of England — surely such a nation must render all foreigners tributary; and her very enemies must help to bear the immense burden of her debt and the enormous accumulation of her taxes.[3]

But Britain's shortcomings were also apparent. Both industrialization and enclosure dislocated the economic order and bred unrest. Artisans such as hand-loom weavers, who could no longer compete with the products of machinery, on occasion smashed the machines rather than seek out new ways of earning a livelihood. In the meantime, cotton spinners vainly petitioned Parliament to legislate a minimum wage on their behalf, and they achieved some wage increases by means of strikes. Villagers who had lost their rights in the common or found their small holdings uneconomical to farm in the aftermath of enclosure, grew as angry as the weavers, and discontent among the lower ranks of society remained intermittently explosive. Some of the well-to-do also felt un-

---

[3]Quoted in William Cunningham, *The Growth of English Industry and Commerce in Modern Times* (1892), pp. 516–517. Cunningham's work, although long out of date, contains much useful detail.

happy. Poor rates tended to edge up steadily during the war years; and that galling invasion of personal liberty, Pitt's income tax, threatened to become a permanent fixture of government finance. Although the war stimulated the expansion of grain growing and boosted the sales of particular manufacturers, some members of the propertied classes acutely felt the burden of taxation that the war had imposed on them.

Others, to judge by literary evidence, lived as if there were no war. The great novelist of the period was Jane Austen; her books explore middle-class country society, which she saw with an amused and keen eye and described in lucid detail. Her characters are entirely absorbed with their own affairs and those of the neighborhood. Except when a regiment of scarlet-clad militiamen is stationed nearby, they move through their daily rounds, flirting, drinking tea, making delightful conversation, with scarcely a hint that the country is in the grip of economic revolution and is standing at bay against Napoleon. Though Miss Austen's two brothers served in the navy throughout the war, the world of her novels is untouched by anything outside itself: It is tranquil and timeless. This tranquility is not the aberration of a single author but the reflection of a significant truth. War, even on the Napoleonic scale, still had a limited impact, as did economic change. Every inhabitant of the British Isles in some way and to some degree experienced the social changes unfolding around them, but the effect was at times too subtle to be perceived. Many Britons continued in the traditional frame of their society, almost unaware that they were living through upheavals that would fascinate historians.

If Jane Austen deliberately focused her attention on only one aspect of her world, William Wordsworth spoke for others passionately involved in the struggle against France. The poet had changed his tune. The young man who had regarded the French as heroes had become a middle-aged patriot who regarded them as "slaves, vile as ever were befooled by words," and who gloried in Britain's isolated stand against the enemy.

> Another year!—another deadly blow!
> Another mighty Empire overthrown!
> And We are left, or shall be left, alone;
> The last that dare to struggle with the Foe
> 'Tis well! from this day forward we shall know
> That in ourselves our safety must be sought;
> That by our own right hands it must be wrought;
> That we must stand unpropped, or be laid low
> O dastard whom such foretaste doth not cheer!

Rational calculations gave little cause for cheer. Although the tsar's *volte-face* meant little to Britain in military terms, because his fleets were insignificant and his armies no more amphibious than the French, it meant a great deal in commercial terms. He closed the ports of Russia to British goods and agreed to bully the other Baltic states into doing likewise. He thereby enabled Napoleon to implement on a large scale a project with which the emperor had already been experimenting — to cut off Britain's entire trade with Europe. Out of the Tilsit settlement came the far-reaching design for economic warfare known as the Continental System.

The Continental System (1807–1809)

His invasion plans foiled, Napoleon sought to use economic weapons to bring Britain to terms. The French military offensive had given the emperor direct or indirect control of a large part of the European coastline, and with Russian help he could control much of the rest; the few holes that remained did not seem difficult to plug. The emperor intended to answer the British naval blockade by a blockade on shore, enforced in every port of the continent and extending like a gigantic dike from the Baltic to the Black Sea. This dike, he reasoned, would accomplish two purposes simultaneously. On the one hand, eliminating France's greatest competitor would give French products a virtual monopoly of the European market. On the other hand, damming the flow of British manufactures would turn the island's greatest strength into a fatal weakness. Britain's economy had become so dependent on exporting goods to continental Europe, Napoleon believed, that it must either export or go bankrupt. Once its markets were cut off, its machines would go idle, factory owners would rage, hungry workers would riot, and pressure on the government in London would mount until its government was forced to capitulate. This was the design, and it determined the whole future of the war.

The Continental System could succeed only on two conditions. One, the accord with Alexander had to continue, for only his collaboration made the dike complete and kept central Europe docile. Two, Napoleon needed to make his power effective along the vast stretch of European coast that lay outside the Russian orbit. His system had to operate in every saltwater port that had good communications with the interior — along a European coastline stretching all the way from northern Germany to southern Italy. He soon discovered, however, that he could almost never enforce a strict embargo through satellite governments. They were too weak, even if they were willing, to suppress the smuggling of British goods. He was compelled to bring in his own bureaucracy of customs officers, backed by troops, which meant extending his dominions; this he did over the next four years. The attempt to make his economic system work involved him in ever greater expansion of his political system, until in the end even he overreached himself.

The ink had scarcely dried on the Tilsit agreement before Napoleon began plotting further moves. He directed his attention to two corners of Europe that were far apart but vital to his schemes. One was Scandinavia, where he intended to revive the old idea of a naval coalition, with Denmark as its focus, to seal off the Baltic from British penetration. The other was the Iberian peninsula, where Portugal had fallen into his bad graces because of its traditional friendship with Britain, and Spain seemed ripe for absorption into his system. If British goods were excluded from the Baltic and from Portugal and Spain, as they already were from the Low Countries, France, and Italy, the blockade would be complete, at least in theory. The islanders would presumably face a choice of ruin or surrender.

London recognized the danger in the Baltic and responded at once. In September 1807 a powerful British expedition attacked Copenhagen for the second time, bombarded the city into surrender, and sailed away with the entire Danish fleet. Whatever its justification as self-defense, this act was almost Napoleonic in its brutality; but it did accomplish its purpose, for the Baltic remained open. In November, when Napoleon's troops were massed at the gates of Lisbon, another British squadron convoyed the Portuguese fleet and royal family to refuge in Brazil. The Royal Navy had become adept at filching fleets from under the emperor's nose.

Almost simultaneously, London counterattacked on another front by tightening the operation of its blockade. A series of orders in council re-defined to Britain's benefit — and therefore narrowly curtailed — the right of neutrals to freedom of the seas. The complex provisions of the orders were not designed to ruin neutral commerce, which was vital to the British themselves, but to control and profit by it while diverting it from the enemy. Neutral ships were encouraged to trade with Britain and were prohibited from trading with any continental state that excluded British ships and goods, unless they had first called at a British port and received a license. The principal impact of the restrictions was on the United States, the only remaining neutral that had a large carrying trade. Ameri-can merchant captains faced a dilemma. If they disobeyed the restric-tions, they risked capture by British men-of-war; if they obeyed them, they became fair game for French privateers at sea and customs officials on land. United States opinion was incensed against both sides, and the only question was which was the greater enemy.

To the peoples incorporated into the Continental System, the answer to that question grew clearer with every month that passed. For them Napoleon was the enemy. Britain had what they wanted, the products of the Industrial Revolution and the produce of the overseas world — silk and sugar and coffee and spices and a thousand other commodities. These imports were in such demand that the black market flourished even as prices soared. Britain offered European consumers the satisfaction of their material wants. Napoleon offered them, in return for tightening their belts and forgoing their wants, the benefits of the French Revolu-tion enforced by French arms; and the benefits that he conferred at bayo-net point had increasingly less appeal. "We come to give you liberty and equality," announced one of his marshals to a newly subjugated people, "but don't lose your heads about it. The first person who stirs without my permission will be shot." Before this kind of pronouncement, the sins of the Royal Navy paled into insignificance.

A year after Tilsit, Napoleon for the first time encountered a challenge by a people in arms. His troops crossing Spain, ostensibly to subjugate

Portugal, were actually intended to win him the entire peninsula. In the spring of 1808, he kidnapped the Spanish royal family and elevated his own brother Joseph to the vacant throne. He failed to reckon with the nature of the Spaniards; a majority of whom had no taste for the reforms that King Joseph dangled before them. By French standards, Spain's monarchy may have been reactionary and its church and aristocracy unenlightened, but numerous Spaniards demonstrated their willingness to fight for their institutions. Revolt germinated almost overnight. In June a French army of 20,000 men surrendered to the Spanish rebels, and the shock waves rippled throughout Europe. King Joseph discovered what the British had learned a century earlier from their attempt to install Archduke Charles in Madrid — that foisting a regime on the Spanish against their will was a dangerous game.

Napoleon fumed at the Spanish resistance. But having no idea of the hornets' nest he had roused, he supposed that suppression would be easy. He knew that the Spanish irregulars, or guerrillas, could not stand up to his troops in the field. He did not know that those troops faced difficulties that in the end would prove insuperable. Communications with France, thanks to the British navy, were almost entirely by land; and the roads south from the Pyrenees ran over a series of mountain ranges where guerrillas could take a heavy toll of men and supplies. The Spaniards also sought aid in their drive to oust their new rulers. They appealed to the British, who responded at once, and so began the Peninsular War that would grind on for the next five years.[4]

The war gave Britons two new opportunities to use their resources, one commercial, the other strategic. The collapse of the Bourbon regime at Madrid loosened Spain's hold on its American empire, which began to disintegrate. Spanish colonists, hungry for manufactured goods, opened their ports to the British and so gave them, at the moment when Napoleon's blockade began to produce serious economic repercussions at home, the market that British merchants had coveted for a century. It was too limited a market to end their difficulties altogether, but it did help to tide them over the most critical phase.

Britain's other opportunity was strategic. After years of landing expeditionary forces on the continent and having them chased back into the sea, the British obtained the chance to use their army effectively. Control of the Spanish coast enabled them to strike where they pleased, supply their troops, and evacuate them if need be; the Spaniards' hatred of the French gave the British a base of popular support. The redcoats alone, or the Spanish irregulars alone, might have been crushed, but not the two in

---

[4]The classic history of the Peninsular War, written by a historian who was also a participant, is Sir William F. P. Napier, *History of the War in the Peninsula and in the South of France, from the Year 1807 to the Year 1814*, 5 vols. (1828–1836). Two briefer but reliable modern accounts are David Gates, *The Spanish Ulcer: A History of the Peninsular War* (1986), and Part II of Elizabeth Longford, *Wellington: The Years of the Sword* (1969).

conjunction. For the first time since 1793, Britain's army received an opportunity to prove itself.

It was a different kind of army from that of the French. The British, untouched by social revolution, had maintained their eighteenth-century military structure. Since the beginning of the war, however, they had taken great pains to overhaul it: They had improved the pay, drill, and equipment of the troops; reorganized their administration; and introduced riflemen and rangers to operate on their own as scouts and skirmishers. The artillery had adopted Major Henry Shrapnel's new explosive shell; the infantry had become so skilled in marksmanship that the volley of a British line had a devastating impact. Britain still had an eighteenth-century army — small, professional, and highly trained — but it had matured into a far more effective instrument.

A reformed army with unreformed leaders would have been useless. "In war *men* are nothing," wrote Napoleon in the summer of 1808; "it is a *man* who is everything." The British hitherto had not produced a man worth mentioning; their generals, in contrast to Nelson and his "band of brothers," had been almost uniformly incompetent. At the beginning of the Peninsular War, however, a new leader came on the scene. Though not yet in command, he had talents comparable with Marlborough's a century before. Just as the navy had had the luck of finding genius at the climax of its struggle against France, so now the army had the same good fortune.

Arthur Wellesley, the younger son of a minor Irish nobleman, had his way to make in the world like most younger sons. He elected the army and in 1796 was sent with his regiment to India. There fortune smiled on him, for in 1797, Pitt appointed his older brother, by then Lord Wellesley, as governor-general. In the next eight years, the two Wellesleys made names for themselves. Indian princes, inspired by the French, were in revolt, but the governor-general, despite the fears of the East India Company directors, promptly took the offensive. He waged a series of wars, in which his younger brother performed brilliantly, that affirmed and enhanced Britain's position as the paramount power in India. By 1805 Lord Wellesley's work was done, but his brother's was only beginning.

In August 1808 Arthur Wellesley landed in Portugal with a small army. He defeated a French force guarding Lisbon and might have annihilated it if he had not been superseded by a blunderer who threw away most of the fruits of victory. Wellesley and his inept superior were recalled; the command in Portugal devolved on Sir John Moore, who advanced into Spain to aid the insurgents. But Napoleon by now had crossed the Pyrenees with 250,000 men. He destroyed the Spanish levies and reached Madrid, where he heard that a British army of only 27,000 menaced his flank. The prospect of capturing it turned him away from his plan for reducing the rest of Spain, and he set out on one of his lightning pursuits. Moore, racing to the sea and the waiting transports, moved even faster, however, until the disgusted emperor turned over the chase to a subordinate and returned to France. Moore reached his destination, Corunna, early in January 1809; there he turned on his pursuers and repulsed them in an action that cost him his life. But he had saved his army and distracted Napoleon from the best opportunity the French ever had to conquer Spain.

The emperor's return to France had been prompted by news that Austria was again preparing for hostilities. He had defeated the Austrians three times, but they refused to stay down. Now that he was embroiled in Spain and the exactions of his Continental System were ending his popularity in Germany, the Austrians hoped that the time had come for revenge. They fought alone, however, and Napoleon brought them to heel in a single campaign. Yet he met tougher resistance than ever before, for he now fought a people as well as a government. When the two together defied him, they gave pause even to the *Grande Armée*.

As Napoleon's involvement in Spain had encouraged Austria to turn on him, so his consequent involvement on the Danube gave new life to the Spanish rising. In the meantime, the British attempted to aid the Austrians in the summer of 1809 by sending 40,000 men to capture Antwerp, a city that Napoleon had transformed into the most important French naval base in northern Europe. The question of how to hold the city, once captured, did not arise because the expedition failed ignominiously. The troops would have been invaluable to Wellesley, who had returned to Portugal in the spring as commander-in-chief. Without them he had only 25,000 regulars and could make no lasting impression. He advanced on Madrid and won victories that earned him a peerage as Lord Wellington, but his Spanish allies proved unreliable, and he barely managed to extricate himself and retreat to Portugal. There he awaited the emperor's next assault, for in the autumn, Napoleon, having crushed Austria, began to pour troops back across the Pyrenees. It was the dismal end to a dismal year.

The British Counterattack (1810–1811)

Fortunately for Lord Wellington, the French elected to conquer Spain before moving against him, providing him many months in which to prepare his defense. Wellington's plans rested on the assumption that the French forces would have to live off the countryside — moving like locusts and stripping each region of everything edible — while his own forces, if they held Lisbon, could continue to be supplied by sea. Wellington therefore fortified the approaches to Lisbon and created an effective transport service. He also built up an excellent staff and an improved medical corps. He drilled his troops to a high level of efficiency, and he strengthened the anti-French forces by supervising the training of an army of 10,000 Portuguese troops as well. His gift for military organization represented what Thomas Carlyle was to define as genius, "the transcendent capacity for taking trouble." Nothing that concerned the smooth functioning of an army escaped his eye. He was never popular with his men (nor did he care to be), but he was as meticulous in watching over their needs as he was remorseless in his demands on them.

The test of his preparations came in September 1810, when Marshal André Masséna began his long-heralded invasion of Portugal with more than 60,000 French veterans. Wellington fell back on Lisbon, fighting as he went, while the Portuguese peasants laid waste their farms in the invaders' path. In October Masséna's advance halted abruptly. Before him loomed the lines of Torres Vedras, fortifications that ran across the neck of the Lisbon peninsula for almost thirty miles, from the Atlantic to the Tagus River. The marshal was helpless. The lines were too strong to be stormed by assault, and he could not starve out the defenders while their navy commanded the sea. For the French, on the other hand, the land offered no subsistence, and only a trickle of supplies from Spain broke through the swarms of Portuguese irregulars operating in their rear. Masséna held out until the spring of 1811, while his starving army dwindled; then he retreated by a route already picked bare of food during his advance. Wellington harassed his rear, and guerrillas hung on his flanks. He lost 25,000 men and returned to Spain with an army of scarecrows.

His retreat had serious repercussions. With his usual public fanfare, Napoleon had ordained that the British should be swept into the sea, but instead the emperor had suffered a disaster to his arms and prestige. French morale in Spain sank, and Spanish morale toughened; the tide of war in the peninsula had turned. The subject peoples of Europe began to hope again, and the Russian tsar took a more independent tone than he had since the Treaty of Tilsit. What Napoleon later called the Spanish ulcer began to drain the health of his empire.

Not the least important, Wellington's success made an impact at home, where good news found welcome ears. By the beginning of 1811, Britain was in a dangerous state. King George III had lost for good his sight and his sanity, and his eldest son had been named to reign in his place as Prince Regent. The prince was popular primarily with the sycophants who surrounded him. The prince's younger brother, the duke of York, commander-in-chief of the army, had been driven from office by a noisome scandal; and the country was governed by a ministry with few discernible talents. After the death of Pitt and Fox, only two men of real ability remained — Lord Castlereagh at the War Office and George Canning as foreign secretary. The public distrusted them both; they loathed each other; and in 1809 their quarreling forced them simultaneously from office. For the next three years, the government headed by Prime Minister Spencer Perceval, run by mediocrities and riven by factions, offered no clear-cut policy at home or abroad.

The immediate danger by 1811 was at home, for Britain was at last feeling the full effect of the Continental System. Commerce was little impaired, but the industrial population suffered almost precisely the hardships that Napoleon had anticipated. Raw materials were in desperately short supply, and prices soared accordingly; the market value of silk almost quadrupled, with wool, timber, and hemp not far behind. An unusually poor harvest drove food prices up as well; in 1812 the price of wheat in some areas rose from ten to twenty-five shillings a bushel, and

Wellington as Liberator   After the British army drove the French out of Madrid in 1812, Wellington was presented with the keys to the city. *(The Victoria and Albert Museum)*

the threat of hunger loomed. Bankruptcies came thick and fast, unemployment ran rife, and riots became commonplace. A worker's job was a life-and-death matter; a smoldering resentment of machines, blamed for curtailing employment and depressing wages, finally broke into violence.

At the end of 1811, organized bands of men, masked and working at night, began to destroy knitting frames and other textile machinery throughout the Midlands. Local opinion supported the rioters, and their activities spread. Their leader was said to be a mysterious "General Ned Ludd," who may or may not have existed; and from him they took the name of Luddites.[5] At first they abstained from bloodshed, but before long, when some of their men were shot by the soldiery, they retaliated with murder. The government sent 12,000 troops into the disordered counties, and in a mass trial at York in 1813, seventeen leaders were sentenced to hang and six others to be shipped to Australia. The movement then disintegrated, although it revived briefly after the war. Some Luddites sought to incite an insurrection against the government, and they

[5]Malcolm I. Thomis, *The Luddites* (1970), provides a reliable account.

rejoiced in May 1812 at the news of the assassination of Prime Minister Perceval in the lobby of the House of Commons. (The assassin was not a Luddite but the agent of an Anglo-Russian trading company whose business had been ruined by the war.) The Luddites hoped to return to a bygone era before machines had complicated life; they embodied the old England protesting against the new. The protest was hopeless, but for the moment it terrorized employers and scared the government. How long, many wondered, would the common people endure their miseries?

Many politicians took a gloomy view. They recognized the popular hardships as real and dangerous and knew that radical agitation made the most of the danger. The nation seemed close to ruin, and defeatism once more permeated the air. Why continue the war, when many British leaders believed in their heart of hearts that Napoleon was invincible on land and that the British army would go on repeating in Spain the failures that had dogged it since 1793? The struggle, they argued, was hopeless. This mood grew so strong in Westminster that Wellington, during his campaign against Masséna in Portugal and Spain, expected at any moment to have his army called home. But the government continued to support a British army of more than 50,000 men on the Iberian peninsula and, by means of subsidies, a Spanish and Portuguese army of comparable size, all under Wellington's command. By the end of 1811, moreover, an oft-disheartened British public had come to realize that its cold and taciturn general had a gift for victory.

While the army redeemed itself in Spain, the navy gathered new conquests. Guadeloupe and Martinique in the West Indies, Java in the East Indies, Mauritius and the Cape of Good Hope — all over the world the colonies of France and its satellites fell into British hands. Around the European coast — on Heligoland in the North Sea, on Malta, Sicily, and the Ionian Islands in the Mediterranean — bases were established for blockading squadrons and for smuggling British goods into the continent. Napoleon had no answer but wider and more stringent control. He annexed to France a strip of territory on the northeast, running through the Low Countries and the North Sea coast of Germany to Lübeck on the Baltic, and on the southeast he incorporated Piedmont, the Papal States, and the eastern coast of the Adriatic; his brother-in-law Murat, king of Naples, ruled all of Italy that was not annexed. The French grip on the coastline seemed secure.

Yet in the process of tightening his grip on that coastline, the emperor added to the number of his enemies. Annexing the Papal States roused against him a power that he could not understand — that of a gentle and unbending old man who excommunicated him and became his prisoner; the sight of the pope at the imperial chariot wheels deeply offended Catholic Europe. Napoleon's intrusion into Germany, and his increasingly overt domination of his satellites there, waked in opposition to him a new sense of German nationalism, particularly among the young, while in the Italian peninsula, politically unified for the first time since the days of Rome, nationalistic dreams also stirred. The emperor had forcibly disseminated the revolutionary fervor of nationalism throughout Europe, and now such fervor began to work against him.

The American and Russian Wars (1812)

While the Napoleonic system stretched French power to the breaking point, Britain also paid a price for its method of making war. The British became embroiled in a second Anglo-American conflict. From their viewpoint, the conflict was no more than a regrettable but minor by-product of the great struggle in Europe, but in American eyes it was momentous. The War of 1812, the first on which the new republic embarked, confirmed the emotions in which the United States had been born: hatred of Britain became part of orthodox American patriotism. That hatred and reciprocal British resentment would poison the relationship between the two countries for several generations and obscure the magnitude of their common interests.

The war grew directly out of the struggle in Europe. As European neutrals disappeared into the maw of the French empire, Britain swept their flags from the seas, and the United States prospered by inheriting the bulk of the continent's carrying trade. But the Americans inevitably fell foul of the navy that brought them their business. They needed more and more ships, hence more and more seamen; and they offered high wages. Soon they were attracting deserters from the Royal Navy, which was also expanding and desperate for sailors. British press gangs abducted for service Americans who could not prove their citizenship, while British men-of-war stopped and searched American vessels and appropriated any of the crew thought to be deserters. The United States protested, but London refused to mend its ways. For the British, manning the fleet was a matter of self-preservation.

For years the two great European belligerents had imposed more and more restrictions on neutral trade, which roused a resentment in the United States that brought it to the verge of war in the 1790s, first against Britain and then against France. But the crises passed, partly because American commerce thrived despite all trammels, and primarily because the European struggle did not yet focus on economic warfare. After 1806 things changed. Neither Britain nor France would permit a neutral to give comfort to its enemy; each aimed at manipulating American trade for its own purpose and exerted increasing pressure to that end. Here Britain was at a disadvantage. Sea power, usually far less conspicuous than land power, was for once more visible. While Napoleon confiscated American merchantmen in the distant ports of France, British warships invaded American territorial waters and outraged national pride.

The United States, caught between the upper and the nether millstone, at first attempted to escape by putting an embargo on all foreign trade, but the effect at home was ruinous. As the next step, the United States in-

"Johnny Bull in a Fret"   During the War of 1812, an American cartoonist gloats over the manner in which the world's largest navy has been stung by American ships like the *Wasp* and the *Hornet*. *(The Historical Society of Pennsylvania)*

formed France and Britain that American trade would be open to whichever one abandoned its restrictive policy, and closed to the other. Napoleon pretended to rescind his decrees in compliance; he duped President Madison, who believed that the French were acting in good faith and that the British would not act at all. Ultimately London did act; it repealed the Orders in Council that had forbidden the United States to carry goods from the French colonies to France. But a few days earlier, on June 18, 1812, the United States Congress, antagonized beyond endurance and animated by "war hawks" hoping to annex Canada, had declared war against Britain.

It was a needless conflict, provoked by prickly emotions on the American side and haughty ineptitude on the British; neither contestant had an intelligible war aim. The Americans had the will to conquer Canada, but not the power. Neither did they have the strength to achieve their ostensible goal: the right to trade as they pleased. For Britain, fighting for its existence, would not compromise the effectiveness of its blockade unless compelled to do so, and the United States Navy of that day could not compel anyone. As for the British, they had no goal; they lacked both the will and the power to conquer the United States. Moreover, they could ill afford a contest that further strained their resources, already spread thin, and that offered them nothing in return.

The conduct of operations was as faulty as the logic that had caused them. An American attempt to invade Canada was a fiasco. A British raid on the Chesapeake accomplished nothing except to burn public buildings in the new capital at Washington, thereby further embittering the Americans, and inspiring *The Star-Spangled Banner.* The infant United States Navy won a number of minor actions, on inland lakes and at sea, that jolted British complacency and elated the American public but had little effect on the outcome of the war. A British attack on the mouth of the Mississippi had no effect at all; veterans of Wellington's peninsular army were defeated in the Battle of New Orleans, which started Andrew Jackson on his road to the White House but which was fought after the war had ended. Peace came in December 1814 with the Treaty of Ghent. As if to emphasize the pointlessness of the conflict, the treaty kept discreetly silent on all the issues out of which hostilities had arisen.

Whereas Americans came to view the war as a landmark, in Britain it became no more than a footnote to the saga of the Napoleonic Wars.[6] It was a sideshow, played out just when the great drama on the continent reached its climax. In the years 1812–1814, Napoleon made his supreme gamble for the mastery of Europe, and by the time the Treaty of Ghent was signed, his empire had shrunk to a Mediterranean island. Small wonder, then, that events in the United States received scant attention overseas.

The declaration of war by the United States in June 1812 coincided almost to the day with the opening of Napoleon's gamble, his invasion of Russia. In his view, a change in Russian policy forced him to adopt this plan. Soon after the Tilsit agreement, Tsar Alexander's enthusiasm for his new ally had begun to cool, as conflicts of interest between the two became more and more apparent. Napoleon's activities in Germany disturbed the tsar, for they undermined Russia's influence in an area of concern for half a century. Napoleon's encouragement of Polish nationalism was still more disturbing because it hit closer to home. In the eighteenth-century partitions of Poland, Russia had absorbed vast territories that it could lose if the Poles reasserted themselves. Last but not least, the tsar's embargo on trade with Britain cut into his popularity at home and strained the Russian economy. For political and economic reasons, he prepared to break the Tilsit accord, and in 1811 he issued a series of decrees that reopened his ports to British goods.

This defiance struck at the foundation of the Continental System and addled Napoleon. He had thought of Russia as a planet revolving about himself, but now it threatened to move into a new course. Either he could let it go and abandon his method of war against Britain just when it seemed to chalk up successes, or he could force Russia back into orbit. For him the dilemma left no choice. Both his nature and his position precluded retreat; he had to push on.

He did not delude himself that coercing Russia would be easy, and for the task he gathered the greatest army that Europe had ever seen. Its core

---

[6]The place of the War of 1812 in British history is illustrated by the (perhaps apocryphal) anecdote of a modern Englishman's reaction when told that his compatriots had once burned Washington: "Really? I knew of course that we burned Joan of Arc, but George Washington —?" American historians have written most of the books about the conflict. Donald Hickey's *The War of 1812* (1989) is an excellent recent account.

comprised 250,000 French veterans, but large contingents of Germans, Italians, Poles, and other nationalities brought the total to 600,000; Prussia and Austria, bullied into alliance, provided another 50,000 to guard the flanks of the invasion. In the whole of continental Europe, only one small power stood out in opposition. The Napoleonic Marshal Bernadotte, whom his master had recently installed as crown prince of Sweden, defied him and allied with the tsar. But Sweden was in no position to give effective help, and neither was Britain; Russia stood alone against a continent in arms.

In June 1812, Napoleon's vast horde crossed the Russian frontier and rolled eastward. It failed by a narrow margin to encircle the defending army, which fell back before it and, like the Portuguese, laid waste the countryside. In mid-September the French entered Moscow, and there they stayed for a month. They were in much the same position that Masséna had been in before Lisbon: The enemy hung on their flanks, their lines of communication were stretched to the limit, and they faced starvation. Napoleon's overtures for peace met with silence. He had to retreat. As soon as he did so, his whole supply system disintegrated, and his nightmare began. In December he reappeared in the west, and only then did Europe learn what lay behind the rumors that had circulated for weeks. Out of the host that had entered Russia, some 20,000 men returned, and they were more dead than alive. Half a million had disappeared, and with them went the foundation of the Napoleonic empire.

The Fall of Napoleon (1813–1815)

Even the catastrophe in Russia did not break Napoleon's hold on the French people. He hurried back to Paris and by the spring of 1813 had succeeded in raising a new army of 200,000 to meet the onslaught that he knew was coming. Alexander had not halted on his own frontiers but continued westward, and his advance roused the Germans to a national war of liberation from their oppressor. Prussia joined the tsar, Crown Prince Bernadotte crossed from Sweden, and in the summer of 1813, Austria, thanks in part to British pressure and loans, threw in its lot with the allies. In the course of twenty-five years of war, successive British governments subsidized its allies to the tune of £65 million; half of this sum was expended during the final five years of the fighting.[7] Napoleon triumphed in several battles in 1813, but with his raw troops he could not win the campaign; never had he so sorely missed the 200,000 veterans fighting in Spain. In October Swedish, Russian, Austrian, and Prussian armies converged upon him at Leipzig and, in the three-day Battle of the Nations, broke his hold on central Europe. With the remnants of his

---

[7]Such "foreign aid" proved highly significant, although it constituted for Britain only 8 percent of the total cost of the wars, some £830 million. See John M. Sherwig, *Guineas and Gunpowder: British Foreign Aid in the Wars with France, 1793–1815* (1969).

forces, he fell back behind the Rhine. His empire was gone, and only France remained.

Meanwhile Wellington, after two years of fluctuating success and failure against superior numbers, had finally expelled the enemy from Spain. At the close of 1813, he crossed the Pyrenees in the first invasion of French soil since 1792. His adversary, Marshal Nicolas Soult, put up a skillful and dogged defense but had fewer and fewer troops as Napoleon called for reinforcements to hold the eastern frontier. By April 1814, the British were in Toulouse. There they learned that the war was over. During the spring, Napoleon, in eastern France, had fought one of the most brilliant campaigns of his career, but against odds that even genius could not overcome. On March 30 his capital surrendered, and on April 11 he abdicated. In return for giving up the crowns of France and Italy, he was made sovereign of the minuscule Mediterranean island of Elba, off the coast of Italy. Bourbon rule was reestablished in France under the late king's brother, who was proclaimed as Louis XVIII; in the autumn the powers convened at Vienna to make peace.

The diplomats faced a staggering task. A few reactionaries might imagine that the world of 1789 would reemerge with all its trappings of monarchy and privilege, and that the map of 1789 would be re-created; but that world and that map were gone. New concepts of nationalism, or representative government and individual rights, had infiltrated the length and breadth of the continent; they could be contained, perhaps kept from growing rapidly, but not rooted out. The crazy-quilt pattern of little states in Germany and Italy had been destroyed, the partition of Poland undone. Neither Russia, Austria, nor Prussia wanted to restore the old map in its entirety, for each hoped to aggrandize itself.

The peacemakers confronted two problems, each of which challenged their statesmanship. First, they had to protect the new order that they sought to build, which would necessarily include France, from the subversion of French revolutionary ideas. Second, they needed to adjust the spoils of victory among the continental powers without precipitating another war. Prussia, Austria, Russia, and Britain had bound themselves together in the Quadruple Alliance to arrange the settlement and then to cooperate in maintaining the peace. Yet soon after the sovereigns and plenipotentiaries met at Vienna, peace hung by a thread. Russia and Prussia wanted to make annexations in central Europe that Britain, Austria, and France threatened to oppose by force. The powers averted war through compromise, thanks in large part to the skillful diplomacy of Klemens von Metternich, the minister who had directed Austrian policy since 1809, and to Viscount Castlereagh, who had taken over the post of British foreign secretary in 1812. But the shrewd observer on Elba had taken note of the crisis.

Napoleon concluded that his enemies were about to fly at each other's throats and that France would welcome his return. From all over Europe, his veterans, released from captivity, had come home to find themselves cold-shouldered by the Bourbon government. Many of them longed to have him back, and with them he could build such an army as he had not had since 1812. The reduction of France to its prerevolutionary frontiers, furthermore, outraged French patriots and endangered the regime of Louis XVIII, who had only the humdrum virtues of peace and retrenchment to offer a nation that had so long feasted on glory. The king, unknown to his people after his years of exile, impressed them like a pigmy replacing a giant. Some of them yearned to have the giant again; few would lift a finger to oppose his return.

In March 1815, Napoleon landed in the south of France. Three weeks later he was installed in the Tuileries, while the Bourbons fled again into exile. But the emperor knew that he was not yet master of the country: The people, he said, "have let me come just as they let the others go." To win support, he had to prove himself, again by the sword. His return had united the quarreling allies, who had outlawed him as an enemy to the peace of the world; their forces began to converge on France. He had the material for rebuilding the *Grande Armée*, but he did not have the time, for 170,000 Russians and 250,000 Austrians were lumbering slowly but inexorably toward the eastern frontier. Close at hand in Belgium were 120,000 Prussians under Marshal Gebhard Blücher, and to the west of them, barring the road to Brussels, a polyglot force of 100,000 men in British pay. These allied armies logistically determined the outline of Napoleon's plan of campaign. He had to strike into Belgium, divide and destroy the enemy there, and then deal with the Austrians and Russians.

Wellington, now a duke, had served as Britain's representative at the Congress of Vienna; he was hastily recalled and put in command of the improvised forces guarding Brussels. They were a far cry from his peninsular veterans, most of whom had been shipped to the United States and had not yet returned. Every soldier available in the British Isles was sent to him, but he had only 30,000 of them. The remaining 70,000 comprised a scratch collection of Dutch, Belgians, and Germans, some raw recruits and some veterans of Napoleon's armies; their fighting spirit and even loyalty were doubtful. The Iron Duke would need all his imperturbability to organize for battle.

Napoleon moved at top speed. He had to, because each of the two armies before him roughly equaled his in size. His only hope lay in outmarching them, getting between them and driving them apart, and then crushing each in turn. His first target was Blücher. On June 16, while a French detachment under Marshal Michel Ney held off the British at Quatre Bras, the emperor with his main force fell on the Prussians at Ligny and cut their army in two. Napoleon assumed that it was shattered and would retreat eastward; he sent a corps under Marshal Emmanuel Grouchy in pursuit and then turned to destroy Wellington. The duke barely managed to extricate his army and retire hastily northward from Quatre Bras, hunting a position strong enough to defend. On June 17 a torrential rain slowed his pursuers, and that evening the British commander found what he wanted: a low ridge south of the village of Waterloo. There he turned at bay.

**The Duke of Wellington
(1769–1852)**   The portrait
is by Sir Thomas
Lawrence, ca. 1814. *(The
Victoria and Albert
Museum, London)*

Unlike Napoleon, Wellington knew that the entire Prussian army
had halted nearby and would come to his aid. It had not been demoralized
by the Battle of Ligny, and it had retreated not eastward but northward to
Wavre, on a route roughly parallel to the British; Grouchy had lost touch
with his quarry and was miles away. However, the Prussians moved
slowly — far more slowly than Wellington had supposed they would —
and everything depended on whether the duke could hold until they arrived. His position was strong and gave scope for the kind of defense at
which he excelled. In front he had little protection, for the slope was gentle, but behind, where the ground fell away to the north, he could maneuver his reserves under cover and out of sight of the enemy. In artillery and
cavalry, he was much weaker than they, and he relied chiefly on the firepower of the British infantry.

After delaying until almost noon of June 18, Napoleon put that
power to the test by ordering a frontal attack. Marshal Soult had
learned from his Spanish experience how costly such an attack could
be, and he cautioned his chief. The emperor's reply was both brutal and
unrealistic: "Because you have been beaten by Wellington, you think
him a great general. And I tell you that Wellington is a bad general, that
the English are bad troops, and that this will be a picnic for us." He
soon learned better, and he did not forget the lesson. "The Duke of
Wellington," he confessed a few weeks after the battle, "is fully equal

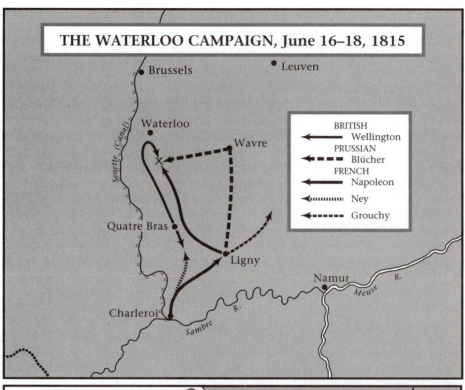

THE WATERLOO CAMPAIGN, June 16–18, 1815

Brussels

Leuven

Waterloo

Wavre

Senette (Canal)

BRITISH
Wellington
PRUSSIAN
Blücher
FRENCH
Napoleon
Ney
Grouchy

Quatre Bras

Ligny

Namur

Meuse R.

Charleroi

Sambre R.

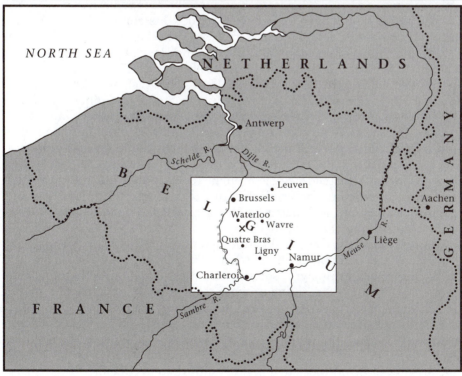

NORTH SEA

NETHERLANDS

Antwerp

Schelde R.

Dijle R.

B
E
L
G
I
U
M

Leuven

Brussels

Waterloo

×G

Wavre

Quatre Bras

Ligny

Namur

Charleroi

Meuse R.

Liège

Aachen

GERMANY

FRANCE

Sambre R.

to myself in the management of an army, with the advantage of possessing more prudence."

In the heat of the battle, Napoleon showed no prudence at all, and little finesse: His sole aim was to overwhelm resistance by sheer mass. In the early afternoon, his columns broke through Wellington's center, scattering a force of Dutch and Belgians in wild confusion. British reserves counterattacked, however, and drove his columns back. Then the emperor threw in his cavalry, some 15,000 under Marshal Ney, in three waves of assault that, though torn by artillery fire, flowed up the slope and poured through gaps in the enemy line. The defenders formed squares, within which the artillerymen took refuge. French round shot ripped the squares, but they held. The attack broke against them twice, reformed and broke again, until by six in the evening it was spent. Wellington had committed his last reserves. Napoleon had not; although his right was by then heavily engaged against the Prussians, who at long last had arrived from Wavre. He made one more effort in the center with the Guards, the elite of his army. They too failed, and the last tide of the empire ebbed down the hill.

Wellington ordered his whole line forward. As it swept into the valley and the Prussians broke through on the flank, the French army dissolved in a rout. All night the panic-stricken remnant fled down the roads toward France. The British were too exhausted to follow, but the Prussian cavalry took up a relentless pursuit. The emperor, his face streaked with tears, tried time and again to make a stand. But his authority was gone, and at last he gave up and led the race to Paris.

Although he had no thought of surrender, his compatriots disagreed; his own legislature forced him to abdicate. The French provisional government threatened to arrest him if he did not leave the country at once, and the Prussians hunted him in order to shoot him. He fled to the port of Rochefort, hoping to escape to the United States, but the wind was against him, and the British were waiting for him. Their blockade, which had done so much to bring him to the end of the road, now claimed his person. He surrendered to the captain of H.M.S. *Bellerophon*, and with supreme effrontery wrote to the Prince Regent, as "the most powerful, the most constant, and the most generous of my enemies," to claim asylum in England. Instead he was brought to Plymouth but not permitted ashore, then exiled to the small British island of St. Helena, in the south Atlantic more than a thousand miles off Africa. There he lived for six years before dying of cancer in 1821.

His second defeat and abdication essentially provided a postscript to his first defeat in 1814, as the Battle of Trafalgar was a postscript to the preceding naval campaign. But the Hundred Days of 1815 also determined, as Trafalgar did, much of what came after. Europe came together in a new unanimity born of the final, unexpected French aggression. Bonapartism was discredited in France for a generation to come. The fallen emperor of 1814 was a hero to many, but the man who fled from Waterloo to Paris, then from his own countrymen to the *Bellerophon*, was not. Lastly, the prestige of Britain rose to a higher point than ever before.

When Napoleon called the British, as personified in the Prince Regent, "the most powerful, the most constant, and the most generous of my enemies," he was wrong only on the last point. They were not generous to him, beyond frustrating the Prussian hope of putting him before a firing squad. They had no cause to be generous: He represented to them the same force of ruthless imperialism that they had fought ever since the French Revolutionaries had begun to expand into all Europe. In battling that force, they had not always been constant or powerful. Yet they had proved more constant than any other people, in part because they were less vulnerable, and had fought on alone when the future seemed without promise. Their naval power had slowly but surely increased until it held the continent in a vise, and their military power, for fifteen years the laughingstock of Europe, had redeemed itself in the Peninsular War and the Waterloo campaign. The Spaniards had helped in one, the Prussians in the other; but the hero of both was Wellington. He had reached the zenith of his reputation, and his country was at the start of its greatest influence in the world. After ten years, events had borne out the prophecy in Pitt's last public speech: "England has saved herself by her own exertions, and will, as I trust, save Europe by her example."

CHAPTER 13

The Twilight of Aristocracy

As Napoleon marched toward Waterloo, far away on the Danube the diplomats and sovereigns were winding up their business at the Congress of Vienna, so that after Waterloo all that remained was for Europe to make peace with France. This was done in the autumn, as part of the general settlement. French frontiers were reduced to those of 1790, before any of the revolutionary conquests. The nation was obliged to return to their former owners the art treasures that Napoleon had filched from all over Europe, to pay an indemnity, and to permit a multinational allied army under the command of the duke of Wellington to occupy France's northern and eastern frontier area until all treaty provisions had been fulfilled. These terms were far from punitive. The victors had no wish to inspire a new revolution in France or to undermine the security of the Bourbon dynasty, which had been restored in the person of Louis XVIII. Only a peace that was tolerable to France could endure.

The Settlement of 1815

The allies did all they could to prevent a recurrence of French aggression. In their territorial arrangements at Vienna, they erected barriers across the two principal routes by which France, since the seventeenth century, had invaded central Europe. The first route, the one that concerned Britain deeply, was through the Low Countries. Here the Belgian provinces, under Austrian control until 1792, were joined with the Dutch provinces, which had been independent before the wars, to form the kingdom of the Netherlands. The peacemakers hoped that this new state would be large and strong enough to repel French attack; to make security doubly sure, they gave to Prussia the area of the Rhineland immediately to the east, so that, if need be, Prussian armies could again march into Belgium as Blücher had done. The second invasion route from France was into northwestern Italy. Here, in the upper Po valley, the allies enlarged the kingdom of Sardinia to serve as an Italian equivalent to the kingdom of the Netherlands. Austria took on the same supporting role as Prussia in the north by acquiring the provinces of Lombardy and

The Great Hyde Park Fair (1814)   Londoners celebrate the end of a generation of war with France. *(John R. Freeman & Company Ltd.)*

Venetia that occupied the lower valley of the Po. In the rest of the peninsula, the old non-Italian dynasties were restored. North of the Alps, the German states, considerably reduced in number, joined together in the German Confederation; one of its members was Hanover, enlarged and converted from an electorate into a kingdom, of which the aged and insane George III was king.[1] In the east, Russia gained the lion's share of Poland, largely at the expense of Prussia; the latter received compensation with part of Saxony as well as the Rhineland.

These arrangements, relatively minor as they seemed on the map, shaped the future of Europe. Sardinia became the only Italian state both ruled by a native Italian dynasty and strong enough to influence the affairs of the peninsula. Austria, the dominant power there, by shifting from the

---

[1]The Hanoverian crown, unlike the British, descended only in the male line. At the accession of Queen Victoria in 1837, consequently, the Hanoverian throne went to her uncle, the Duke of Cumberland, the fifth (and oldest surviving) son of George III. He became King Ernest of Hanover, and the dynastic connection between the two countries that had begun in 1714 was thus broken. Helpful general works dealing with the period covered by this chapter include the first two volumes of Eli Halévy, *A History of the English People in the Nineteenth Century*, 2nd ed., 6 vols. (1949–1952); Asa Briggs, *The Age of Improvement, 1783–1867* (1959); and Eric J. Evans, *The Forging of the Modern State: Early Industrial Britain, 1783–1870* (1983). Norman Gash's *Aristocracy and People: Britain, 1815–1865* (1979) is particularly useful in clarifying the policies of the central government, while James J. Sack, *From Jacobite to Conservative: Reaction and Orthodoxy in Britain, c. 1760–1832* (1993), sets the assumptions of post-1815 Tories within a broader context.

The Congress of Vienna (1815) A painting by Jean-Baptiste Isabey. The duke of Wellington stands at the extreme left. Austria's Prince Metternich is pointing toward the seated Lord Castlereagh. France's Prince Talleyrand is seated at the right with his arm on the table. *(Bild-Archiv der Osterreichischen National-bibliothek, Wien)*

Netherlands to the Po, relinquished its old role of protecting the German states against France. Prussia assumed that role by acquiring the Rhineland. Thereby the Prussians also gained, quite inadvertently, the area that would play a crucial role in the future industrialization of Germany. Russia advanced westward into the heart of the continent and subsequently played a more important part in European power politics than ever before.

Britain had little direct concern with most of these territorial adjustments and so could afford to be detached. Its principal aims in the peacemaking proved less controversial than those of the land powers. The British believed that their own security depended on the Low Countries being secure from French aggression; they desired a lasting, and therefore an equitable, settlement with France; and they wanted an end to the international slave trade. (At Vienna, Lord Castlereagh, the British foreign secretary, obtained international agreement on a statement condemning that practice; and he subsequently put pressure on the Dutch, the French, the Spaniards, and the Portuguese to abide by their pledges.) Their final objective at Vienna was to safeguard Britain's communications with India. At the end of the war, the British occupied the colonies of almost all the maritime states and therefore had a strong means of persuasion during the peacemaking: Only if British wishes were met could the former owners feel sure of regaining their possessions. The British had their way on almost every point and gave up the bulk of their conquests. In the West Indies, they retained a few small islands won from France; in the North Sea, Heligoland; and in the Mediterranean, Malta and a protectorate over the Ionian Islands. To guard the route to India, Britain kept the former French island of Mauritius, off the coast of Africa, and two erstwhile Dutch possessions, Cape Colony and Ceylon, for which the British paid compensation to the kingdom of the Netherlands.

That compensation was nothing to what Cape Colony would cost them in the long run, for there they were buying trouble. The Cape of Good Hope was a valuable possession, largely because it yielded the fruit and vegetables that prevented scurvy. Ships on the long voyage to or from India made Capetown a port of call in order to preserve the health of their crews. But the colony was populated by Boers — Dutch who had settled there since the seventeenth century and who had kept their old ways; and they soon proved to be among the most intractable inhabitants of the British Empire. A majority of the Boers clearly had no desire to live under British administration. Anglo-Boer tensions flared intermittently throughout the century and in the 1890s were to provoke the greatest imperial crisis since the American War of Independence.

The Congress of Vienna had restored peace to the continent, and it left none of the "Big Five" of the day — Russia, Prussia, Austria, France, and Britain — with a major grievance. Yet there were people who lived in these lands and in smaller states outside them who proved less happy with the Vienna settlement.

Napoleon's armies had destroyed the *anciens régimes* all over Europe and had aroused the revolutionary idea of nationalism, particularly among inhabitants of the German and Italian states. In the years after 1815, revolts would break out periodically that aimed either to alter the territorial settlement of 1815 or to liberalize the regimes that had arranged it. To German nationalists, who had dreamed that the War of 1813 would lead to unification, the loosely structured German Confederation was a poor sop; to Italian nationalists the change from French to Austrian hegemony was no sop at all. This frustration of nationalism was not accidental; one powerful man at Vienna had designed it that way. Prince Metternich, the Austrian chancellor, was a Rhinelander by birth but a Viennese by policy; and the policy of Vienna necessarily opposed unification in Germany or Italy. The Austrian Empire, composed of Germans, Hungarians, Poles, Czechs, and a host of smaller minorities, constituted the living denial of nationalism. A united Germany would deprive the Habsburgs of the influence that they had exerted there since the fifteenth century, and a united Italy would deprive them of Lombardy-Venetia. Those losses would represent only the beginning; the end would see the breakup of the empire itself into its constituent national parts. The French virus menaced the very existence of the state over which Metternich presided; for more than thirty years after the Congress of Vienna, therefore, he tried to guard against the danger, until it materialized in the great revolution of 1848.

Because the other great powers also feared, in varying degree, a resurgence of French revolutionary ideas, their leaders saw themselves as part of a single community, which they described as the Concert of Europe. Whenever a nationalist uprising of comparable threat to the peace arose, they agreed to assemble in a congress like that at Vienna and to consult as to how to react against the danger. What has sometimes been called the "congress system" scarcely deserves the name of system. It had no formal organization, no agreement on methods of coercion or even of procedure; it committed its members to nothing except to meet together. Yet the Vienna settlement also promoted the international management and navigation of river systems such as the Rhine and the Danube, and it regulated many questions of diplomatic procedure. In international relations, therefore, it marked a significant break with the anarchic world of the eighteenth century. After twenty-five years of war during which five million Europeans had died, the continent's leaders formally recognized that all the powers had a common stake in maintaining peace.[2] "The immediate object," declared Lord Castlereagh, "is to inspire the states of Europe with a sense that the existing concert is their only perfect security, . . . and that their true wisdom is to keep down the petty contentions of ordinary times and to stand together in the support of the established principles of social order."

Tsar Alexander attempted to Christianize this new spirit of unanimity. In the autumn of 1815, he announced that he had formed a Holy Alliance with the emperor of Austria and the king of Prussia. The members of this new body bound themselves in indissoluble fraternity to act according to the precepts of Christ, and they invited other sovereigns to join them. "Sublime mysticism and nonsense" was Castlereagh's private comment, and the Prince Regent politely declined to join, as did the pope. Although other European heads of state accepted the tsar's invitation, only Russia, Austria, and Prussia ever took the alliance seriously, and for them it soon became more reactionary than holy. Yet the Holy Alliance helped to keep the peace among the three great powers of Central and Eastern Europe, and Britain remained tied to them in the Quadruple Alliance formed against Napoleon in 1814. After a probationary period, France was in 1818 admitted as a fifth partner. These were the powers at the center of the congress system.

Britain's Breach with the Concert (1815–1823)

A concert is as a concert does, and the fundamental question was how the new order would operate. This question of what means to employ in keeping peace lies at the core of any such international collaboration and has

---

[2]In *The Transformation of European Politics, 1763–1848* (1994), Paul W. Schroeder emphasizes the manner in which the Vienna settlement helped make the nineteenth-century European world far more peaceful than that of the previous century. See, especially, pp. 575–582.

since arisen in the League of Nations and the United Nations. It has no easy answer. A threat to peace is most difficult to assess correctly at just the moment when it is easiest to deal with — in its early stages. At that moment, the collaborating powers risk doing either too little or too much — too little if they allow a real threat to grow until it gets out of hand; too much if they regard every alteration of the status quo in any country as a threat that justifies intervention to reestablish "principles of social order." In the latter case, their policing to maintain peace becomes a tyrannical suppression of change. Castlereagh recognized this difficulty from the first. Keeping the peace was one thing; supporting internal misgovernment where it existed was quite another. Britain's collaboration with its allies would depend on whether they preserved the distinction between the two.

At first all went smoothly. After 1818, however, when the Congress of Aix-la-Chapelle withdrew allied troops from France and admitted their former enemy to full standing in the Concert, the mood of the continental powers began to change. Liberals, restive under their static regimes, resorted to sporadic violence; Tsar Alexander had posed for three years as their champion, but he began to waver erratically; Metternich turned to repression as the only security. In 1819 the Spanish army, with which the king of Spain had hoped to regain his American colonies, revolted against him and touched off a revolution that spread from Spain to Portugal, the Kingdom of the Two Sicilies, and Sardinia. Metternich responded by convoking the Congress of Troppau, where in November 1820 the Holy Alliance got down to work. Prussia, Austria, and Russia bound themselves to intervene in any state where a revolution endangered its neighbors, and a few months later Austrian troops moved against the two Italian culprits. This action was based on sound logic, for revolution had in fact proved itself highly contagious and confirmed Metternich in his conviction that the only way to preserve the peace and social order of Europe was to intervene before trouble got out of hand.

But Castlereagh strongly dissented. He took much the same stand that his mentor, Pitt, had adopted toward France before 1793 but carried it further; he denied that the Holy Alliance had the right to interfere in the domestic affairs of independent states. In taking this position, one might argue, Castlereagh could not help himself. The Spanish and Italian revolutionaries were moderates who demanded the kind of constitutional parliamentary regime of which Britain had long stood as the chief exemplar; and no minister responsible to the Mother of Parliaments could well have agreed that such a system menaced the social order. Yet, Castlereagh and his colleagues, who sometimes feared revolution at home, required courage to defend it abroad and to admit the right of a people to change their form of government. For the moment, however, their stand was merely verbal, and while they protested, the continental powers acted. Austrian arms made Italy safe for reaction, and in 1822 the Congress of Verona authorized France to do likewise in Spain. A French army then crossed the Pyrenees, restored Spain's imperious monarch, and stood guard while he wreaked his vengeance on the rebels.

Many Britons welcomed the prospect of weakening diplomatic ties with the continent. Sydney Smith, a prolific contributor to the prestigious Whig journal, the *Edinburgh Review*, expressed such isolationism in a private letter in 1823:

> . . . For God's sake, do not drag me into another war! I am worn down, and worn out, with crusading and defending Europe, and protecting mankind; I *must* think a little of myself. I am sorry for the Spaniards — I am sorry for the Greeks — I deplore the fate of the Jews; the people of the Sandwich Islands are groaning under the most detestable tyranny; Bagdad is oppressed; I do not like the present state of the Delta; Tibet is not comfortable. Am I to fight for all these people? The world is bursting with sin and sorrow. Am I to be champion of the Decalogue, and to be eternally raising fleets and armies to make all men good and happy? We have just done saving Europe, and I am afraid that the consequence will be, that we shall cut each other's throats. . . . If there is another war, life will not be worth having.[3]

George Canning, who succeeded Castlereagh at the Foreign Office upon the latter's suicide in 1822, was a different kind of isolationist from Smith. The change in foreign ministers influenced the style of British policy more than its underlying direction. Canning had a gift for drama, in words and actions, that his predecessor had lacked; and where Castlereagh had regretted Britain's alienation from its allies, Canning welcomed it. He did not believe in the Concert of Europe; "it will necessarily involve us deeply," he had warned, "in all the politics of the continent, whereas our true policy has always been not to interfere except in great emergencies, and then with a commanding force." Early in 1823, he was encouraged to think that the Concert had begun to break apart and that international relations would revert to a wholesome state — "every nation for itself, and God for us all."

The France that had invaded Spain impressed Canning, however, as behaving uncomfortably like the France of Louis XIV. The ascendancy of the French in Madrid was bad enough; worse still was the possibility that they would go on to regain for their new protégé the Spanish American empire, in which Britain had so long been interested. The Holy Alliance considered the Spanish colonists as revolutionaries whose virus had once infected the mother country and might do so again; the sooner they were brought to heel the better. The British government, in contrast, considered them as independent *de facto* and held that Spain had lost its claim to them and that France had none.

The crisis revealed a strong community of interest between Britain and the United States, for Washington also objected strongly to European intervention in the western hemisphere. The Americans wanted to loosen the ties between the New World and the Old: They had recently recognized the colonies as independent, as Britain had not, and

---

[3]W. H. Auden, ed., *The Selected Writings of Sydney Smith* (1956), pp. 323–324.

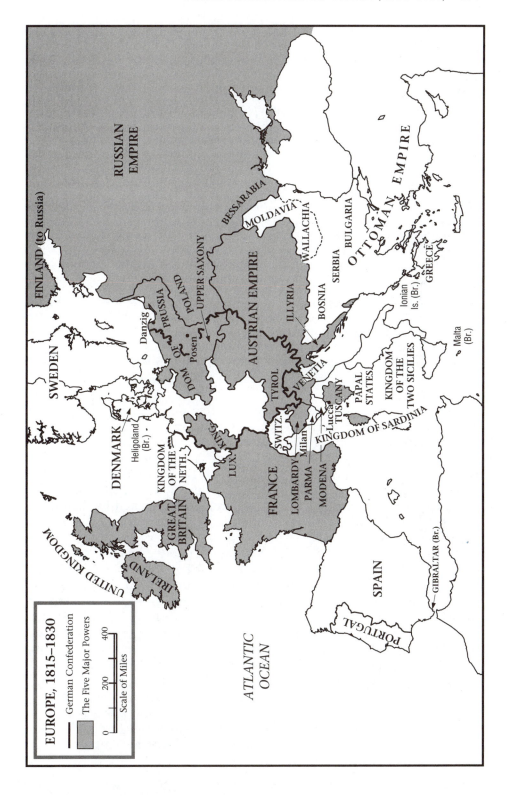

EUROPE, 1815–1830

— German Confederation

The Five Major Powers

Scale of Miles

0   200   400

RUSSIAN EMPIRE

FINLAND (to Russia)

SWEDEN

OTTOMAN EMPIRE

BESSARABIA

MOLDAVIA

WALLACHIA

BULGARIA

SERBIA

BOSNIA

GREECE

Ionian Is. (Br.)

Malta (Br.)

POLAND

UPPER SAXONY

PRUSSIA

Danzig

Posen

DOM OF

AUSTRIAN EMPIRE

ILLYRIA

TYROL

VENETIA

SWITZ.

Milan

LOMBARDY

PARMA

MODENA

Lucca

TUSCANY

PAPAL STATES

KINGDOM OF THE TWO SICILIES

KINGDOM OF SARDINIA

DENMARK

Heligoland (Br.)

KINGDOM OF THE NETH.

KING.

LUX.

FRANCE

GREAT BRITAIN

UNITED KINGDOM

IRELAND

ATLANTIC OCEAN

SPAIN

PORTUGAL

GIBRALTAR (Br.)

had determined to do all in their power to keep them so. The United States, with no army or navy worth the name, had negligible physical power, but Britain possessed the "commanding force" of which Canning had spoken. While repression had been confined to Europe, he had been limited to protests; now that it threatened to reach across the Atlantic, he could act. In October 1823, he brusquely informed the French government that Britain would not tolerate intervention in America. This ultimatum proved decisive because it was backed by the force of the Royal Navy.

Meanwhile in Washington, as the trend of British policy became unmistakable, President James Monroe recognized and rose to a great opportunity. On December 2, before he knew of Canning's ultimatum to Paris, he delivered to Congress the message known ever since as the Monroe Doctrine. In it he proclaimed that the United States would not interfere in the internal affairs of any European state or of an existing colony in America but would oppose both European interference in any independent American state and future European colonization on either American continent. The doctrine was a bold gesture. With its proclamation, the United States seemed to throw the mantle of its protection, by fiat, over the entire hemisphere. In fact, the president had no mantle to throw. Instead he appropriated, by dexterous timing, the mantle of British sea power. For the rest of the century, with one brief interlude, the Royal Navy rather than the American gave teeth to the Monroe Doctrine.

Although the American government had taken action unilaterally rather than in public partnership with Canning, the British made no objection to Monroe's policy. They had little wish to gain more colonies themselves in the Americas and less desire to see European powers do so. They were glad to share with the United States the onus of defying the Holy Alliance. The crisis evaporated, for the French did not dream of challenging Monroe's words when backed by Canning's threat. Reaction was stopped, as the Napoleonic system had been, at the water's edge.

By the mid-1820s, the British had thus separated themselves from a Concert of Europe eager to repress all political reform movements that threatened the status quo. At the same time, Britain remained very much affected by events on the continent. During the 1830s, indeed, British statesmen were often to contrast the "liberal West" (Britain, France, and sometimes Spain and Portugal) with the "reactionary East" (Russia, Prussia, and Austria). Neither bloc became monolithic, however, and cooperation across the east-west divide proved possible in numerous instances. In the meantime, Canning had reminded Britain's European neighbors that his nation's interests remained worldwide and were in no way limited to the continent. Britain's past history and current concerns worked to draw the island kingdom away from the Concert and, as Thomas Jefferson said in 1823, to "bring her mighty weight into the scale of free government."

The Tory Reaction (1815–1822)

The ministry that carried out this momentous shift in British foreign policy became, ironically enough, notorious for its fear of popular freedom at home. Since Fox's death, the reform impulse that came to be known as liberalism[4] had been in eclipse. Under the pressure first of war and then of postwar economic dislocation, and haunted by fears of a British uprising comparable to the French Revolution, the ruling classes had grown increasingly apprehensive and averse to new ideas. The Whigs who remained faithful to the tradition of Fox had dwindled to a small minority, doomed to what seemed permanent opposition. Divided among themselves, they offered a wide range of criticism but no coherent program. The shifting groups of politicians who held office during the war years had set their faces against institutional change and had come to stand for an often repressive conservatism. By 1812, when Lord Liverpool formed an administration that lasted until 1827, these heirs of William Pitt the Younger were generally known as Tories. In Parliament, the opposition Whigs, little as they could agree on specific measures, insisted on the need for change, and a handful of self-professed Radicals proved yet more vocal. The Tories sought to maintain the constitutional status quo as a safeguard against revolution, and, as long as they heeded those groups in society most strongly represented in Parliament, they maintained their power.

The heyday of this static conservatism was the first decade of the Liverpool ministry, from 1812 to 1822. The prime minister himself seemed undynamic and undistinguished, but clearly he kept an oft-divided cabinet working in tandem, for it fell apart rapidly after his retirement and death. Three men in his cabinet had chief responsibility for governmental policy: Lord Eldon, a diehard conservative who was Lord Chancellor; Henry Addington, now Lord Sidmouth, who was home secretary; and Lord Castlereagh, the foreign secretary and chief government spokesman in the House of Commons. Under the leadership of this triumvirate, the cabinet, particularly between 1816 and 1819, followed a repressive policy almost worthy of Metternich. The liberties of British citizens were more drastically curtailed than in any other peacetime period of modern history.

The government was motivated by fear, and it had every reason to be frightened by the postwar problems that beset the kingdom. The sudden curtailment of wartime expenditures helped to throw the economy into depression, while the debt contracted to conduct the war cast its shadow over peacetime budgets for many years. Since 1793 the net annual

---

[4]Although the word *liberal* had long been used as a synonym for "unrestricted" or "generous," it was only after 1815 that it became identified — by its opponents — with a particular political point of view or party. Spaniards resisting the reactionary King Ferdinand called themselves the *Liberales,* and members of the Tory government came to apply the label to Whigs and Radicals. Not until the mid-1840s did many Whigs themselves begin to accept the label. By then it had entered the political vocabulary of much of Europe.

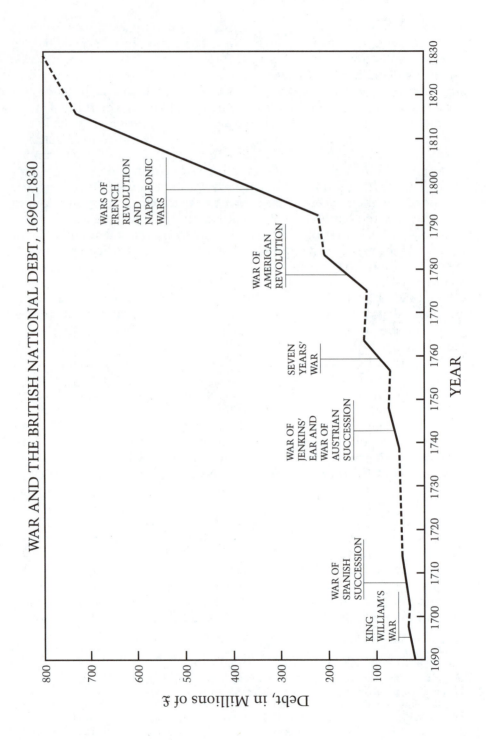

WAR AND THE BRITISH NATIONAL DEBT, 1690–1830

revenue — from customs and excise, various forms of taxation, crown land rents, and so on — had increased more than fourfold, thanks in part to the introduction of the income tax in 1798; and by 1815, this revenue approached £83 million per annum. In 1816 the Liverpool government bowed to public pressure and abolished the income tax, which had been an emergency war measure, and the annual revenue soon fell off to a mere £58 million. The struggle with France had cost Britain, in subsidies to its allies and the expenses of its own operations, more than £830 million. This sum (admittedly in somewhat inflated pounds) added up to almost four times the outlay for all the nation's wars between 1739 and 1783. In large part, the nation had raised the money by loans; as a result, the national debt had more than tripled during the twenty-two years of fighting. By the time of Waterloo, the debt had climbed to £860 million. The carrying charges on this sum remained virtually constant even as the revenue declined; before long, therefore, more than half the annual budget went to servicing the debt and another £5 million to paying veterans' pensions. What Castlereagh called an "ignorant impatience of taxation" rendered the government's financial position more difficult in peacetime than it had been during the war.

The Bank of England had long since suspended payment in gold and issued only paper currency. A host of country banks that had recently sprung up, some with shaky assets, also put out bank notes. The effect was twofold: first, to debase the value of the currency and hence encourage wartime inflation; and second, to produce great financial instability. The worth of the paper notes, even those of the Bank of England, fluctuated from month to month, and prices rose and fell accordingly. Business was a gamble for all concerned, until an act of Parliament in 1819 ordered the Bank of England to resume the payment of gold and silver for bank notes on demand. The immediate effect of this step was deflationary, and critics condemned it as a discouragement to trade. On balance, however, it promoted financial stability, and the gold standard soon became a tenet of Victorian orthodoxy.

The private sector of the economy suffered as bad a strain as the public. During the war, the problem of the food supply, with European imports sharply reduced, had grown acute. Only by transforming erstwhile wasteland into cropland and by enclosing some three million additional acres could the nation feed its population. For British landlords and their tenant farmers, peace brought disaster, because imported grain, or "corn" in British parlance, sent domestic grain prices tumbling. The landed interest had long used Corn Laws to maintain a stable market in grain, but the Corn Law of 1815 introduced the novel principle of prohibition: No foreign grain was to be imported at all unless the domestic price rose to ten shillings a bushel. The law sparked immediate tumult.

Mobs of protesters ranged through the streets of London, insulting members of Parliament and threatening cabinet ministers; the young Lord Palmerston, secretary of war, defended his town house by arming the servants with shotguns. More significant if less dramatic opposition to the government came from manufacturers. They protested that the high price of grain, and hence of bread, would inflate wages and thereby raise the cost of production and the price of the finished goods, which businessmen had to market abroad in competition with foreign products. British industry, therefore, would be penalized for the sake of British agriculture. Parliament held to its course. For the time being, the landed interest turned a deaf ear to argument, but intense debate over the future of the Corn Laws would recur at intervals until it reached a climax in the 1840s. On one side were the industrialists and the workers in town and country, the chief consumers of bread. On the other side were the landlords and the farmers.

When the harvest was good, as it was in 1815, even the most stringent of Corn Laws could not prevent the domestic price of grain from falling. Prices shot up again during the next three years; a violent volcanic eruption in the East Indies helped to bring on the coldest summers (and the worst grain harvests) that England and continental Europe had experienced in several generations. English laborers had good cause therefore to lament the high price of bread. They had many other grievances as well. Despite Napoleon's best efforts, during the war Britain had come to supply the needs of much of the outside world for manufactures; its exports in the year before Waterloo had become three times as great as in 1792. During that same period, moreover, Britain's population had risen by some 35 percent. The end of the war brought the termination of government war contracts and the return to civilian life of more than 330,000 soldiers and sailors. Together with a temporary downturn in the continental demand for British goods, these events help explain the high degree of unemployment and destitution that beset the land intermittently between 1816 and 1819.

The government was ill prepared to cope with a sudden increase in the number of paupers. It regarded Corn Laws and currency acts as within its domain but did not dream of a nationally administered program of demobilization and either industrial or agricultural reconversion. The consequences of a return to peace were, to officialdom, the concern of the counties and the localities. And there the problems were legion. The Justices of the Peace grappled with a great many more matters than they had fifty years before. Justices had played a major role in military recruiting during the war with France and had also been given responsibility for supervising the manner in which parish overseers of the poor safeguarded the welfare of soldiers' wives and families. A sharp wartime and postwar increase in crime, especially among juveniles, had forced them to devote more time to apprehending and trying suspects and more money to enlarging and maintaining jails. (For example, the county jail of Warwick, which had housed 41 prisoners back in 1775, had to accommodate 351 sixty years later.) The central government, furthermore, was imposing on each county an increasing number of administrative duties such as the registration of savings banks and friendly societies, supervision of turnpike trusts, annual reports on assignments performed.

The English poor-law system came under increasing attack during the years after 1815.[5] Its cost seemed staggering, and the effect of the Speenhamland system (described in Chapter 11) of supplementing wages out of public funds seemed, where it operated, to be pernicious. The employer who did not have to pay a living wage was liberated from whatever social conscience he might possess, and the laborer had no incentive to work when the lazy and diligent were treated alike. The wage earner, who received an extra dole for each child, was invited to be fruitful and multiply. Families may not truly have been largest where the poor law allowance was most generous; but for contemporaries the forebodings of Thomas Malthus in his *Treatise on Population* (first published in 1798) seemed amply confirmed: The population was still growing at least as rapidly as the food supply; state intervention, however humanitarian in intent, simply encouraged the poor to have larger families; and the taxpayer financed the population explosion. Between 1803 and 1818, the cost of poor relief rose by more than 400 percent, from £4.25 million to £18 million, yet the agricultural laborer, in the regions where the Speenhamland system operated, became almost synonymous with the pauper. The Scottish poor-law system, traditionally less generous, appeared equally ineffective in meeting genuine human needs.

The eighteenth-century working classes, far from supine, had aired their grievances in riots and other forms of direct action. Industrial laborers, particularly in the wool trade, had combined in associations to hinder the introduction of machinery and keep up the wages of hand labor. These associations, the ancestors of the modern trade unions, had petitioned Parliament, conducted strikes, bargained with employers, and in general become so controversial as to precipitate a series of repressive statutes. The most important of these was a wartime measure, the Combination Act of 1799, which gave employers a potentially powerful weapon. It prohibited all labor unions as conspiracies "in restraint of trade" on pain of three months' imprisonment of those who joined. Magistrates enforced the act erratically, however, and craft workers such as tailors, building workers, and shipwrights formed successful trade unions in time of war. Manchester cotton spinners and Lancashire calico printers also conducted successful strikes in 1818. In fact, a Home Office official complained that year that the Combination Act "was almost a dead letter while conspiracy is increasing on every side." Political radicals continued to decry the act as a major grievance, however. In time of depression, with wages falling and jobs scarce, unions tended to disintegrate and laborers either accepted their lot or, on occasion, turned to violence.

The government had no way of knowing which the workers would do, acquiesce or agitate. It is difficult, in today's era of mass communications,

---

[5]In *The Idea of Poverty: England in the Early Industrial Age* (1984), Gertrude Himmelfarb summarizes and analyzes the debate from the 1770s to the 1840s about how best to deal with poverty and pauperism.

to grasp how little communication existed at that time between the rulers and the ruled. The masses had few ways to communicate with Westminster. The popular press was still in its infancy; petitions to Parliament, even if read, seldom revealed a consensus among the petitioners. Riots did not provide a tactful way of making a point to authority, but to some Britons they seemed the only way. The central government, in turn, had no reliable method for feeling the pulse of the masses. Spies and informers, though widely used, tended to produce evidence that they thought their employers wanted. Investigations by parliamentary committees and so-called Royal Commissions (which included experts other than peers and Members of Parliament) grew increasingly common. Although they took voluminous testimony from witnesses called from all over the country, months and even years might elapse between appointment and final report. The local magistrates who sometimes sought the advice of the Home Office in London necessarily reflected their own fears and prejudices. The amateurs who still governed Britain may have had better means of gathering information than their grandfathers had had,[6] but when they tried to gauge the mood of the underrepresented majority, they found it difficult to decide whether a particular plot was a storm in a teacup or a portent of revolution. And *if* revolution was brewing, the authorities had to nip it in the bud, for they lacked the force to put down a full-blown insurrection. Even metropolitan London still lacked a police force in the modern sense. The regular army at the disposal of the government was surprisingly small, and it could not readily rely on the often ill-trained local militia.

The traumatic difficulties that beset postwar Britain — rapid demobilization, a burdensome national debt, an unstable currency, intermittently poor harvests, and large-scale unemployment — led to widespread misery and numerous acts of violence. In the course of the year 1816, the Luddites again took to smashing machinery in the Midlands; mobs rioted in London, displaying the revolutionary French tricolor, and on one occasion pillaged firearms and invaded the heart of the city. Some of the agitation was respectable; thus the sober Corporation of London petitioned the Prince Regent for financial retrenchment and parliamentary reform. During the following winter, secret committees of both houses of Parliament made alarming reports, whereupon the government suspended habeas corpus, banned seditious meetings, and ordered local magistrates to prosecute authors of dangerous pamphlets. For a time the agitation died down — less because of these measures than because of economic improvement — but soon the depression returned, and with it political unrest.

In August 1819, a meeting of some 60,000 people convened in St. Peter's Fields in Manchester. The crowd was unarmed and included many women and children, but participants carried banners demanding annual Parliaments, universal suffrage, and "liberty or death." Henry Hunt, a well-known rabble-rouser popularly known as "Orator Hunt," mounted

---

[6]A major example is the decennial census of population begun in Britain in 1801.

The "Battle of Peterloo" (1819) An engraving by George Cruikshank. *(City of Manchester Art Galleries)*

the platform to harangue the concourse. At that point the magistrates panicked and ordered mounted militia — ill-trained local shopkeepers in uniform — to arrest the speaker. The men charged in with drawn sabers, and pandemonium erupted. The violence left eleven people dead and more than four hundred wounded — sabered or trampled in the crowd.

The shock of the "Manchester Massacre," also derisively nicknamed from St. Peter's Fields "the Battle of Peterloo," reverberated through the country and beyond. From the safe distance of Italy, the young republican, Percy Bysshe Shelley sent a call to revolution:

> Rise like Lions after slumber
> In unvanquishable number —
> Shake your chains to earth like dew
> Which in sleep had fallen on you —
> Ye are many — they are few.

At home even moderate opinion was outraged, and Lord Liverpool privately questioned the good judgment of the Manchester magistrates. He and other members of the government felt compelled, however, to give them full support in public and to promote in Parliament in the autumn of 1819 the passage of the "Six Acts." Among British reformers, those acts became notorious as the highwater mark of post-1815 political repression. The legislation resurrected Pitt's policies of the late 1790s, but this time without the excuse of war. The acts banned unauthorized military drilling and provided for the seizure of firearms, muzzled the cheap press by imposing a stamp duty not only on newspapers but also on political pamphlets, and limited freedom of assembly in the open air to meetings held under official auspices. This legislation, much of which expired or was repealed within a few years, proved far more potent as a symbol of repression than as an effective barrier to the numerous pamphlets and cartoons that continued to criticize the government of the day.

The events of 1816–1819 appeared to reveal as never before the distance between the propertied classes and the masses. Well-off Britons, smelling revolution in the air, closed ranks in self-defense. In Parliament the Whigs, with few exceptions, were acquiescent; party labels meant nothing when oligarchy itself was threatened. Outside Parliament businessmen and magistrates, if Peterloo is a fair sample, eagerly supported the government. A Lancashire merchant boasted to a radical leader about how the people had been kept in their place: "The sons of bitches had eaten up all the stinging nettles for ten miles round Manchester, and now they had no greens for their broth. . . . Damn their eyes, what need you care about them? How could I sell you goods so cheap if I cared anything about them?" Economic forces alone scarcely account for such bitter brutality.

It would be misleading, however, to overemphasize the profound gulf between the rich and the poor, because British society retained numerous intermediate ranks. The complexities of the social structure were demonstrated by Patrick Colquhoun, the Scottish-born London magistrate, whose *Treatise on the Wealth, Power, and Resources of the British Empire* (1814) constitutes an early-nineteenth-century counterpart to Gregory King's late-seventeenth-century estimates. Unlike King, Colquhoun included both Scotland and Ireland in his calculations (summarized in the table that follows) and, in surveying the social gradations of the United Kingdom, he could make use of official census statistics.

The last two designated groups — the military population — almost disappeared after 1815, when the size of the army and navy declined by more than four-fifths, and veterans distributed themselves among Colquhoun's seven classes. His other estimates, however, even though they fail to distinguish between agricultural and industrial workers or between the different portions of the United Kingdom, remain a useful guide to the social structure of Britain in the postwar era.

The Prince Regent and Regency England

During this era the head of state in fact, though not in name, was the Prince Regent, who acted for his father from 1811 and became King George IV when the old man finally died in 1820. In typically Hanoverian fashion, the prince had rebelled continually against the king's tutelage, and for the greater part of three decades, father and son were hardly on speaking terms. They could not have been more different. George III had been sim-

POPULATION AND SOCIAL STRUCTURE OF GREAT BRITAIN, ACCORDING TO
PATRICK COLQUHOUN, 1814

Classes	Heads of families	Total persons comprising their families
Highest Orders		
1st. The Royal Family, the Lords Spiritual and Temporal, the Great Officers of State, and all above the degree of a Baronet, with their families	576	2,880
Second Class		
2d. Baronets, Knights, Country Gentlemen, and others having large incomes, with their families	46,861	234,305
Third Class		
3d. Dignified Clergy, Persons holding considerable employments in the State, elevated situations in the Law, eminent Practitioners in Physic, considerable Merchants, Manufacturers upon a large scale, and Bankers of the first order, with their families	12,200	61,000
Fourth Class		
4th. Persons holding inferior situations in Church and State, respectable Clergymen of different persuasions, Practitioners in Law and Physic, Teachers of Youth of the superior order, respectable Freeholders, Ship Owners, Merchants and Manufacturers of the second class, Warehousemen and respectable Shopkeepers, Artists, respectable Builders, Mechanics, and Persons living on moderate incomes, with their families	233,650	1,168,250
Fifth Class		
5th. Lesser Freeholders, Shopkeepers of the second order, Inn-keepers, Publicans, and Persons engaged in miscellaneous occupations or living on moderate incomes, with their families	564,799	2,798,475
Sixth Class		
6th. Working Mechanics, Artisans, Handicrafts, Agricultural Labourers, and others who subsist by labour in various employments, with their families	2,126,095	8,792,800
Menial Servants		1,279,923

Classes	Heads of families	Total persons comprising their families
Seventh, or Lowest Class		
7th. Paupers and their families, Vagrants, Gipsies, Rogues, Vagabonds, and idle and disorderly persons, supported by criminal delinquency	387,100	1,828,170
	3,371,281	16,165,803
The Army and Navy		
Officers of the Army, Navy, and Marines, including all Officers on half-pay and superannuated, with their families	10,500	69,000
Noncommissioned Officers in the Army, Navy, and Marines, Soldiers, Seamen, and Marines, including Pensioners of the Army, Navy, &c., and their families	120,000	862,000
Total	3,501,781	17,096,803

ple in his tastes and financially prudent. Young George loved to gamble and to spend lavishly; he perpetually fell into debt and time and again had to be bailed out by his parents or Parliament. George III had provided a model of marital fidelity; his son moved from one affair to another, both before and after his marriage in 1795 to his cousin, Princess Caroline of Brunswick, from whom he separated within less than a year. George III was by conviction a political conservative, but his son made a firm friend of the elder monarch's keenest political antagonist, Charles James Fox.

When the future regent was a boy, his tutor prophesied that he would become "either the most polished gentleman or the most accomplished blackguard in Europe — possibly both"; the prediction was a shrewd one. George indulged himself on a lavish scale and made no attempt to hide his excess. During the Napoleonic Wars, when most Britons endured short rations, he boasted the best French chef of the day and invited guests to routine meals in which they might choose among 116 different dishes served in nine different courses accompanied by a multitude of wines. (On special occasions, the dinners would be even more elaborate.) It is little wonder that even statutory limitations on the freedom of the press failed to protect the corpulent Prince Regent from savage caricatures and lampoons.

Yet he had another side. Unlike his father, he possessed both wit and easygoing charm. Moreover, he acquired a sense of royal showmanship that pleased a fashionable society long repelled by his father's court and that at times attracted even the fickle London populace. George saw to it, for example, that his realm celebrated the end of the Napoleonic Wars with a state visit by Tsar Alexander I of Russia and King Frederick

King George IV: Royal Showman or Royal Reprobate? *Left:* The fashionable monarch. *(The Granger Collection) Right:* The king as symbol of decadence. The cartoon by George Cruikshank (1820) quotes King Solomon: "Give not thy strength unto women, nor thy ways to that which destroyeth kings." *(Graphic Works of George Cruikshank, selected and with an introduction by Richard A.* Vogler; Dover Books, 1979)

William III of Prussia to a London brightly illuminated by gaslight. For the occasion, he had Hyde Park transformed into a vast pleasure garden: Oriental temples, towers, pagodas, and bridges were erected there; mock naval battles were fought on the Serpentine; balloon ascents were staged; and, in the midst of a tremendous display of fireworks, a specially constructed 100-foot-high Castle of Discord "with all its horrors of fire and destruction" was magically converted into a delightful Temple of Concord. Royal showmanship was not confined to London. George made successful state visits to Scotland and Ireland, which his Hanoverian forebears had studiously ignored for more than a century. In fact, he won a popularity in Edinburgh and Dublin, perhaps because his visits were brief, that he rarely evoked in London. Not all of his showmanship was ephemeral: He was a patron of some of the best architects, authors, and painters of his day. With his encouragement, Henry Holland transformed the prince's London home, Carlton House Terrace, into one of the finest palaces in Europe, while John Nash planned Regent Street, the broad, curving avenue that leads to Regent's Park, to this day one of the world's most charming parks. At a cost of many hundred thousand pounds, Nash also rebuilt Buckingham Palace. When a Radical M.P. criticized such extravagance "at a time when bread can scarcely be found for a large portion of our population," the chancellor of the exchequer responded that such censure was peculiarly inappropriate on the day that George IV had presented his father's magnificent book collection to the nation — to form the basis of what is today known as the British Library. The king became the chief patron of Sir Thomas Lawrence, the leading Regency portrait painter; was an admirer of Jane Austen, who dedicated *Emma* to him; and befriended Sir Walter Scott.

Like Sir Walter, George was in his own way a Romantic, and Romanticism had come into vogue. The new mood took many forms. Back in the 1790s, Scotland's prolific Robert Burns had written scores of poems, most in a Scottish dialect, rejoicing in the foibles and fancies of ordinary people; he fit his words to the old Scottish folk tunes that he transcribed. His adaptation of *Auld Lang Syne* was, in due course, to become a nostalgic international anthem. The poet William Wordsworth was an English exponent of the virtues of nature and of the unlettered villager; Percy Bysshe Shelley lashed out at tyranny in politics, religion, and social convention; Lord Byron, one of the best-known literary figures of Europe and the idol of Romantics, celebrated the lonely, melancholy, recklessly passionate hero who sought adventure in exotic climes. They were all part of the Romantic movement. So too was a revival of the Gothic: in tales of mystery and horror, in the novels of Scott, in a veneration of the ruins of medieval abbeys, and in the reintroduction of Gothic architecture. George, too, felt the appeal of long-ago events and far-off cultures. His Stuart predecessors fascinated him; he had Windsor Castle restored in what the architects thought was the original style. He also built the Royal Pavilion at Brighton, an Arabian Nights extravaganza with exotic domes even on its stables.

The Prince Regent may have had romantic inclinations, but some of his actions impressed his critics as both unromantic and unregal. In January 1820, George III, condemned by Shelley as that "old, mad, blind, despised, and dying King," finally expired. The prince became king in his own right and immediately precipitated a crisis that shook the monarchy, revivified Whig opposition, and gave the masses a chance to show that their anger was still a force to be reckoned with. George IV's wife, Princess Caroline, had lived on the continent for the previous six years, touring Italy in the company of an entourage headed by an impoverished Italian aristocrat. Her dress and her behavior had inspired intense gossip, and in 1820 she infuriated George by hurrying home to London to be crowned by his side as queen. The king knew that a divorce trial in the church court would open him to damaging countercharges. He therefore asked his ministers to introduce *A Bill to deprive Her Majesty Caroline Amelia Elizabeth of the Title, Prerogatives, Rights, Privileges, and Pretensions of Queen Consort of this Realm, and to dissolve the Marriage between his Majesty and the said Queen.* Immediately the Whigs took up the queen's cause for its political value, and London rallied to her with wild enthusiasm. If Caroline was vulgar, foolish, and of questionable morals, her husband's morals left no room for question. George IV had followed the example of Charles II and had made no attempt to conceal his profligacy. No matter what his wife had done, he had done worse; in

Jane Austen In novels such as *Pride and Prejudice* (1813) she cast a keenly observant, ironic eye on early nineteenth-century English country society. (The engraving is based on a sketch by Jane Austen's sister.) *(Bettmann/Corbis)*

the eyes of most Britons, especially British women, she was the injured party. In an address to Caroline formulated by "the Ladies of Edinburgh," they pointed out that the

> principles and doctrines now advanced by your accusers do not apply to your case alone, but if made a part of the law of the land, may hereafter be applied as precedent by every careless dissipated husband to rid himself of his wife, however good and innocent she may be; and to render his family, however amiable, illegitimate. . . .[7]

---

[7]Cited in Tamara Hunt, "Morality and Monarchy in the Queen Caroline Affair," *Albion* (Winter 1991), p. 716. The article provides a helpful brief introduction to the case and the cause. See also Thea Holme, *Caroline* (1980). Until the mid-twentieth century, most biographies of George IV were distinctly hostile, but Roger Fulford, *George the Fourth,* rev. ed. (1949), is judicious, and Joanna Richardson, *George IV: A Portrait* (1970), eminently favorable. E. A. Smith also provides a multi-dimensional assessment in *George IV* (1999). In *The Prince of Pleasure and His Regency, 1811–20* (1969), the literary critic J. B. Priestley has compiled an entertaining and lavishly illustrated survey of the era. Mark Girouard furnishes an informative and richly illustrated introduction to the impact of romanticism on nineteenth-century English society in *The Return to Camelot: Chivalry and the English Gentleman* (1981).

The Royal Pavilion at Brighton   The pavilion symbolizes regency romanticism as fashioned by architect John Nash. *(Royal Pavilion, Art Gallery and Museums, Brighton)*

When the bill for divorce was introduced into Parliament in the summer of 1820, the king was in fact on trial; as the weeks passed, it became ever clearer what the verdict would be. The most brilliant of Whig lawyers defended the queen, the idol of the populace, and excitement mounted into a threat of revolution. In November the bill was dropped, amid tumultuous rejoicing. For the last time, a king had persuaded his ministers to introduce a measure at his personal behest; and the minority party, with public opinion behind it, had defeated him.[8] The lesson was not lost on the Whig party. One of their younger members, Lord John Russell, remarked that "the Queen's business had done a great deal of good in renewing the old and natural alliance of the Whigs and the people, and of weakening the influence of the Radicals with the latter." The Whigs of the 1820s had strayed a long way from the old alliance, personified in Charles James Fox; and they began to realize that renewing it might prove politically profitable.

But the profit was delayed, because by 1822 the Tories were showing a new vitality and a fresh willingness to remember Edmund Burke's dictum that "a state without the means of change is without the means of its conservation." Canning, Castlereagh's successor as foreign secretary and leader of the House of Commons, appeared far more open-minded on

---

[8]Though he lost the battle, King George IV won the war. The Privy Council ruled that Caroline, because she had long lived separately from the king, might not be crowned queen. After she had accepted a large financial settlement from the ministry, Caroline became less of an object of popular pity. In July 1821, she was excluded from both the elaborate ceremony in Westminster Abbey and the lavish coronation banquet in Westminster Hall, and she died — of natural causes — only a few weeks later.

the need for reform. Lord Sidmouth, who had taken the odium for enforcing the Six Acts, had resigned as home secretary and was replaced by the son of a Lancashire cotton manufacturer, Robert Peel. Peel developed a strong distrust of any Toryism that did not move with the times. William Huskisson, one of the ablest financiers of his day, became the new president of the Board of Trade. The era of fearful repression was giving way to a more optimistic period of pragmatic legislation.

Crisis in the Near East (1821–1830)

After 1822 both foreign and domestic policy began to shift. Canning's interference with the Holy Alliance in 1823 over the issue of the rebellious Spanish American colonies was only the beginning of Britain's concern with rebels. In 1821 the Greeks had revolted against their rulers, the Ottoman Turks; from this revolt came a crisis that tormented Europe for a decade. Until 1825 the decrepit Ottoman Empire tried without success to regain control of Greece, in a war that was one of grisly atrocities on both sides. But a wave of sympathy for the Greeks swept over Europe. The ruling class of Britain and the continent had been nurtured on the classics and, knowing little or nothing of modern Greece, saw in rough peasants the ancient Spartans and Athenians. The cause not only aroused the sympathy of the classicists but also appealed, in its exotic wildness, to devotees of Romanticism. Philhellenes, or supporters of the Greeks, soon sprouted up everywhere from Russia to the American frontier.

Lord Byron set his seal on the revolt. He wrote about it in a tone that blended nostalgia for the Greeks' past with anxiety about their future, a combination calculated to rouse Philhellenes to a frenzy.

> The isles of Greece! the isles of Greece
>   Where burning Sappho loved and sung,
> Where grew the arts of war and peace,
>   Where Delos rose, and Phoebus sprung!
> Eternal summer gilds them yet,
> But all, except their sun, is set. . . .
>
> Fill high the bowl with Samian wine!
>   Our virgins dance beneath the shade —
> I see their glorious black eyes shine;
>   But gazing at each glowing maid,
> My own the burning tear-drop laves,
> To think such breasts must suckle slaves.
>
> Place me on Sunium's marbled steep,
>   Where nothing, save the waves and I,
> May hear our mutual murmurs sweep;
>   There, swan-like, let me sing and die:
> A land of slaves shall ne'er be mine —
> Dash down yon cup of Samian wine!

Lord Byron (1788–1824)
The romantic poet (as painted by Richard Westfall in 1813) called on his countrymen to help restore the Greece of old. *(The Granger Collection)*

Byron not only wrote; he also took action. In 1823 he traveled to Greece to help the insurgents, and in 1824 he gave his life for them in a botched military assault. He died, not singing on the promontory of Sunium but at Missolonghi from fever, and he proved to be worth even more to the cause dead than alive. He became the hero-martyr of the Philhellenes. They sent money, supplies, and volunteers to the Greeks until the war took on the aspect of an international crusade.

Although the idealism that stirred such excitement put pressure on the great powers to intervene in Greece, they were not accustomed to acting on idealism. Their policies rested on calculations of interest, and in this case the interaction of their interests was enormously complex. But the underlying forces at work are clear in retrospect and merit examination if only because they led ultimately to the onset of a world war in 1914.

The geographical focus of these forces was the Ottoman Empire. For almost 200 years, its dominions had been shrinking, and the sultan's government, the Sublime Porte at Constantinople, had been growing more feeble. By the 1820s, Russia had conquered the north coast of the Black Sea and pressed toward the mouth of the Danube; the Serbs had revolted in the Balkans before the Greek rising and had gained substantial autonomy; and the sultan's ambitious vassal in Egypt, Mohammed Ali, had assembled an effective army and navy with which to build an empire for himself. The Ottoman state appeared on the verge of disintegration.

But the great powers could not allow it to disintegrate before they had agreed on dividing the spoils, and agreement proved impossible. Russia longed for Constantinople and the sultan's Balkan provinces, in order to open the straits and get access through the Aegean to the Mediterranean. The Austrians feared Russian expansions into the Balkans; the British opposed a Russian naval base in the Mediterranean; the French sought to recover the influence that Napoleon had briefly exercised in the eastern Mediterranean. For all three powers, the shaky Ottoman Empire served as a barrier against the tsar. They therefore found it difficult to support the Greek revolt against the sultan.

In 1824–1827, the crisis deepened. First the sultan called in Mohammed Ali's army and fleet. The Egyptians set to work, with efficient ferocity, to end the Greek rebellion by exterminating the rebels, whose only hope soon lay in intervention by the powers. At the end of 1825, Tsar Alexander died. His successor, Nicholas I, made clear that he would intervene alone if need be on behalf of his fellow (Eastern Orthodox) Christians. In that case, Russia would probably turn Greece into a satellite. Metternich grumbled at that prospect, but his refusal to assist any nationalist rebels included the Greeks. France and Britain had no desire to undermine the Ottoman edifice either, but they dared not let Russia proceed alone. To keep some influence on events, they decided to cooperate with the tsar in whatever measures might prove necessary. The Holy Alliance of the three eastern powers gave way for the moment to a new triangular grouping of Russia, France, and Britain.

In August 1827, Canning died. His successors tried to retreat into what looked like the safety of inaction, but events were out of their control. In October a combined squadron of Russian, French, and British men-of-war, which had been sent to the Greek coast, observed the Turko-Egyptian fleet in the Bay of Navarino. The allied admirals felt uncertain as to what they had been sent to do, but the question became academic when the enemy fleet fired on them. They returned the fire and wiped out the foe.

The Battle of Navarino saved the Greeks, but it roused consternation in London. At the beginning of 1828, the duke of Wellington became prime minister. He strongly opposed any action that would impair Ottoman power, particularly if Russia reaped the benefit, and had the king express to Parliament his hope that the battle, "this untoward event," would not interrupt Britain's friendly relations with its "ancient ally," the Porte. The sultan was unimpressed by this apology and called for a holy war against the powers that had destroyed his fleet. Russia responded by launching a war of its own against the Turks, and for the moment both of Britain's contradictory objectives — to protect the Greeks and to preserve the Ottoman Empire — appeared out of reach.

Britain escaped utter diplomatic defeat by an unforeseen factor — the fighting power of the ragged and ill-equipped Turkish army. After the Russian troops had sustained a number of reverses, Nicholas became more amenable. Metternich now urged an independent Greece, and Wellington, much against his will, was persuaded to agree. The negotiations between the powers dragged on until the spring of 1832, when at long last Greece was formally established as a sovereign kingdom under the guarantee of Britain, France, and Russia. Meanwhile, in 1829, the Russo-Turkish war had ended in the Treaty of Adrianople. The agreement considerably strengthened Russian influence in the Balkans outside Greece and proportionately weakened Ottoman control. There for the moment the eastern question rested.

The issue was far from closed, however. For almost a hundred years, it reopened periodically, bringing with it wars and the threat of wars. The settlement of the Greek phase left an uneasy three-cornered balance of power in the eastern Mediterranean among Russia, Britain, and France, which operated for a time to British advantage. Another crisis would erupt in 1840; yet another in the 1850s, which led to the Crimean War; and one more in the 1870s. Somehow the Ottoman Empire remained alive, not because the great powers relished its existence but because they could not agree on how to divide its inheritance.

Moderate Toryism (1822–1827)

The period 1822–1827, with Liverpool still prime minister but Canning the leading figure in the ministry, saw legislative change that foreshadowed the upheaval of the 1830s. The Tories were as unwilling as ever to alter the constitution of Parliament or of the Church of England, but they were prepared to amend the criminal law, statutes affecting trade unions, and the Corn Laws.

The first change, initiated by Robert Peel, came in the criminal code. As early as 1819, Peel had made a name for himself as a rising financier by regularizing the currency and providing for the resumption of specie payments. Now, as home secretary, he carried through a significant program to amend the substantive law and the system of law enforcement. The abolition of the death penalty for all but the most serious offenses curtailed the high degree of discretion that judges had previously exercised in sentencing; the average number of executions per year declined within a decade from 108 to 61. The punishment for minor offenses was mitigated also, and more than a hundred separate statutes concerned with larceny were consolidated into a single act. Peel, who was as much concerned with deterring crime as with altering the criminal law, proposed for London a metropolitan police force, directly responsible to the Home Office, with headquarters at Scotland Yard. Peel had helped to establish such a police force in Ireland during the previous fifteen years, but many Londoners initially greeted the proposal with hostility as an invasion of English liberties. Parliament adopted the plan for metropolitan London in 1829, however, and encouraged the setting up of local police forces in cities and towns elsewhere in the country during the 1830s and 1840s.[9]

---

[9]The story is told in detail in Stanley H. Palmer, *Police and Protest in England and Ireland, 1780–1850* (1988).

VALUE OF BRITISH EXPORTS, 1825

(in millions of £s)

£ 8.5

£ 6.1

£ 7.0

£ 7.3

£ 5.8

£ 3.6

£ 0.4

NORTHERN	SOUTHERN	AFRICA	ASIA	U.S.	CANADA	REST OF
EUROPE	EUROPE				& BRIT.	WESTERN
					W. INDIES	HEMISPHERE

Derived from B. R. Mitchell and Phyllis Deane, eds., *Abstract of British Historical Statistics* (1962), p. 313.

The Combination Act of 1799, never easy to enforce, was repealed in 1824, and employers and employees alike were freed to organize as they pleased. The change sparked an epidemic of strikes and lockouts, which precipitated a new statute in 1825 that continued to permit combinations "for the sole purpose of consulting upon and determining the rate of wages and prices." Such combinations were illegal if they involved violence, intimidation, molestation, or obstruction. Penalties were imposed on employees who used force against their employers or who coerced fellow workers to join a trade union. Under the law of 1825, such a union was not illegal, provided that it was voluntary and uncoercive, but its power to strike, to picket, and to safeguard its funds was left in legal limbo. Most Members of Parliament wanted to establish what became a concept sacred to most Victorians, freedom of contract. By this process, an employee, without outside interference, might contract with his employer on any mutually acceptable terms. Neither the state nor the union but the law of supply and demand would determine the rate of wages.

Victorian economic doctrine was also foreshadowed in the reforms instituted by William Huskisson, the president of the Board of Trade. In principle he was for his day an advanced free-trader; and although in practice he proceeded cautiously, the sum of his achievements proved impressive. He relaxed the Navigation Acts, primarily to stimulate the trade of the British colonies and thereby cement their loyalty to the mother country; he changed the Corn Laws to reduce the tariff on imported colonial grain; he also lowered tariffs on foreign manufactured goods and, even more drastically, on foreign raw materials, and in the process he dealt a lethal blow to smuggling. British trade boomed.

The prosperity that followed, however, brought in the short run a wave of speculation almost as wild as the South Sea Bubble, and in 1826 a crash came that was almost as shattering as that when the Bubble burst. The resultant unemployment was aggravated by bad harvests, and hunger stalked the countryside. Much foreign grain was in storage, waiting for the domestic price to rise to that stipulated in the Corn Laws. Parliament hastily authorized the sale of this grain and thereby tacitly admitted that the Corn Laws worked a hardship on the nation. Two years later, a sliding scale of duties was introduced, decreasing as grain prices rose on the domestic market; and this principle remained operative until 1846. Parliament was willing to compromise in an emergency, but it remained committed to safeguarding the prosperity of the landed interest.

The Disruption of the Tories (1827–1830)

For the moment, the question of the Corn Laws was overshadowed by political developments. Early in 1827, a stroke incapacitated Lord Liverpool, the head of the government since 1812, and a bitter battle ensued for the succession. Canning won, at the cost of disrupting his party. Rank-and-file Tories distrusted his liberal views, especially on Catholic emancipation, and also distrusted him. He was too brilliant for the more pedestrian, and he could not blunt the shafts of his wit. Every time he delivered a major speech, it was said, he made an enemy for life. When he was named prime minister, six of his colleagues resigned, including Peel and Lord Eldon; and Tories harassed him more than Whigs during his term of office. His tenure was brief. In August 1827 he died, and without him his few followers could not carry on. After a short interlude, the duke of Wellington in January 1828 formed a government that appeared to be a return to the Toryism of an earlier day. But, torn by factions and haunted by Canning's ghost, that Toryism was dying, and the duke felt compelled to surrender its principles one by one.

The first surrender seemed primarily symbolic. The new cabinet grudgingly accepted a Whig bill, introduced by Lord John Russell in 1828, to raise the growing body of religious dissenters — non-Anglican Protestants — to full citizenship by repealing the Test and Corporation Acts that barred them from local and national office. This legislation of the Cavalier Parliament had lost most of its teeth after 1727, thanks to annual suspending acts, but had remained on the books as a nostalgic Tory symbol of the day when Anglicans had monopolized political power.[10] Repeal had a chiefly psychological rather than legal impact: It gave new force to the movement for Catholic emancipation. If Protestants outside the established church deserved full recognition, why not Roman Catholics?

The man who posed this question dramatically was Daniel O'Connell. Ever since 1801, some Irish Catholics had agitated for the repeal of the union that had failed to grant them full citizenship. O'Connell, a successful Dublin lawyer, had recently come to the fore as the leader and organizer of their discontent. He welcomed not only gentlemen but also tenant farmers — who paid dues of a penny a month — into his Catholic Association, an increasingly powerful pressure group that utilized the cause of "emancipation" to sharpen its members' consciousness of their Irish identity. O'Connell was a big man in every way — in body and intellect and humor — and he was as patient as he was astute. He had no faith in persuading the British by logic or coercing them by violence; instead, he aimed to generate irresistible political pressure, and in this he succeeded. In 1828 he stood for Parliament from the Irish county of Clare, and experts were startled to discover that a Catholic might legally be nominated and even elected, though he might not sit. The Anglo-Irish gentry solidly opposed the candidate, and they were used to controlling county elections. But hundreds of freeholders marched to the polls, blessed by their priests, to vote for O'Connell. He was triumphantly returned.[11]

The Clare election put Wellington's government in a serious dilemma. The duke and Peel, his leader in the House of Commons, were against Catholic emancipation on principle; so were the king and the great majority of the House of Lords. But to refuse to seat O'Connell might well have led to new rebellion in Ireland — over an issue that had the support of at least half the members of the House of Commons. The followers of Canning, true to his memory, championed the Irish cause, as did most Whigs. Wellington ultimately succeeded in overcoming the opposition of the House of Lords, but only after adding to the measure a number of "securities": O'Connell's Catholic Association would be suppressed; the right to vote in Irish counties would be sharply curtailed; Roman Catholic M.P.'s would have to take an oath denying the right of the pope to interfere in Britain's domestic affairs. On such conditions, professing Roman Catholics could henceforth take seats in Parliament and hold virtually all government offices. Before the measure became law, Wellington and Peel

---

[10]See Chapter 2. In *Pulpits, Politics and Public Order in England, 1760–1832* (1989), Robert Hole traces the manner in which the revival of dissenter influence undermined the Anglican domination of political power. The fullest account of the revival of non-Anglican Protestants may be found in Michael R. Watts, *The Dissenters* (Vol. 2: *The Expansion of Evangelical Nonconformity, 1791–1859*) (1995).

[11]For the details see Fergus O'Ferrall, *Catholic Emancipation: Daniel O'Connell and the Birth of Irish Democracy, 1820–1830* (1986). Also relevant are Charles Chenevix Trench, *The Great Dan: A Biography of Daniel O'Connell* (1984); G. I. T. Machin, *The Catholic Question in English Politics, 1820–1830* (1964); and Wendy Hinde, *Catholic Emancipation: A Shake to Men's Minds* (1992).

Daniel O'Connell (1775–1847)   Ireland's "Liberator" (as depicted by George Hayer) after his admission to the United Kingdom Parliament. *(The Granger Collection)*

had still to overcome the resistance of King George IV, who, like his father, felt convinced that such a measure violated his coronation oath. When his chief ministers threatened to resign, the king, realizing that he had no alternative ministers to turn to, reluctantly agreed.

The effect was profound. Emancipation created in the House of Commons a third party, composed of thirty or more of Ireland's 100 members of Parliament. Primarily Roman Catholics, they followed O'Connell's lead. They were committed neither to Whig nor Tory principles but solely to the interests of Ireland as they understood those interests. Under different names and with a varying number of adherents, such an Irish third party would play for more than a century a role in British politics out of all proportion to its numbers. The way in which O'Connell had achieved his ends showed that efficient organization, backed by the threat of violence but operating within legal channels, could force the hand of a reluctant British government, and the lesson was not lost on the Irish. In domestic politics, the emancipation crisis constituted a further step in the disruption of the Tory party that had begun at Liverpool's retirement. Wellington and Peel were discredited with their own rank and file, and the Canningites were driven into coalition with the Whigs. While the impetus to change accelerated, the barriers to it were revealed as feeble when the king and the House of Lords, those champions of the status quo, gave way before the ministry. The path lay open for changing the structure of Parliament itself, and the drive for reform began that would culminate in 1832.

The Tory defenses crumbled rapidly. In June 1830, George IV performed what many of his subjects regarded as his one good deed — he died. Whatever his virtues as a patron of the arts, as a monarch he had proved opinionated, meddlesome, and inconsistent, and he had brought the popularity of the crown to its nadir in modern times. Despite his sympathy for Fox in his earlier years, he had become an adamant opponent of constitutional reform. His younger brother, who succeeded him as William IV, posed a far less ponderous obstacle. He was a bluff and genial man, with some pretensions to liberalism but little political common sense, and as conscientious and well-meaning as he was irresolute.

His accession necessitated a new parliamentary election, which coincided with a revolution in France. It was a moderate revolution, like that in England in 1688, and out of it came not a Jacobin Reign of Terror but a staid bourgeois regime with a moderate king, Louis Philippe. Developments in Paris made a deep impression across the Channel. If even the volatile French could change their government without opening the floodgates of democracy and chaos, surely the British could.

In the new Parliament the Tories had a shaky majority, which melted away as soon as Wellington made clear that he would not consider any measure of constitutional reform. He stood for a Toryism adamant against further concessions, and his speech in the House of Lords in November 1830 served as its funeral oration. Parliament as it then existed, he said,

> possesses the full and entire confidence of the people. I will go further. If at the present moment I had imposed upon me the duty of forming a legislature . . . for a country like this, in possession of great property of various descriptions, I do not mean to assert that I could form such a legislature as we possess now, for the nature of man is incapable of reaching such excellence at once, but my great endeavor would be to form some description of legislature which would produce the same results.

At a time when a popular clamor for political reform was again widespread and often backed by holders of "great property of various descriptions," the duke could only extol the surpassing excellence of the status quo. Two weeks later he was forced to resign, and the battle for reform began.

The Reform Program

Many Britons of the post-1815 era believed that what their land truly required was a reform of the spirit. The evangelical revival discussed in Chapter 10 was in full flower, and many Britons sought to combat the hedonism and permissive morality of the aristocratic Regency era. They saw salvation in a more rigorous personal moral code, in more faithful attendance at church or chapel, in a multiplication of Sunday schools for all children, and in a greater devotion to family life.

At the same time, the disintegration of the Tory party in the late 1820s and the return of a Whig ministry enabled all manner of groups in British society to argue in favor of political reform as well. Radical pressure groups once again proposed a program of universal suffrage for all adult males. Numerous middle-class pressure groups urged political reform also but change of a less drastic order. Yet the process of industrialization and urban growth had vastly altered the social geography of the kingdom, and many magnates of foundry and mine and mill found it absurd that cities such as Manchester and Birmingham continued to lack direct representation in the House of Commons. They might fear the prospect of universal manhood suffrage, but they sought a more direct share of power for themselves.

Until the accession of George III, the composition of the House of Commons, despite all the anomalies of rotten boroughs, had borne some rough relationship to the distribution of wealth and population. The country had still been chiefly engaged in trade and agriculture, and a case could be made for a legislature in which commercial interests were represented but in which the landed interest predominated.[12] But by the time George III died, a vast new interest had come into being, and it had no representation worth the name. The great industrial centers lay in parts of the British Isles that had hitherto been sparsely populated and in which parliamentary boroughs were few and far between. Many mushrooming cities sent no members to Parliament, and the barons of industry who dominated those cities had at best an indirect voice in national politics.

The Tories felt disinclined to tamper with a constitutional arrangement that apparently had stood the test of time. Although their leaders saw themselves as championing the interests of both commerce and industry, and although their ranks included a few scions of industrialists, such as Robert Peel, the party was dominated by the landed interest. The heads of the great territorial houses still made up the bulk of the peerage, and their relatives and dependents the bulk of the House of Commons. That house could not be enlarged to take in the clamorous outsiders without becoming hopelessly unwieldy. The only way to accommodate them lay in disenfranchising scores of rotten boroughs and thereby depriving numerous borough-mongers of their influence and many Members of Parliament of their seats.

The Whig leaders also had aristocratic social connections and landed roots, but they differed from the Tories in one important respect. Their party was out of power. They had been out since the days of Fox, and clinging to their old ways gave them little chance of getting in again. A political party that feels itself condemned to perpetual wandering in the wilderness is a party prepared to consider a change in the rules of the po-

---

[12]For the composition of the eighteenth-century House of Commons, see Chapter 4.

litical game, if such change offers hope of tasting once more the fruits of office. So it was with the Whigs. In the course of the 1820s, they not only clung to the tradition of civic and religious liberty identified with Charles James Fox, but they also embraced the cause that some of their party had advocated forty years earlier, parliamentary reform, and by 1830 they were its champions. They had no sympathy with a program seeking universal manhood suffrage (in their judgment a prelude to the despoilment of the rich by the poor). Nevertheless, they were fully prepared to harness popular enthusiasm to a measure extending the privilege of the franchise to hitherto excluded property owners.

The Whigs' political program had two parts — the rationalization of the franchise and the reapportionment of borough representatives. Landed property, they argued, deserved no more influence in government than any other form, and voting qualifications should be adjusted so that all men of substance had a voice. The existing electoral system seemed far too arbitrary: some boroughs had only a handful of voters whereas in democratic constituencies like Westminster most adult males voted. If the seats from the smaller boroughs were awarded to the newly populous areas, then the system would reflect far more equitably the realities of wealth and population.

The long-term effects would be sweeping, as both conservatives and radicals well knew. Once admit the principle that the constitution needed amending, then no amendment could be considered permanent; the same logic that impelled the first change would lead inexorably to others, in a never-ending process of innovation. Removing the rotten boroughs would shake the gentry's control of local government; unseating the gentry there would be a prelude to attacking their economic power as maintained by the Corn Laws; destroying the Corn Laws in the interest of the people at large would lead to enfranchising the masses, and then how would any kind of property be safe? This line of thinking triggered the Tory's dread of reform and the radical's enthusiasm for it. In part, but only in part, both Tories and radicals were to be proved right.

Epilogue

When the Whigs introduced their Reform Bill in March 1831, Britain had reached a watershed in its history. No previous ministry of the crown had ever proposed to Parliament such a deliberate and drastic constitutional revision. The Glorious Revolution and the Hanoverian accession had certainly brought drastic change, but it had not been deliberate; the intent had been to safeguard the existing constitution. In the eighteenth century, the gradual and subtle process of constitutional growth had gone largely unperceived by the oligarchs themselves. They had not deliberately created the cabinet or the rotten borough or government by "interests" but had merely used the means that came to hand for conducting the business of the state. "In what we improve," Burke had said, "we are never wholly new; and in what we retain, we are never wholly obsolete." He spoke for a ruling class that had proved itself capable of moving with the times, slowly and hesitantly, but that had no thought of revolution even by statute.

The question at issue was whether traditional landed aristocrats would be willing to share with merchants and industrialists the power that they sought. The Reform Act of 1832 brought about such a readjustment. It broadened a largely landed aristocracy into an oligarchy that incorporated other sources of wealth. When the settlement of 1832, which both Whigs and Tories hoped would be permanent, was altered radically in the Reform Bill of 1867, the whole principle of oligarchy was eroded as well. In the meantime, the first Reform Bill had opened the door to other changes — in local government, in the administration of the central government, in poor relief, in colonial and commercial policy, and in the organization of popular pressure groups agitating on behalf of numerous causes, including a further expansion of the franchise.

Landed aristocrats were to play an important role in British life for another hundred years, but a survey of the age of landed aristocracy in its heyday may reasonably end in 1830. The tumult that followed Wellington's resignation that autumn belongs as much to a new age that was dawning as to the twilight of the old. The Britain of 1830 was a far cry from that of Lord Chesterfield. The frock coat and top hat had replaced the finery of a gentleman's brocade and sword and wig. Rural meadows frequented by grazing cows had become the site of factories run by steam engines and surrounded by workers' slums. The workshop of the world produced a bustle of activity, and portents loomed everywhere of the greater bustle to come. The first Atlantic crossing by a steamship, British-built, had occurred in 1827; and in 1830 the opening of a rail line between Liverpool and Manchester, designed to carry passengers, inaugurated the railroad age. Steam and machinery, as they came into their own, were making the social order of the eighteenth century more and more archaic.

That eighteenth-century society need not evoke nostalgia, but it does demand respect. Aristocrats ruled Britain as never before or since; they loved their country, and by and large they served it well. The list of their accomplishments is long, and a few examples in conclusion may stand as a summary of their rule. They did not resolve the Irish problem, but they did consolidate the British Isles into a single kingdom. In the face of distress and disaffection at home, they ultimately prevailed in the "Second Hundred Years' War" against the French, and they successfully directed the armies and the navies that had helped their land become a world power. They maintained an economic structure both stable and flexible enough to accommodate a rapid growth of population and the introduction of new trades and industries. They developed a national framework of taxation, administration, and law that made it possible for the new economy to prosper. They governed in a manner that was sometimes lax, sometimes repressive, and that was characterized more by amateur improvisation than by bureaucratic planning but that permitted, in the long run, the growth of individual freedom. Their self-confidence matched their energy. They had a refinement and sureness of taste that made both the Jacobean and the Victorian eras seem boorish by comparison, and they were experts in the fine art of living.

Most important of all, they knew by instinct when their power was ebbing and were able to surrender it with good grace rather than battling to the death. They possessed a saving gift for compromise, which may be one of the humdrum but is also one of the great political virtues; and by compromising, they made peaceful change possible. Their best epitaph is the observation of a shrewd foreigner, Prince Louis Napoleon, the heir and eventual successor of his uncle as Napoleon III: "In England you make reforms," said the prince; "in France we make revolutions."

Appendix

Monarchs, 1685–1837

James II (VII of Scotland)	1685–1689	George III	1760–1820
William III	1689–1702	George IV	
and Mary II	1689–1694	as Prince Regent	1811–1820
Anne	1702–1714	as King	1820–1830
George I	1714–1727	William IV	1830–1837
George II	1727–1760		

Population England (minus Monmouthshire)

YEAR	ESTIMATED POPULATION[1]	PERCENTAGE CHANGE IN PREVIOUS TEN YEARS
1691	4,931,000	—
1701	5,058,000	+2.6
1711	5,230,000	+3.4
1721	5,350,000	+2.3
1731	5,263,000	−1.6
1741	5,576,000	+5.6
1751	5,772,000	+3.5
1761	6,147,000	+6.5
1771	6,448,000	+4.9
1781	7,042,000	+9.2
1791	7,740,000	+9.9
1801	8,664,000	+11.9
1811	9,868,000	+13.2
1821	11,491,000	+15.3
1831	13,299,000	+14.7

	ENGLAND & WALES	SCOTLAND	IRELAND	TOTAL UNITED KINGDOM
1761	6,569,000	1,265,000[2]	—	
1771	7,052,000	—	3,530,000	
1781	7,531,000	—	4,048,000	
1791	8,247,000	1,500,000	4,753,000	14,500,000
1801	9,156,000	1,599,000	5,216,000	15,972,000
1811	10,322,000	1,824,000	5,956,000	18,102,000
1821	12,106,000	2,100,000	6,802,000	21,008,000
1831	13,994,000	2,374,000	7,767,000	24,135,000

[1]Estimates based on E. A. Wrigley and R. S. Schofield, *The Population History of England: A Reconstruction* (1981).

[2]Alexander Webster's Census of 1755 cited in B. R. Mitchell, *European Historical Statistics, 1750–1970* (1978). The remaining statistics in this table are drawn from Chris Cook and John Stevenson, eds., *British Historical Facts, 1760–1830* (1980).

Ministries, 1714–1830

DATE BEGUN	USUAL NAME OF MINISTRY	FIRST LORD OF THE TREASURY	SECRETARY OF STATE (South Dept.)	SECRETARY OF STATE (North Dept.)
1714	Stanhope	OCT. 1714: Halifax	SEP. 1714: Townshend	SEP. 1714: Stanhope
		MAY 1715: Carlisle		JUN. 1716: Methuen
		OCT. 1715: Walpole	DEC. 1716: Stanhope	APR. 1717: Addison
		APR. 1717: Stanhope	APR. 1717: Sunderland	MAR. 1718: Craggs
		MAR. 1718: Sunderland	MAR. 1718: Stanhope	MAR. 1721: Carteret
1721	Walpole	APR. 1721: Walpole	FEB. 1721: Townshend	APR. 1724: Newcastle
			JUN. 1730: Harrington	
1742	Carteret	FEB. 1742: Wilmington	FEB. 1742: Carteret	
1744	Pelham	AUG. 1743: H. Pelham	NOV. 1744: Harrington	
1746	Bath	FEB. 1746: Bath	FEB. 1746: Granville	FEB. 1746: Granville
1746	Pelham	FEB. 1746: H. Pelham	FEB. 1746: Harrington	FEB. 1746: Newcastle
			OCT. 1746: Chesterfield	JUL. 1748: Bedford
			FEB. 1748: Newcastle	JUN. 1751: Holderness
1754	Newcastle	MAR. 1754: Newcastle	MAR. 1754: Holderness	MAR. 1754: Robinson
				NOV. 1755: H. Fox
1756	Pitt-Devonshire	NOV. 1756: Devonshire		DEC. 1756: W. Pitt
1757	Pitt-Newcastle	JUN. 1757: Newcastle		JUN. 1757: W. Pitt
1761	Bute		MAR. 1761: Bute	OCT. 1761: Egremont
		MAY 1762: Bute	MAY 1762: G. Grenville	
			OCT. 1762: Halifax	
1763	Grenville	APR. 1763: G. Grenville	SEP. 1763: Sandwich	SEP. 1763: Halifax
1765	Rockingham	JUL. 1765: Rockingham	JUL. 1765: Grafton	JUL. 1765: Conway
1766	Chatham	AUG. 1766: Grafton	MAY 1766: Conway	MAY 1766: Richmond
				JUL. 1766: Shelburne
1768	Grafton		JAN. 1768: Weymouth	OCT. 1768: Weymouth
			OCT. 1768: Rochford	
1770	North	JAN. 1770: North	DEC. 1770: Sandwich	DEC. 1770: Rochford
			JAN. 1771: Halifax	
			JUN. 1771: Suffolk	NOV. 1775: Weymouth
			OCT. 1779: Stormont	NOV. 1779: Hillsborough

DATE BEGUN	USUAL NAME OF MINISTRY	FIRST LORD OF THE TREASURY	HOME SECRETARY	FOREIGN SECRETARY
1782	Rockingham	MAR. 1782: Rockingham	MAR. 1782: Shelburne	MAR. 1782: C. J. Fox
1782	Shelburne	JUL. 1782: Shelburne	JUL. 1782: Sydney	JUL. 1782: Grantham
1783	Fox-North	APR. 1783: Portland	APR. 1783: North	APR. 1783: C. J. Fox
1783	Pitt	DEC. 1783: W. Pitt	DEC. 1783: Temple	DEC. 1783: Temple
			DEC. 1783: Sydney	DEC. 1783: Leeds
			JUN. 1789: W. W. Grenville	
			JUN. 1791: H. Dundas	JUN. 1791: Grenville
			JUL. 1794: Portland	
				FEB. 1801: Hawkesbury
1801	Addington	MAR. 1801: H. Addington	JUL. 1801: Pelham	
			AUG. 1803: C. P. Yorke	
1804	Pitt	MAY 1804: W. Pitt	MAY 1804: Hawkesbury	MAY 1804: Harrowby
				JAN. 1805: Mulgrave
1806	All the Talents	FEB. 1806: Grenville	FEB. 1806: Spencer	FEB. 1806: C. J. Fox
				SEP. 1806: Howick
1807	Portland	MAR. 1807: Portland	MAR. 1807: Hawkesbury	MAR. 1807: G. Canning
1809	Perceval	OCT. 1809: S. Perceval	NOV. 1809: R. Ryder	OCT. 1809: Bathurst
				DEC. 1809: Wellesley
1812	Liverpool	JUN. 1812: Liverpool	JUN. 1812: Sidmouth	MAR. 1812: Castlereagh
			JAN. 1822: R. Peel	SEP. 1822: G. Canning
1827	Canning	APR. 1827: G. Canning	APR. 1827: W. Sturges Bourne	APR. 1827: Dudley
			JUL. 1827: Lansdowne	
1827	Goderich	AUG. 1827: Goderich		
1828	Wellington	JAN. 1828: Wellington	JAN. 1828: R. Peel	JUN. 1828: Aberdeen

Bibliography

Bibliographies and Reference Works

Annual Bibliography of British and Irish History. Since 1975.

Bibliographies of British Statesmen. Volumes have been published on Edmund Burke, Charles James Fox, George Grenville, the duke of Newcastle, and William Pitt (earl of Chatham). 1991–1997.

Brown, Lucy, and Ian Christie, eds. *Bibliography of British History, 1789–1851.* 1977.

Bruce, Arthur. *Bibliography of the British Army, 1660–1914.* 1985.

Cannon, John, ed. *The Oxford Companion to British History.* 1997.

Chaloner, W. H., and R. C. Richardson, eds. *British Social and Economic History: A Bibliographical Guide.* 3rd ed. 1996.

Cook, Chris, and John Stevenson, eds. *British Historical Facts, 1688–1760.* 1989.

———. *British Historical Facts, 1760–1830.* 1980.

Davies, Godfrey, ed. *Bibliography of British History: The Stuart Period.* 2nd rev. ed. 1971.

Dictionary of National Biography. 1882–1900.

Falkus, Malcolm, and John Gillingham, eds. *The Historical Atlas of Britain.* 1982.

Greene, Jack P., and Pole, J. R., eds. *The Blackwell Encyclopedia of the American Revolution.* 1991.

Griffiths, Dennis, ed. *The Encyclopedia of the British Press, 1422–1992.* 1992.

Kanner, Barbara. *Women in English Social History, 1800–1914: An Essay and Guide to Research.* 3 vols. 1987–1990.

———, ed. *The Women of England from Anglo-Saxon Times to the Present: Interpretive Bibliographical Essays.* 1979.

Mitchell, Brian, ed. *British Historical Statistics.* 1988.

Morrill, J. S., ed. *Seventeenth Century Britain, 1603–1714.* Critical Bibliographies in Modern History. 1980.

Schlatter, Richard, ed. *Recent Views on British History.* 1984.

Smith, Robert A., ed. *Late Georgian and Regency England, 1760–1837.* Bibliographical Handbook. 1984.

Winks, Robin, ed. *The Oxford History of the British Empire: Historiography.* 1999.

General Works

Baugh, Daniel, ed. *Aristocratic Government and Society in Eighteenth-Century England: The Foundations of Stability.* 1975.

Baxter, Stephen, ed. *England's Rise to Greatness.* 1983.

Black, Jeremy, ed. *Britain in the Age of Walpole.* 1984.

———. *British Politics and Society from Walpole to Pitt, 1742–1789.* 1990.

Briggs, Asa. *The Age of Improvement, 1783–1867.* 1959.

Bryant, Arthur. *The Years of Endurance, 1793–1802.* 1942.

———. *The Years of Victory, 1802–1812.* 1945.

———. *The Age of Elegance, 1812–1822.* 1950.

Cannon, John, ed. *The Whig Ascendancy: Colloquies on Hanoverian England.* 1981.

Churchill, Winston S. *A History of the English-Speaking Peoples*, Vol. 3. 4 vols. 1956–1958.

Clark, George N. *The Later Stuarts, 1660–1714.* Vol. X. The Oxford History of England. 2nd ed. 1956.

Colley, Linda. *Britons: Forging the Nation, 1707–1837.* 1992.

Connolly, S. J. *Religion, Law, and Power: The Making of Protestant Ireland, 1660–1760.* 1992.

Dickinson, H. T., ed. *Britain and the French Revolution, 1789–1815.* 1989.

Evans, Eric J. *The Forging of the Modern State: Early Industrial Britain, 1783–1870.* Vol. IV. Foundations of Modern Britain. 1983.

Ferguson, William. *Scotland: 1689 to the Present.* 1968.

Gash, Norman. *Aristocracy and People: Britain, 1815–1865.* New History of England. 1979.

Halévy, Elie. *A History of the English People in the Nineteenth Century*, Vols. 1 and 2. 6 vols. 2nd ed. 1949–1952.

Holmes, Geoffrey, ed. *Britain After the Glorious Revolution.* 1969.

———. *The Making of a Great Power: Late Stuart and Early Georgian Britain, 1660–1722.* 1993.

———, and Daniel Szechi. *The Age of Oligarchy: Pre-Industrial Britain, 1722–1783.* 1993.

Inwood, Stephen. *A History of London.* 1998.

Jenkins, Geraint H. *The History of Wales.* Vol. 4: *The Foundations of Modern Wales, 1642–1780.* 1987.

Jones, J. R. *Country and Court: England, 1658–1714.* New History of England. 1978.

Langford, Paul. *A Polite and Commercial People: England, 1727–1783.* The New Oxford History of England. 1989.

Lecky, W. E. H. *A History of England in the Eighteenth Century.* 8 vols. 1878–1890.

Lenman, Bruce. *Integration, Enlightenment, and Industrialization: Scotland, 1746–1832.* 1981.

Marshall, Dorothy. *Eighteenth-Century England, 1714–1783.* A History of England, edited by W. N. Medlicott. 2nd ed. 1975.

Mitchison, Rosalind. *A History of Scotland.* 2nd ed. 1982.

———. *Lordship and Patronage: Scotland, 1603–1745.* 1983.

Ogg, David. *England in the Reigns of James II and William III.* 1955.

Owen, John B. *The Eighteenth Century, 1714–1815.* Norton Library History of England. 1974.

Plumb, John H. *England in the Eighteenth Century.* 1963.

Smout, T. C. *A History of the Scottish People, 1560–1830.* 1972.

Speck, W. A. *Stability and Strife: England, 1714–1760.* New History of England. 1977.

Trevelyan, George Macaulay. *England Under Queen Anne.* 3 vols. 1930–1934.

Trevelyan, George O. *The American Revolution.* 4 vols. 1905–1912.

Watson, J. Steven. *The Reign of George III, 1760–1815.* Vol. XII. The Oxford History of England. 1960.

Willcox, William B. *Star of Empire: A Study of Britain as a World Power, 1485–1945.* 1950.

Williams, Basil. *The Whig Supremacy, 1714–1760.* Vol. XI. The Oxford History of England. 2nd ed. 1962.

Woodward, E. Llewelyn. *The Age of Reform, 1815–1870.* Vol. XIII. The Oxford History of England. 1938.

Legal, Constitutional, and Political History

Ashley, Maurice. *The Glorious Revolution of 1688.* 1966.

Beattie, John M. *Crime and the Courts in England, 1660–1800.* 1986.

———. *The English Court in the Reign of George I.* 1967.

Brewer, John. *Party Ideology and Popular Politics at the Accession of George III.* 1976.

———, and John Styles, eds. *An Ungovernable People: The English and Their Law in the Seventeenth and Eighteenth Centuries.* 1980.

Brock, W. R. *Lord Liverpool and Liberal Toryism, 1820–1827.* 2nd ed. 1967.

Bucholz, Robert. *The Augustan Court: Queen Anne and the Decline of Court Culture.* 1993.

Butterfield, Herbert. *George III and the Historians.* 1957.

Cannon, John. *Aristocratic Century: The Peerage of Eighteenth-Century England.* 1984.

Chester, Norman. *The English Administrative System, 1780–1870.* 1981.

Christie, Ian R. *Myth and Reality in Late Eighteenth-Century Politics and Other Papers.* 1970.

———. *Stress and Stability in Late Eighteenth Century Britain: Reflections on the British Avoidance of Revolution.* 1985.

———. *Wilkes, Wyvill and Reform.* 1962.

Colley, Linda. *In Defiance of Oligarchy: The Tory Party, 1714–60.* 1982.

Cone, Carl B. *Burke and the Nature of Politics.* 2 vols. 1957–1964.

———. *The English Jacobins.* 1968.

Cookson, J. E. *Lord Liverpool's Administration: The Crucial Years, 1815–1822.* 1975.

Cotter, William R. "The Somerset Case and the Abolition of Slavery in England," *History* (February 1994).

Cruickshanks, Eveline, ed. *By Force or by Default? The Revolution of 1688–89.* 1989.

———, and Jeremy Black, eds. *The Jacobite Challenge.* 1988.

Daiches, David. *Scotland and the Union.* 1977.

Davis, Richard. *Political Change and Continuity, 1760–1885: A Buckinghamshire Study.* 1972.

De Krey, Gary Stuart. *A Fractured Society: The Politics of London in the First Age of Party, 1688–1715.* 1986.

DeLacy, Margaret. *Prison Reform in Lancashire, 1700–1850: A Study in Local Administration.* 1986.

Foord, Archibald S. *His Majesty's Opposition, 1714–1830.* 1964.

Gilmour, Ian. *Riots, Risings and Revolution: Governance and Violence in Eighteenth-Century England.* 1992.

Goodwin, Albert. *The Friends of Liberty: The English Democratic Movement in the Age of the French Revolution.* 1979.

Harling, Philip. *The Waning of "Old Corruption": The Politics of Economical Reform in Britain, 1779–1846.* 1996.

Harris, Tim. *Politics Under the Later Stuarts, 1660–1715.* 1993.

Harvie, Christopher. *Scotland and Nationalism: Scottish Society and Politics, 1707–1977.* 1977.

Hill, B. W. *The Growth of Parliamentary Parties, 1689–1742.* 1976.

———. *British Parliamentary Parties, 1742–1832.* 1985.

Hinde, Wendy. *Catholic Emancipation: A Shake to Men's Minds.* 1992.

Holdsworth, William S. *A History of English Law,* Vols. 10–16. 16 vols. 3rd ed. 1922–1938.

Holmes, Geoffrey. *British Politics in the Age of Anne.* Rev. ed. 1987.

———. *The Trial of Doctor Sacheverell.* 1973.

Horwitz, Henry. *Parliament, Policy, and Politics in the Reign of William III.* 1977.

Hunt, Tamara. "Morality and Monarchy in the Queen Caroline Affair." *Albion* (Winter 1991).

Jones, Clyve, ed. *A Pillar of the Constitution: The House of Lords in British Politics, 1640–1784.* 1989.

Jones, George Hilton. *Convergent Forces: Immediate Causes of the Revolution of 1688 in England.* 1990.

Jones, J. R., ed. *Liberty Secured? Britain Before and After 1688.* 1992.

———. *The Revolution of 1688 in England.* 1972.

Keir, David L. *The Constitutional History of Modern Britain, 1485–1950.* 1953.

Kenyon, J. P. *Revolution Principles: The Politics of Party, 1689–1720.* 1977.

Landau, Norma. *The Justices of the Peace, 1679–1760.* 1984.

Langford, Paul. *The Excise Crisis: Society and Politics in the Age of Walpole.* 1975.

———. *Public Life and the Propertied Englishman, 1689–1798.* 1991.

Laqueur, Thomas. "The Queen Caroline Affair." *Journal of Modern History* (September 1982).

Machin, G. I. T. *The Catholic Question in English Politics, 1820–1830.* 1964.

Middleton, Richard. *The Bells of Victory: The Pitt-Newcastle Ministry and the Conduct of the Seven Years' War, 1757–1762.* 1985.

Midgley, Clare. *Women Against Slavery: The British Campaign 1780–1870.* 1992.

Mitchell, Austin. *The Whigs in Opposition, 1815–30.* 1967.

Monod, Paul Kleber. *Jacobitism and the English People, 1688–1788.* 1989.

Morris, Marilyn. *The British Monarchy and the French Revolution.* 1998.

Namier, Lewis B. *England in the Age of the American Revolution.* 1933.

———. *The Structure of Politics at the Accession of George III.* 2nd ed. 1957.

———, and John Brooke. *The House of Commons, 1754–1790.* 3 vols. History of Parliament Series. 1964.

O'Ferrall, Fergus. *Catholic Emancipation: Daniel O'Connell and the Birth of Irish Democracy, 1820–30.* 1986.

O'Gorman, Frank. *The Emergence of the British Two-Party System, 1760–1832.* 1982.

———. *The Rise of Party in England: the Rockingham Whigs, 1760–82.* 1975.

———. *The Whig Party and the French Revolution.* 1967.

———. *Voters, Patrons and Parties: The Unreformed Electorate of Hanoverian England, 1734–1832.* 1990.

Palmer, Stanley H. *Police and Protest in England and Ireland, 1780–1850.* 1988.

Pares, Richard. *King George III and the Politicians.* 1953.

Peters, Marie. *Pitt and Popularity: The Patriot Minister and London Opinion During the Seven Years' War.* 1981.

Petrie, Sir Charles. *The Jacobite Movement.* 3rd ed. 1959.

Philip, Mark, ed. *The French Revolution and British Popular Politics.* 1992.

Phillips, John A. *Electoral Behavior in Unreformed England.* 1983.

Plumb, J. H. *The Origins of Political Stability in England, 1675–1725.* 1967.

Prall, Stuart E. *The Bloodless Revolution: England, 1688.* 1972.

Reitan, E. A., ed. *George III: Tyrant or Constitutional Monarch?* 1964.

Riley, P. W. J. *The Union of England and Scotland: A Study in Anglo-Scottish Politics of the Early Eighteenth Century.* 1979.

Robbins, Caroline. *The Eighteenth-Century Commonwealthman.* 1959.

Rogers, Nicholas. *Whigs and Cities: Popular Politics in the Age of Walpole and Pitt.* 1990.

Rudé, George. *Wilkes and Liberty.* 1962.

Sack, James J. *From Jacobite to Conservative: Reaction and Orthodoxy in Britain, c. 1760–1832.* 1993.

———. *The Grenvillites, 1801–29; Party Politics and Factionalism in the Age of Pitt and Liverpool.* 1979.

Schwoerer, Lois G. *The Declaration of Rights, 1689.* 1981.

———, ed. *The Revolution of 1688: Changing Perspectives.* 1992.

Sedgwick, Romney. *The House of Commons, 1715–1754.* 2 vols. History of Parliament Series. 1970.

Speck, W. A. *Reluctant Revolutionaries: Englishmen and the Revolution of 1688.* 1989.

Straka, Gerald M., ed. *The Revolution of 1688 and the Birth of the English Political Nation.* 2nd ed. 1973.

Thomas, P. D. G. *The House of Commons in the Eighteenth Century.* 1971.

Thompson, Edward P. *Whigs and Hunters: The Origins of the Black Act.* 1978.

Thorne, R. G., ed. *The House of Commons, 1790–1820.* 5 vols. History of Parliament Series. 1986.

Walker, David M. *A Legal History of Scotland*. Vol. V: *The Eighteenth Century*. 1998.

Webb, Sidney, and Beatrice Webb. *English Local Government from the Revolution to the Municipal Corporation Act*. 9 vols. 1906–1929.

Williams, E. Neville. *The Eighteenth Century Constitution, 1688–1815: Documents and Commentary*. 1960.

Wilson, Kathleen. *The Sense of the People: Urban Political Culture in England, 1715–85*. 1995.

Economic and Social History

Altick, Richard D. *The Shows of London*. 1978.

Ashton, Thomas S. *An Economic History of England: The Eighteenth Century*. 1955.

———. *The Industrial Revolution, 1760–1830*. Rev. ed. 1964.

Black, Jeremy. *The British and the Grand Tour*. 1985.

Bohstedt, John. *Riots and Community Politics in England and Wales, 1790–1810*. 1983.

Borsay, Peter. *The English Urban Renaissance: Culture and Society in the Provincial Town, 1660–1770*. 1989.

Briggs, Asa. *The Power of Steam*. 1982.

Brown, Ford K. *Fathers of the Victorians*. 1961.

Buck, Anne. *Dress in Eighteenth Century England*. 1979.

Carpenter, J. Kenneth. *The History of Scurvy and Vitamin C*. 1986.

Carswell, John. *The South Sea Bubble*. 1960.

Chambers, J. D. *Population, Economy, and Society in Pre-Industrial England*. 1972.

———, and G. E. Mingay. *The Agricultural Revolution, 1750–1880*. 1966.

Clapham, John H. *An Economic History of Modern Britain*, Vol. 1. 3 vols. 1930–1938.

———. *The Bank of England*. 2 vols. 1944.

Clark, Anna. *The Struggle for the Breeches. Gender and the Making of the English Working Class*. 1995.

Clarkson, Leslie. *Death, Disease, and Famine in Pre-Industrial England*. 1975.

Cockburn, J. S., ed. *Crime in England, 1550–1800*. 1977.

Corfield, Penelope J. *The Impact of English Towns, 1700–1800*. 1982.

Cowherd, Raymond G. *Political Economists and the English Poor Law*. 1977.

Crafts, N. F. R. *British Economic Growth During the Industrial Revolution*. 1985.

Crouzet, Francois. *The First Industrialists: The Problem of Origins*. 1985.

Daunton, Martin J. *Progress and Poverty: An Economic and Social History of England, 1700–1850*. 1996.

Davidoff, Leonore, and Catherine Hall. *Family Fortunes: Men and Women of the English Middle Class, 1780–1850*. 1987.

Deane, Phyllis. *The First Industrial Revolution*. 2nd ed. 1979.

———, and W. A. Cole. *British Economic Growth, 1688–1959: Trends and Structure*. 2nd ed. 1967.

Dickson, P. G. M. *The Financial Revolution in England: A Study in the Development of Public Credit, 1688–1756.* 1967.

Dobson, C. R. *Masters and Journeymen: A Prehistory of Industrial Relations, 1717–1800.* 1980.

Drescher, Seymour. *Capitalism and AntiSlavery: British Mobilization in Comparative Perspective.* 1986.

Earle, Peter. *The Making of the English Middle Class: Business, Society and Family Life in London, 1660–1730.* 1989.

Ehrman, John. *The British Government and Commercial Negotiations with Europe, 1783–1793.* 1962.

Emsley, Clive. *British Society and the French Wars, 1793–1815.* 1979.

Flinn, M. W. *British Population Growth, 1700–1850.* 1970.

———. *Origins of the Industrial Revolution.* 1966.

———. *The History of the British Coal Industry.* Vol. 2. *1700–1830: The Industrial Revolution.* 1984.

Floud, Roderick, and Donald N. McCloskey, eds. *The Economic History of Great Britain Since 1700.* 3 vols. 2nd ed. 1994.

Fox, Celina, ed. *London: World City, 1800–1840.* 1992.

George, M. Dorothy. *Hogarth to Cruikshank: Social Change in Graphic Satire.* 1967.

———. *London Life in the Eighteenth Century.* 1925.

Gillis, John R. *For Better, For Worse: British Marriages, 1600 to the Present.* 1985.

Girouard, Mark. *Life in the English Country House: A Social and Architectural History.* 1978.

Gwynn, Robin D. *Huguenot Heritage: The History and Contribution of the Huguenots in Britain.* 1985.

Hammond, John L., and Barbara Hammond. *The Town Laborer, 1760–1832: The New Civilization.* 1917.

———. *The Skilled Laborer, 1760–1832.* 1920.

———. *The Village Laborer, 1760–1832: A Study in the Government of England Before the Reform Bill.* 4th ed. 1932.

Hargreaves, E. L. *The National Debt.* 1930.

Hartwell, R. M. *The Industrial Revolution and Economic Growth.* 1971.

Hay, Douglas, et al. *Albion's Fatal Tree: Crime and Society in Eighteenth-Century England.* 1975.

———, and Nicholas Rogers. *Eighteenth-Century English Society.* 1997.

Hecht, J. Jean. *The Domestic Servant Class in Eighteenth-Century England.* 1956.

Hibbert, Christopher. *King Mob: The Story of Lord George Gordon and the Riots of 1780.* 1958.

Hill, Bridget. *Women, Work, and Sexual Politics in Eighteenth-Century England.* 1989.

Hilton, Boyd. *Corn, Cash, Commerce: The Economic Policies of the Tory Governments, 1815–1830.* 1978.

Himmelfarb, Gertrude. *The Idea of Poverty: England in the Early Industrial Age.* 1984.

Hobsbawm, E. J. *Industry and Empire*. 1968.

Hodgkin, Eric. *Birmingham: The First Manufacturing Town in the World, 1760–1840*. 1989.

Holmes, Geoffrey. *Augustan England: Professions, State, and Society, 1680–1730*. 1982.

Houston, R. A. *Social Change in the Age of Enlightenment: Edinburgh, 1660–1760*. 1994.

Hunt, Margaret. *The Middling Sort: Commerce, Gender, and the Family in England, 1680–1780*. 1996.

Jones, D. W. *War and Economy in the Age of William III and Marlborough*. 1988.

Koditschek, Theodore. *Class Formation and Urban Industrial Society: Bradford, 1750–1850*. 1990.

Landes, David. *The Unbound Prometheus: Technological Change and Industrial Development in Western Europe from 1750 to the Present*. 1969.

Laslett, Peter. *The World We Have Lost: England Before the Industrial Age*. 1965.

Lees, Lynn Hollen. *The Solidarities of Strangers: The English Poor Laws and the People, 1700–1948*. 1998.

Lewis, Judith S. *In the Family Way: Childbearing in the British Aristocracy, 1760–1860*. 1986.

McKendrick, Neil, John Brewer, and J. H. Plumb. *The Birth of a Consumer Society: The Commercialization of Eighteenth-Century England*. 1984.

Malcolmson, R. W. *Popular Recreation in English Society, 1700–1850*. 1973.

Mantoux, Paul J. *The Industrial Revolution in the Eighteenth Century in England*. Rev. ed. 1928.

Marshall, Dorothy. *English People in the Eighteenth Century*. 1956.

———. *The English Poor in the Eighteenth Century: A Study in Social and Administrative History*. 1926.

Marshall, J. D. *The Old Poor Law, 1795–1834*. 1968.

Mathias, Peter. *The First Industrial Nation*. 2nd ed. 1983.

———. *The Transformation of England: Essays in the Economic and Social History of England in the Eighteenth Century*. 1979.

Mingay, G. E. *English Landed Society in the Eighteenth Century*. 1963.

———. *The Agrarian History of England and Wales*. Vol. 6: *1750–1850*. 1989.

———. *The Gentry: The Rise and Fall of a Ruling Class*. 1976.

Mitchell, B. R. *Economic Development of the British Coal Industry, 1800–1914*. 1984.

Mokyr, Joel, ed. *The British Industrial Revolution: An Economic Perspective*. 2nd ed. 1998.

Morgan, Marjorie. *Manners, Morals and Class in England, 1774–1858*. 1994.

Mui, Hoh-Cheung, and Lorna H. Mui. *Shops and Shopkeeping in Eighteenth-Century England*. 1989.

Munsche, F. B. *Gentlemen and Poachers: The English Game Laws, 1671–1831*. 1981.

Musson, A. E., and Eric Robinson. *Science and Technology in the Industrial Revolution*, 1969.

Neal, Larry. *The Rise of Financial Capitalism: International Capital Markets in the Age of Reason.* 1991.

Neale, R. S. *Class in English History, 1680–1850.* 1981.

O'Brien, Patrick. *Power With Profit: The State and the Economy, 1689–1815.* 1991.

———, and Roland Quinault, eds. *Industrial Revolution and British Society.* 1993.

Oldfield, J. R. *Popular Politics and British Anti-Slavery: The Mobilization of Public Opinion Against the Slave Trade, 1787–1807.* 1995.

Olsen, Donald J. *Town Planning in London: The Eighteenth and Nineteenth Centuries.* 1964.

Owen, David. *English Philanthropy, 1660–1960.* 1964.

Perkin, Harold. *The Origins of Modern English Society, 1780–1880.* 1969.

———. *The Structured Crowd: Essays in English Social History.* 1981.

Pinchbeck, Ivy. *Women Workers and the Industrial Revolution.* 1930.

———, and Margaret Hewitt. *Children in English Society.* 2 vols. 1969–1972.

Plumb, J. H. *The Commercialization of Leisure in Eighteenth-Century England.* 1973.

Pollock, Linda. *Forgotten Children: Parent-Child Relations from 1500 to 1900.* 1983.

Porter, Roy. *English Society in the Eighteenth Century.* The Pelican Social History of Britain. 1982.

———. *Health for Sale: Quackery in England, 1660–1850.* 1989.

———. *London: A Social History.* 1995.

———. *Mind-Forg'd Manacles: A History of Madness in England from the Renaissance to the Regency.* 1987.

——— and G. S. Rousseau. *Gout: The Patrician Malady.* 1998.

Quinlan, Maurice J. *Victorian Prelude.* 1941.

Richards, Eric. *A History of the Highland Clearances: Agrarian Transformations and Evictions, 1746–1886.* 1982.

Rosenberg, Nathan, and L. E. Birdzell, Jr. *How the West Grew Rich: The Economic Transformation of the Industrial World.* 1986.

Rostow, W. W. *The Stages of Economic Growth: A Non-Communist Manifesto.* 3rd ed. 1990.

Royster, Charles. *A Revolutionary People.* 1979.

Rudé, George. *Criminal and Victim: Crime and Society in Early Nineteenth-Century England.* 1986.

———. *The Gordon Riots.* 1974.

———. *Hanoverian London, 1714–1808.* 1971.

———. *Paris and London in the Eighteenth Century.* 1973.

Rule, John. *Albion's People: English Society, 1714–1815.* 1992.

———. *The Vital Century: England's Developing Economy, 1714–1815.* 1992.

Salaman, Radcliffe. *The History and Social Influence of the Potato.* New ed. 1985.

Schwarz, L. D. *London in the Age of Industrialization: Entrepreneurs, Labour Force, and Living Standards, 1700–1850.* 1992.

Shammas, Carole. *The Pre-Industrial Consumer in England and America.* 1990.

Sharpe, Pamela, ed. *Women's Work: The English Experience 1650–1914*. 1998.

Snell, K. D. M. *Annals of the Labouring Poor: Social Change and Agrarian England, 1660–1900*. 1985.

Starr, Douglas. *Blood: An Epic History of Medicine and Commerce*. 1999.

Stevenson, John. *Popular Disturbances in England, 1700–1870*. 1979.

Stone, Lawrence. *Broken Lives: Separation and Divorce in England, 1660–1857*. 1993.

———. *The Family, Sex, and Marriage in England, 1500–1800*. 1977.

———. *Road to Divorce: England, 1530–1857*. 1990.

———. *Uncertain Unions: Marriage in England, 1660–1753*. 1992.

———, and Jeanne Stone. *An Open Elite? England, 1540–1880*. 1984.

Taylor, A. J., ed. *The Standard of Living in Britain in the Industrial Revolution*. 1975.

Taylor, P. A. M., ed. *The Industrial Revolution in Britain: Triumph or Disaster?* 2nd ed. 1970.

Thirsk, Joan. *The Agrarian History of England and Wales*. Vol. 5: *1640–1750*. 2 Parts. 1984.

Thomis, Malcolm I. *The Luddites*. 1970.

———. *Responses to Industrialization: The British Experience, 1780–1850*. 1976.

———. *The Town Laborer and the Industrial Revolution*. 1975.

———, and Peter Holt. *Threats of Revolution in Britain, 1789–1848*. 1977.

Thompson, E. P. *Customs in Common: Studies in Traditional Popular Culture*. 1992.

———. *The Making of the English Working Class*. 1963.

Thompson, F. M. L., ed. *The Cambridge Social History of Britain, 1750–1950*. 3 vols. 1990.

Traill, Henry D., ed. *Social England: A Record of the Progress of the People . . . by Various Writers*, Vols. 4–6. 6 vols. 1893–1897.

Trevelyan, George Macaulay. *English Social History*. 3rd ed. 1946.

Trumbach, Randolph. *The Rise of the Egalitarian Family: Aristocratic Kinship and Domestic Relations in Eighteenth-Century England*. 1978.

Turberville, A. S. *English Men and Manners in the Eighteenth Century*. 2nd ed. 1929.

Turner, Michael. *Enclosures in Britain, 1750–1830*. 1984.

Vickery, Amanda. *The Gentleman's Daughter: Women's Lives in Georgian England*. 1998.

Weatherill, Lorna. *Consumer Behavior and Material Culture in Britain, 1660–1760*. 1988.

Wells, Roger. *Wretched Faces: Famine in Wartime England, 1793–1801*. 1988.

West, E. G. "Literacy and the Industrial Revolution." *Economic History Review* (August 1978).

Whatley, Christopher. *The Industrial Revolution in Scotland*. 1997.

Wilson, Charles. *England's Apprenticeship, 1603–1763*. 1965.

Woodforde, James. *Country Parson: James Woodforde's Diary, 1759–1802*. 1985.

Wordie, J. R. "The Chronology of English Enclosure, 1500–1914." *Economic History Review* (November 1983).

Wrigley, E. A. *Continuity, Chance and Change: The Character of the Industrial Revolution in England.* 1988.

———, and R. S. Schofield. *The Population History of England, 1541–1871: A Reconstruction.* Rev. ed. 1989.

Intellectual, Religious, and Cultural History

Altick, Richard D. *The English Common Reader.* 1957.

———. *The Shows of London.* 1978.

Baer, Marc. *Theatre and Disorder in Late Georgian London.* 1992.

Black, Jeremy. *The English Press in the Eighteenth Century.* 1987.

Bossy, John. *The English Catholic Community, 1570–1850.* 1975.

Bostridge, Ian. *Witchcraft and Its Transformations, c. 1650–1750.* 1997.

Brewer, John. *The Pleasures of the Imagination.* 1997.

Broadie, Alexander, ed. *The Scottish Enlightenment: An Anthology.* 1997.

Cannadine, David. *Class in Britain.* 1998.

Clark, Jonathan. *The Language of Liberty, 1660–1832: Political Discourse and Social Dynamics in the Anglo-American World.* 1994.

Curl, James Stevens. *Georgian Architecture.* 1993.

Currie, R., et al. *Churches and Churchgoers: Patterns of Church Growth in the British Isles Since 1700.* 1977.

Daiches, David, and others, eds. *A Hotbed of Genius: The Scottish Enlightenment, 1730–1790.* 1986.

Davies, Horton. *Worship and Theology in England,* Vol. 3, *1690–1850.* 1961.

Dickinson, H. T. *Liberty and Property: Political Ideology in Eighteenth Century Britain.* 1978.

Endelman, Todd M. *The Jews of Georgian England, 1714–1830: Tradition and Change in a Liberal Society.* 1979.

Gascoigne, John. *Cambridge in the Age of the Enlightenment.* 1990.

Gay, Peter. *The Enlightenment: An Interpretation.* 2 vols. 1967–1970.

Gilbert, Alan D. *Religion and Society in Industrial England: Church, Chapel, and Social Change, 1740–1914.* 1976.

Girouard, Mark. *The Return to Camelot: Chivalry and the English Gentleman.* 1981.

Halévy, Elie. *The Growth of Philosophic Radicalism.* 1928.

Harris, R. W. *Reason and Nature in the Eighteenth Century, 1714–1780.* 1968.

———. *Romanticism and the Social Order, 1780–1830.* 1969.

Haydon, C. *Anti-Catholicism in Eighteenth-Century England.* 1993.

Hempton, David. *Methodism and Politics in British Society, 1750–1850.* 1984.

———. *The Religion of the People: Methodism and Popular Religion, c. 1750–1900.* 1996.

Henriques, Ursula. *Religious Toleration in England, 1787–1833.* 1961.

Hole, Robert. *Pulpits, Politics and Public Order in England, 1760–1832.* 1989.

Humphreys, A. R. *The Augustan World: Society, Thought, and Letters in Eighteenth-Century England.* 1954.

Jacob, Margaret. *The Newtonians and the English Revolution.* 1976.

Laqueur, Thomas Walter. *Religion and Respectability: Sunday Schools and Working Class Culture, 1780–1850.* 1976.

Laski, Harold. *English Political Thought from Locke to Bentham.* 1920.

LeMahieu, D. L. *The Mind of William Paley: A Philosopher and His Age.* 1976.

Liesenfeld, Vincent J. *The Licensing Act of 1737.* 1984.

Maccoby, Simon. *English Radicalism,* Vols. 1 and 2. 5 vols. 1935–1955.

Newman, Gerald. *The Rise of English Nationalism: A Cultural History, 1740–1830.* Revised ed. 1997.

Paulson, Ronald. *Popular and Polite Art in the Age of Hogarth and Fielding.* 1979.

Pittock, Murray G. H. *The Invention of Scotland: The Stuart Myth and Scottish Identity, 1638 to the Present.* 1991.

Plumb, J. H., ed. *Man and Society in Eighteenth Century Britain.* 1968.

Pocock, J. G. A. *Virtue, Commerce, and History: Essays on Political Thought and History, Chiefly of the Eighteenth Century.* 1985.

Priestley, J. B. *The Prince of Pleasure and His Regency, 1811–1820.* 1969.

Pruett, John. *The Parish Clergy Under the Later Stuarts: The Leicestershire Experience.* 1978.

Quennell, Peter. *Romantic England: Writing and Painting, 1717–1851.* 1970.

Rendall, Jane. *The Origins of the Scottish Enlightenment, 1707–1776.* 1978.

Rogers, Katharine M. *Feminism in Eighteenth-Century England.* 1982.

Rupp, Gordon. *Religion in England, 1688–1791.* 1986.

Semmel, Bernard. *The Methodist Revolution.* 1974.

Sher, Richard B. *Church and University in the Scottish Enlightenment.* 1985.

Soloway, Richard A. *Prelates and People, 1783–1852.* 1969.

Spadafora, David. *The Idea of Progress in Eighteenth-Century Britain.* 1990.

Speck, W. A. *Society and Literature in England, 1700–60.* 1984.

Stephen, Leslie. *History of English Thought in the Eighteenth Century.* 2 vols. 3rd ed. 1902.

Stromberg, Roland. *Religious Liberalism in Eighteenth-Century England.* 1954.

Summerson, John. *Architecture in Britain, 1530–1830.* 7th ed. 1983.

———. *Georgian London.* Rev. ed. 1988.

Sykes, Norman. *Church and State in England in the XVIIIth Century.* 1934.

Thomas, Keith. *Religion and the Decline of Magic.* 1971.

Trussler, Simon, ed. *The Cambridge Illustrated History of the British Theatre.* 1994.

Vann, Richard T. *The Social Development of English Quakerism, 1665–1755.* 1969.

Vincent, David. *Literacy and Popular Culture in England, 1750–1914.* 1989.

Virgin, Peter. *The Church in the Age of Negligence.* 1989.

Waterhouse, Ellis. *Painting in Britain, 1530–1790.* 4th ed. 1978.

Walvin, James. *The Quakers: Money and Morals.* 1997.

Watts, Michael R. *The Dissenters.* Vol 1: *From the Reformation to the French Revolution.* 1978. Vol. 2: *The Expansion of Evangelical Nonconformity, 1791–1859.* 1995.

Webb, Robert K. *The British Working Class Reader, 1790–1848.* 1955.

Willey, Basil. *The Seventeenth Century Background: Studies in the Thought of Age in Relation to Poetry and Religion.* 1934.

———. *The Eighteenth Century Background: Studies on the Idea of Nature in the Thought of the Period.* 1941.

Imperial, Diplomatic, and Irish History

Anstey, Roger. *The Atlantic Slave Trade and British Abolition, 1760–1810.* 1975.

Baylin, Bernard. *Ideological Origins of the American Revolution.* 1967.

Bayly, C. A. *Imperial Meridian: The British Empire and the World, 1780–1830.* 1989.

Beckett, J. C. *The Making of Modern Ireland, 1603–1923.* 2nd ed. 1981.

Black, Jeremy. *British Foreign Policy in the Age of Walpole.* 1985.

Bonwick, Colin. *The American Revolution.* 1992.

Bradley, James E. *Popular Politics and the American Revolution in England.* 1986.

Cain, P. J., and A. J. Hopkins, *British Imperialism: Innovation and Experience, 1688–1914.* 1993.

Christie, Ian R. *Crisis of Empire: Great Britain and the American Colonies, 1754–1783.* 1966.

———, and Benjamin Labaree. *Empire or Independence, 1760–1775: A British-American Dialogue on the Coming of the American Revolution.* 1976.

Connolly, S. J. *Religion, Law, and Power: The Making of Protestant Ireland, 1660–1760.* 1992.

Cullen, L.M. *An Economic History of Ireland Since 1660.* 1972.

Curtin, Philip D. *The Atlantic Slave Trade: A Census.* 1969.

Davis, Ralph. *The Industrial Revolution and British Overseas Trade.* 1979.

Derry, John. *English Politics and the American Revolution.* 1976.

Drescher, Seymour. *Econocide: British Slavery in the Era of Abolition.* 1977.

Elliott, Marianne. *Partners in Revolution.* 1982.

Eltis, David. *Economic Growth and the Ending of the Transatlantic Slave Trade.* 1987.

Gipson, Lawrence H. *The British Empire Before the American Revolution* (1748–1776). 15 vols. 1958–1970.

———. *The Coming of the Revolution, 1763–1775.* 1956.

Hancock, David. *Citizens of the World: London Merchants and the Integration of the British Atlantic Community, 1735–1785.* 1995.

Harlow, Vincent T. *The Founding of the Second British Empire, 1763–1793.* 2 vols. 1952–1964.

Horn, D. B. *Great Britain and Europe in the Eighteenth Century.* 1967.

Hughes, Robert. *The Fatal Shore.* 1987.

Langford, Paul. *The Eighteenth Century, 1688–1815.* Modern British Foreign Policy Series. 1976.

Lawson, Philip. *The East India Company: A History.* 1994.

Lecky, W. E. H. *A History of Ireland in the Eighteenth Century*. Edited by L. P. Curtis. 1972.

Marshall, P. J. *East India Fortunes: The British in Bengal in the Eighteenth Century*. 1976.

———. *The Impeachment of Warren Hastings*. 1965.

———. *Problems of Empire: Britain and India, 1757–1813*. 1968.

———, ed. *The Oxford History of the British Empire: the Eighteenth Century*. 1998.

McCaffrey, Lawrence. *Ireland: From Colony to Nation State*. 1979.

McDowell, R. B. *Ireland in the Age of Imperialism and Revolution, 1760–1801*. 1980.

Miller, P. N. *Defining the Common Good: Empire, Religion and Philosophy in Eighteenth Century Britain*. 1994.

Moody, T. W., and Q. E. Vaughan, eds. *Eighteenth-Century Ireland, 1691–1800*. Vol. IV. A New History of Ireland. 1986.

Moon, Sir Penderel. *The British Conquest and Dominion of India*. 1989.

———. *Warren Hastings and British India*. 1947.

Perkins, Bradford. *Prologue to War: England and the United States, 1805–1812*. 1961.

Ritcheson, Charles R. *Aftermath of Revolution: British Policy Toward the United States, 1783–1795*. 1969.

Rose, John Holland et al., eds. *The Cambridge History of the British Empire*, Vols. 1–2. 8 vols. 2nd ed. 1929–1936.

Schroeder, Paul W. *The Transformation of European Politics, 1763–1848*. 1994.

Schweizer, K. W. *Britain, Prussia and the Seven Years' War*. 1989.

Scott, H. M. *British Foreign Policy in the Age of the American Revolution*. 1990.

Semmel, Bernard. *The Rise of Free Trade Imperialism*. 1970.

Seton-Watson, R. W. *Britain in Europe, 1789–1914*. 1937.

Sosin, Jack M. *Whitehall and the Wilderness: The Middle West in British Colonial Policy, 1760–1775*. 1961.

Steele, Ian K. *The English Atlantic, 1675–1740: An Exploration of Communication and Community*. 1986.

Stone, Lawrence, ed. *An Imperial State At War: Britain from 1689 to 1815*. 1994.

Sutherland, Lucy S. *The East India Company in Eighteenth-Century Politics*. 1952.

Szechi, Daniel. *The Jacobites: Britain and Europe, 1688–1788*. 1994.

Temperley, Harold. *The Foreign Policy of Canning, 1822–1827*. 1925.

Thomas, Hugh. *The Slave Trade: The History of the Atlantic Slave Trade, 1440–1870*. 1997.

Thomas, P. D. G. *British Politics and the Stamp Act Crisis: The First Phase of the American Revolution, 1763–1767*. 1975.

———. *The Second Phase of the American Revolution, 1767–1773*. 1987.

Walvin, James. *Making the Black Atlantic: Britain and African Diaspora*. 1999.

Ward, Adolphus W., and George P. Gooch, eds. *The Cambridge History of British Foreign Policy, 1783–1919*, Vol. 1. 3 vols. 1922–1923.

Webster, Charles K. *The Congress of Vienna*. Rev. ed. 1934.

———. *The Foreign Policy of Castlereagh*. 2 vols. 1925–1931.

Whelan, Frederick G. *Edmund Burke and India: Political Morality and Empire.* 1997.

Williamson, James A. *A Short History of British Expansion.* 2 vols. Rev. ed. 1943–1945.

Woodruff, Philip. *The Men Who Ruled India: The Founders.* 1954.

Military and Naval History

Anderson, Fred. *The Crucible of War: The Seven Years' War and the Fate of Empire in British North America, 1754–1766.* 1999.

Baugh, Daniel A. *British Naval Administration in the Age of Walpole.* 1965.

Black, Jeremy. *War for America: The Fight for Independence, 1775–1783.* 1992.

Bond, Gordon. *The Grand Expedition: The British Invasion of Holland in 1809.* 1979.

Brewer, John. *Sinews of Power: War, Money, and the English State, 1688–1783.* 1989.

Cookson, J. E. *The British Armed Nation, 1793–1815.* 1997.

Cordingly, David. *Under the Black Flag: The Romance and Reality of Life Among the Pirates.* 1997.

Corbett, Julian S. *England in the Seven Years' War: A Study in Combined Strategy.* 2 vols. 2nd ed. 1918.

Cresswell, John. *British Admirals of the Eighteenth Century: Tactics and Battles.* 1972.

Duffy, Michael. *Soldiers, Sugar and Seapower: The British Expeditions to the West Indies and the War Against Revolutionary France.* 1987.

Elliott, Marianne. *Partners in Revolution.* 1982.

Fortescue, John W. *History of the British Army,* Vols. 1–10. 13 vols. in 20. 1899–1930.

Gates, David. *The Spanish Ulcer: A History of the Peninsular War.* 1986.

Glover, Michael. *Wellington as Military Commander.* 1968.

Glover, Richard. *Britain at Bay: Defense Against Bonaparte, 1803–14.* 1973.

———. *Peninsular Preparation: The Reform of the British Army, 1795–1809.* 1963.

Hall, Christopher D. *British Strategy in the Napoleonic War 1803–1815.* 1992.

Hayter, Tony. *The Army and the Crowd in Eighteenth-Century England.* 1978.

Hickey, Donald. *The War of 1812: A Forgotten Conflict.* 1989.

Hill, J. R., ed. *The Oxford Illustrated History of the Royal Navy.* 1996.

Kennedy, Paul M. *The Rise and Fall of British Naval Mastery.* 1976.

Kopperman, Paul E. *Braddock at the Monongahela.* 1976.

Levack, Brian P. *The Formation of the British State: England, Scotland, and the Union, 1603–1707.* 1987.

Lynn, John A., ed. *Tools of War: Instruments, Ideas, and Institutions of Warfare, 1445–1871.* 1990.

Mackesy, Piers. *The War for America, 1775–1783.* 1964.

———. *The War in the Mediterranean, 1803–1810.* 1957.

———. *War Without Victory: The Downfall of Pitt, 1799–1802.* 1984.

Mahan, Alfred T. *The Influence of Sea Power upon History, 1660–1783.* 32nd ed. 1928.

———. *The Influence of Sea Power upon the French Revolution and Empire.* 2 vols. 10th ed. 1898.

Marcus, G. J. *The Age of Nelson: The Royal Navy, 1793–1815.* 1971.

———. *Heart of Oak: A Survey of British Sea Power in the Georgian Era.* 1975.

Myerly, Hughes Scott. *British Military Spectacle: From the Napoleonic Wars through the Crimea.* 1996.

Oman, Charles W. C. *A History of the Peninsular War.* 7 vols. 1902–1930.

Parker, Geoffrey. *The Military Revolution: Military Innovation and the Rise of the West, 1500–1800.* 1988.

Rodger, N. A. M. *The Wooden World: An Anatomy of the Georgian Navy.* 1986.

Sherwig, John M. *Guineas and Gunpowder: British Foreign Aid in the Wars with France, 1793–1815.* 1969.

Speck, W. A. *The Butcher: The Duke of Cumberland and the Suppression of the 45.* 1982.

Wallace, Willard M. *Appeal to Arms: A Military History of the American Revolution.* 1951.

Western, J. R. *The English Militia in the Eighteenth Century: The Story of a Political Issue, 1660–1802.* 1965.

Biography

Ashley, Maurice. *James II.* 1978.

Ayling, Stanley. *The Elder Pitt, Earl of Chatham.* 1976.

———. *George the Third.* 1972.

———. *John Wesley.* 1979.

Barnett, Correlli. *Marlborough.* 1974.

Bartlett, J. C. *Castlereagh.* 1967.

Bate, W. Jackson. *Samuel Johnson.* 1977.

Baxter, Stephen B. *William III and the Defense of European Liberty, 1650–1702.* 1966.

Beaglehole, J. C. *The Life of Captain James Cook.* 1974.

Bence-Jones, Mark. *Clive of India.* 1974.

Black, Jeremy. *Pitt the Elder.* 1992.

Boswell, James. *The Life of Samuel Johnson, LL.D.* 1791.

Brooke, John. *King George III.* 1972.

Brown, Peter Douglas. *William Pitt, Earl of Chatham.* 1978.

Browning, Reed. *The Duke of Newcastle.* 1975.

Campbell, R. H., and A. S. Skinner. *Adam Smith.* 1982.

Churchill, Winston S. *Marlborough, His Life and Times.* 6 vols. 1933–1939.

Cobban, Alfred. *Edmund Burke and the Revolt Against the Eighteenth Century.* 2nd ed. 1960.

Coupland, Reginald. *Wilberforce: A Narrative.* 1923.

Derry, John W. *Castlereagh.* 1976.

———. *Charles James Fox.* 1972.

Dickinson, H. T. *Walpole and the Whig Supremacy.* 1973.

Ehrman, John. *The Younger Pitt.* 3 vols. 1969, 1983, 1996.

Elliott, Marianne. *Wolfe Tone: Prophet of Irish Independence.* 1989.

Flexner, Eleanor. *Mary Wollstonecraft: A Biography.* 1972.

Fulford, Roger. *George the Fourth.* Rev. ed. 1949.

Furneaux, Robin. *William Wilberforce.* 1974.

Gash, Norman, *Lord Liverpool.* 1984.

——. *Mr. Secretary Peel: A Life of Sir Robert Peel to 1830.* 1961.

——. *Peel.* 1976.

——, ed. *Wellington: Studies in the Military and Political Career of the First Duke of Wellington.* 1990.

Green, David. *Queen Anne.* 1971.

——. *Sarah, Duchess of Marlborough.* 1967.

Gregg, Edward. *Queen Anne.* 1979.

Grundy, Isobel. *Lady Mary Wortley Montagu: Comet of the Enlightenment.* 1999.

Hamilton, Edith. *William's Mary.* 1972.

Harris, Frances. *A Passion for Government: The Life of Sarah, Duchess of Marlborough.* 1992.

Hatton, Ragnhild. *George I: Elector and King.* 1978.

Hawke, David Freeman. *Paine.* 1974.

Hedley, Olwen. *Queen Charlotte.* 1975.

Hibbert, Christopher. *George III: A Personal History.* 1998.

——. *George IV, Prince of Wales, 1762–1811.* 1972.

——. *George IV, Regent and King, 1811–1830.* 1974.

Hill, Bridget. *The Republican Virago: The Life and Times of Catharine Macaulay, Historian.* 1992.

Holme, Thea. *Caroline: A Biography of Caroline of Brunswick.* 1980.

Jones, James Rees. *Marlborough.* 1993.

Kemp, Betty. *Sir Robert Walpole.* 1976.

Kenyon, John P. *The Stuarts: A Study in English Kingship.* 1959.

Kronenberger, Louis. *The Extraordinary Mr. Wilkes.* 1974.

Lang, Paul Henry. *George Frederick Handel,* 1970.

Lawson, Philip. *George Grenville: A Political Life.* 1984.

Lock, F. J. *Edmund Burke.* Vol. 1 (1730–1784). 1999.

Longford, Elizabeth. *Wellington: The Years of the Sword.* 1969.

——. *Wellington: Pillar of State.* 1973.

McLynn, Frank. *Charles Edward Stuart: A Tragedy in Many Acts.* 1988.

Macalpine, Ida, and Richard Hunter. *George III and the Mad Business.* 1969.

Mack, Maynard. *Alexander Pope.* 1986.

Marshall, Dorothy. *John Wesley.* 1965.

Marshall, Rosalind K. *Bonnie Prince Charlie.* 1988.

Miles, Dudley. *Francis Place, 1771–1854: The Life of a Remarkable Radical.* 1988.

Miller, John. *James II: A Study in Kingship.* 1977.

Mingay, G. E., ed. *Arthur Young and His Times.* 1975.

Mitchell, L. G. *Charles James Fox.* 1992.

Mossner, Ernest Campbell. *The Life of David Hume.* 2nd ed. 1980.

Nowlan, Kevin B., and Maurice R. O'Connell, eds. *Daniel O'Connell: Portrait of a Radical.* 1984.

O'Brien, Conor Cruise. *The Great Melody: A Thematic Biography and Commented Anthology of Edmund Burke.* 1992.

Ogg, David. *William III.* 1956.

Oman, Carola. *Nelson.* 1947.

Osborne, John W. *William Cobbett: His Life and Times.* 1966.

Perry, Ruth. *The Celebrated Mary Astell: An Early English Feminist.* 1987.

Phillipson, Nicholas. *Hume.* 1989.

Plumb, John H. *The First Four Georges.* 1956.

———. *Sir Robert Walpole.* 2 vols. 1956, 1960.

Pollock, John. *Wilberforce.* 1977.

Porter, Roy. *Gibbon.* 1988.

Postgate, Raymond. *That Devil Wilkes.* 1930.

Quennell, Peter. *Hogarth's Progress.* 1955.

Richardson, Joanna. *George IV: A Portrait.* 1970.

Rock, Henry D. *Reasonable Enthusiast: John Wesley and the Rise of Methodism.* 1989.

Rodger, N. A. M. *The Insatiable Earl: A Life of John Montague, Fourth Earl of Sandwich, 1718–1792.* 1993.

Schofield, Robert E. *The Enlightenment of Joseph Priestley: A Study of His Life and Work from 1733 to 1773.* 1997.

St. Clair, William. *The Godwins and the Shelleys: The Biography of a Family.* 1989.

Schwoerer. Lois G. *Lady Rachel Russell: "One of the Best of Women."* 1988.

Shellabarger, Samuel. *Lord Chesterfield and His World.* 1951.

Smith, E. A. *George IV.* 1999.

Stone, George W., and George M. Kahrl. *David Garrick: A Critical Biography.* 1980.

Sundstrom, Roy A. *Sidney Godolphin: Servant of the State.* 1992.

Thomas, Peter D. G. *John Wilkes: A Friend to Liberty.* 1996.

———. *Lord North.* 1975.

Trench, Charles C. *The Great Dan: A Biography of Daniel O'Connell.* 1984.

Turner, F. C. *James II.* 1949.

Uglow, Jenny. *Hogarth: A Life and a World.* 1997.

Wain, John. *Samuel Johnson.* 1974.

Wallas, Graham. *The Life of Francis Place, 1771–1854.* 4th ed. 1925.

West, E. G. *Adam Smith: The Man and His Works.* 1976.

Whiteley, Peter. *Lord North: the Prime Minister Who Lost America.* 1996.

Wickwire, Franklin, and Mary Wickwire. *Cornwallis: The American Adventure.* 1970.

———. *Cornwallis: The Imperial Years.* 1980.

Wilkes, John W. *A Whig in Power: The Political Career of Henry Pelham.* 1964.

Willcox, William B. *Portrait of a General: Sir Henry Clinton in the War of Independence.* 1964.

Williams, Basil. *The Life of William Pitt, Earl of Chatham.* 2 vols. 1913.

Index